Ripe

Ripe

A cook in the orchard

NIGEL SLATER

Photographs by Jonathan Lovekin

TEN SPEED PRESS

Berkeley

Copyright © 2010 by Nigel Slater
Photographs copyright © 2010 by Jonathan Lovekin

Published in the United States by Ten Speed Press, an imprint of the
Crown Publishing Group, a division of Random House, Inc., New York.
www.crownpublishing.com
www.tenspeed.com

Originally published in hardcover in Great Britain as *Tender, Volume II:*
A Cook's Guide to the Fruit Garden by Fourth Estate, a division of HarperCollins
Publishers, London, in 2010

Ten Speed Press and the Ten Speed Press colophon are registered trademarks
of Random House, Inc.

First Ten Speed Press edition, 2012

Library of Congress Cataloging-in-Publication Data
Slater, Nigel.
  Ripe : a cook in the orchard / Nigel Slater ; photography by Jonathan Lovekin.
     p. cm.
  Includes index.
  Summary: "A comprehensive guide to growing and cooking with fruit,
featuring more than 300 recipes for sweet and savory dishes"—Provided by
publisher.
  1. Cooking (Fruit) 2. Cookbooks. I. Title.
  TX811.S58 2012
  641.6′4—dc23
                          2011043551

ISBN 978-1-60774-332-3
eISBN 978-1-60774-333-0

Printed in China

Cover design by Colleen Cain
Interior design by BLOK

10 9 8 7 6 5 4 3 2

First United States Edition

Introduction

And then there was fruit. I always knew that if ever I found a space in which to grow a few knobbly vegetables of my own, some of it would be set aside for fruit: wild strawberries with flowers like tiny, brilliant stars; amber and bronze apples with russet skins; dusky blueberries in old terra-cotta pots; maybe a black currant bush or two for jam. What I had not expected was to find myself with a virtually blank canvas, an opportunity to plant not only fruit bushes but some space for trees too, a row of raspberry canes, and even a vine.

Ten years on, permanently teetering on the edge of chaos, this garden creaks under the weight of my overenthusiastic planting. There is barely an inch of ground to spare. From white currants and golden raspberries to purple figs and red gooseberries, my pocket handkerchief of urban space is bursting at the seams. Give me a couple of feet more and I'll show you space for a crab apple with blossom the color of a loganberry fool.

There is a moment, sometime around the middle of September, when this garden, this diminutive *hortus conclusus* I have made in an 1820s London terrace, truly becomes the garden of my dreams. The leaves are turning from green to gold, amber, and rust, the last of the fruits hang crimson and smoky blue on the trees, the pumpkin-colored dahlias and Michaelmas daisies have collapsed like drunks across the gravel path. The garden darkens to the color of ginger cake, here and there a shot of saffron, brilliant ochre, or deepest crimson. The colors, I would guess, of the Vatican at prayer.

The last berries, apples, and plums, wet and almost rotting from the late sun and autumn rain, lend a mellow, alcoholic scent to the space, like the dregs of an abandoned glass of wine. The garden is falling asleep with an air of damp tobacco and wood smoke, but it is still abundant too, with late blackberries, damsons, and a grapevine at breaking point. Each year I race to get to those blackberries before the feast of Michaelmas, when the devil is said to piss on them.

Growing many, though sadly not all, of my own vegetables is a deeply pleasurable thing to do. Watering the tomatoes and the runner beans is now as much a part of my life as taking a shower, but although I produce far less of my own fruit than I do vegetables, curiously they give me even more joy. Walking round the garden late on an autumn morning, pushing past the spiders' webs that festoon the pathways and plucking those last, wine-colored berries from their blackened canes is as good as life gets. A moment of intense well-being, and even more so when the time has been stolen from a busy schedule.

This space at the back of my house could so easily have been a lawn. Instead, I have ended up with a back garden laden with sensual pleasures. A bough of yellow plums the size of a blackbird's egg; an apple tree whose fruit is snow white flushed with rose pink; loganberries as dark and sultry as a glass of Pinot Noir; and grapes that hang outside the kitchen wall like bunches of jet beads. There are sherbet-sharp gooseberries and piercingly tart sticks of rhubarb; fat black figs and raspberries the color of a glass of Sauternes. Their pleasures are brief, and yes, there is always a struggle to get there before the birds and the squirrels, but it is hard to find a mulberry more exquisite than the one you have grown for yourself, a strawberry more sweet, or a fig more seductive.

Why grow your own fruit?

While I cannot imagine my little garden without its cane teepee of runner beans and their scarlet flowers, or its chipped pots of random tomatoes, it is a simple truth that more of the garden's space is given over to fruit with each passing year. The potatoes that basked in the luxury of their own bed now share it with gooseberry bushes and three crowns of rhubarb; the beet patch is constantly invaded by ever more varieties of strawberry; the Jerusalem artichokes have, no doubt to everyone's relief, been partly replaced by raspberry canes.

Vegetables remain at the heart and soul of this fifty-five yard (fifty-meter) plot but, as the infant plums and pears mature into fully grown trees and the loganberries climb up their blue steel wires, the focus of the garden is shifting toward being a slightly more fragrant and sensual place.

The supermarkets may carry more varieties of locally grown apples and pears than they used to but they are a long way off being as interesting as a farm stand or the apple stall of a farmers' market as somewhere to pick up the week's supply of fruit. The clinical, bright aisles of even the most user-friendly chain store can never hope to approach the sight and smell of a farmers' market on a misty autumn morning.

I cannot be the only one who generally finds supermarket fruit somewhat characterless—a testament to sweetness and shelf life. By growing my own fruits I not only have the chance to grow lesser-known varieties spurned by the big boys as being unproductive, short-lived, or, dare I say it, too characterful, but also that of experiencing them straight from the tree, bush, or plant. But there is much, much more pleasure to growing fruit than that of a strawberry on the lips. The haunting silhouette of a bare tree against a winter sky; the first breaking buds; the childlike pleasure of an avalanche of cherry blossom and then, as the fruit ripens over the coming weeks, watching its progress like a hawk eyeing its prey. To bring a home-grown apple or a palm full of raspberries in from the garden is a different experience altogether from that of taking them off a supermarket shelf. And isn't that what we all want—food that brings us the most possible pleasure and delight?

Like interesting salad leaves and bright, vital greens, fruit is a massive part of what I eat. But, in truth, I could never satiate my need for berries and currants on my own soil alone. I wish I could. Not to mention the fact that the British blueberry, currant, and blackberry season, though longer now than at any time in its history, still lasts no more than a few weeks. Where I would never touch a spring cabbage out of season or be tempted by the call of a bunch of airfreighted asparagus, I do supplement our own fruits' short seasons with those from elsewhere. As a result, I buy far more of my berries from supermarkets and produce stores than I would like. Growing at least some of my own is, I suppose, partly a tiny attempt to redress that.

And as anyone who has dug their own potatoes from the earth or twisted a ripe plum from its stem knows, growing your own is as addictive a drug as almost anything else out there.

The trees

The fruit trees were the first to go in. My initial list, as absurdly long as a spoiled child's Christmas list, included a Nottingham medlar for which there was no obvious use and a King James mulberry from which I was told to expect no fruit for a decade. (They were right.) The others, Mirabelle de Nancy plums, Rouge de Bordeaux figs, Merryweather damsons, Vranja quinces, Durondeau pears, and Count Althann's gages, were from a list made more out of romanticism than practicality. As with my first purchase of rose bushes, I bought those whose names I happened to like and the order was put together with no thought for space, pollination, or correct location. I was soon to learn a hard and painful lesson.

The idea was tempting. A space at the end of the garden, past the vegetable patch with its Peter Rabbit lettuces and clumps of Joseph's Coat chard, would be a small, enclosed orchard. A cloister within a cloister, if you like. Even though I knew the word *orchard* was a ridiculous exaggeration, I hadn't quite envisaged how I would get things so very wrong.

Trees grow. A fact that, in his overexcitement, this newbie gardener had overlooked. At first I put an apple, a plum, a damson, a quince, and two nut trees in a space small enough in which to park a car. Branches tangled, blossoms merged, roots entwined, the damson almost suffocated under the prolific, arching branches of the hazelnuts. The squirrels bounced from one tree to the next like kids practicing parkour, taking every fruit and nut in their path.

The apple was moved, at great cost to my back, its thick roots dug out with a garden fork and the more fragile ones scrabbled out with my bare hands, to a place where it could at last spread its branches. The nuts were coppiced, their long twigs recycled as climbing frames for the runner beans; the plum was pruned to disentangle it from the nearby quince. Trees, it seemed, need to breathe just as we do.

One by one, I moved the fruit trees around the garden: a pear to one bed, a plum to another, finding each one a new home among the flowers and vegetables. One fig ended up in a lead-lined hole in the stone terrace, another climbing up strings nailed into the scullery wall. Within a year or so they were happy, each with a bit of space to call its own, their blossoms bringing bees and butterflies to the fruits and vegetables underneath, and shade to those beds that needed it. The exception is, I suppose, the medlar, whose canopy is now so thick that the bed beneath it is good only for rhubarb and gooseberries.

A garden without at least one apple tree is probably no garden at all, but one happy tree is better than several without the room to thrive. This garden has seen three. The first, a Discovery, was the first tree on my list. The young tree, barely three feet high, was planted with white phlox underneath in an attempt to realize a haunting childhood memory of the smell of ripe apples mixed with the powdery scent of fading *Phlox paniculata*. (As an eight-year-old, I would reach down through the phlox to pick up the fallen apples, and the scent of the fruit and flowers was unforgettable.) I succeeded, too: the earliest apple ripens just as the second flush of flowers starts to fade. I cannot overemphasize the effect this small success had on me. For years I had walked around with this childhood scent in my head. And now here it was in a garden of my own making.

The second, a Blenheim Orange, the apple of the Benedictine monasteries, was a more than appropriate choice as it turned out—more than one observer has described this space as having the air of a monastery garden. The blossom was exquisite, the fruit large, its skin green, orange, and russet. I loved the tree's extraordinary crooked shape, like an old man in a fairy tale. I almost cried the day I returned home to find it had been ripped up, its branches hideously snapped by unknowing scaffolders who had no choice but to squeeze their long rods through my tiny orchard.

And then there was the Court Pendu Plat. A flat-topped apple, whose late blossom never quite coincides with that of the Discovery and so rarely bears fruit. The world of pollinators, and the idea that apple trees often need a mate, was a mystery to me in those days.

A little homework led me to choosing a pear tree with a suitable friend as pollinator. It had been suggested that rather than being home to a large tree, the garden might fare better with an espalier—a tree whose branches were carefully trained to reach out along wires attached to a wall. For once, I did things properly, getting stiff wires fastened to a south-facing wall close to the house by someone more of an expert than me. The tree arrived and its young, whippy branches were tied along the wires. (At first the diagrams in pruning manuals were as strange to me as those in a car maintenance book. Yet once the pruning shears are in your hand things become clearer, the diagrams suddenly start to make sense.)

My little Doyenne du Comice pear fruited within two years, and now, eight years on, has branches spreading four feet or more along the wall. The idea of espaliered trees has something of the grand kitchen garden about it, yet it makes total sense for a tiny urban garden like mine. Did I mention the garden looks much bigger in photographs than it is? Well, it does. Its mate, a Winter Nelis, has blossoms like a snow flurry and, in autumn, leaves the color of bitter orange marmalade. The pears, as hard and crisp as the Comices are soft and luscious, are often still hanging on the tree on Christmas Eve. They are wonderful poached slowly with maple syrup and vanilla or sliced up and dropped into mulled perry.

Of all the trees in this garden, it is the plums with which I am most enamored. Their names are lovable—Crimson Drop, Mirabelle de Nancy, Oullins Gage, and Old Transparent—but their fruit is superb too. They are worth growing for their color alone: amber freckled with crimson; opal with flashes of mauve; chartreuse, rust, and vermilion. On a sunny day in late July they hang translucent on the tree, as if lit by a candle. Their flesh becomes soft and melting and the juice honey-sweet, a sticky golden nectar. If I could have just one tree it would be a plum.

After my Discovery apple, the second tree on the list was a damson. The trees are brittle and their growth slow. They need a firm hand with the pruning shears if they are not to run wild, but their blossom is the most delicate of all the plums, like that of a fairy's wing. I knew, even ten years ago, that cold January morning I dug the deep, wide hole for my Farleigh damson, I would never get enough fruit for more than a crumble, and I still don't. No matter. The single dessert, its purple fruit bubbling up through the oatmeal crust, is as welcome as the dusky, blue-black fruit and that tissue-paper blossom each spring.

The bushes

Trees are but part of the story. The fruit bushes have been more of a success than I had ever dreamed. Any garden can squeeze in a raspberry cane or two (a friend has planted a couple just for the kids). Sadly, there simply isn't room in my patch for more than one or two of each hue of currant, or for more than two or three rows of berries. None of which seems to matter. The fruits somehow become all the more precious for their scarcity. When I was a child, there wasn't a garden on the block that didn't have a few currant bushes at the end of it. Often as not, down by the runner beans past the washing line. Mine are closer to the house, where I can keep an eye on their progress. The daily walk around the garden, pulling up the odd weed or leading a snail to a happier place, is a year-round bonus.

The day the fruit bushes arrived was one of the most disappointing of my life. At that stage, I had no idea how unpromising a young, bare-rooted plant would look when taken from its cardboard package. Wrapped in a nest of coarse, damp straw and tied in a bundle with unbreakable orange twine, they were very different from the lush bushes whose berries, hanging like jewels, I had envisaged when I placed the order. The day was bitter too, as cold as I can remember, and by four o'clock, with sleet coming sideways at me, I gave up planting my little brown sticks and toasted crumpets with ridiculous amounts of butter to make myself feel better.

Within six months my sticks had turned into a fizz of green leaves and even fruited in their first year. Not many, granted, but enough to convince me I was heading in the right direction (better gardeners would have had the sense to remove the first fruits to give the bushes a chance to build a strong root system). The raspberries were worse, a bundle of kindling that, in a final moment of disillusionment, I was invited to cut to the ground as soon as they were planted. Those Autumn Bliss raspberries have gone on to become one of the most magical parts of this little space. Huge, deep-red berries heavy with perfume (roses, Beaujolais, who can say?) hang down from late August until the first frosts. They have recently been joined by Autumn Gold, a yellow variety, and a loganberry with its prolific stems and fruit the color of sloe gin. And yes, there are now blueberries in terra-cotta pots too.

I recently found that first fruit order, smudged with garden soil and yellow as nicotine, in an old box of papers. On it were the Careless gooseberry bushes that did so well for the best part of eight years. They have recently been replaced with three Hinnomaki bushes in red, green, and gold. They fruited, just enough to tease, in their first year.

Fruit bushes have much to be said for them in even the smallest garden. They show off the seasons: the peaceful gray stems of winter, spring's stinging green, the spritz of those tiny summer flowers, and then the fruits that slowly ripen from hard and opaque to shimmering, translucent gold.

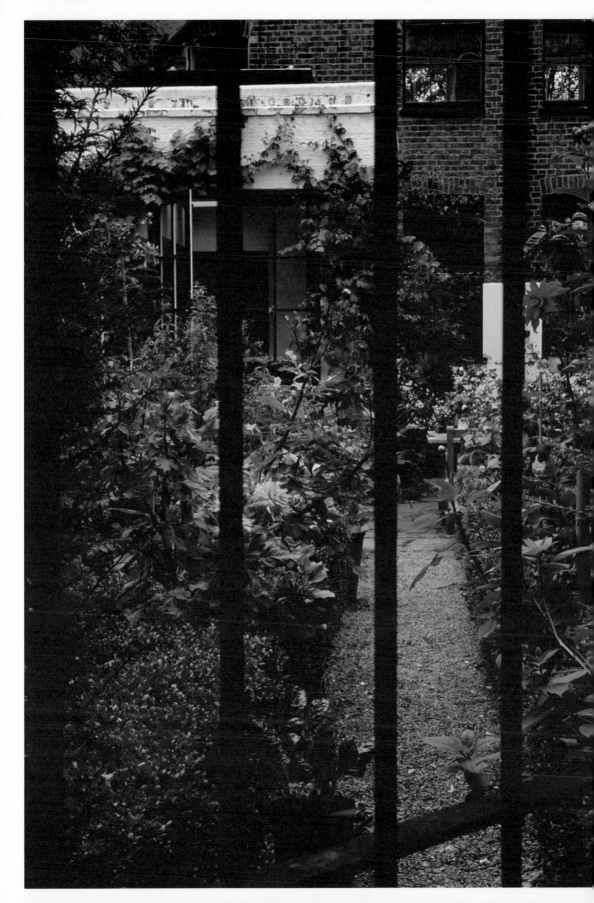

The plants

At first I had no wish for strawberries other than the wild ones with fruit the size of midget gems. They started sweetly, a gift from a friend, and as dainty and hidden as a snowdrop, but pretty soon profligate seedlings had escaped all over the garden. Two years on from planting and I was pulling them up like weeds (to be honest, I still am). Now they are contained in a vast pot around the *Magnolia stellata*, where they grow lush, with leaves so thick they successfully hide the fruits from the blackbirds' eyes. Their spring green is one of the freshest of all, and occasionally in autumn a golden orange leaf appears.

An annual trip to the Chelsea Flower Show is never complete without the heady scent of strawberries caught in the heavy air of the Great Pavilion. Tantalizing—you cannot touch them, let alone taste them—but you can still breathe in their sugary richness. A few years ago I fell for one called Florence, quite rare at the time, and ordered a dozen plants. Such a revelation was the flavor of those first home-grown strawberries that I started a small patch in the hottest of the six vegetable beds. Joined by Mara de Bois, Gariguette, and, later, Ken Muir's Chelsea Pensioner, my little patch is now an essential part of the garden. Hiding behind the runner beans as they do, they announce their presence if not by their poster-paint colors then by the scent they give off on a baking-hot July afternoon.

The cloudberry is the one that got away. I hopefully phone the gardener in the Scottish Highlands each year, a polite inquiry, but am always unlucky. Yet again a few weeks too early or a day too late. One day I will get my hands on these beautiful berries that dot the Scandinavian countryside and make such superlative jam. They are part of my wish to bring the fruit of the hedgerow into this garden to accompany the elders and the wild blackberry. That, or I will hide some plants in my suitcase.

The vine

I have seen grapevines clamber over rickety, painted sheds on inner city allotments, dominate Victorian greenhouses on country estates, and wind their tendrils over neat suburban pergolas, but it never crossed my mind to have one in my own garden.

The grapevine seems to belong to the Mediterranean. Like the olive trees on every balcony in new apartment blocks, they seem curiously out of place here. Yet we have grown vines in Britain for hundreds of years and we can make very good wine here too. I took a chance and ordered one. Well, two actually. Not interested in homemade wine, I went for the Fragola, or strawberry grape, a thick-skinned variety that has extremely juicy fruits with flesh the texture of melting jelly.

The kitchen has double doors that open flat on parliament hinges. Either side of them is a space begging for a climber. While wisteria and roses were possibilities, this bit of wall seemed perfect for a grapevine. Planted deeply, in somewhat stony soil, they couldn't be happier, and now regularly produce eighty small bunches between them. What is more, they sprout downy, rose-pink buds in early April in perfect harmony with their dove-gray stems. In autumn, although they lack the stunning colors of other varieties of vine, their fading gold leaves look suitably somber against the matte black of the doors.

A word about blossom

My earliest memory is of blossom and staring up into branches so crammed with pink petals you couldn't see the sky. Cherry probably. One of those frilly, overabundant varieties that are best viewed from a distance. The flowering cherry so beloved of the 1960s suburban garden, and a world away from the single, white cherry blossom I now love.

When I was a teenager, my father would take me along the "blossom routes" that ran like maypole ribbons though the Shropshire countryside. Seeing them as vast white curds, like snow clouds resting on thick trunks, I would climb up with my head out of the sunroof of the car, flurries of petals hitting me in the face and getting stuck to my lips. It was when he would pull up the car and we would get out and walk through the orchards that I got to admire their bent, wicked-witch shapes and lichen-encrusted branches.

There was blossom at home too. First, the three apple trees set into neatly trimmed rings in the lawn, then the orchard at the top of our new garden—plum, golden gage, pear, damson, and wonderful, crisp apples. When I first drew the London garden out in my notebook, a spectacular show of pure white blossom in April and May was just as much my aim as the fruits that followed. Blossom is all about hope—a promise of good things to come.

A half century on from that first pink cherry tree, I am obsessed by the flowers of the fruit tree. I seek out the fragile, butterfly-wing petals, from the sloes in the hedgerows around Sissinghurst to the wild apricots that grow on the hillsides outside Kyoto. Where orchids and lilies are the ultimate blooms for some, the sight and scent of frost-white plum blossom against a gray branch is what sets this heart racing.

Buying fruit trees, bushes, and plants—a few notes

I must say that I have found fruit specialists to be more rewarding hunting grounds than garden centers. They tend to hold more interesting varieties and often have wise proprietors and staff who are generous with their advice. If you have the transport, you can often go and choose your tree; if not, they will send them by post.

Be warned that it is the least interesting trees that are sent by post, the sort whose branches will fit neatly into their uniform packaging. They obviously need to pick trees that won't get damaged in transit. If you want something with a bit of character, you might do better to go there and pick one out for yourself.

Buying by mail order has its advantages, and I have had both surprises and disappointments. My first blueberry plants were lanky and unpruned—I would never have bought them had I seen them first—but a fig tree was unexpectedly fine, its branches held secure on canes and even a few infant fruit in place.

I can read a specialty fruit list like a novel, but we should be careful not to get carried away. Evocative, poetic names are infinitely tempting. Curled up by the fire with a catalogue, I would sometimes imagine a larger garden altogether, a place with room for a Michaelmas Red apple and a D'Arcy Spice, a Peasgood's Nonsuch and a Nutmeg Pippin; not just a Careless gooseberry but a Catherine and a Keepsake too, not to mention a Floribunda crab apple and a Jules Guyot pear. Oh and what about that Sanctus Hubertus plum or a white-fleshed pear called Moonglow? Imagine biting into that one freezing, starlit night in the garden.

My advice, as with ordering vegetable seeds, is to make your list at night but do not send it. Look at it again the following day when you can delete your wilder flights of fancy. A loquat? What was I thinking?

And, just as this book went off to press, I heard that finally, after years of searching, I had secured six little cloudberry plants from Scotland.

The recipes

Just as savory dishes made up the bulk of the recipes in this book's companion, *Tender*, baking, cakes, and desserts form the heart and soul of this volume. This is as it should be. Fruit has an inherent sweetness that makes it more appropriate for sweet recipes than for savory ones. But just as we dipped our toes into the world of beet cakes and pumpkin scones in that book, this one has a host of savory dishes too—a pan-fry of venison with blueberries, pork with pears, and spareribs with a cooling lime and peach salsa, to name just three. There is duck served with damsons, lamb stewed with quinces, and quite a few recipes for rabbit, pheasant, and partridge.

That said, you should find nothing to raise an eyebrow in this collection, no flights of fancy, no strawberry sauce with chicken to upset the family at suppertime. Despite many an enthusiast's insistence that rhubarb works in a beef stew or that peaches make a nice sauce for chicken (and I am sure they do), I have generally kept away from fruit's more unusual applications. Some may say that I haven't been experimental enough and I take that accusation on the chin, but I wanted to produce a collection of recipes that were useful and delicious rather than extraordinary and seasoned with the zeal of the evangelist. I hope I have the balance right.

Where I have used fruits with meat or (very, very occasionally) fish, then I would like to think it is because the inclusion was relevant rather than revelatory. I will leave it to you to experiment further.

Meat and fruit

The meat dishes of the Middle East have long been sweetened or given bite with appropriate fruits: a casserole of lamb that benefits from the sweet acidity of the apricot; quail roasted with a scattering of jewel-like pomegranates; sizzling steak cut into strips and tossed with tart green grapes; roast duck smeared with golden quince paste. Classical French cooking includes a sauté of chicken with apples, cream, and Calvados; the famous *porc aux pruneaux*; and the much derided but oh-so-delicious duckling à l'orange that can be so good when made with the correct bitter Seville fruits.

In autumn, Scandinavian cooks feast on salads of bacon and plums, veal with rhubarb, and the ever-popular meatballs with a compote of lingonberries. Only the Italians resolutely refuse to mix fruit with meat on a regular basis—apart of course from the ever-present lemons—until you get further down south into Sicily, where oranges and raisins appear as a matter of course. It is worth remembering, however, that their beloved tomatoes and zucchini are both fruits.

British cooks, once happy to serve fruits with their main-course meats (Elizabethan cooks made much use of them), have become a little wary. Where a sharp applesauce has always been welcome with pork, and sometimes gooseberry too, it has taken a long time to get our collective palate to accept that there is more to rhubarb than fool.

If I am unsure whether a particular fruit will work with meat or game, I apply a simple rule. If the two regularly share a landscape, then maybe the combination is worth trying. The chances are that grouse, deer, and partridge will have eaten the wild berries that pepper the hedges and moors that are part of their habitat. Most game birds are happy to indulge themselves on elderberries, just as pigeons do on my plums. If the idea of adding fruit to a recipe sounds plausible, then I am happy to explore

it. There have been some wonderful surprises, such as the venison with blueberries on page 158.

The marriage of fish and fruit is generally too controversial even for me. I just don't get it. Sole with bananas simply doesn't do it for me. But cut the fattiness of a marinated herring with a crisp, wincingly sharp apple salad the way the Swedish do, or fry mackerel with rhubarb or gooseberries to slice through the oily flesh, and then I think we could be on the same page. But I freely admit to being less happy with the marriage of fruit and fish than some more open-minded cooks.

Ten years ago, finding myself with an unwanted lawn, I set about digging it up with the hope of growing some of my own fruits and vegetables. Five years later, shortly after *The Kitchen Diaries* was published, I set out to chronicle what I grew and to learn more about the possibilities that can arise once you stick your trowel in the soil or push a seed into a pot.

In that short time my tiny plot has established itself as a place that, while coming up laughably short of the self-sufficient, nevertheless enriches my life and well-being more than this book can ever tell. Not just when I twist an apple off the tree on an autumn morning or get pink-fingered from picking raspberries on a July afternoon; not only when there is a dish of roast tomatoes with my own-grown garlic and thyme in the oven, or when I ladle out a bowl of carrot soup, but in myriad other ways too. The enrichment of my life that comes from watching a pear slowly ripen on the branch, the bud of a potato opening to reveal a fragile flower of the softest lilac, or when the greens of the garden turn from gold to amber and darkest bronze. I have always said that the joy of food should go way beyond the plate and it does.

Now I couldn't imagine life without some sort of allotment, a window box, or a few pots in which to plant something, however small. What I grow here is a drop in the ocean of my daily needs, but you know what? I really don't care. The pleasure I get from growing a crisp, white-tipped radish in a pot is pleasure enough for me.

As I sit here now at the summer solstice, watching my little patch of strawberries ripen, the still-green Crimson Drop plums swelling on the trees and yet another sowing of beans pushing their swan's necks through the soil looking hopefully for one of my rickety cane affairs, I have to say that I am probably closer to my food, and more respectful of it, than I had ever thought possible. The pleasure, let me tell you, is immeasurable.

A note on the US edition

In editing this book for an American audience, we sought to do two things: one, to make it as much a treasure trove of information, inspiration, and solid cooking advice for Americans as it is for its original British audience; and two, to retain the book's engaging style and tone. To that end, the recipes and cooking instructions have been Americanized, so that ingredients, terminology, and measurements are familiar to US readers. We have retained the metric measures from the original edition for readers whose cooking style includes measuring by weight and/or using metric units. Any errors or omissions belong to the American publisher, Ten Speed Press.

A small number of ingredients used in these recipes are unfamiliar or hard to find in the States, and these deserve a little discussion here. **Golden baker's sugar** is small-crystal raw (unrefined) sugar, and it can be expensive or difficult to find. Raw sugar with a larger crystal, such as **demerara** or **turbinado**, can be whizzed in a food processor into smaller crystals and used in its stead. **Golden syrup** is a pure sugarcane syrup, the flavor of which is essential to a classic treacle tart, among other dishes. It can be found online, and other pure cane syrups or sweet syrups without additives may be substituted, though the flavor will not be the same. **Muscovado sugar** is a soft, moist brown sugar with a distinctive flavor; regular soft brown sugar may be used in its place, but the flavor will lose something. **Sloe gin** is a cottage or artisanal product in Britain, made by infusing gin with sloes, the bracingly sharp fruit of the blackthorn. Commercially made American versions are no substitute, as they are artificially flavored and colored, and overly sweetened. Choose a British brand, such as Plymouth, or, if you are lucky enough to have some homemade, use that.

The "allotments" referred to occasionally in these pages are small parcels of land leased to private citizens in England (and Europe) by local government entities for the purpose of growing food crops. Allotments differ from community gardens in that they are not worked by a group of people, but by the individual to whom the land is leased.

The author gardens in London, and his plant choices and experiences of climate and season reflect that. In each chapter's section on fruit varieties, US-friendly cultivars are denoted with asterisks. The descriptions of a fruit's flavor, texture, and other qualities can be used as a guide in the produce market when choosing a US variety that will work well in a particular context.

Apples

 The most interesting apples are probably
to be found in private gardens, farmyards,
and monasteries, their skins a tapestry of moss
green, sage, and amber, their flesh crisp,
acid-sweet, and full of character. Perhaps they
will be copper or deepest crimson, or etched
here and there with a web of russet as rough as a
farmer's hand. They may be known as Christmas
Red or D'Arcy Spice, Fenouillette Gris or
Peasgood's Nonsuch, or maybe their names have
been lost in time. The trees will be loved too,
for their lichen-encrusted branches, tissue-frail
blossom, and quiet benevolence.

The apples of commerce can be good too, but I have had more fun at
farm stands and farmers' markets than at neon-lit superstores. I prefer to
rummage through wooden crates for my Pippins, happy to go home with
bags of misshapen fruit of all sizes: plump ones for breakfast, majesties for
baking, and a few the size of baubles for snacking on.

Apples lack the seductive qualities of the peach and the mystery of
the pomegranate, but they make up for it in no-nonsense appeal. I have
never met anyone who doesn't like an apple. Yet from early spring until late
summer I rarely touch them, except in a sugar-crusted pie or a slick of sauce
to cut the richness of the Sunday roast. From the first Discovery in August
to the last of the Cox's in February, I eat an apple every day, sometimes
two, three even—tiring only once I have seen the pink and white froth of
blossom of the new year's growth.

I was brought up with munificent Bramleys and reliable Cox's, but took
them for granted. Only when I got my own garden and planted first a rose-
hued Discovery, then a Blenheim Orange and an ancient and late-flowering
Court Pendu Plat did I appreciate their finer qualities, the possibilities of
flavor—strawberry, walnut, nail polish—and the satisfaction of picking the
right variety for the right job.

There is probably an apple for every occasion: the Ribston Pippin for an aromatic crunch, the russet-skinned Ashmead's Kernel to munch with a wedge of Cheddar, an Emneth Early for a frothy pudding, and an Orleans Reinette for an open *tarte fine*. There are apples with subtle hints of pineapple, raspberry, or hazelnut and others with the pronounced astringency of a pear drop. Some could probably charm their way into our shopping bags by their names alone: Michaelmas Red, Pig's Nose, and Cornish Honeypin. Others still by their looks, such as the Christmas Pearmain or the extraordinarily apt Catshead.

An apple's character is prone to change as the season progresses. Many deepen in flavor after picking, as their starch turns to sugar and their notes of nutmeg, aniseed, or pineapple come to the fore. Others simply become soft and woolly. I have had more than a few of those. A fruit that disappointed on the tree may, by Christmas, be sublime, with all its credentials on show—the Pippins and the honey-scented Cornish Gilliflower being cases in point.

An apple in the garden

The apple tree originated in Central Asia, and its wild ancestor is found in the mountains there to this day. Many a tree will fruit within a year or two of planting, and they are well suited to a domestic garden—some take up barely more space than an umbrella clothesline (and the blossom is prettier than even your fanciest pair of underwear). Thanks to Barrie Juniper at Oxford University and DNA analysis, we know that our domestic apple probably originated from a single species still growing on the north slopes of the Tian Shan mountains in northern China. This perhaps explains why I prefer apples from a cold climate.

The apple is part of Norse mythology, a gift to the gods for eternal youth, and has long been associated with fertility. This, of course, is the tree of life, but to Christians it is the tree of the Knowledge of Good and Evil (*mala*, the Latin plural for apple, is identical to that for "evil"). Not for nothing, then, is this the forbidden fruit.

Apple trees for the garden come as dwarf and standard, fans and espaliers, cordons and bushes, and a few sizes and shapes in between. There are some 7,500 known cultivars, though the choice at the garden center will not be large. Specialty nurseries are the places to look for the older, often more interesting varieties. They send out young trees in the dead of winter, the perfect time to plant, before the sap rises.

My semidwarfing (M26 rootstock) apples were a wise choice for a small town garden, though more by luck than good judgment on my part. They stand at roughly my height, their silhouettes twisting against the winter sky. These are not the large, uniform trees of commercial orchards.

An apple tree in blossom is a magical sight in any garden—the petals getting caught on the breeze and occasionally falling in flurries, like snow. Apple blossom and the young leaves burst early, and can occasionally be caught by frost, but look enchanting against the gray bark and silver skies of early spring.

A tree will often need a friend if it is to bear fruit, and, more importantly, a compatible variety that flowers at around the same time. I have the earliest and latest of varieties at home, which is probably why my crop can be hit and miss. Wise cooks will plant more than one variety to keep them going through the autumn.

An apple in the kitchen

Once we take an apple into the kitchen—for a pie, perhaps—its flavor becomes only slightly less important than that of an apple eaten straight from the tree. You might lose the very top notes, the subtlest hint of raspberry, say, or nutmeg, but the backbone of sharpness or intense sweetness will remain. It may even sing louder than in the raw fruit.

It is worth considering which might be the best apple for the job. A slice of pork crackling needs a sharp bite to offset its rich fattiness; a dish of poached apples will possess an extraordinary elegance when made with a batch of early Discovery; a baked apple needs plenty of acidity to balance the brown sugar and vine fruits with which it is traditionally stuffed. But what is most important to the cook is whether an apple is the sort to keep its shape or not. Will the fruit stay in one piece or will it expand in a balloon of snowy bubbles?

Talk of "cooking" apples and "eating" apples is confusing and full of anomalies. Many varieties cross over between dessert and cooking. A crisp Howgate Wonder, for instance, is as happy with cheese as it is under the crust of pie. You can cook with any apple, but whether it is a wise choice is another matter. I tend to think of *Malus domestica* as dividing into two kinds—those that will look good in soldierly slices under the glaze of a fruit tart, and those that will melt into a sweet, fragrant slush.

Varieties

We have grown well over 2,000 varieties of apple in this country. I would dearly like to list the characteristics of each deserving one but that would constitute a hefty book in its own right (I occasionally have to remind myself that whatever else it may be, *Ripe* is principally a cookbook). For a full discussion of apple varieties, you cannot do better than Joan Morgan and Alison Richard's *Book of Apples* (Ebury Press, 1993). It barely leaves my side in autumn, and it is here that I check the history and tasting notes of, say, Hoary Morning or Mrs. Wilmott. It is a directory, but this is also where you will find out that D'Arcy Spice is traditionally picked on Guy Fawkes Day and that the Norfolk Beefing was dried in bread ovens and used by bakers. An extraordinarily detailed and important work.

The Internet, too, has rich pickings. Where else would you learn that you have been looking in the wrong place for the Manaccan Primrose (it is found almost exclusively around the Lizard in Cornwall) or that, despite its delicious name, Buttery d'Or (or Buttery Door or Buttery Dough) is best as a cider apple?

I have instead split the most popular apple varieties (and those we are most likely to come across during the Apple Day celebrations around October 23 each year) into what I feel are the most useful categories for the cook—apples that hold their shape, those that froth, and those that have a unique affinity for eating as they are, or with cheese.

The frothing apples

A baked apple, its skin split, the top half rising like a beret, is best achieved with an acidic variety. The list includes Golden Noble,* Kentish Fillbasket, Emneth Early, Monarch, Charlotte, Newton Wonder, Lord Derby, and the Carlisle and Keswick Codlins. Most of these I have met at some point in my cooking life; others, such as Edward VII and the Eynsham Dumpling, I have never even seen on sale, let alone poured custard over. Then, of course, there are the seedlings: Bramley, Dumelow's, and Pott's.

If you are in Cornwall with nothing much to do on an October afternoon, you might like to go in search of the Colloggett Pippin. You will be in with a good chance if you pronounce it Clogget and are within sight of the Tamar. The Cornish have a habit of shortening place names the way children shorten those of their best friends.

An apple that will bake nicely without collapsing is the Grenadier, but it carries a hefty dose of sweetness too. My own reverence is kept for Peasgood's Nonsuch, a generous, beaming apple with the geniality of a pumpkin. Handsome, striped, and slightly russetted, it combines cloudlike froth and deep flavor. The tart, complex Roxbury Russet,* a favorite of Thomas Jefferson, takes well to the oven too, as do the sweet-yet-tangy Honeycrisp,* the spicy, juicy Esopus Spitzenburg,* and the tart Northern Spy.*

Keeping their shape—apples for an open tart or a good, stiff purée

The variety of apple we use is, of course, a matter of taste, but occasionally the choice can be crucial. Attempt to make a tart in the French manner, with fine pastry and overlapping slices of fruit, using a frothing apple such as Bramley and you will fail. A fruit that keeps its shape when cooked is essential if the characteristic neatness of classic French pâtisserie is to be preserved. French pastry chefs don't really do wobbly. That means a Charles

Ross, James Grieve, Gravenstein,* or, if you find one, a Cravert. A Granny Smith* will behave well too, and its lack of sweetness will balance the fruit jelly you will inevitably use as a glaze.

The drier the flesh of an apple, the more likely it is to retain a semblance of its shape. Annie Elizabeth, still popular in the Midlands, is just about perfect for this, but I wish you good luck in tracking her down. Golden Pippin will work, though my own pick is Blenheim Orange,* with its lightly flattened top and flushed skin the timid orange of an October sunset.

Firm, creamy-yellow-fleshed fruits are also worth a thought as stewing apples, becoming tender and almost canary yellow when simmered with a little sugar, while not exploding into a mass of foam.

Apples for cheese

Away from the stove, there are apples to be chosen to eat with cheese, which can be a lifelong and pleasure-filled hunt. The marriage of fruit and cheese is a very personal one, and only you can say whether Adam's Pearmain is the one for a wedge of Cheddar, or the Beeley Pippin works better with a six-month-matured Caerphilly than it does with a newly made goat cheese. As with pairing food and wine, there is no right and wrong.

A lump of cheese and an apple is a regular lunch in our house; more often than not with a bowl of soup—a mildly spiced parsnip soup, a jagged lump of Cheddar, and a Cox's* being a favorite January lunch.

I tend to prefer the aromatic apples with cheese—those whose notes may include a subtle breath of hazelnuts, aniseed, pear drops, or a faintly herbal inflection. Aromatic apples are not the easiest of fruits to find, being mostly older, less sweet varieties. With the exception of Ashmead's Kernel,* which I have occasionally spotted in supermarkets, these are farm-stand varieties, or ones to jostle for, elbow to elbow, at the farmers' markets. Cornish Gilliflower,* Alfred Jolibois, Ribston and Beeley Pippins, Carlswell's and Ellison's Orange, D'Arcy Spice,* Orleans Reinette,* Easter Orange (though I have yet to taste it), Jupiter, and Suntan are what I call cheese apples.

*Available from US sources.

Apples and...

Fennel Both the bulb and the seeds will introduce a welcome breath of aniseed to an apple salad.

Cinnamon The knee-jerk spice for apples it may be, but with good reason. Any dessert application will benefit from a generous pinch of the ground spice, particularly where brown sugar is involved.

Nutmeg Just the most diminutive grating will lend a homey warmth to a sweet recipe.

Dark sugars The butterscotch notes of light muscovado and the treacly tones of dark muscovado marry well with the sharper varieties of apple.

Berries The sharper fruits such as black currants, elderberries, and loganberries are better partners for the apple than sweet strawberries or raspberries.

Blackberries Apple and blackberry is probably the ultimate pairing of fruits. A partnership that feels like part of our national identity.

Honey Use to brush an apple tart after baking or instead of sugar when sweetening stewed apples.

Maple syrup Pour over baked apples or blend into a purée. Use to glaze wafer-thin apple tarts straight from the oven.

Brandy I am not one for including much alcohol in recipes, but brandy with the fruit of the apple tree is an exception. A very successful match.

Cheese I have gone into detail about this masterful match elsewhere, but a highlight of any Saturday shopping trip in autumn is when we buy a bag of apples from the farmers' market, then try them out with different cheeses. This is the way I discovered the delights of munching Discovery and goat cheese and Egremont Russet with a piece of Double or (very rare) Single Gloucester. It's a good family-around-the table game.

Nuts The nut family is never happier than when in the presence of apples, especially in cakes. Hazelnuts, almonds, and walnuts are more successful than Brazils or pistachios.

Butter The preferred cooking medium with this ingredient, though if oil is a necessity, then use peanut, hazelnut, or walnut rather than olive or sunflower.

Dried fruits Slices of yellow Russet and a lump of British cheese on a piece of raisin-freckled fruit bread is a great midmorning pick-me-up and much better for us than tiramisu.

Pork Any sharp apple will cut the fatty notes of pork, but the silkiest sauces tend to come from the large fruit such as Grenadier, Peasgood's, and the like.

Sage A difficult herb to marry with fruit, but apples and sage get on well. A couple of leaves tucked into the filling of a pie with a cheese crust is worth a try.

* The fatty qualities of roast pork are best balanced with a dab of sauce made from the Bramley-style fruits, but other meats will benefit too: duck, goose, and pork sausages take on a lighter feel in the mouth with a smear of apple purée.
* Apple and game is well worth trying, especially pheasant and mallard. Apples flatter the dark character of venison too, particularly if you stir a spoonful of red currant or rowan (small, tart pome fruit) jelly into the gravy.
* Mackerel, grilled until its skin crisps, is just as happy with applesauce as it is with gooseberry.
* Most varieties can be used as a flavoring in a sausage hotpot, but only as a gem to find hidden in the rich gravy, not as a main ingredient, where their effect would be too sweet.
* Try a couple of "cookers" in a pork casserole, cut into thick slices and added halfway through cooking.
* The wedlock of apples and ham works in many ways. An apple jelly makes a fine accompaniment for cold honey-baked ham; thinly sliced Russets are refreshing in a ham sandwich made with granary-style bread; a piercing purée of Bramley-type fruit will enliven a plate of warm poached ham; ham steaks become infinitely more interesting with the addition of a spot of applesauce.
* Some varieties store more comfortably than others. Nothing quite beats the traditional slatted wooden storage racks, but then, few of us have the room nowadays. Wrapping them in newspaper seems to succeed, as does nicking a few polystyrene apple trays from your produce market (it works well enough for their crummy old imports). The crucial point is to prevent the fruits touching one another. Apart from the risk of bruising, if the skins are nestling too close to one another, a single bad apple will spread like wildfire through the whole box.
* Any type will keep better under refrigeration. I have kept even the most temperamental apples in a plastic bag in the bottom of the fridge for weeks. To avoid loss of flavor, bring the fruit to room temperature before eating.
* When deciding which apple to use for which job, check its sugar content. The sweeter the apple, the more likely it is to keep its shape. The sharper the apple, the more likely it is to collapse.

Pheasant with apples and cider or verjuice

The sharp character of some of our apples (Grenadier, early Worcester, Peasgood's Nonsuch, and, of course, the Bramley) offers a knife-edge with which to cut the rich, fungal taste of game birds. Pheasant, partridge, and wild duck are all flavors that benefit from the bite of damsons, sour cherries, bitter oranges, or a good sharp apple.

As a teenager, I probably ate more pheasant than I have ever done since. We lived in deepest Worcestershire, Dad was a good shot (he trained as a gunsmith), and the birds would often loiter on the lawn, a shimmer of bronze in the autumn light, asking to be lunch. The traditional way to get around the lack of natural fat in game birds is to cover their breasts with fatty bacon, so it melts and bastes the birds as they roast. But moisture in the pan can work too, in the form of wine or stock, so that the air inside the oven is moist.

To this end, I find a batch of small apples tucked around the bird can help. The fruits split and froth up in the pan, issuing sweetness and, hopefully, a shot of cider-spritz into the juices present in the roasting pan (there are often onions and bacon in there, too). To the pan, I add liquid such as cider or, just as suitable, a glass of verjuice—the light, fruity liquid ('tain't wine, 'tain't vinegar) made from unfermented grapes. It can be difficult to find, so I buy two bottles when I see it. Its extraordinary mellow-sharpness, if there can be such a thing, feels as if it were invented for the lean meat of the pheasant.

enough for 2
medium onions – 2
unsmoked bacon slices – 4, cut into short lengths
butter
sage leaves – 3 or 4
verjuice, dry cider, or white vermouth – 1 cup (250ml)
a pheasant
bay leaves – 2
small, tart apples – 4 to 6

Peel and coarsely chop one of the onions and put it into a roasting pan with the bacon and a little butter. Leave to cook over medium heat until the bacon fat has turned opaque and the onion is starting to soften. This is a ten-minute job. Add the sage, then pour in the verjuice, cider, or vermouth.

While the bacon is cooking, preheat the oven to 425°F (220°C). Rub the pheasant all over with a little butter, salt, and black pepper. Cut the remaining onion in half and tuck it inside the cavity with the bay leaves. Place the buttered bird on top of the softened onions; slit the apples around their middles, then tuck them around the bird and roast for fifteen minutes.

continued

Lower the heat to 350°F (180°C) and continue cooking for thirty to forty minutes, depending on the bird's size. It should be juicy, very slightly pink inside, and the skin should be amber-gold. The aromatics in the pan should have the deep, appley scent of autumn, especially if you have used cider for want of verjuice.

To serve, I tend to put the bird on the table in its roasting pan, deal out the apples, bacon, and onion, carve the bird as best as I can—usually something of a hatchet job—then spoon over the thin, flavorsome juices from the pan.

Blood sausage with apple and mustard sauce

A properly made blood sausage is a fine thing if you can find one: coarse, soft, and silky. If soft, handmade blood sausage escapes you, then head for a boudin noir, the French version, which has the necessary open texture and generous seasoning.

> *enough for 2, maybe with a crisp cabbage or celery root salad*
> a little oil
> blood sausages – 2, about 7 ounces (200g) each
> bacon slices – 4
> small sweet apples – 2

Preheat the oven to 400°F (200°C). Pour a thin film of oil into an ovenproof pan. Put in the blood sausages, bacon, and the whole apples. Roll the sausages in the oil, then bake for twenty minutes or so, until they are meltingly soft inside and the apple has fluffed up. Serve with the mustard cream sauce below.

A quick mustard sauce

Warm ⅔ cup (150ml) of cream in a small saucepan with a couple of sprigs of thyme and 2 teaspoons of whole-grain mustard. When the sauce is thoroughly hot but not boiling, add a palmful of chopped parsley. Season carefully and serve with the blood sausage and apple above.

Pot-roasted guinea fowl with sausage and apple

The guinea fowl, the intruder alarm of the farmyard, is not a large bird. I usually count on one being enough to serve two, with some left for picking at the next day (good with a crisp apple salad). Add a few substantial bits and pieces—sausages maybe, a few onions—and you can stretch it to three.

enough for 2 or 3
medium onions – 2
butter – a thin slice
olive oil – 2 tablespoons
thick fresh sausages – 4
medium potatoes – 2
a large guinea fowl
apples – 3, about 1⅓ pounds (600g)
bay leaves – a couple
brandy – 2 tablespoons

Preheat the oven to 400°F (200°C). Peel the onions and cut them in half, then into thick segments. Put them in a large, heavy casserole or Dutch oven—one to which you have a lid—with the butter and olive oil and leave to color over medium heat. Slice the sausages into three and add them to the pan, then stir from time to time to keep them from sticking. Peel the potatoes, cut them into large chunks, and add them to the pan. Continue cooking until the onions are soft and golden, the potatoes are pale gold, and the sausages have colored nicely. Push everything to one side of the pan, put in the bird, breast side down, and let it color briefly, then turn it over and do the underside.

Meanwhile, peel the apples, core them, and cut them into thick chunks. Drop them into the pan, then season with the bay leaves and some salt and coarsely ground black pepper. Tip in the brandy and leave to bubble furiously for a minute or two. Cover with a lid and put in the oven. Leave for forty minutes, then remove the lid. The fowl should be golden on all sides. Check that it is ready by inserting a skewer deep into its thigh. If the juices run clear, then it is done. If there is any sign of blood, then put it back in the oven for a few minutes.

Pork chops for an autumn night

Magic tends to occur when French cooks get their hands on apples, pork, and the cream jug. Though in fairness, they usually resort to a slug of Calvados too, the intense, almost bitter apple brandy that has been part of Normandy cooking since the sixteenth century. Usually not one for cream with red meat, I am nevertheless fond of a dish of pork that has been roasted or sautéed until its sugars—the ones that have caramelized on the surface of the pan—are sticky like toffee and can be stirred into cider and thickened with cream. On the side, you need nothing more than watercress and a few pale potatoes, boiled until their cut edges start to fray.

enough for 2
thyme – leaves from 4 bushy sprigs
black peppercorns – 6
olive oil – 2 tablespoons
pork chops – 2
large, sharp apples – 2
butter – a thick slice
sugar – a scant tablespoon
hard cider – a generous ¾ cup (200ml)
heavy cream – ⅔ cup (150ml)

Strip the thyme leaves from their stems and chop them finely, then tip them into a mortar together with the peppercorns and half a teaspoon of sea salt. Pound with the pestle, slowly mixing in the oil until you have a loose paste.

Scrape this marinade into a shallow dish and turn the pork chops in it until they are coated on both sides. Leave them to marinate in a cool place for a good hour—longer if you have it.

Peel the apples, remove the cores, and cut the flesh into large dice. Melt the butter in a shallow pan and add the apples and sugar, leaving them to cook until golden and approaching tenderness. It's worth turning them now and again with a spoon, gently, so they do not crush, and letting them take on an even color. Lift them out and set aside.

Return the pan to the heat, lower in the chops and their oil, and let them cook over medium heat until they are done to your liking (probably about five minutes on either side) and have formed a slightly sticky, golden residue on the surface of the pan. Lift them out and keep warm. Pour the cider into the pan and stir to dissolve the pan-stickings. Leave to bubble and reduce until there are just a few tablespoons left—a matter of three or four minutes or so.

Pour in the cream, whisk lightly to mix it with the cider, and let the mixture bubble briefly. Return the chops and apples to the pan. This is not a thick sauce, but one that will soak neatly into the accompanying boiled potatoes.

Stuffed pork belly with apples

Belly pork, with or without its wide, flat bones, is a regular in my kitchen. It is one of the cheaper cuts and roasts more successfully than the bargain cuts from other animals tend to. As I was buying a piece the other day, my butcher, Mr. Godfrey, suggested I stuff it with apples and sausage meat. I did, and the result was sumptuous.

enough for 6
pork belly – 3¼ pounds (1.5kg), boned and scored
plump, herby fresh sausages – 5
a large, sharp apple
small sage leaves – 6
a little oil or pork dripping
a large glass of hard cider

Preheat the oven to 425°F (220°C). Lay the pork belly flat on a work surface. Remove the sausages from their skins and put the sausage meat into a bowl. I am tempted to suggest a little more salt and black pepper, but you alone will know the seasoning of your butcher's best. Peel, core, and coarsely chop the apple, then stir it into the sausage meat with the whole sage leaves (the leaves are cooked whole so they add a subtle note and you can remove them as you carve).

Put the sausage meat down the center of the pork, then roll the meat up to form a thick cylinder. Tie with kitchen string down its length to secure the stuffing. Unless you are very professional at tying meat up, it will bulge out here and there, but no matter. Lightly oil the base of a roasting pan, lay the rolled pork in the pan, and season the skin thoroughly with salt and pepper. Roast in the preheated oven for twenty minutes, then lower the heat to 400°F (200°C) and continue cooking for forty to fifty minutes, until the juices run clear.

Remove the meat from the pan and keep warm. Pour off much of the fat from the roasting pan (there will be quite a lot) and put it over medium heat. Pour in the cider and bring to a boil, scraping at the pan-stickings and stirring them to dissolve them into the cider. Check the seasoning. Carve the pork and serve with the hot pan juices.

A casserole of apple and rabbit

A sweet, apple-rich stew for a cool autumn evening—mild and soothing to the point of verging on the soporific.

enough for 4
dried flageolet or haricot beans – 8 ounces (250g), about 1¼ cups
olive oil – 3 tablespoons
rabbit pieces on the bone – 8
fresh sausages – 4, cut into quarters
medium onions – 2
dessert apples – 14 ounces (400g)
rosemary – 3 sprigs
all-purpose flour – 2 tablespoons
a bay leaf or two
hard cider, stock, or, at a push, water – 2 cups (500ml)
heavy cream – 3 tablespoons
cider vinegar – a tablespoon, or more to taste

Soak the beans overnight in cold water. Drain and bring to a boil in fresh unsalted water. Let them simmer for approximately forty minutes, checking their progress now and again. How quickly they are ready will depend on the age of your beans. Drain and set aside.

Preheat the oven to 375°F (190°C). Warm 2 tablespoons of the olive oil in a shallow ovenproof pan, add the rabbit pieces and the sausages, and let them color nicely on all sides. While the rabbit is cooking, peel and coarsely chop the onions, core and chop the apples, and remove the rosemary needles from their stems and chop them.

Remove the meat to a plate and add the onions to the pan, letting them soften. Introduce the apple, allowing it to color on all sides, adding the remaining oil if necessary. Stir in the chopped rosemary, flour, bay leaf, and some salt and pepper. Continue cooking for a few minutes to cook out the raw taste of the flour, then pour in the cider or stock. Let the liquid bubble for a couple of minutes, stirring to dissolve any crusty bits from the pan. Stir in the drained, cooked beans.

Cover with a lid, place in the oven, and bake for forty-five minutes to an hour. Check that the meat is tender, then stir in the cream and cider vinegar. The sauce should be quite sweet, but if it is too much so, then add more cider vinegar. Check the seasoning, adding more salt, pepper, and vinegar as necessary. Serve in shallow bowls.

A hotpot of sausage and apples

A rich and heartwarming supper for a freezing night. I tend to go for a fairly plain pork sausage here, just a plump, good-quality banger, but a slightly garlicky one might work too. Any apple will do, but a dessert apple is less likely to collapse than a "cooker."

enough for 4
dried flageolet or haricot beans – 8 ounces (250g), about 1¼ cups
onions – 3
olive oil – 2 tablespoons
large garlic cloves – 3
fennel seeds – 2 small pinches
bay leaves – 2
thick, nicely seasoned pork sausages – 8
large dessert apples – 2
all-purpose flour – 2 tablespoons
Madeira or medium-dry sherry – a glass
stock – 4 cups (a liter)
whole-grain mustard – 2 tablespoons

Soak the beans overnight in cold water. Drain and bring to a boil in fresh unsalted water. Let them simmer for about forty minutes, checking their progress now and again. Drain and set aside.

Peel the onions, cut them in half, then cut each half into six or so thick segments. Warm the olive oil in a Dutch oven over low to medium heat. Put the onions in the pan and leave them to color lightly, stirring them from time to time so that they don't stick or burn.

While the onions are cooking, peel and finely slice the garlic, then add it to the onions with the fennel seeds and bay leaves. Push the mixture to one side of the pan (if your pan is on the small side, then remove the onions and return them later). Cut the sausages into short lengths, add them to the pan, and lightly brown them on all sides. Meanwhile, peel, core, and quarter the apples. Cut them smaller if you wish, but be mindful that the smaller they are, the more likely they are to break up. Mix the sausages with the onions (if you removed the onions, return them to the pan now), then stir in the flour and the apples. Cook for five minutes or so, then gradually pour in the Madeira or sherry and stock, stirring. Add half the mustard, season, and leave at a low simmer for a good twenty-five minutes.

Add the beans to the sauce, season with salt and black pepper, and simmer the mixture gently for twenty to twenty-five minutes. It is ready when the sausages are fully cooked and much of the liquid has evaporated. Stir in the second spoonful of mustard and continue to simmer for a minute or two, remembering that mustard loses its interest if cooked for too long.

Cheese and apple puffs

There are some who might call these *pithiviers aux pommes et au fromage*.
Well, they are cheese and apple puffs to me. Store-bought pastry is fine here,
though a homemade version could be even better. One per person is enough
for a light lunch. But I think they need a salad to offset their richness;
something with the bitterness of endive or watercress would be perfect. You
could use pretty much any cheese here, but the blues from Strathdon or
Lanark would be more than worth a try. I used Bramleys for this because
that is what I had around, but I see no reason why a sweeter apple couldn't
be good, too.

enough for 4
puff pastry – 1 pound (500g)
apples – 14 ounces (400g)
the juice of half a lemon
blue cheese, such as Gorgonzola – 6 ounces (175g)
an egg

Preheat the oven to 400°F (200°C). Roll the pastry out thinly. Using a bowl
or small plate as a template, cut out eight disks and put four of them on a
baking sheet. Put the others aside.

Peel and core the apples, then slice them thinly, dropping them into the
lemon juice as you go. Cut the cheese into small cubes and toss it with the
apple slices. Season with salt and pepper, then divide the mixture between
the four pastry disks. Lightly beat the egg and brush the edges of the pastry.

Roll the remaining circles of pastry out just a little more, then lay them
over the apples and press tightly to seal the edges together. Brush with
beaten egg and bake for fifteen to twenty minutes or until the pastry is deep
gold. Leave them to settle for a few minutes before eating.

Rollmop herrings with beet and apple

The acid crunch of a green apple sits well with vinegary rollmop herrings. A mouthful as refreshing as being splashed by a wave. A Russet would work well here with the slightly sweet dressing, of which there may be a little left over for the next day, but it is difficult to make less.

enough for 2
cooked beets – 2, about 7 ounces (200g)
medium apples – 2
marinated herrings (rollmops) – 4
small spinach or chard leaves – 4 handfuls

for the dressing
white wine vinegar – a tablespoon
olive oil – 3 tablespoons
chopped dill – a tablespoon
heavy cream – a tablespoon
whole-grain mustard – a teaspoon

Cut the beets into thin wedges. Thickly slice and core the apples. Unroll the herrings and cut them into quarters across their length to give short, fat pieces. Wash the spinach or chard leaves thoroughly, tear them up into manageable pieces or shred them with a large knife, then add them to the beets, apples, and herring.

Make the dressing by dissolving a pinch of salt in the vinegar, then whisking in the olive oil, dill, cream, and mustard. A little black pepper won't go amiss.

Gently toss the salad ingredients and the dressing, avoiding the temptation to overmix, then serve.

Apple rabbit

Welsh rarebit—or rabbit, call it what you will—is traditionally made with ale. I like a lighter, nonalcoholic version for this recipe, where I have hidden some fried apples under the blanket of melted cheese. The classic recipe is served after a meal as a savory, but to my mind this also makes a very fine light lunch, served with a crisp, wintry salad on the side (frisée, Belgian endive, watercress) and maybe some fruit to follow.

enough for 2 as a light snack, 4 as a savory
large apples – 2
butter – a thick slice
farmstead cheese – 2½ ounces (75g)
heavy cream – 6 tablespoons
whole-grain mustard – 2 teaspoons
bread – 4 small slices

Halve the apples, remove the cores, and cut the fruit into thick segments. Warm the butter in a shallow pan and, once it starts frothing, lower in the slices of apple. Leave them to cook until they are golden and thoroughly tender. Remove and drain on paper towels.

Meanwhile, grate the cheese coarsely, put it in a bowl, and stir in the cream, mustard, and a light grinding of salt and pepper. I always take care not to overmix at this point. The cream and cheese mixture can easily "seize" with too much stirring.

Toast the bread lightly on both sides, so that it is gold rather than brown. Distribute the apples over the bread, spoon over the cheese sauce, then place under a hot broiler until bubbling.

I find Welsh rarebit always tastes best when the edges of the toast are slightly burnt. The mixture of creamy cheese, mustard, and crisp, black-edged toast is sublime.

A mildly spiced applesauce

You could serve this with pork or eat it with yogurt, at breakfast.

half a cinnamon stick
cloves – 2
juniper berries – 4
a strip of orange zest – about 1½ inches (4cm) long
unfiltered apple juice – 1⅔ cups (400ml)
fairly tart apples – 2 pounds (1kg)
light brown sugar – 3 tablespoons
butter – 1 tablespoon

Put the cinnamon, cloves, juniper berries, and orange zest in a piece of cheesecloth and tie with string. Bring the apple juice to a boil, lower the heat, and add the spice bag. Allow to simmer for half an hour or until it has considerably reduced. Remove and discard the spice bag. It has done its work.

Peel, core, and coarsely chop the apples, then add them to the reduced apple juice. Add a grinding of salt and the sugar, cover, and simmer until the apple is soft and slushy. Taste and add a little more sugar if you wish. Stir in the butter and serve.

The classic applesauce

A slush of sharp apples is still the finest accompaniment for roast pork and its crackling. At least, I have yet to find anything more appropriate.

large, sharp apples, such as Grenadier, Peasgood's Nonsuch, or
    Roxbury Russet – 3 or 4
superfine sugar – 2 tablespoons
the juice of a lemon

Peel, core, and coarsely chop the apples. Put them in a medium-sized enameled or stainless steel pan with the sugar, lemon juice, and a tablespoon or two of water. Let them cook down, covered by a lid and stirred regularly, until soft and fluffy. Check them for sweetness; they might need a little more depending on the season. Beat with a wooden spoon until no lumps remain, then serve with pork.

Applesauce with clove and orange

Make the classic sauce as above but add a couple of cloves to the apples as they cook, then a fine grating of orange zest once they have started to soften.

Apple and horseradish sauce

I first came across this in Sweden, sharing a plate with some grilled herring. Fabulous.

enough for 6 or more
large, sharp apples – 3 or 4
the juice of half a lemon
superfine sugar – 2 tablespoons
a small piece of horseradish root, to give 2 tablespoons grated

Peel, core, and coarsely slice the apples. Put them in a medium-sized enameled or stainless steel pan with the lemon juice, sugar, and a couple of tablespoons of water. Let them soften over medium heat, covered by a lid and stirred regularly until they have fallen into a pale golden slush. Stir in the grated horseradish and beat with a wooden spoon until no lumps remain.

Apple and rhubarb purée with almond brittle

An invigorating start to an icy morning. The brittle is quite optional but its crunch makes a satisfying contrast to the silken purée.

enough for 4

for the purée
rhubarb – 14 ounces (400g)
superfine sugar – 2 tablespoons
orange juice – 3 tablespoons
sweet apples, such as Cox's – 1 pound (500g)

for the brittle
blanched almonds – 2½ ounces (75g), about ½ cup
superfine sugar – scant ⅓ cup (75g)
water – 5 tablespoons

To make the purée, preheat the oven to 400°F (200°C). Cut the rhubarb into short pieces and put it in an ovenproof dish. Scatter over the sugar, then add the orange juice and bake for twenty to twenty-five minutes, until it is soft enough to crush (you could cook it over medium heat, if you prefer). Mash with a fork. While the rhubarb is cooking, peel the apples, core them, and cook with a couple of tablespoons of water, no sugar, over medium heat. Crush to a purée with a fork.

To make the brittle, tip the nuts into a shallow pan and toast over high heat for a minute or two, until golden. Put the sugar into a small, heavy-bottomed saucepan with the water and bring to a boil. Leave to bubble fiercely, without stirring, until the syrup changes to a rich brown. Tip in the toasted nuts, then pour the mixture carefully onto a lightly oiled nonstick baking sheet and leave to harden.

Smash the brittle into small pieces and set aside. Serve the two crushed fruits mixed together, scattered with broken almond brittle.

A deeply appley apple crumble

Any apple is suitable for a crumble. A dry variety such as a russet just needs some moisture—a splash of apple juice, perhaps, some lemon, or a spot of brandy. Others will collapse into a frivolous cloud under the sand-and-pebbles crust, some will keep their shape.

A sublime crumble is probably one where the fruit lies somewhere between thick juice and soft nuggets of flesh. For me, the filling should be a mixture of barely recognizable chunks on the verge of collapse and a sort of sweet slush the texture of melting snow. This is easier to achieve with the larger apples, such as Howgate Wonder, Peasgood's, Lord Derby, and Gravenstein. Blenheim Orange works well if still young and juicy, as does Suntan, a cringeworthy name for a fine cooking apple. Bramleys will do.

I can't begin to imagine the number of apple crumbles I have made over the years, the first aged nine, while my mother ironed my flannelette sheets on the other side of the kitchen (if heaven has a smell, then it is that of warm ironing and apple crumble).

Part of the deep, toe-tingling pleasure of cooking is that of constantly tweaking a much-loved recipe, and none more so than the apple crumble. My latest move on the classic instructions has been to caramelize the fruit lightly in a frying pan before I cover it with the sweet rubble of butter, flour, and sugar. It's a worthwhile step forward. The flavor seems all the more pronounced for that bit of caramelization. If the apples are tight and not producing much juice, then you know you need to add something in the way of moisture before you cover them with the crumble. The result will be less of a gamble.

I like a crust of mixed texture—a little sand, some gravel-sized lumps, and some larger, crumbly, buttery pebbles. This is easily achieved by scattering a spoonful or two of water over the crumble mixture and shaking it back and forth. The crumble will form clusters of different-sized grains. Another method is to squeeze the crumbs together in your hands before you scatter it.

And no, I'm not sure the world needs another recipe for apple crumble either, but it is something I have worked on repeatedly over the years and I want to share it with you. There is much, much pleasure to be had in a simple thing, perfectly made.

enough for 4

for the filling
cooking apples – scant 2 pounds (850g)
half a lemon
golden baker's sugar – scant ⅓ cup (75g)
butter – 2 tablespoons (30g)

for the crumble
butter – 6 tablespoons (95g)
all-purpose flour – scant ⅔ cup (150g)
golden baker's sugar – scant ¼ cup (45g)

Peel and core the apples, cut them into plump chunks (about ¾ inch [2cm] on each side) and toss them with the juice of the lemon half and the sugar.

Melt the butter in a shallow pan over frisky heat. When it starts to sizzle, tip in the apples and sugar and let the fruit color lightly. It is essential not to move the apples around too much. Let the sugar caramelize here and there, so the fruit is golden in patches. There should be a faint smell of toffee. Stir them gently.

Lift the apples out and put them into a baking dish, about 6 cups (1.5 liters) in capacity, together with the pan juices. If there are any sticky bits in the pan, add a dash of lemon juice or water and stir until they dissolve. Tip among the apples. Preheat the oven to 350°F (180°C).

Make the crumble by rubbing the butter into the flour with your fingertips (you could happily use a food processor here). When the mixture looks like fine breadcrumbs, stir in the sugar. Add a tablespoon of water, shake the crumble mixture until some of it sticks together in gravel-sized lumps, then tip it over the apple. Bake for forty-five to fifty minutes, until lightly colored.

Early autumn apples on hot toast

You could feel it: something wonderful was happening. The air had a ciderlike note, part sweet, part rotten. Shoppers hugged knobbly brown paper bags to their chest. I felt the need to hurry in case I missed something. Around the corner, outside the cheese shop, customers jostled around a stack of open wooden crates. The first of the autumn's apples had arrived.

A sucker for a Russet, I buy them by the bagful. Any will do: Egremont, Ashmead's Kernel, or St. Edmund's Pippin. Rosemary Russet is a treat and a half. The aniseed notes of its flesh flatter a lump of Gloucester or a jagged crumb of Caerphilly. Heat will sometimes bring out a hidden waft of orange. I roll them over and over in my hand too, rubbing their scabby roughness with my thumb.

I arrived home with a mixed bag of early Russets, some deeply craggy early Cox's, two-mouthful Worcesters, and a handful of the regrettably named Scrumptious. After I had crunched enough, I sliced yet more of them up, keeping their skins intact, and let them soften in a pan with enough butter and sugar to give them a thin coating of caramel. Then I tipped them onto fresh toast and spooned unpasteurized yellow cream over them.

makes 2 rounds of toast
small dessert apples – 4
a little lemon juice
butter – 3 tablespoons (50g)
golden baker's sugar – 2 slightly heaping tablespoons
a handful of raisins or golden raisins
a knifepoint of ground cinnamon
2 slices of toast, made from brioche, nut and raisin bread, or
    soft white bread

Quarter the apples and core them, but leave the skin on. Slice the apples thickly, then toss them with a little lemon juice. It will keep their flesh from browning and balance the sugar you are going to add.

Melt the butter in a shallow pan. Before it froths, stir in the sugar and leave to bubble for a minute or two. Introduce the apples, letting them cook for five minutes or so over medium heat until soft. Stir in the raisins and cinnamon.

Have the toast ready. I like it to be hot and lightly crisp. As soon as the apples are soft and lightly coated in caramel, tip them over the toast. A tub of cream, thick and yellow, would be quite wonderful here.

An apple crisp

A lighter crust, more open and less rich than that of a crumble, can be achieved using breadcrumbs instead of flour. It will also suit those who have convinced themselves they can't make pastry.

A couple of years ago, on finding myself with a batch of less than fresh bread in need of a home, I took the step of reducing all except the crusts to coarse breadcrumbs, packing them loosely into plastic freezer boxes (I seem to remember they were old yogurt tubs), and keeping them in the freezer. Throughout the next month or two, I would dip into this squirrel store of breadcrumbs to mix with a stuffing or to make fishcakes or gremolata, and on a couple of occasions to top a crumble. Storing breadcrumbs is a habit I have slipped into, and one I recommend to anyone whose heart sinks when they see the line "2 ounces (50g) fresh white breadcrumbs" in a recipe.

enough for 6
sharp apples, such as Bramley, Peasgood's Nonsuch, or Northern
    Spy – about 2 pounds (1kg)
a knifepoint of ground cinnamon
soft white bread – 4 ounces (125g)
light muscovado sugar – ⅓ cup, packed (75g)
butter – 5 tablespoons (75g)
heavy cream, to serve

Preheat the oven to 375°F (190°C). Peel and core the apples and cut them into thick slices. Drop the fruit into a buttered shallow casserole or baking dish and toss very gently with the ground cinnamon. Please don't overdo the cinnamon, otherwise your crisp will taste like a sticky bun.

Whiz the bread to coarse crumbs in a food processor. I like them not too fine—more of a soft rubble than a fine sand. Mix the breadcrumbs and sugar and cover the apples loosely with the mixture. Melt the butter in a small pan, then pour it over the crumbs, making certain to soak them all. Bake for thirty-five minutes, until the apples are soft and melting and the crumbs on top are golden and crisp.

Serve with heavy cream.

A deep cake of apples with cinnamon and nutmeg

We could fall out debating whether this is a cake or a pie. Whatever we decide to call it, the result is extraordinarily deep. The recipe needs a little care: the pastry is extremely fragile and you will feel as if you are peeling apples for England. But the finished cake is truly splendid. Just the thing to make on a wet autumn day.

enough for 8 at least

for the pastry
butter – 1 cup minus 2 tablespoons (200g)
golden baker's sugar – 1 cup (200g)
a large egg
all-purpose flour – 3 cups plus 2 tablespoons (400g)
baking powder – a heaping teaspoon
a little milk and sugar, to finish

for the filling
sweet dessert apples – 4 pounds (1.8kg)
a lemon
golden baker's sugar – 2 tablespoons
a knifepoint of ground cinnamon
a little grated nutmeg

cold heavy cream, to serve

To make the pastry, cut the butter into chunks and put it in a stand mixer with a paddle attachment. Add the sugar and beat until pale and creamy. Break the egg into a cup, mix it gently, then add to the butter and sugar, mixing thoroughly. Mix together the flour and baking powder, then add carefully and slowly to the butter mixture. Stop as soon as the flour is incorporated. Remove the dough, put it on a lightly floured board, and roll into a fat sausage. Wrap in wax paper or plastic wrap and chill for half an hour.

Meanwhile, peel the apples. As you finish each one, drop it into a bowl of cold water in which you have squeezed the juice of half the lemon. Quarter the apples, then core and thickly slice them, dropping them back into the acidulated water as you go. Drain the apples and put them into a large, heavy-bottomed saucepan with the sugar, cinnamon, nutmeg, and the juice of the remaining lemon half. Bring to a boil, then turn down to a simmer and continue until the apples are tender but still hold their shape—about ten to fifteen minutes over medium heat with the occasional stir. Leave them to cool.

Very lightly butter an 8-inch (20cm) springform cake pan. Remove the pastry from the fridge, cut off a little less than a third of it and return that to the fridge. Cut thick slices from the large piece of pastry and use them to line the base and sides of the cake pan, pressing it firmly into the corners and patching any tears or cracks. The pastry should be quite thick. Chill for twenty minutes. Preheat the oven to 400°F (200°C).

Line the cake pan with a sheet of wax paper or parchment paper and half-fill with pie weights. This will keep the pastry in place. Put a baking sheet in the oven and, when it is hot, put the lined cake pan on it (the heat will help the pastry cook underneath). Bake for fifteen minutes, remove, and leave to cool slightly, then remove the paper and pie weights. Take care not to tear the pastry. Return the pan to the oven for five minutes without the weights and paper. Remove and leave to cool down a little. Turn the oven down to 350°F (180°C).

Fill the pastry shell right up to the rim with the apples, holding back as much of the liquid as possible. Roll out the remaining pastry to fit the cake and place it over the top. Patch any holes and gently press the raw pastry onto the edges of the cooked. Cut three slits in the top of the pastry to let out the steam (though they will close on cooking). Brush the top with a little milk.

Bake on the hot baking sheet for forty-five minutes, until the top is nut brown. Remove from the oven, dust with a little superfine sugar and leave to settle down for a good fifteen minutes. Run a thin spatula around the edge to free the pastry from the pan, but leave the cake in place for now. When the cake is thoroughly cool, carefully remove it from the pan. You will need a sharp knife and a jug of cream.

Whole wheat apple and marmalade cake

A good, reliable cake that will keep for a day or two, the sort you find at village-fête cake stalls.

enough for 8
butter – a scant cup (220g), at room temperature
light muscovado sugar – a scant cup (210g)
eggs – 4
whole wheat flour – 2 cups (250g)
baking powder – a slightly heaping teaspoon
ground cinnamon – half a teaspoon
apples – 7 ounces (200g) peeled weight
golden raisins or raisins – ⅔ cup (100g)
orange marmalade – 6 tablespoons (125g)
finely grated zest of an orange
demerara sugar

Preheat the oven to 325°F (160°C). Use baking parchment to line an 8-inch (20cm) round springform cake pan. Beat the butter and sugar together in a stand mixer until light, fluffy, and pale coffee colored. Meanwhile, lightly beat the eggs with a fork. Sift together the flour, baking powder, and cinnamon. Core and coarsely chop the apples. They should be under ⅓ inch (1cm) square. Toss the chopped apples with the raisins and stir in the marmalade and orange zest.

Add the beaten eggs a little at a time to the creamed butter and sugar, introducing a spoonful of flour if the mixture starts to curdle. Gently but firmly fold in the rest of the flour. Fold in the fruit and marmalade mixture. Spoon into the prepared cake pan, scatter a fine layer of demerara over the top, and bake for an hour and fifteen minutes, until a skewer comes out moist but without any cake mixture sticking to it. Cool before serving.

A cake of apples and zucchini

enough for 8 at least
butter – 1 cup minus 2 tablespoons (200g)
superfine sugar – 1 cup (200g)
eggs – 2
zucchini – 5 ounces (150g), about 2 small ones
a small apple
all-purpose flour – generous 1½ cups (200g)
a pinch of salt
½ teaspoon baking powder
a pinch of ground cinnamon
pecans – 2 ounces (60g), ½ cup chopped
golden raisins – ½ cup (80g)

Preheat the oven to 350°F (180°C). Butter and line the bottom of a loaf pan measuring 8 by 5 inches (20cm by 12cm) and 3½ inches (9cm) deep.

Cream the butter and sugar until light and fluffy. Lightly beat the eggs and beat them in a little at a time, making sure each bit is fully incorporated before adding the next. Coarsely grate the zucchini and apple. Squeeze them with your hands to remove any excess moisture, then add to the mixture. Mix the flour, salt, baking powder, and cinnamon together and gently fold them into the mixture. Stir in the nuts and raisins. Transfer to the lined loaf pan and bake for about an hour, until golden and firm to the touch. Allow to cool in the pan before turning out.

Marmalade apple tart

As much as I like contemporary eating, I warm to the tastes and smells of food from other times. This sticky open tart, like oat flapjacks and pea and ham soup, smells of a different era. Appropriately enough, you will need an old-fashioned pie pan for this, with a rim around the edge.

enough for 6

for the pastry
butter – 5 tablespoons (75g)
golden baker's sugar – ⅓ cup (75g)
an egg yolk
all-purpose flour – 1¼ cups (150g)
a little milk

for the filling
sweet dessert apples – about 2 pounds (850g)
half a lemon
golden baker's sugar – a tablespoon
marmalade – ¾ cup (250g)

heavy cream, to serve

To make the pastry, cut the butter into chunks and put it in a stand mixer fitted with the paddle attachment. Add the sugar and beat until pale and creamy. Mix in the egg yolk. Add the flour carefully and slowly to the mixture, stopping as soon as it is incorporated. Check the texture of the dough, adding a very little milk if necessary to bring it to a nice rolling consistency. Remove the dough from the bowl, put it on a lightly floured board, and shape it into a fat sausage. Wrap in wax paper or plastic wrap and chill in the fridge for half an hour.

Meanwhile, peel the apples. As you finish each one, drop it into a bowl of cold water into which you have squeezed the lemon half. Coarsely chop them and put back into the acidulated water as you go.

Drain the apples, put them into a large, heavy-bottomed saucepan with the sugar and bring to a boil. Turn down to a simmer, and cook until the apples are tender and have all but lost their shape—about twenty or thirty minutes over medium heat with the occasional stir. Leave them to cool.

Very lightly butter the pie pan. Remove the pastry from the fridge, cut it into thick slices, and use them to line the pan, pressing the dough firmly into the corners and patching any tears or cracks. The pastry should be quite thick. Prick it lightly with a fork, then chill for twenty minutes. Preheat the oven to 400°F (200°C). Place a baking sheet in the oven.

Put the chilled pastry shell on the hot baking sheet and bake for twenty minutes, until lightly biscuit colored. Remove from the oven and turn the heat down to 350°F (180°C). Fill the pastry shell with the apple purée. Warm the marmalade in a small pan, then spoon it on top of the apple and return to the oven for thirty to thirty-five minutes. Serve warm, with cream.

Apple custard tart

Cartons of ready-made custard come in two sorts: one full of sugar, coloring, and thickeners; the other, marginally more expensive, that is simply eggs, sugar, cream, and vanilla. Go for the latter if you want to make this heavenly pie—and if you can find it. Otherwise, make your own custard—there is a recipe on page 493.

> tart cooking apples – 2½ pounds (1.15kg)
> butter – 5 tablespoons (75g)
> frozen puff pastry, thawed – 13 ounces (375g)
> ready-made or homemade custard – 1⅔ cups (400g)
> a large egg yolk, beaten
> milk – 2 tablespoons
> superfine sugar, for dusting

Peel, core, and thinly slice the apples. Melt the butter in a shallow pan over medium heat, then toss the apples in it. As the apples start to soften—a matter of five or six minutes—remove them from the heat and leave to cool.

Preheat the oven to 400°F (200°C). Put a baking sheet in the oven. Unroll the pastry and cut it in two, one piece slightly larger than the other. Roll out the smaller piece and trim it into an 11-inch (28cm) circle. Lay this in a floured deep metal tart pan, 9½ inches (24cm) in diameter. Roll out the second piece of pastry into a 13-inch (32cm) circle and set it aside.

Pour the custard onto the apples and toss gently. Pile the mixture onto the pastry in the tart pan in an even mound. Brush the edge of the pastry with the beaten egg yolk. Lay the second piece of pastry over the apples, then pinch the edges together firmly all the way round. There will inevitably be some leakage but it will be contained in the dish.

Mix together the milk and the remaining beaten egg yolk and brush the pastry with it. Scatter superfine sugar over the top, cut a small hole in the center to let the steam out, then place the pan on the hot baking sheet and bake for about forty-five minutes to an hour, until golden brown.

Treacle tart with russet apples

Warm treacle tart—the deep, stick-to-your-spoon variety—remains on my list of desert-island dishes. I experiment with the basic recipe, sometimes making a humble, tin-plate-style tart (for which see *The Kitchen Diaries*) and on other occasions producing a thicker version such as the one here.

The unrelenting sweetness of the genre needs something cold and sharp alongside. I serve mine with ice cream or crème fraîche, or a big jug of heavy cream. But in the depths of autumn, when this sort of dessert is almost compulsory, some brightly flavored apple, cooked until soft and sticky, is a pleasing change of step. Needless to say, I do serve both the apples and the crème fraîche. Golden syrup (a by-product of sugarcane refining) is harder to find in North America than in the UK, but the flavor of this tart depends on using it (rather than substituting corn syrup).

enough for 8

for the crust
vegetable shortening – 2½ tablespoons (35g)
butter – 2½ tablespoons (35g)
all-purpose flour – 1¼ cups (150g)
water – roughly 2 tablespoons

for the filling
golden syrup – 2 cups plus 2 tablespoons (675g)
the zest and juice of a small lemon
fresh coarse white breadcrumbs – 9½ ounces (270g), about 6 cups

for the apples
medium Russet apples – 4
a little superfine sugar
cloves – 2

Make the pastry in the usual way, rubbing the fats into the flour with your fingertips until the mixture resembles coarse breadcrumbs, then bringing it together with a little water to form a soft ball of dough. Alternatively, mix the ingredients together in a food processor.

Roll the pastry out, using a little flour so it does not stick, and use it to line a deep-sided 8-inch (20cm) tart pan with a removable bottom. I always take great care to push the pastry deep into the corners. Put on a baking sheet and in the fridge to chill.

Preheat the oven to 400°F (200°C). Pour the syrup into a saucepan over medium heat. It takes an age to empty a whole can, so I tend to write my name with the golden syrup at this point. Stir in the lemon juice and breadcrumbs, then pour into the uncooked pastry shell. It should come almost to the rim. Slide the tart into the oven and bake for fifteen minutes. Turn the heat down to 350°F (180°C) and continue cooking for a further fifteen to twenty minutes, until lightly firm.

While the tart is cooking, cut each apple into six or so pieces, removing the core as you go. I leave the skin on, but it is up to you. Put the apples in a pan with a little sugar, the cloves, and a couple of tablespoons of water, bring to a boil, then lower the heat so the apples simmer to an all-over softness. Stir from time to time and add a little more water if necessary, until the fruit is sticky and golden. Remove from the heat and put aside to cool. Serve with the tart.

A tart of mincemeat and apples

A simple tart, yet one that is also thoroughly festive. I serve this as a Christmas dessert, with cream, but it works as a cake too. In which case I would serve it strudel-style, with coffee and whipped cream on the side.

> *enough for 6*
> cooking apples – 14 ounces (400g)
> superfine sugar – 2 heaping tablespoons
> puff pastry – 17½ ounces (500g)
> mincemeat – 14 ounces (400g)
> beaten egg

Peel the apples, core them, and cut them into small, thin slices. Put into a wet saucepan with the sugar and leave to simmer gently until the sugar has melted and the apples are tender but not quite collapsed. Preheat the oven to 400°F (200°C).

Cut the pastry in half and roll out each piece to measure 14 by 6 inches (36 by 16cm). Place one half on a nonstick baking sheet, or one lined with parchment paper, then place the mincemeat in a wide line down the center of the pastry, leaving a margin around the rim. Place the apples on top (any juice should be left in the pan), then brush the edges of the pastry with some of the beaten egg. Lay the second piece of pastry on top, pressing the edges firmly to seal. Trim any ragged edges, crimp them with a fork if you wish, then decorate with any trimmings of pastry if the mood takes you. Brush with more of the beaten egg, cut four or five small slits in the top of the pastry, and bake for twenty to twenty-five minutes, until golden and crisp. Serve warm, with cream.

Apfelstrudel

There is apple in neat, thin slices, golden raisins the size of pistachios, the warm Christmastide note of ground cinnamon, and drift upon drift of snow-white confectioners' sugar. There are crisp leaves of pastry and, should I feel the need, a little pot of whipped cream at its side. As I press my fork down on the folds of crackling pastry, the scent of late autumn slowly fills my corner of the room. I have coffee too, in a tiny, thick-sided cup, and a newspaper on a stick of which I can read barely a single word.

I have a love of Europe's timeworn cafés. Those hallowed rooms heavy with the scent of chocolate, cinnamon, burnt sugar, and marzipan. The tables that are just that bit too small, too dinky; the long, white aprons and fraying leather purses of the waiting staff; the creaking chairs and well-trampled wooden floors. Each has its specialty—a deep apple cake in Stockholm; cheesecake in Budapest; chocolate cake in Vienna; and in Berlin the mother and father of *apfelstrudel*. Believe me when I say I will be happy to die with a pastry fork in my hand.

In Germany and Austria I have been offered cream, custard, and ice cream with my hot strudel. It's a hard decision to have to make. I generally take it without any accompaniment, then regret it, wishing I had gone for the vanilla ice cream. The addition of a little apricot jam in the filling is purely mine and not at all traditional.

enough for 6

for the filling
sweet apples – 1¾ pounds (800g)
the zest and juice of a lemon
apricot jam – 3 tablespoons
superfine sugar – ¼ cup (50g)
a pinch of ground cinnamon
golden raisins – ⅓ cup (50g)
sliced almonds – ½ cup (50g)

for the pastry
butter – 10 tablespoons (150g)
fresh white breadcrumbs – 3 ounces (80g), scant 2 cups
filo pastry – 10 sheets
confectioners' sugar, for dusting

Peel, core, and quarter the apples, then cut each quarter into very thin slices. Toss them with the lemon zest and juice, the jam, sugar, and cinnamon. Add the raisins and sliced almonds. Preheat the oven to 400°F (200°C).

Melt the butter in a small frying pan, then pour a good half of it into a small bowl. Add the breadcrumbs to the butter remaining in the pan and fry them until they are golden and crisp. Tip them out onto a paper towel.

Place a large sheet of wax paper or a clean kitchen towel on a work surface. Place two sheets of filo side by side, long sides slightly overlapping. Brush with some of the melted butter and scatter over two heaping tablespoons of the toasted breadcrumbs. Place another two sheets of pastry on top but in the opposite direction. Brush them too with butter and scatter with breadcrumbs and continue, alternating the direction of the pastry each time, until all ten sheets are used up. Scatter any remaining breadcrumbs over the top sheet of pastry.

With the long edge of the pastry nearest you, pile the apple filling onto the nearest third of the pastry. Make sure the edge is well buttered, then roll up the pastry into a fat sausage, keeping the filling in place as you roll. Squeeze the open edges together to seal the filling inside. Slide it onto a flat baking sheet. Brush with butter and bake for thirty minutes or so, until the pastry is thoroughly crisp. Dust with confectioners' sugar and serve.

Warm rice with cinnamon, apple, and maple syrup

A pudding as comforting as an old teddy bear.

enough for 4
Arborio, Carnaroli, or other risotto rice – 5 ounces (150g), about ¾ cup
water – 2 cups plus 2 tablespoons (500ml)
whole milk – 2 cups plus 2 tablespoons (500ml)
a good pinch of ground cinnamon
a large apple
superfine sugar – 3 tablespoons
maple syrup

Put the rice in a small pan and cover it with the water. Bring to a boil, then simmer until the water has almost entirely evaporated. Keep an eye on it. Pour in the milk, bring back to a boil, then turn down to a simmer and partially cover with a lid. Leave for about fifteen minutes, stirring regularly and keeping a watch on the liquid level. It should still be very creamy at the end. Stir in the cinnamon, adding more to taste if you wish.

Grate the apple, peeling it if you wish, then stir it into the rice together with the sugar. Leave for five minutes, during which time some of the remaining liquid will be absorbed, then serve, pouring the maple syrup over as you go—at least two tablespoons for each.

Baked apples with apple ice cream

Baked apples, originally cooked in the fading heat of a wood-fired oven, are almost unique to the northern hemisphere. We have a history of growing the varieties whose acid flesh rises, soufflélike, from their skins: Howgate Wonder, Dumelow's Seedling, Bramley. Generously proportioned apples, with skins tough enough to hold back the billowing froth that peeps at their brim.

We have stuffed their chiseled hollows with mincemeat, buttered breadcrumbs and syrup, or turned them into deep wells of molten honey. We wrap them in pastry and call them dumplings. Wise cooks score around the apples' tummies, so that rather than exploding, they emerge from the oven with beaming smiles, their contents intact. A jolly dessert for a bitterly cold night.

Any apple will bake—a Russet can be deeply aromatic when stuffed with a walnut of butter and a clove or two—but the drier and more yellow the flesh, the less likely it is to puff up. Cox's have a tendency to explode.

It is, I find, not easy to know when to serve a baked apple. Too often they appear at Sunday lunch, a dish slid into the oven when the roast comes out, a meal unlikely to leave any of us needing more. In our house, the baked apple, with its blackened skin and snow-white froth, tends to appear after a bowl of thick soup, possibly of white beans or pumpkin, most usually on a short, frosty day with a sulfurous sky.

My mother offered cream with her baked apples, her replacement Bird's custard. My own preference is for ice cream, a shocking contrast to the searing heat of the apple's flesh. Vanilla works in its usual calming manner, and praline made an interesting change, but in the autumn of 2007 I made an ice cream from the apples themselves. The result was delicate and full of warm bonhomie.

enough for 4, with more than enough ice cream for later

for the ice cream
sharp apples – 2¼ pounds (1kg)
golden baker's sugar – 1 cup (200g)
light or heavy cream – 1⅔ cups (400ml)
egg yolks – 4

for the baked apples
large dessert apples – 4
a little butter

To make the ice cream, peel the apples, core them, and cut into thick slices. Put them in a heavy-bottomed saucepan with half the sugar and let them stew slowly over medium to low heat (they need no water, but keep an eye on them so they don't burn). Once a little juice has formed in the bottom of the pan, cover with a lid and leave to simmer gently for twenty minutes or so, stirring from time to time, until the apples are fluffy. Mash with a fork and leave to cool.

Bring the cream to a boil. Beat the egg yolks and remaining sugar in a heatproof bowl until thick, then pour in the hot cream and stir. Rinse the saucepan and return the custard to it, stirring the mixture over low heat until it starts to thicken slightly. It won't become really thick. Cool the custard quickly—I do this by plunging the pan into a shallow sink of cold water—stirring constantly. Chill thoroughly, then mix with the cold mashed apple. Pour into your ice-cream maker and churn according to the manufacturer's instructions. It will seem quite a thick mixture. Scoop into a plastic, lidded box and freeze until you are ready.

To bake the apples, preheat the oven to 400°F (200°C). Remove the apple cores with a corer if you don't wish to do battle with them at the table. Score the fruits around their tummies with a sharp knife. Put them into a small roasting pan or baking dish in which they will fit snugly. Drop a tablespoon of butter into each hollow and bake for forty to fifty minutes, until the apples are puffed up and golden. Serve with the ice cream.

Baked apples with mincemeat and brandy

Apple brandy has been made in this country since the 1700s and of late has been undergoing something of a revival. It is my first choice for adding to baked apples, or indeed any apple recipe that might benefit from a touch of alcohol, if for no other reason than that it feels right. Of course, French-made Calvados, or even an "ordinary" cognac, is fine here too.

enough for 4
4 very large or 8 smaller apples
mincemeat – 6 to 8 tablespoons
apple brandy – 6 tablespoons

Preheat the oven to 400°F (200°C). Score each apple lightly around its tummy with a sharp knife. You want to split the skin so the apple doesn't explode in the oven. Remove the core of each apple with an apple corer or a small knife. Put the fruit in a shallow baking dish or roasting pan. Mix the mincemeat with 2 tablespoons of the apple brandy, then spoon as much of the mixture as you can into the hollows in the fruit. If there is any mincemeat left over, put it into the roasting pan. Pour in the remaining brandy and bake until the apples have puffed up and started to split open, revealing a fluffy interior of baked apple. This will take about forty-five minutes to an hour, depending on the variety of apples.

Judging a baked apple for doneness is best accomplished with the eye rather than by the clock. A baked apple ready to eat will have risen so much that its skin has split open into a wide smile and the interior is turning to fluff and frothing around the edges.

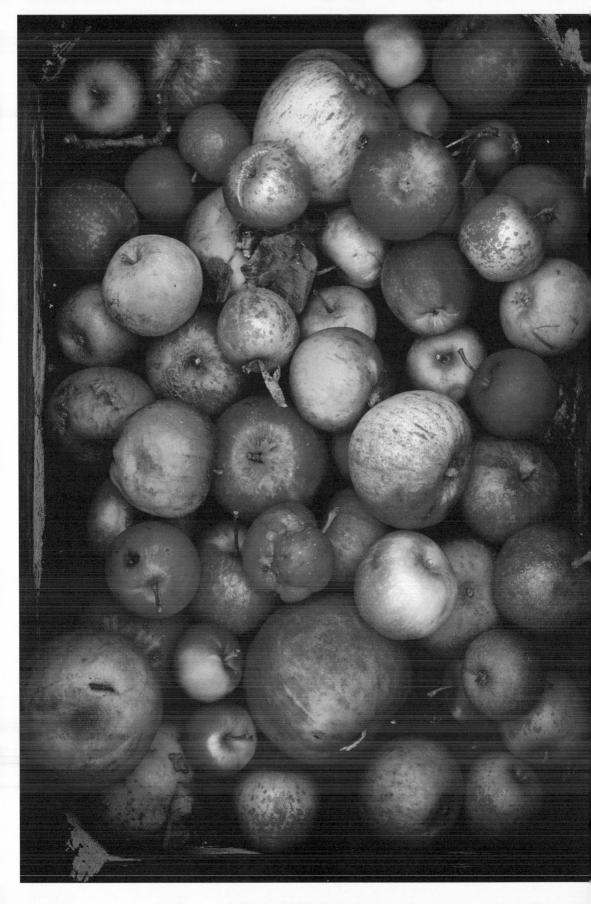

An apple in the hand

Lastly, a fruit not to trap between two layers of piecrust, fold into whipped cream or nibble with a piece of Wensleydale, but a fruit to eat for its own sake. This should be a very special apple, one whose flesh packs as much acidity as sweetness, whose notes are complex and come at us in waves. An apple so good you could eat its core.

For me, there has to be an icelike crunch, followed by an element of sharpness and that slight acidity that gets you at the corner of your mouth as you take the first bite. I am in the minority. The ancient sharp apples are considered of little interest commercially, with North Americans and Europeans supposedly preferring sweet, dull-tasting fruit with no apparent flavor other than that of sugar. It is interesting that these modern flavorless apples are also those that perform well in terms of high yield, having a tolerance for storage and long transport, a uniform shine, and an unchallenging character. In other words, manna for the supermarket chains. So perhaps it is not what we want to buy that ensures the popularity of mediocre fruit so much as what they wish to sell us.

Each to his own, but I would like to put in a word for the Russets. The web of rough skin that sits like fine sandpaper on the surface of the apple, softening the rusts, umbers, and crimsons of the skin, offering an extra texture to delight the hand and the tongue. Blenheim Orange, Braddick's Nonpareil, Claygate Pearmain, the Egremont and Golden Russet, Ribston Pippin, Ross Nonpareil, St. Edmund's Pippin, and Tydeman's Late Orange can usually be relied upon and, in season, are not impossible to find. Beyond the lacework of rough skin will be apples of extraordinary interest, with hints of nut and spice.

Each season, an apple passes my lips that I insist is the best I have ever tasted. It could be a late Cox's Orange Pippin, a particularly honeyed Pitmaston Pineapple, a Christmas Pearmain with its dusty crimson skin, or, more usually, a frustratingly anonymous apple from someone's fruit bowl. At that moment it is the perfect apple, the one I have been looking for all my life. Until, that is, I find the next one.

A few quick ideas

A salad of blood sausage and apple

If you have a lovely blood sausage, then you might like to use it in an autumn salad. I did this the other week, marrying the savory sausage to crisp young Cox's.

Cut the sausage into fat chunks, about 1½ inches (4cm) long. Get a trace of oil hot in a shallow nonstick pan and brown the pieces nicely all over. Remove them to a warm plate, covered with foil, as they become ready or push them to one side of the pan. Add a little more oil or some butter to the pan if necessary, then add slices of apple, cored but not peeled, and let them color nicely.

Have ready a bowl of spinach and watercress leaves, rinsed and shaken dry. Mix a dressing of peanut oil, smooth French mustard, and cider vinegar and toss gently with the leaves, apple, and hot blood sausage. A more robust alternative could use shredded and lightly cooked Savoy cabbage. I might save that one for the colder weather.

Vanilla ice cream with hot mincemeat and applesauce

If there is one sensation I love, it is hot sauces over cold ice cream. Great favorites are coffee over vanilla and hot chocolate sauce over coffee ice cream. This is a Christmas version of that marriage.

Core and coarsely chop three small apples. I prefer not to peel them for this recipe. Put them into a small pan with a couple of tablespoons of brandy or Calvados and warm over low heat until the apple has softened. If you cover the pan with a lid, this will take about eight to ten minutes, but it is a good idea to check regularly that they are not boiling dry. When the apple is very tender, stir in 15 ounces (425g) of mincemeat and bring almost to a boil.

Put two or three small balls of ice cream into each of four dishes and pour over the hot sauce. Serve immediately.

A cinnamon crème fraîche for baked apples

Preheat the oven to 350°F (180°C). Score four apples around their tummies, cutting just through the skin. Put them in an ovenproof dish. Wet the fruit with a tablespoon or so of water, then scatter a little sugar over them and dot with butter. Bake for forty minutes or so, depending on the size of the apples.

Just before you remove them from the oven, put a generous ¾ cup (200ml) of crème fraîche in a small nonstick pan, add two level tablespoons of golden baker's sugar or superfine sugar and a knifepoint of ground cinnamon and bring almost to a boil. As soon as the sugar has dissolved, remove from the heat and serve over the apples.

Stewed apples with black currants

Perhaps my favorite use for a black currant compote is to fold it into stewed apples. First peel and core five large apples, slice them thickly, then let them cook over low heat with a couple of tablespoons of sugar and barely two tablespoons of water. When they start to froth, switch off the heat and leave to cool. Chill thoroughly.

Divide the apples among four dishes and fold in a small amount of stewed black currants, so that it leaves a purple ripple running through the apples. Pour over cream or yogurt and serve.

Apricots

A fine apricot, rich, intense, fragrant, is perhaps the rarest of all fruits. So rare, in fact, that I briefly considered its exclusion in this collection, but to have done so would have been to give up on what can be a sublime and memorable fruit. This is a fruit as soft and tender as a baby's cheek, with a scent that is part honey, part almond. A fruit whose flesh has notes of peach, brown sugar, and orange blossom and an opportunity for pleasure that is too good to miss. Coupled with the new popularity of apricot cordons being bought for the home garden, and a slowly warming climate, *Prunus armeniaca* has secured its place in these pages.

But note that I said "a fine apricot." You know, apricots have been spoiled by commerce, with its need for a lengthy shelf life and its constant obsession with size and sweetness. I know of no fruit or vegetable whose character and reputation has been so spoiled by the greed and ignorance of commercial growers and the supermarkets they supply. I am not as critical as some of modern commerce but in this instance it deserves it. Even a trip to France to witness at first hand the progress of the modern apricot industry did not convince me. My idea of progress was very different from theirs.

Anyone who has given up on the modern apricot, with its heart of watery cotton wool, would be heartened at coming across the real thing. A fine apricot will have a cluster of dots, freckles of ruby, rust, and chocolate, around its shoulders. It may have a dime-sized patch of rough skin. Within its velvet skin, it will glow a deep, intense orange, as if lit by a candle flame. You will be able to tease the two halves apart with a single pull, at which point it will almost certainly lose a bead or two of juice. The flesh will be soft and sumptuous, very different from the hard, modern apricot with its sunset blush that so often leads us up the garden path.

The apricot came to us from China, and was probably cultivated well before 2000 BC. Its name, *Prunus armeniaca*, is understood to have come from the Greeks, who supposed, incorrectly as it turned out, that the fruit originated in Armenia. The word *apricot* is linked to the Roman *praecocium,* meaning "precocious," referring to the fact that it ripened so early. It is this early ripening that is the cause of so many of the fruit's problems. Such early blossom and fruits are truly at the mercy of the weather.

The reason this exquisite fruit is here at all is down to Henry VIII's gardener, who brought it from Italy in 1542. Although grown throughout Iran, China, Japan, America, and southern Europe, it will, given a warm wall and a bit of luck, do rather well here too.

An apricot in the garden

Just one more wall. That is all I ask, a wall on which to train the branches of an apricot tree. A wall that is in full sun, sheltered from early frosts yet open enough for the blossom to tempt the bees. They can be grown as large trees, but training against a wall is a more popular method, providing reflected warmth and making for easier picking.

Apricot blossom is pure white and comes in March, three weeks or more before the leaves open. A roll of row cover fabric will prevent the frost from doing its worst to the buds. Keep an ear open for the weather forecast. The fabric should be removed during the day to allow pollination to take place. That said, it is still very early in the year and many insects are yet to get out of bed, so pollinating by hand is wise. I have seen it done and it is not difficult.

An apricot will not bear fruit on new wood; it must be one or two years old. They can be pruned in spring and summer. Choose a dry day (winter pruning may result in diseased wood, as it does in plums and damsons). In most cases this will be to remove any growth that cannot be tied neatly back against the wall in an open fan shape.

The fruit is best ripened on the tree if possible, which will mean keeping the birds at bay. Like apples, apricots are ready when they can be removed from the twig with one firm twist. Should they refuse, hold fire a day or two. Although they are some of the earliest stone fruits on the market, British-grown varieties tend to appear in late summer.

Varieties

The varieties named on supermarket packages are often modern hybrids suited to the climate of South Africa, Chile, France, or wherever they are grown. I list the most successful for growing in our climate.

Moorpark* The most popular variety here, Moorpark is happy in our hit-and-miss climate and can generally be relied upon. Ripening in early August, it has a good color with plenty of red freckles. Likes a south-facing wall.

Blenheim* A pale-fleshed but deeply flavored variety first grown at Blenheim Palace in the 1840s. Best grown in plenty of sun, this is often thought of as our finest variety. August ripening.

Isabella A chance find in Gloucestershire, hardy and apparently of good color and flavor (I have yet to taste this one).

Golden Glow A pale-yellow apricot discovered in 1985 growing on the Malvern Hills, not far from where I spent my childhood. It is said to be very hardy and a good cropper.

Gold Cott I am less than impressed with this vigorous modern variety, but it has been bred for our climate and is generally reliable.

Hemskirke Rather like Moorpark but less prone to die back. Bright-orange flesh with a reddish blush; the fruit should be ripe by late July.

Petit Muscat Small fruits of an intense flavor.

Gold Kist* A generous bearer, the tree produces big, deep-orange-fleshed fruits with wonderful flavor; especially good for jam and for drying.

*Available from US sources.

An apricot in the kitchen

The apricot is one of the more successful additions to savory recipes. More versatile than the plum, the fig, or even the pear, its lack of sugar and faint back-note of acidity give a lot more scope for mixing with meat and game. Lamb, duck, and pork are especially comfortable with apricots, and for once we have a fruit that appeals with rice, couscous, and lentils, though I would keep it well away from fish.

Middle Eastern cooking is rich in apricot recipes. I had a heady lamb tagine in Marrakech, thick with golden raisins, mint, and pickled lemon. A French version, with rosemary and garlic, is surprisingly satisfying too. A slow-simmered casserole of duck and apricots makes a welcome change from the more usual oranges, while a salad of duck skin and blood orange will brighten up a winter's day.

In desserts, the apricot excels where the peach fails, having a snap of acidity missing in the sweeter fruit. Where a peach tart may cloy, one of apricots will shine brightly in the mouth, always offering a note of freshness to balance the buttery pastry. An apricot puff pastry tart is one of the most enduring pieces of pâtisserie, but it also works in a more homely crumble.

A warm couscous, comforting, frugal, grounding, is infinitely more interesting when it contains a few apricots. I would include pistachios, golden raisins, and sometimes mint, too. Apricots also work in a rice salad, which cannot be said of many fruits, especially if you have some caramelized onions in there for balance.

Wherever possible, I keep the pit in. Not in a tart, where its presence would intrude, but whenever I poach the fruit for a compote, and I always leave a few in when making jam. The stone is the heart and soul of the fruit and its faint almond note seems, like cooking a piece of meat on the bone, to work a little magic.

Apricots and...

Rice No fruit works so well with the nutty flavor of rice. Use apricots fresh in a rice salad with mint and golden raisins or add the poached fruits to a rice pudding.

Pistachios The apricot's natural affinity for this mauve and green nut can be exploited in a rice pilaf or by scattering the chopped nuts across the glaze of an apricot tart.

Almonds A marriage of antiquity and quiet perfection. A tart with a heart of ground almonds; a Danish pastry with sliced nuts on its glacé icing surface; a single kernel floating on an apricot compote. The almond and the apricot are as true a culinary friendship as you will ever find.

Cinnamon A dusting of ground cinnamon is worthwhile on a dish of baked apricots, as is a whole stick tucked into a dish of the poached fruit.

Honey Despite, or perhaps because of, the apricot's honeyed tones when truly ripe, a spoonful of the real thing is a successful sweetener in place of sugar. Try a trickle over the fruits before you bake them.

Lamb Perhaps the most welcome of meat and fruit partnerships. Tuck fresh or dried apricots into a lamb casserole or tagine, or offer a salsa of the chopped fruit with mint and watercress to serve with grilled chops. Used as a stuffing, the fruit will work with pork or turkey too.

Brandy I'm never one to use many spirits in the kitchen, but the apricot does nevertheless like a drop or two. Sprinkle over apricots for baking or add to the sugar and water when stewing.

Yogurt The apricot feels much more at home with yogurt than with cream, as you might expect of something with such a heritage.

* Unlike some soft fruits, apricots will go on to ripen after picking, though there may be a small loss of flavor. Ideally, though, we should leave them to ripen on the tree.
* An apricot kernel, the small, flat nut at the center of the pit, adds an almond note to cooked apricots and jams. Use only one or two per recipe. In large amounts, the prussic acid they contain can be poisonous.
* Apricot jam is the correct one to use in a classic Sachertorte.
* The distinctive flavor of the crisp, light amaretti di Saronno comes from ground apricot kernels.
* Apricot leather is a Middle Eastern specialty, rather like fruit-flavored jelly. You can melt it down for a tart glaze.
* To make a glaze suitable for fruit tarts, warm apricot preserve in a small pan with a squeeze of lemon juice or a spoonful of brandy, then push it through a sieve. Apply with a pastry brush.
* The smartest way to gauge an apricot's flavor is by smell rather than color. The more headily fragrant the fruit, the more chance of it being what you are hoping for.

An apricot pilaf

The scented steam emerging from white basmati puttering in a covered pot; the homely note of warm, sweet spices; the top notes of fresh, clean mint. If ever smell alone could bring us to the table, then this is it. Add to that the sharp, fruity note of fresh apricots and you have an olfactory feast of the first order. I have eaten this as a side dish to lamb cutlets from the broiler and as a quietly pleasing main course.

enough for 4 as a side dish
white basmati rice – 1 cup (200g)
butter – 3½ tablespoons (50g), plus an extra tablespoon
bay leaves – 3
green cardamom pods – 6, very lightly crushed
black peppercorns – 6
a cinnamon stick
cloves – 2 or 3, but no more
currants – 2 ounces (50g), scant ⅓ cup
apricots – 7 ounces (200g)
green onions – 4
mint – 2 or 3 sprigs
sliced almonds – 2 tablespoons

for the yogurt sauce
chopped mint – 2 tablespoons
a pinch of ground cinnamon
thick, natural yogurt – ¾ cup (200g)
olive oil – 2 tablespoons

Wash the rice three times in a bowl of cold water, moving the grains around in the water with your fingers. Cover with fresh water and set aside for ten minutes.

Melt the 3½ tablespoons of butter in a saucepan, then add the bay leaves, cardamom pods, peppercorns, cinnamon stick, cloves, and currants. Stir them around in the butter for a minute or two, until the fragrance wafts up. Drain the rice and add it to the warmed spices, then pour in one-third inch (1cm) of water and bring to a boil. Season with salt, cover with a lid, and turn the heat down to a simmer. Pit and coarsely chop the apricots. Trim and finely slice the green onions. Chop the mint.

After ten minutes, remove the lid and gently fold in the chopped apricots, green onions, and mint. Replace the lid and continue cooking for a further two or three minutes, until the rice is tender and all the water has been absorbed. Leave, with the lid on but the heat off, for two or three minutes. Toast the almonds in a nonstick pan until golden.

Remove the lid and add the remaining tablespoon of butter and the almonds. Fluff gently with a fork.

For the yogurt sauce, mix the mint, cinnamon, and a little salt into the yogurt, then stir in the oil. Spoon the sauce over the pilaf and serve.

Spiced apricot couscous

The apricot takes nicely to a little spice, and not just the sweet cinnamon stick and pinks-scented clove but the cardamom pod and chile too. All the flavors it was brought up with.

I like apricots in a couscous, fat nuggets of fruit flecked through grain as soft and comforting as a cashmere blanket. This is something to sit beside lamb that you have cooked slowly until its fibers fall grainily from the bone, or peppers that have been stuffed simply with rice and herbs.

enough for 8
large shallots – 2 (or a medium onion)
butter – a thick slice
half a cinnamon stick
green cardamom pods – 6
dried chile flakes – a good pinch
apricots – 7 ounces (200g)
golden raisins – a handful

for the couscous
couscous – scant 1 cup (150g)
olive oil – a tablespoon
hot vegetable stock – 1 cup (250ml)
harissa paste – 2 tablespoons
a preserved lemon
cilantro – a small bunch

Peel and chop the shallots, then cook them in the butter over medium heat for ten minutes or so, until soft and golden. Stir in the cinnamon stick, cardamom pods, chile flakes, and a grinding of salt and black pepper. Halve, pit, and chop the apricots and add to the pan with the raisins and a cupful of hot water. Leave to simmer gently for ten to fifteen minutes, until the apricots are truly soft.

Put the couscous in a heatproof bowl with the olive oil. Pour over the hot stock and cover with a lid. Leave for ten minutes, then fluff up the grains with a fork, stirring in the harissa paste and the finely chopped skin of the lemon (you can discard the inner pulp, if you wish). Fold the cooked apricots into the couscous, then chop the cilantro and fold it in too.

A tagine of lamb with apricots

Of all the fruit and meat marriages, this is the one that appeals to me most. Meat, spices, and apricots probably work better together than any combination since roast pork and applesauce.

> *enough for 4*
> diced lamb shoulder – 2¼ pounds (1kg)
> ground cinnamon – 2 teaspoons
> ground cumin – 2 teaspoons
> ground turmeric – 2 teaspoons
> sweet paprika – a tablespoon
> hot paprika – a teaspoon
> olive oil – 2 tablespoons
> onions – 3
> garlic cloves – 4
> golden raisins – scant ½ cup (60g)
> honey – 2 tablespoons
> saffron threads – 1 teaspoon
> stock – 3 cups (750ml)
> chopped tomatoes – two 14-ounce (400g) cans
> apricots – 12 ounces (350g)
> a preserved lemon
> cilantro leaves – a handful
> mint leaves – a small handful

Toss the cubed lamb in half the ground spices and leave for at least four hours. Overnight would be ideal.

Preheat the oven to 325°F (160°C). Warm the olive oil in a deep, heavy-bottomed baking dish and add the seasoned meat in small batches. Remove when it is browned nicely on all sides. Peel and coarsely chop the onions, then peel and finely slice the garlic. Add to the pan with the remaining spices and allow to soften and color lightly. Stir regularly over medium heat so that the spices flavor the onions but do not burn.

Add the raisins, honey, saffron threads, stock, tomatoes, and apricots, then return the meat to the pan. Bring to a boil, season with salt and black pepper, then cover with a lid and place in the oven. Cook for two and a half hours.

Cut the preserved lemon in half and discard the interior pulp. Finely chop the skin and stir into the tagine. Lift out the meat with a slotted spoon and boil the sauce over high heat until it is reduced and thick, then stir in the coarsely torn cilantro and mint leaves. Return the meat to the sauce and serve.

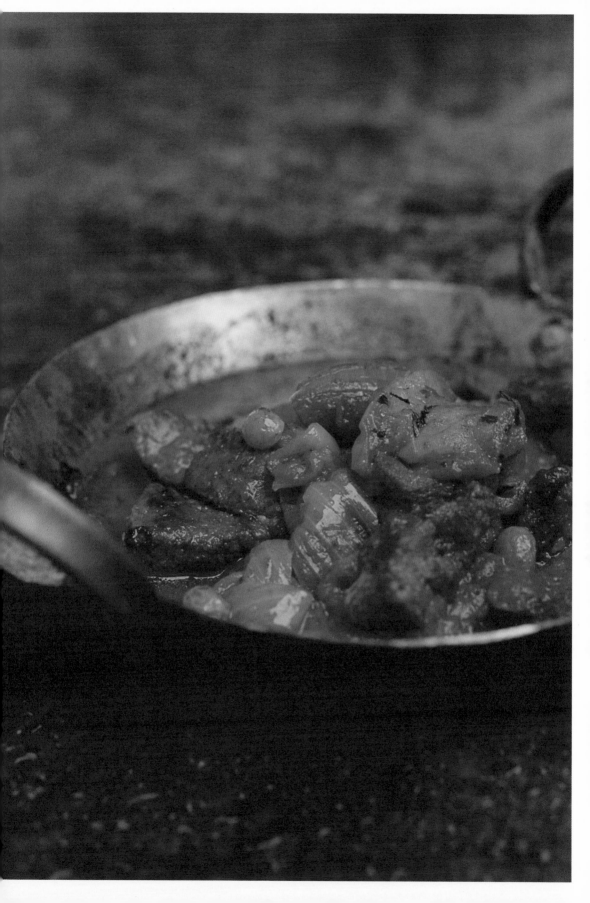

A "Frenchified" casserole of lamb, apricots, and rosemary

enough for 4
olive oil – 2 tablespoons
butter – a thick slice
cubed shoulder or leg of lamb – 2¼ pounds (1kg)
pancetta or bacon, in one piece – 5 ounces (150g)
onions – 2
carrot – a smallish one
garlic cloves – 2
tomato paste – a tablespoon
all-purpose flour – a tablespoon
white wine – 2 glasses
bay leaves – a couple
rosemary – 4 short, bushy sprigs
a strip of orange zest from half an orange
small apricots – 12

Warm the olive oil in a large, heavy-bottomed casserole or Dutch oven. The heat should be quite high. Drop in the butter and, when it starts to froth, add the cubed meat. Let the meat brown a little on each side, then remove it to a dish with a slotted spoon. While the lamb browns, cut the pancetta or bacon into small cubes, peel and coarsely chop the onions and carrot, and peel and slice the garlic.

Tip the bacon into the pan, let it cook over slightly lower heat until the fat turns gold, then add the onions, carrot, and garlic. Let the vegetables cook until they are just lightly colored, then stir in the tomato paste and flour. Leave for three or four minutes, with the occasional stir, then pour in the wine. Bring to a boil, scraping at the bottom of the pan with a wooden spoon to dissolve the pan-stickings (so much flavor there), then add the herbs and orange zest. Return the meat to the pan, turn the heat down, season with salt and black pepper, and leave to simmer, partially covered by a lid, for an hour, with the occasional stir.

Halve and pit the apricots and add them to the pot. Continue to simmer for thirty minutes. The casserole is ready as soon as the meat and apricots are tender, but it would taste even better the next day.

Guinea fowl with apricots, orange, and Szechwan pepper

The lean, slightly gamey meat of the guinea fowl has an affinity with fruit—it is very successful with apples and Calvados, and with plums too—though the addition of apricots here was done on a whim. One of those thoughts you wish you had had earlier in life. The hint of acidity in the apricots is good with this dark, rich meat.

enough for 2
butter – a thin slice
olive oil – 2 tablespoons
a large guinea fowl – about 3¼ pounds (1.5kg)
medium onions – 2
medium carrots – 2
celery – a stalk or two
a clove of garlic
Szechwan peppercorns – a teaspoon
all-purpose flour – a heaping tablespoon
stock – 2½ cups (600ml)
orange zest – 4 long strips
bay leaves – a couple
star anise – 3
apricots – 8

Preheat the oven to 400°F (200°C). Melt the butter in the oil in a large, deep casserole. Cut the guinea fowl in half through the backbone, salt and pepper it, then color it lightly on both sides in the butter and oil. Remove and set aside.

Peel the onions and cut them in half and then into thick segments. Put them in the pan in which you browned the guinea fowl and leave to color over medium heat. Scrub and coarsely chop the carrots, trim and coarsely chop the celery, then add them to the onions. Peel the garlic, crush and add it. Toast the peppercorns in a dry frying pan, then crush or grind fairly finely and add them to the pan together with the flour. Continue cooking for three or four minutes, then pour in the stock.

Bring to a boil, then turn down to a simmer. Season with salt, pepper, orange zest, bay, and star anise. Return the guinea fowl to the pan. Halve, pit, and chop the apricots, then slip them into the sauce. Cover with a lid, transfer to the oven, and bake for fifty minutes. Serve the guinea fowl surrounded by its sauce and vegetables.

Roast pork with apricot and pine nut stuffing

A boned shoulder is an economical cut of pork and a sound candidate for stuffing and roasting for a Sunday lunch. I get the butcher to remove the bones (you can put them in the pan with the roast, if you wish; it will lead to tastier pan juices). I also ask the butcher to score the fat for crackling. Spinach is the vegetable for this one, and maybe a leafy summer salad with which to wipe up the juices from your plates.

enough to serve 6 generously
a boned shoulder of pork – at least 5½ pounds (2.5kg), skin scored
rosemary – 3 sprigs
apple juice – a generous ¾ cup (200ml)
stock – a generous ¾ cup (200ml)

for the stuffing
butter – a thin slice
a medium onion
apricots – 8
pine nuts – 3 heaping tablespoons
rosemary – a tablespoon of chopped needles
lemon zest – a tablespoon
fresh white breadcrumbs – 2 ounces (60g), about 1⅓ cups
an egg – beaten

Make the stuffing: melt the butter in a large pan, peel and coarsely chop the onion, and fry it in the butter for ten minutes, until soft and pale gold. Pit and coarsely chop the apricots and stir them into the onion with the pine nuts, rosemary, lemon zest, breadcrumbs, and beaten egg. Season with salt and pepper, then set aside. Preheat the oven to 425°F (220°C).

Put the pork shoulder skin-side down on a large cutting board. Spread the stuffing over the surface (you might have a little left over, in which case cook it in lumps around the roast). Roll the meat up as best you can, tying it securely in several places with kitchen string.

Place in a roasting pan, tucking the rosemary underneath, then rub the skin with salt. Roast for twenty-five minutes, reduce the heat to 325°F (160°C), and cook for another two hours.

Remove the pork from the pan, put it on a warm dish, and cover it loosely with foil (covering it too tightly will soften the crackling). Pour most of the fat from the roasting pan, leaving the darker juices behind (there won't be many). Put the pan over medium heat and pour in the apple juice, scraping away at any crusty bits on the pan as it bubbles. Pour in the stock, let it boil and reduce by half, then season and pour into a warm pitcher.

Carve the meat and serve with the apple gravy.

Baked apricots with fresh cheese

There was an unforgettable afternoon last summer when a dish of sugared apricots, still warm from the oven, was passed around the garden table with a plate of small, snow-white fresh cheeses. We sat, barefooted on the searing hot stone, scooping up the warm juices with our spoons.

enough for 4
apricots – 12
golden baker's sugar or vanilla sugar – 3 tablespoons
soft, fresh cheeses, such as Petit Suisse, mascarpone, caprini freschi,
      or fromage frais

Preheat the oven to 350°F (180°C). Halve the apricots and discard all but one or two of their pits. Lay the fruit snugly in a shallow baking dish, dust with the sugar, then tuck in an apricot pit or two. Pour over just enough water to wet the sugar, then cover with a lid of some sort. Bake for an hour, until the fruits are soft and deeply colored.

Serve them warm, in small dishes, with a little soft fresh cheese.

Broiled apricots with mascarpone

Ripe fruits of deepest orange are the only ones to use here.

enough for 2
seriously ripe apricots – 6
mascarpone – 3 ounces (80g)
superfine sugar – 4 tablespoons

Get a broiler really hot. Cut the apricots in half and remove their pits. Place them hollow-side up on a broiler pan lined with foil. Spoon the mascarpone into the hollows, spoon half of the sugar on top, and place under the broiler. Leave for four or five minutes, then add the remaining sugar.

Return them to the broiler until the mascarpone has melted and the sugar has formed a partial crust. Eat immediately.

Slim apricot tarts

At the height of summer, we often eat around the zinc table in the garden. While everyone is wiping the roasting juices from their plates with a few soft salad leaves, I sometimes take the opportunity to slip a tray of paper-thin apricot tarts into the oven. It's a feel-good moment, partly because for once I feel like an organized cook. True, a certain amount of prep is required: the apricots need to be cooked and left sleeping in their syrup; the pastry has to be cut; the oven has to be on. Yet it is a rather wonderful moment, bringing to the table a tray of warm, slim pastries, their crusts holding a handful of melting apricot halves.

enough for 2
apricots – 8
sugar – 2 tablespoons
puff pastry – 7 ounces (200g)
apricot jam – 4 tablespoons

Put the apricots into a small saucepan, add the sugar and enough water just to cover the fruit, and bring to a boil. Lower the heat and simmer for ten minutes, until the fruit is soft and tender. It must be soft enough to crush between your fingers. Drain, halve, and discard the skins and pits. The skins should slide off effortlessly. Preheat the oven to 425°F (220°C). Place a baking sheet in it to get hot.

Roll the pastry out to ⅛ inch (3mm) thick, which is thinner than you would normally expect. Cut two rounds of pastry approximately 6 inches (15cm) in diameter. Score a wide rim around the outside of each one, about a third of an inch (1cm) in from the edge, taking care not to cut right through the pastry. Place the apricots flat-side down on the pastry, steering clear of the rim of each tart.

Take the hot baking sheet from the oven, lift the tarts onto the baking sheet with a large, flat spatula, and bake for ten to twelve minutes, until the pastry is puffed and golden. Warm the apricot jam in a small saucepan and brush it over the tarts. Eat warm or cool.

An iced apricot and black currant terrine

You could get away with using store-bought meringues for this, but if you wish to make your own, then use the recipe for rose water meringue in the Black currants chapter. Ideally, omit the rose water and bake the meringue on a lined baking sheet as six or eight individual meringues; that way you will have a good balance of crisp shell and gooey middle. You will need 7 ounces (200g) of them, so keep the remainder for another day.

enough for 6
black currants – 7 ounces (200g)
superfine sugar – 2 tablespoons
water – 2 tablespoons
ripe apricots – 4
heavy cream – 2 cups (500ml)
meringues – 7 ounces (200g)

You will need a freezer-safe plastic or metal box approximately 9½ by 5 inches (24 by 12cm) and 3 inches (7cm) deep, lined with plastic wrap.

Pull the black currants from their stems and put them in a small saucepan with the sugar and water. Bring to a boil, leave to simmer for five minutes, until the fruits start to burst, then boil hard for two minutes, until the liquid has reduced a little. Remove from the heat and allow to cool.

Slice the apricots in half, remove the pits, and chop the fruit into small pieces. Whip the cream until it is thick, but stop short of whipping it so far that it will stand in peaks. It should still be able to slide very slowly from the whisk. Crumble the meringues into small chunks—not to a fine powder— then fold them gently into the whipped cream with the chopped apricots. Pour into the lined box. Pour the black currants on top, then gently swirl them through the mixture. Fold the overhanging plastic wrap over the top and freeze for at least four hours.

To serve, cut into thick slices with a sharp knife.

Apricot betty

The hot dessert has a place in summer as long as it contains fruit—at least that is my thinking. Classic winter recipes are worth trying with summer ingredients, such as steamed pudding with damsons, rice pudding with blueberries, or, in this instance, a betty made with summer fruits. This is even better with a little cream to flatter the hot, crisp crust and meltingly tender fruit.

enough for 4
ripe apricots – 1⅔ pounds (750g)
superfine sugar – 2 tablespoons
butter – scant 2 tablespoons (25g)

for the crumb layer
butter – 5 tablespoons (75g)
maple syrup or golden syrup – 2 brimming tablespoons
soft white breadcrumbs – 4½ ounces (125g), about 2⅔ cups
light soft brown sugar – ½ cup, lightly packed (100g)

Preheat the oven to 350°F (180°C). Cut the apricots in half and remove the pits. Lightly butter a baking dish, add the apricots, and sprinkle lightly with the sugar. Add the butter, cut into small cubes.

To make the topping, put the butter and syrup into a saucepan and let them melt slowly. Mix the breadcrumbs and sugar together. Pour over the melted butter and golden syrup, then pour this mixture over the apricots. Bake for thirty minutes, until the crust is crisp and the fruit is fully tender.

Classic almond apricot tart

A classic from the pâtissier's window. Some cream—thick, yellow and unpasteurized—is needed here. Or possibly crème fraîche. Either way, it should be offered with generosity.

enough for 6

for the filling
apricots – 6
superfine sugar – a scant cup (180g), plus 2 tablespoons
sherry (dry or medium-dry), or marsala if you have it – 2 tablespoons
butter – ¾ cup (180g)
large eggs – 2, lightly beaten
all-purpose flour – ⅔ cup (80g)
ground almonds – 1⅓ cups (150g)

for the pastry crust
cold butter – ⅔ cup (150g)
all-purpose flour – 2 cups (250g)
superfine sugar – 2 tablespoons
an egg yolk

Halve and pit the apricots. Put them in a bowl and add the two extra tablespoons of sugar and the sherry or marsala.

For the pastry, rub the butter into the flour with your fingertips or in a food processor. The mixture should resemble fine, fresh breadcrumbs. Stir in the sugar, egg yolk, and a tablespoon or two of water to bring the mixture together into a firm dough. Pat into a ball, flatten with a rolling pin, then roll out on a floured work surface. Use to line a 9½-inch (24cm) tart pan with a removable bottom, trim any overhanging pastry, then leave to chill in the fridge for thirty minutes. Preheat the oven to 400°F (200°C).

To make the filling, cream the butter and sugar together until smooth and pale. Add the lightly beaten eggs a little at a time, adding a tablespoon of the flour if there is any sign of curdling. Mix in the ground almonds and flour.

Remove the pastry shell from the fridge, line it with wax paper, and fill with pie weights, then bake for fifteen to twenty minutes, until the edges are dry and pale. Carefully lift out the paper and pie weights and return the pastry shell to the oven for five minutes, until the entire surface feels dry to the touch. Turn the oven down to 350°F (180°C).

Spread the almond paste over the bottom of the pastry shell. Arrange the apricots evenly on the almond paste (they will sink as they cook) and bake for twenty-five to thirty minutes. Allow to cool a little before attempting to remove the tart from the pan.

A simple apricot jam

A fresh-tasting jam that is best kept in the fridge.

> *enough for two pint (500g) jars*
> apricots – 2 pounds (1kg)
> granulated sugar – 1½ pounds (750g)
> the juice of half a lemon

Halve, pit, and quarter the apricots. Break open a couple of the pits and extract the small, bitter kernel within. Put the apricots into a large steel or enameled pot, add the sugar, and bring to a boil. Turn down the heat and let the fruit and sugar simmer enthusiastically for twenty-five minutes, until the fruit is soft. Skim off any foam that rises to the surface and discard. Test to see if the jam is ready by dropping a small spoonful on a fridge-cold saucer and placing it in the fridge. If a skin forms within a minute or two, it is ready. Stir in the lemon juice, add the two apricot kernels, and transfer to Mason jars. Seal and store in the fridge.

A few recipes for canned and dried apricots

When apricots are halved, pitted, and dried, they take on an intense flavor with a welcome edge of acidity. Rather than becoming a shadow of its fresh self, a dried apricot develops true character and is often used in place of the fresh fruit in pastries and cakes. No inferior ingredient this, but rather a hint of what the fresh fruit was like before it had the life bred out of it. I can eat dried apricots like sweets. I include a couple of recipes for them without apology.

Turkey with pistachio and apricot stuffing

I suggest you order the turkey leg a couple of days before you need it. Ask the butcher to bone it and remove the sinews. A large leg should weigh about four pounds (1.8kg), and when stuffed will feed six.

enough for 6
a small to medium onion
fresh white breadcrumbs – 5 ounces (150g), about 3 cups
soft dried apricots – 2½ ounces (75g)
shelled pistachio nuts – 1½ ounces (45g), ⅓ cup
interesting sausages – 12 ounces (350g)
thyme leaves – a tablespoon or so
grated zest of a small lemon
parsley leaves – a handful, chopped
a large turkey leg, boned, sinews removed, ready for stuffing
olive oil
vermouth – a glass

Peel the onion, chop it finely, and put it in a mixing bowl. Stir in the fresh breadcrumbs. Chop the dried apricots and the pistachios, then add them to the bowl. Slit the sausage skins and peel them away, then mix the meat in with the other ingredients. Add the thyme, lemon zest, and parsley, then season thoroughly with salt and a little pepper.

Preheat the oven to 325°F (160°C). Put the turkey leg skin-side down on a work surface and pound out the meat with a rolling pin or meat pounder to roughly ⅓ inch (1cm) thick (there will inevitably be holes and tears). It needs to be thin enough to roll into a thick sausage when stuffed. Spread the stuffing over the meat, pushing it almost to the edge. Roll up the meat to give a long, fat sausage, then secure with string at 1¼-inch (3cm) intervals.

Place the meat in a roasting pan, moisten with olive oil, cover with foil, and roast for two hours. It is done when the juices run clear when tested with the point of a skewer.

Remove the meat to a warm place to rest (such as the switched-off oven), covered with foil, and tip most of the fat from the roasting pan, leaving behind the darker residue and any crusty pan-stickings. Put the roasting pan and its juices over medium to high heat, pour in the vermouth, and stir to dissolve the gooey flavors stuck to the pan to make a thin, delicious gravy. Simmer for a few minutes, taste for seasoning, and pour into a warm pitcher.

Put the meat on a carving board, slice thickly onto warm plates, and serve with the hot pan juices.

A cake for midsummer

Raspberries and apricots are rippled through the soft, almond-rich crumb of this pretty cake. The very essence of summer. I sometimes add a few rose petals and an extra handful of raspberries at the last moment, or perhaps a light scattering of confectioners' sugar.

enough to serve 8 to 10
butter – ¾ cup (175g)
golden baker's sugar – 1 cup minus 2 tablespoons (175g)
ripe apricots – 7 ounces (200g), 4 or 5
eggs – 2
self-rising flour – 1⅓ cups (175g)
ground almonds – a scant cup (100g)
milk – 2 tablespoons
raspberries – 6 ounces (170g), about 1½ cups

Line the bottom of an 8-inch (20cm) springform cake pan with parchment paper. Preheat the oven to 350°F (180°C).

Cream the butter and sugar together in a stand mixer until pale and fluffy. Halve, pit, and coarsely chop the apricots. Beat the eggs lightly, then add to the creamed butter and sugar a little at a time, pushing the mixture down the sides of the bowl occasionally with a rubber spatula. If there is any sign of curdling, stir in a tablespoon of the flour.

Mix the flour and almonds together and fold in, with the mixer on a low speed, in two or three separate batches. Add the milk, and once it is incorporated, add the chopped apricots and the raspberries.

Scrape the mixture into the cake pan and bake for an hour and ten minutes. Test with a skewer; if it comes out relatively clean, then the cake is done. Leave the cake to cool for ten minutes or so in the pan, then run a thin spatula around the edge and slide it out onto a plate, decorating as the fancy takes you.

Apricot almond cake with apricot purée

An endlessly useful cake, shallow like a single layer of sponge, for use with poached fruits or a plate of strawberries. In summer, I serve it in slim slices with a purée of fresh apricots and an egg-shaped scoop of crème fraîche.

enough for 10 to 12
butter –1 cup plus 2 tablespoons (250g)
superfine sugar – 1¼ cups (250g)
ground almonds – ⅔ cup (75g)
all-purpose flour – ¾ cup plus 2 tablespoons (100g)
soft dried apricots – 3½ ounces (100g)
large eggs – 4, beaten
the grated zest and juice of an organic or unwaxed lemon

for the apricot purée
ripe apricots – 14 ounces (400g)
granulated or superfine sugar – ½ cup (100g)
a lemon

Line the bottom of a shallow 9-inch (23cm) cake pan with parchment or wax paper. Preheat the oven to 350°F (180°C).

Beat the butter and sugar together in a stand mixer until white and fluffy. Mix the almonds and flour together. Whiz the apricots in a food processor until they are very finely chopped. They must be finer than candied peel—almost, but not quite, a purée.

Add the eggs to the butter and sugar mixture a little at a time, with the beater on low. Turn the machine off and add the lemon zest and a third of the almonds and flour, then turn the mixer on low until the dry ingredients are incorporated. Add the second and then the third batch of almonds and flour, switching the machine off each time. If you do this too quickly you will end up with a heavy cake.

Lastly, the machine still on low, mix in the lemon juice and the apricots. Using a rubber spatula, transfer the mixture to the lined cake pan and bake for thirty-five minutes. Run a thin spatula around the edge of the pan, turn the cake out onto sugared wax paper, and leave to cool.

For the purée, put the apricots in a saucepan with the sugar and 4 tablespoons of water. Bring to a boil, turn down the heat to a simmer, and leave to cook for twenty minutes, or until the fruit is very soft. Pour into a food processor and blitz to a smooth purée, or push through a sieve. Sharpen with lemon juice to taste and leave to cool. Serve with the cake.

Apricot and pistachio crumble

I have tried fresh, dried, and canned apricots for this sumptuous dessert and have come to the conclusion that canned, with some of the silky syrup, beats everything else hands down. A pinch of ground cardamom in with the apricots or the crumble topping would be wonderful.

enough for 4
apricots in syrup – three 15-ounce (425g) cans
a tablespoon of butter for the dish

for the crust
shelled pistachio nuts – 4 ounces (125g), about 1 cup
cold butter – ⅔ cup (150g)
all-purpose flour – 2⅓ cups (300g)
demerara sugar – ¾ cup (175g)

Preheat the oven to 350°F (180°C). Grind the pistachios to a point somewhere between the fineness of ground almonds and the coarseness of chopped nuts. They should resemble fine gravel. Rub the butter into the flour until it resembles fresh breadcrumbs, then stir in the ground pistachios and the demerara sugar.

Pile the apricots and 4 tablespoons of their syrup into a buttered baking dish, tucking a few whole pistachios in, if you wish. Tip the topping onto the fruit and bake for thirty to thirty-five minutes, until the crust is crisp and golden, the fruit soft and tender. Take care that the crust doesn't burn (nuts always burn easily)—cover with foil if necessary. Serve hot, with cream.

Baked apricots with lemon tea

One of the most reliable plants in my garden is the lemon verbena bush, coming back from its winter dormancy every May with its slender, rough, lemon-scented leaves. I use them for tea mostly, but occasionally find a use for them in the kitchen. They have much to contribute to a dish of poached fruits, particularly peaches and apricots.

enough for 4
fresh apricots – about 1 pound (500g)
a handful of lemon verbena or 2 lemon verbena tea bags
sugar – 2 to 3 tablespoons
star anise – 2
a vanilla pod

Preheat the oven to 350°F (180°C). Wipe the apricots, cut each one in half, twist them apart, and discard the pits. Lay the halved fruit in a shallow dish, tucking them together snugly.

Put the kettle on, and when it boils, pour enough water into a heatproof measuring cup to come up to 3 cups (750ml). Drop in the leaves or tea bags and leave them for five minutes, then fish them out and throw them away (I put mine in the compost). Stir the sugar into the tea until it has dissolved, then pour it over the apricots, tucking in the star anise and the vanilla pod as you go.

Bake the apricots for about forty minutes, until they are tender. Remove and allow to cool before chilling thoroughly.

Blackberries

Of all of the blossom that fills this garden in
the spring, the blackberry's is the most fragile.
A stiff breeze or an April shower will destroy in
a heartbeat the tissue paper–white petals with
their faint purple blush.

The blackberries are not officially mine,
but cascade over the garden wall and its thick
covering of ivy courtesy of a generous neighbor.
They produce enough fruit for a pie or two,
sometimes a crumble as well, ripening gradually
from mid-July until the first frosts. Picking a late
blackberry on a misty November morning is one
of the great pleasures of the British countryside. In my patch they are no
trouble, except when I snag my arm on their vicious thorns as I walk past on
my way to pick a pear or to take something up to the compost heap. If there
are not enough for a pie, then I throw them in the breakfast muesli, where
they stain the goat's milk yogurt a romantic purple.

Archaeologists have proof of *Rubus fruticosus* having been eaten for
at least 2,000 years. The blackberries in the stores are now both earlier and
juicier than I remember them. I knew them as an autumn fruit, ripening
around the annual return to school, the berries a temptation on the long
walk back home from where the school bus dropped its lone, last passenger.
The fruits were sharp, juicy, and tightly packed. Today I see locally grown
fruit in the stores at the same time as black and red currants, many three
times the size of those I picked as a kid, and fatter, too. (Had it come
earlier in the season, I might have questioned whether the tiny berry of
my childhood was in fact the similar, but smaller, dewberry.) The fruit of
commerce—strawberries, raspberries, red currants, as well as this one—will
continue to get sweeter and larger until someone finally realizes they are
diluted beyond recognition; but why those grown in the wild are also larger
nowadays is a mystery. I remember them as the odd, sharp cluster of berries
that you tipped into an apple pie, a few berries intense enough to flavor even
the largest quantity of apples. I don't recall them being something plump

and sweet enough to put in a bowl and eat with cream. We are lucky we have both at our disposal.

With each acre of green land that disappears under new and doubtless necessary housing estates, the remaining brambles become all the more precious. Collecting berries, with a wicker basket for the regulars, plastic bags for the unprepared, has been a late-summer pastime here for centuries. It may not be the most valuable of our wild food, nor as exciting as finding a cluster of apricot-capped chanterelles, but it is the most common and probably the most appreciated by all the family. Though how many of those bags of purple squish ever become a pie one can only speculate. But the art of reaching over the mounds of thorns and scratchy leaves to get at the fattest berry ("just one more, then I'll go home") is a pleasure in itself. We should probably continue to do it while we can.

There is a little myth and superstition to the bramble. Brave is he or she who picks a bag of blackberries once Michaelmas has passed. It is then, we are told, that the devil is supposed to piss on them. The facts back this up. The cooler weather permits the growth of *Botryotinia*, which can occasionally be mildly poisonous. So once again, an "old wives' tale" proves true.

Blackberries in the garden

Botanically this is not a berry but an aggregate fruit made up of numerous drupelets. Well, it looks like a berry to me. Deer are especially fond of their leaves, while bees dote on their nectar-rich flowers. I rank them as one of my favorite fruits. The blackberry's natural habitat is woodland, meadows, and waste ground, with many plants forming part of our hedgerows. I found some last year in the back lanes of a north London housing estate, together with rusting prams and car tires. A wild feast just waiting to be picked. Blackberries will do very well in the average garden, taking up only as much room as you allow them to. They will climb a hedge or ramble over an unsightly garden feature. "Scrambling" is probably the best description for this perennial's growth, like that of a particularly vigorous climbing rose (the bramble belongs to the family Rosaceae). The plants are not even remotely fussy about their soil and will happily form dense thickets even on wasteland. Like the lemon, the bush has both blossom and ripe fruits at the same time.

You should really get new plants going in the autumn, but a winter-planted one will survive. I have said they will grow anywhere, but they won't complain if you give the ground a little manure as a housewarming present. Those long stems with their powerful thorns that are produced in the first year are generally fruitless, but flower buds will follow in the second year. They like a good winter, by which I mean a long, cold one. It encourages bud production.

Blackberries need some sort of support to scramble up. A makeshift structure knocked up from a couple of poles and horizontal wires will work, or you could train them over a rustic arch. Thornless varieties will save scratched arms and legs, but you can train the long shoots up trellises and pergolas to make their picking more manageable. Mine just fall in great skeins over the hedge. As soon as you get the plants in, cut the canes back to the second visible bud.

They will overwinter in that dormant way that fruit canes do (you will probably think you have killed them), then in spring will send up the first of the new shoots. As these grow, keep tying them in by folding them around the wires or trellis by hand or securing them with pieces of string. When the second winter approaches, ruthlessly cut back all the side shoots on each of the major canes. Come spring, the plant will send up a whole new batch of shoots from ground level. Tie these in as soon as they are long enough.

Varieties

Sylvan* Large fruits on a very thorny and vigorous plant. Ripens midsummer.

Loch Ness* A very popular variety, with a long season from late summer onward. Should keep you supplied with large, richly flavored berries throughout the autumn.

Fantasia Another widely grown variety with a long season. Will keep fruiting until the first frosts.

Oregon Thornless A compact variety, good for the smaller garden. Not overly large, the fruit has a good flavor, approaching that of the wild. Ripens from late August onward and offers pleasing autumn foliage.

Waldo* Needs a bit of protection from high winds, but produces good-quality fruits on disease-resistant plants.

Cherokee* An erect, thorny variety with sweet, large berries that ripen midseason.

*Available from US sources.

The hybrids

The loganberry (*Rubus x loganobaccus*) is a cross between the blackberry and the raspberry. A closer look suggests it may have been the Aughinburgh blackberry and the Red Antwerp raspberry. The deed was done in the late 1880s in Santa Cruz by the horticulturalist James Logan. Legend has it that the fruit is a result of an accident when he was trying to cross two varieties of blackberry. It was introduced into Europe in 1897.

Deep burgundy red in color and less seedy than the blackberry, it is said that the loganberry has a little of both berries in its flavor and I think that is a fairly accurate description. But it also has a vinous quality that makes it richer than both. It makes a particularly sumptuous jam. Slightly earlier than the blackberry, it should be picked from July to September, the fruits ripening in slow succession rather than all at once. They have a habit of hiding under their leaves.

The tayberry is a further cross between the loganberry and the raspberry.
The boysenberry is the result of a threesome between the logan, the raspberry, and the blackberry.

Blackberries in the kitchen

The difference between the wild and cultivated blackberry is extraordinary. The berry you pick from a country lane invariably has the truest flavor, sweet but sharp, winelike and heavy with the warm glow of nostalgia and berry-gathering trips past. The cultivated berry is good enough, plump and handsome, yet sweeter and somehow flat tasting in comparison. While the flavor of a wild berry will linger in the mouth long after the berry itself has gone, the pleasure of the cultivated fruit is short lived. Rather than thinking of the cultivated as an inferior form, I treat it as a different berry altogether, perhaps one to eat with yogurt rather than to be mixed with apples for a pie or eaten from the container on the way home.

Foraging aside, we are more likely to cook with blackberries than to eat them raw. It is unusual to sit down to a dish of them with cream as we might strawberries or raspberries, though one can. There is a quiet beauty in the sight of a pile of blackberries in a celadon blue bowl.

Good though the raw berry can be, they really appreciate warmth, and the addition of cinnamon and brown sugar. Most of all, it is their partnership with apples that is worth exploration. It is rare for a fruit to be so comfortable in the presence of another, but blackberry and apple is one of the great food marriages. A sharp apple is my first choice here, but they all work well enough once the heat gets going and the tree-fruit starts to soften. It is best to introduce your berries only once the apples have softened. Add them too soon and they will overcook. Once the two have been brought together, breathe in, dream of more carefree times, then use them to start the day, in a crumbly-crusted pie, a turnover, or as a filling for the easily shattered crust of a strudel. You can stuff them into a suet crust, tuck them beneath a layer of crumble, or use them to fill pancakes. The mixture likes custard as much as it does cream. And what sight is more tempting on a Sunday afternoon than that of translucent apples, their edges tinged with rich pink, being spooned out of a sugar-dusted pastry crust?

The marriage is partly seasonal and partly an attempt to make a small haul of berries go a long way, but more importantly it is the little explosions of rich, winelike berries amongst the mass of mildly flavored apple that make this such an enduring partnership.

I like forager Mike Irving's idea of adding a little wild mint to a dish of blackberries. In the past I have also had much pleasure from introducing blueberries, whose musky mildness seems to heighten the wild berries' flavor. Blackberries, particularly the slightly tart ones, are gorgeous with ripe melon—the green varieties in this case being even more appealing than the orange-fleshed.

Blackberries and goat's milk yogurt remains a favorite breakfast. They are the second berry I add to my morning smoothie (the blueberry being pretty much essential in this house). Few fruits are quite so uplifting at 7 a.m., though grapefruit comes pretty close. Which reminds me to suggest you take a look at the grapefruit tree in Chelsea Physic Garden if ever you are passing. Sheltered by high walls, it is often loaded down with its crop of golden orbs.

Blackberries and...

Game Only dark-fleshed game works with blackberry. Pheasant, venison, grouse, partridge. Add a few berries to the pan juices when making a game roast, or serve a puddle of sieved berries. Blackberry jelly is rather fine with cold roast pheasant.
Red wine The inkier the better. Simply anoint the berries with a splash of particularly fruity red wine. A little sugar is needed too.
Melon Sweet melon salad, especially Charentais, appears all the sweeter for the inclusion of a few juicy blackberries.
Apple One of the best marriages of all, especially when sheltering under a pastry crust.
Cream The richer and yellower, the better.
Pastry crusts The copious juice of the blackberry sinks delectably into the underside of the crust, giving a slightly moist piece of pastry soaked in juice. I find this the best bit of any fruit pie.

A textured fool of blackberries and apples

The charm of a gooseberry fool—pure, calm, gentle dessert that it is—relies on its smoothness, but other fools can delight by having a small amount of the fruit left whole amid the softly whipped cream. Raspberry, rhubarb, and blackberry all seem to be improved by a ripple of lightly crushed but wholly identifiable fruit in their midst.

The apple and blackberry fool that follows came about by happy accident as late as last autumn (my breakfast poached fruit folded into whipped cream as an emergency dessert). So pleasing was the result that I now make it from scratch, but this is also a kind end for that cold baked apple from the fridge that no one could manage.

enough for 2 or 3
dessert apples – 3 large
water – 3 tablespoons
heavy cream – 1 cup (240ml)
blackberries – 5 ounces (150g), about 1 cup

Peel the apples, core them, and slice them thinly. Put them into a small pan with the water and bring to a boil. Turn down the heat and simmer gently until the apples are tender. They must be completely soft. Leave to cool.

Whip the cream in a fridge-cold bowl until it is just thick enough to hold its shape (I usually stop once it starts to feel heavy on the whisk and it will lie in soft folds).

Crush the apples to a coarse purée with a fork. Lightly crush the blackberries. Fold the fruit into the cream very lightly, so that it is still visible. Pile into glasses.

A salad of blackberries and golden melon

You look at a bowl of jet-black berries and melting, orange-fleshed melon and instantly know the time of year. If the melon is truly ripe and fragrant and the berries are not too sweet, such a dish is a delight for the senses.

Roast partridge with blackberry pan juices

A plate redolent of autumn if ever there was one. The toasted bacon, golden-skinned bird, and glossy, berry-stained juices make this a gorgeous treat to behold.

enough for 4
young, plump partridges – 4
thyme – 6 bushy little sprigs
juniper berries – 12
butter – 7 tablespoons (100g)
unsmoked bacon – 8 thin slices
blackberry, red currant, or rowan jelly – 2 tablespoons
blackberries – 3½ ounces (100g), about ⅔ cup
Madeira or dry marsala – a wineglass

Inspect the birds for any stray feathers. Preheat the oven to 425°F (220°C).

Using a mortar and pestle, mash the thyme leaves with the juniper berries, butter, and a hefty pinch of sea salt and black pepper. Spread the butter all over the birds but particularly on their breasts.

Place each bacon slice on a cutting board, then stretch with the flat of a knife blade to give a longer, thinner slice. Wrap the slices around the birds and place in a roasting pan. Roast for twenty minutes, then peel off the bacon, setting it aside if it is crisp enough or leaving it in the roasting pan if not. Return the birds to the oven for ten minutes.

Remove the pan from the oven and set the birds somewhere warm (I use a large warm plate for this with an upturned bowl on top). Put the roasting pan over medium heat, drop in the jelly and blackberries, and let them soften for a minute, then squash the berries lightly with a fork. Add the Madeira or marsala, stir to dissolve the pan crustings, and season with salt and black pepper. Bring to a boil, put the birds on warm plates, then spoon over the blackberry gravy.

Roast duck legs with squash and blackberry and apple sauce

Duck legs are something I tend to eat far more often than a whole bird. They have a neatness to them, and often seem to work out to be better value. You need just one leg apiece. Recipes for pot-roasting them are rare, but cooked that way the results can be tender in the extreme and a pleasant change from the usual crisp-skinned roast bird or broiled breasts. Soft, moist flesh is the goal here, with the squash soaking up some of the herb-seasoned fat.

enough for 4
small sprigs of thyme – about 8
sea salt
whole black peppercorns
plump duck legs – 4
a small winter squash or pumpkin
bay leaves – 2
blackberry and apple sauce (page 120)

Pull the thyme leaves from their branches (you could leave some stems whole) and pound them with half a teaspoon of sea salt and the same of black peppercorns. I use a mortar and pestle, but a wooden rolling pin (with no handle) in a bowl works too. Season the duck legs generously.

Put the legs in a deep casserole or Dutch oven with a heavy bottom. Place the casserole over medium heat and quickly brown the duck pieces on both sides. The skin should color to a pale amber; the fat should melt to form a shallow film in the pan.

Halve, peel, and seed the squash, pulling away and discarding any coarse fibers from the center. Cut the flesh into thick chunks.

Tuck the pieces of squash alongside the duck legs with the bay leaves, turning them in the seasoned fat as you go. Cover with a lid, then turn the heat to low and leave for forty-five to fifty minutes or so, until you can pull the flesh easily from the bones with a fork. You shouldn't expect the skin to be crisp, but soft, fragrant with thyme, and meltingly tender. The squash should be at the point of collapse.

Transfer the duck legs and squash to warm plates and serve with the blackberry and apple sauce that follows.

A blackberry and apple sauce for pork or duck

Applesauce is something I make in any number of ways: with cooking or eating apples either in a shallow pan with a little water; or by baking the apples whole. The last method, useful if the oven is on for the Sunday roast anyway, seems to give a deeper, more concentrated flavor. The quantity of sugar you add is dependent on the sweetness of the apple variety.

enough for 4
cooking apples – 4 large
blackberries – 5 ounces (150g), about 1 cup
a little confectioners' sugar

Score the skins of the apples around the middle (so that they don't explode) and put them in a baking dish. Bake them at 350°F (180°C)—or whatever temperature your roast is on—for a good forty minutes or so until they have puffed up and the apple is soft and frothy.

Put the blackberries into a small pan, add a tablespoon of stock or water, and bring to a boil. Crush lightly with a fork.

Scrape the flesh from the apples' skin into a bowl. Using a small whisk or fork, beat in the sugar. Stir the crushed blackberries through the apples and serve with the duck above or with a roast shoulder or loin of pork.

Deep-dish blackberry and apple pie

It is almost impossible to think of a dish that so accurately expresses the glories of the British countryside in autumn as a vast, sugar-dusted blackberry and apple pie. It is everything we do so well: apples, wild berries, pastry crusts, and comfort food. Far from what you could call an anglophile, I suddenly feel like waving a little flag.

enough for 6 to 8
for the pastry
all-purpose flour – 2 cups (250g)
butter – 5 tablespoons (75g), cold from the fridge
lard – about 5 tablespoons (75g), cold from the fridge
ice-cold water
a little milk, for brushing

for the filling
good pie apples – 6 large
superfine sugar, to taste
blackberries – 2 or 3 large handfuls

heavy cream, to serve

You will need a traditional two-quart (2-liter) oval pie dish that measures about 13 inches (32cm) in length.

Put the flour into a large mixing bowl with a small pinch of salt. Cut the butter and lard into small chunks and rub into the flour with your thumbs and fingertips. You could do it in a stand mixer but I can't really see why. It only takes a minute by hand. To bring the mixture to a rollable dough, add a little ice-cold water. Start with a tablespoonful, adding it gingerly (too much is difficult to correct), and draw the dough in from the sides to form a ball. You may need a couple of spoonfuls. You are looking for a dough that is firm enough to roll but soft enough to demand careful lifting. Set aside in the fridge, covered with a kitchen towel, for thirty minutes.

Preheat the oven to 400°F (200°C). Roll the pastry out to fit the top of the dish. You need enough extra pastry around the edge to be able to cut off and cover the rim of the dish (plus a few scraps to make some leaves, if you like that sort of thing). The simplest way to do this is to turn the dish upside down on the pastry and score around the top, then score a second line around the outside as wide as the rim.

Peel, core, and quarter the apples, cut them into thick slices or chunks, then put them into the pie dish. Taste them to gauge their sweetness. I like my fruit fairly tart, so add just a surface sprinkling of sugar. The sweet of tooth may want to use anything up to a tablespoon per apple. Add the blackberries and toss them with the apples and sugar. Wet the rim of the dish—water will do—then fix the outer rim of pastry to it, cutting and pasting to fit. Wet it with water or beaten egg. Lift the pastry onto the pie, pressing the edge firmly onto the pastry rim. Crimp it with your thumb and forefinger to seal or by pressing down with the prongs of a fork.

Cut two or three short slits in the center of the pastry to let out the steam and, if you wish, decorate the pie with scraps of pastry cut into leaves. Brush with a little milk and dust with superfine sugar. Bake for forty to fifty minutes, until the pastry is crisp and pale gold, covering it as needed to keep it from browning. Serve with heavy cream.

Little turnovers of blackberry and apple

These sweet little turnovers are good hot or cold. Rather than put sugar in the pastry crust, I have used a traditional pasty pastry recipe but added a wafer-thin crust of sugar as they come out of the oven.

makes 6 small turnovers

for the pastry
lard – 4 tablespoons (55g)
butter – 4 tablespoons (55g)
all-purpose flour – 1¾ cups (225g)
cold water

for the filling
cooking or dessert apples – 2¼ pounds (1kg)
sugar – 4 tablespoons
blackberries – 5 ounces (150g), about 1 cup

a little beaten egg and milk, for glazing
an egg white
superfine sugar
cream or custard, to serve

Put the lard and butter into the freezer for an hour. Grate the fats into the flour and add enough water to make a firm dough—about five tablespoons. Rest for twenty minutes.

Peel the apples, discard their cores, and cut into small chunks. Put them into a saucepan with the sugar and a couple of tablespoons of water and cook over medium heat, stirring regularly, until they start to soften. Tip in the blackberries and set aside. Preheat the oven to 400°F (200°C).

Divide the pastry into six pieces. Roll each into a disk about 5 inches (12cm) in diameter, using a saucer as a template. Brush the edges with beaten egg and milk, then put a small heap of the apple filling on each disk. Fold the dough over to make a semicircle and press hard around the edges to seal.

Transfer the pastries to a baking sheet lined with parchment paper. Brush all over with beaten egg and milk. Cut a couple of steam holes in the top of each pasty to prevent them from bursting. Bake for about forty minutes, until golden.

Lightly beat the egg white with a fork until it starts to froth. Brush lightly over the hot pastries, then scatter with superfine sugar and return to the oven for three or four minutes. Eat warm with cream or custard.

Little fig and blackberry pies

Here is the softest pastry for the juiciest of fruit pies. Don't be tempted to roll it thinly. Cut the pastry into four and pat each piece out lightly, pushing it into the corners of the ramekins. Spoon in the filling, then fold the pastry lightly over the top. Crème fraîche or thick yogurt on the side would be appropriate but not necessary.

enough for 4

for the pastry
all-purpose flour – 1¾ cups (230g)
butter – 10 tablespoons (140g)
confectioners' sugar – a generous ⅓ cup (50g), plus a little more
     for dusting
a large egg yolk

for the filling
blackberries – 8 ounces (250g), about 1¾ cups
large figs – 4
blackberry or red currant jelly – 4 tablespoons, melted
the juice of half a lemon
ground hazelnuts – ½ cup (60g)

You will need four deep tartlet pans about 3½ by 1½ inches (9cm by 4cm).

Put the flour into a mixing bowl and rub in the butter with your fingertips, then mix in the confectioners' sugar and the egg yolk. Bring the dough together and squeeze it into a round, then roll it into a short, fat log before putting it in the fridge for half an hour to chill. I find this pastry works well in the food processor too; first blitz the flour and butter, then mix briefly with the sugar and egg yolk.

Preheat the oven to 400°F (200°C). Rinse the fruit, coarsely chop the figs, and toss with the melted jelly, lemon juice, and ground hazelnuts.

Cut the pastry into four. Flatten each piece on a floured board and use it to line the pans, leaving the excess pastry overhanging the edges. Pile the filling into the tart shells, then loosely fold over the pastry. It should not meet in the center, but instead leave a gap through which the fruit is visible.

Place the tarts on a baking sheet and bake for thirty to thirty-five minutes or so, until the pastry is dark biscuit colored and the fruit is bubbling. Dust with a little confectioners' sugar and eat warm or cool.

Blackberry focaccia

A dough speckled with fruit. It is difficult to know exactly when to eat such a treat—it's too substantial for dessert, so maybe we should file it under tea.

enough for 8
bread flour – 3¼ cups (450g)
quick-rise yeast – 1 package (7g), about 2 teaspoons
sea salt – 1 teaspoon
superfine sugar – 1 tablespoon
warm water – 1½ cups (350ml)

for the topping
blackberries – 8 ounces (250g), about 1¾ cups
olive oil – 2 tablespoons
superfine or demerara sugar – 2 tablespoons
confectioners' sugar, for dusting

Put the flour in a large bowl, add the yeast, the sea salt (if you are using coarse salt, crush it finely first), then the sugar and warm water. Mix with a wooden spoon, then turn the dough out onto a generously floured board and knead lightly for five minutes or so. You need not be too enthusiastic. A gentle pummeling will suffice.

Once the dough feels elastic and "alive," put it into a floured bowl, cover with a clean cloth or plastic wrap, and leave it somewhere warm to rise. It will take approximately an hour to double in size. Once it has, punch it down again, knocking some of the air out. Tip it into a shallow baking pan about 12 inches (30cm) in diameter. Gently knead half the blackberries into the dough, scattering the remaining ones on top. Cover the dough once more and return it to a warm place to rise.

Preheat the oven to 425°F (220°C). Once the dough has expanded to almost twice its size, drizzle over the olive oil, scatter with the sugar, and bake for thirty-five to forty minutes, until well risen, golden brown, and crisp on top. It should feel springy when pressed. Leave to cool slightly before dusting with confectioners' sugar. Cut into thick wedges and eat while it is still warm. It will not keep for more than a few hours.

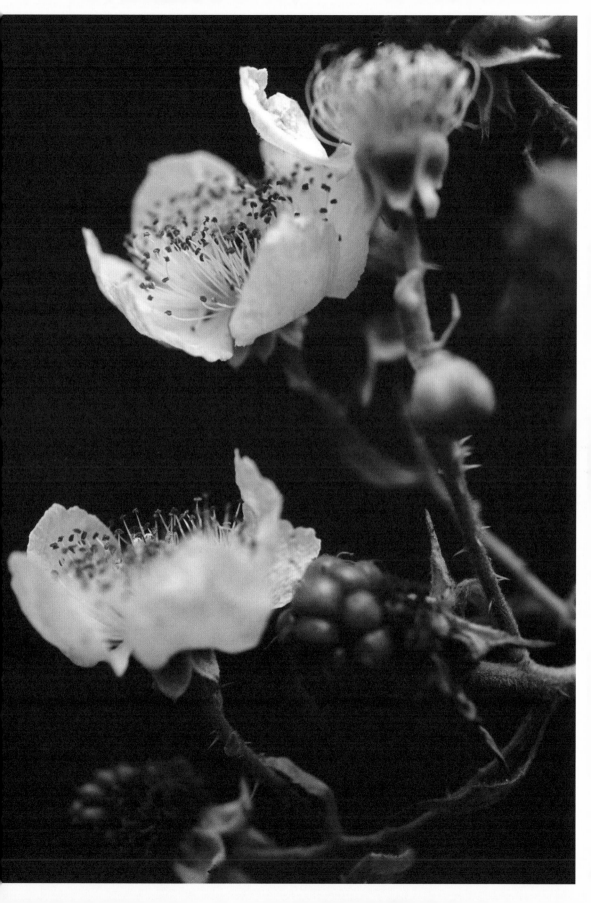

Blackberry bread-and-butter pudding

Autumn is bread-and-butter pudding season, for no other reason than it feels right. I will occasionally add a spreading of apricot jam or a handful of blueberries—even, on one occasion, some broken pieces of chocolate. Best of all, I find, is the addition of large, ripe blackberries. The custard around them curdles slightly, and those that float to the top can catch a little in the heat of the oven, but overall I feel they are a good thing, adding a touch of tart fruitiness to the bland and comforting bread and custard.

enough for 4
white bread – 9 small slices
soft butter
egg yolks – 4
milk – 1¼ cups (300ml)
heavy cream – 1¼ cups (300ml)
golden baker's sugar – ½ cup (100g)
a drop or two of vanilla extract
blackberries – 7 ounces (200g), about 1⅓ cups
a pinch of ground cinnamon

Preheat the oven to 350°F (180°C). Butter the bread on one side and cut it into thick fingers. Beat the egg yolks gently in a bowl and then add the milk, cream, sugar, and vanilla.

Lightly butter a medium-sized baking dish. Place the bread randomly over the dish, scattering the blackberries as you go. Pour over the egg custard and then finally add a mild dusting of cinnamon over the surface. Lower the dish into a roasting pan and pour in enough hot water to come halfway up the sides of the dish. Carefully place in the oven. Bake until the custard has set and the bread is golden, about forty-five to fifty minutes. Take great care removing the pan and its hot water from the oven. Leave to settle before eating.

Blackberry and apple betty

A betty is a crumble made by pouring melted butter and syrup over
a mixture of sugar and breadcrumbs. I find it possibly the most endearing
name for a dessert. All is well with a world where there is a betty on
the table.

enough for 4
cooking apples – 2¼ pounds (1kg), peeled and cored
butter – 2 tablespoons (30g)
blackberries – a couple of large handfuls

for the crumb layer
soft white breadcrumbs – about 4½ ounces (125g), about 2¾ cups
light soft brown sugar – ⅓ cup, packed (75g)
butter – 5 tablespoons (75g)
maple syrup or golden syrup – 4 heaping tablespoons

Preheat the oven to 375°F (190°C). Cut the apples into large chunks, put
them in a pan, and toss with the butter and a couple of tablespoons of water
over medium heat. When they start to soften but are still keeping their
shape, drop in the blackberries, then tip the fruit into a 6-cup (1.5 liter)
baking dish.

   Mix the crumbs and sugar and cover the fruit loosely with the mixture.
Melt the butter and syrup in a small pan, then pour over the crumbs, making
certain to soak them all. Bake for thirty-five minutes, until the apple is soft
and the crumbs are golden and crisp.

A moist cake of apples, blackberries, ground hazelnuts, and cinnamon

The weight of autumn fruit is inclined to make this gorgeous cake sigh
a little in middle. If you are the sort of tightly wound cook who thinks a
sunken cake is a failure then turn away now. We will eat this supremely
moist, cinnamon-scented wonder without you.

   The first time I made this cake I used whole hazelnuts, which I skinned
and toasted before grinding. The toasting gave the cake a deep, nutty
warmth and I recommend it if you have an extra twenty minutes to spare.
Failing that, toast the ground hazelnuts under a hot broiler before you fold
them into the cake batter.

enough for 4 to 6

for the cake
small dessert apples – 2
half a lemon
blackberries – 5 ounces (150g), about 1 cup
butter – 10 tablespoons (150g)
superfine sugar – ⅓ cup (75g)
dark muscovado sugar – ⅓ cup, packed (75g)
eggs – 3 large
all-purpose flour – ⅔ cup (85g)
baking powder – 1½ teaspoons
ground hazelnuts – a scant cup (100g)

for the crumble
cold butter – 3½ tablespoons (50g)
all-purpose flour – ⅓ cup plus 1 tablespoon (50g)
demerara sugar – ¼ cup (60g)
rolled oats – 2 heaping tablespoons
ground cinnamon – a knifepoint

You will need a deep loaf pan, 9 by 5 inches (approximately 22 by 12cm). Preheat the oven to 350°F (180°C). Line the loaf pan on the bottom and sides with parchment. It will keep the cake from sticking. Cut the apples into quarters, core them, then cut into thin (but not paper-thin) slices. Squeeze a little lemon juice over them, then mix lightly with the blackberries.

Put the butter, cut into small pieces, in the bowl of a stand mixer together with the sugars and beat until light, smooth, and pale coffee colored. Break the eggs into a small bowl and whisk them lightly with a fork to break them up. Add them, a little at a time, to the mixture, beating all the time.

Sift the flour and baking powder together, followed by the hazelnuts, then add in two or three batches to the mixture. Transfer to the lined cake pan. Scatter the apples and blackberries over the top and push some of the fruit lightly down through the mixture with your finger.

Make the crumble by rubbing the butter—cut into small pieces—into the flour, either with your fingertips or using a food processor. Stir in the sugar, rolled oats, and cinnamon. Scatter over the top of the cake and bake for about an hour, until a skewer or knitting needle inserted into the center of the cake comes out moist but relatively clean.

Leave the cake to cool completely before removing it from its pan. The cake will improve if wrapped in foil and stored overnight before cutting. But either way you will end up with a moist, crumbly cake that is the very essence of autumn.

Black currants

Without heat, there is little point to the black currant. Along with the other kitchen fruits, the dusty purple damson and the hard, green gooseberry, the black currant needs to be cooked to render it a pleasure. Once warmed, the dull black fruits have an incomparable intensity of flavor. But it is a flavor that must be sweetened if it is not to pucker the lips as tight as a cat's bottom.

There is no gloss to this fruit. It does not sparkle in the market stall like its red and white sisters. There is little clue for the nose or eye that this is the most vivid-tasting fruit of all. An early-eighteenth-century writer insisted they smelled of bedbugs. I am not sure I would know, despite confessing to a romantic predilection for seedy Parisian hotels.

Currants bring back memories like those of no other fruit. They provide, by their flavor and the scent of their pruned wood, a clearer memory of my childhood than any photograph album ever could. Their smell—musky, sour, almost fetid—reminds me of my first bid for freedom, a school holiday job in the fruit fields of Worcestershire, picking tray after tray of small fruit, much of which ended up, apparently, as cordial. Ninety percent of the country's harvest is made into Ribena. My parents were happy for me to drink gallons of the stuff, watered down with lemonade, which to this day I find a refreshing drink with much ice on a blistering summer's day. As a child, I ate them raw, as I do now, toward the end of August when they are plump from the rain.

Our modern, warming climate is not good for this berry, which needs a snap of frost to stimulate its growth. New varieties appear from time to time and it is hoped breeders will come up with one that can thrive in the warm. As fruit goes, the black currant is a recent arrival. I can find no mention of it before the late 1700s. Herbalists welcomed the tar-black berries for their ability to soothe a sore throat—they are still used in cough drops.

A currant is cooked when its skin splits. The chemistry of burst currants, sugar, and heat will give a thick, rich syrup to garnish vanilla ice cream, lubricate a piece of sponge cake, or supply a base for a powerfully flavored sorbet. Such intensity is exploited in crème de cassis, the suave, deep purple liqueur made in Burgundy and used for the most part to jolly up a glass of white wine for drinking outdoors.

It is possible, I suppose, to have too much flavor. A bowl of stewed currants, all purple and punch, is too forceful for some. Temper its power with cream, or with bland stodge in the form of a suet crust, bread, or pastry. A more delicate version of summer pudding, where the fruit is supported by slices of brioche, is a modern answer. I have made many a summer pudding with black currants instead of red. It works as long as you are the sort not afraid to indulge in the cream pitcher.

A mouthful of tart black fruits and crumbly pastry is bliss to me. Pastry that will soak up some of the juice, a deep crumble topping, or an American-style thick cobbler crust has more point than a sweet, thin pastry shell. The juice-soaked crust is, at least to my taste, the reason for this fruit's existence.

A black currant bush in the garden

Once the lawn had been removed and the six soil beds dug and manured, I planted fruit bushes. Ben Lomond is the black currant I grow, and has fruited exceptionally for nine years. The fruits are plump even in a dry year, and stay in good condition on the branch for up to four weeks. They last better there than in the fridge, if they are shaded and you can keep the birds away. A net will help, but you can get into a right old tangle trying to take it off after the stems have inevitably grown through.

Currants love rich, damp soil and a regular dose of manure. The black will tolerate shade, unlike the red, but are not fond of wind. Black currants fruit on old wood. This means careful pruning if you are not to end up with either no fruit (overpruning) or an untidy bush (underpruning). No one wants an untidy bush. I prune out some of the older, weak-fruiting branches or those that cross one another as soon as the fruit has finished in September. This way there are always some old branches for next year's berries and space to allow new growth next spring.

Varieties

I have seen small currants (*Ribes nigrum*) growing wild in Scotland and it is certainly where the cultivated strains do well, though they can still be found in woodland in Cumbria and Yorkshire. Damp is no problem to this fruit. They do very well on the wet side of my garden. There may be as many as 150 varieties all told, but few are ever seen beyond the much-loved and tough-skinned Baldwin and the modern "Bens"—an assortment of cultivars named for the Scottish peaks, Ben Nevis being taller than most.

Baldwin An old variety, vigorous, with sweet, late fruit.
Ben Alder Late flowering, a heavy cropper with juicy fruit.
Ben Lomond* An early "Ben" and still fruiting copiously.
Ben Nevis A tall, upright bush with large, late fruit.
Ben Sareck* A small variety, good for compact gardens.
Ben Connan Large, juicy berries that will stay on the bushes in good condition for a couple of weeks.

*Available from US sources.

Black currants in the kitchen

The fact that the black currant is essentially a cook's fruit, of no interest in the fruit bowl, is partly why I have such affection for it. Actually, it is more like an obsession. I applaud the fact that its appeal isn't instant, like that of a peach or a nectarine. It is part of why I am a cook.

As soon as I see them in the market in their green cardboard baskets, round about the second week in July, I start a sort of personal homage to this fruit. First it's a handful of raw berries on the way home; then a compote of eye-watering richness; then a crumble, a pie, a soggy dome of summer pudding; a potent jam for plain scones or to hold together a buttery sponge; best of all is a shallow pie, its pastry pale and glistening with sugar, its filling hot, velvety, sour. At that point I reach for the cream.

Its short season through July and August can often end in a glut, and you would be wise to freeze a basket or two. Their rich, startling taste will not seem out of place in a winter pie. Robust flavors for cold days.

Once cooked, the black currant has the most strident flavor of any fruit save the damson. You will need a little patience to pull the pearl-sized berries from their stalks. Even more if you are the fastidious type who likes to remove the dried flowers as well. I am not sure it makes enough of a difference to bother. A cook's tip is to run a fork down the stem to remove the fruit but, being a hands-on kinda guy, I prefer holding the end of the stem and plucking at the fruit with my fingers. Black currants are often dusty from the open transport along farm roads and may need a gentle rinse.

It takes barely five minutes to cook a currant. They need just a little water to keep them from burning before their skins pop: three tablespoons per fourteen ounces (400g) of currants is about right. Once their juice has mingled with the necessary sugar they are ready. Boil any longer and you will have jam.

This particular member of the currant family occasionally turns up in savory recipes, especially with game. If it must, then let it be with the darker meats, venison or squab perhaps, the fruit squished into the pan juices with the back of a wooden spoon.

Well worth trying for its subtlety is a quivering lump of black currant jelly left to dissolve in the roasting juices after you have taken the meat out to rest. You can make the jelly at home using the recipe later in this chapter. It is also very good just as it comes, with venison steaks or partridge.

The ubiquitous crumb-edged cheesecake with its thick layer of black currant jam, seen on the counter of virtually every delicatessen in the 1980s, was a clue to how effective this fruit is in the presence of dairy produce. Its mouth-puckering sharpness deals instantly with the cheesecake's tendency to cloy. A modern interpretation might be the cherry cheesecake on page 183, served with a slick of the indigo compote in this chapter.

An early-autumn dessert made with an equal mixture of blackberries and currants will quell the currants' strength. A jam of the fruit is easily set, and is possibly the best thing you can do to a rice pudding. A purple-black sauce is very sexy on a snow-white ice cream. Or on top of a meringue, when you can pull your fork through the cream to make vibrant swooshes on your plate.

Black currants and...

Mint Odd but true. Add a few finely chopped leaves to a black currant purée or to a fruit salad in which very ripe black currants are included.
Vanilla ice cream Spoon a purée of the fruit over vanilla ice cream or stir it into homemade vanilla ice cream after churning and just before it goes into the freezer.
Pastry Where a pastry or crumble crust will do nothing for a red or white currant, they have a certain affinity with the black currant. Use them in a pie, a crumble, or an American-style cobbler. They are the only currants that work in a pie.
Cream and cream cheese If there is a more suitable topping for a cheesecake than a layer of black currants I have yet to find it. Although cream and the poached fruit can curdle on meeting each other, the flavors work together in surprising harmony. Black currant jam is my favorite of all preserves for piling aboard scones and clotted cream.
Oats A layer of black currant jam is generally a welcome thing to find in the middle of a thick flapjack, or baked sweetened oat bar. A dollop on an oatcake spread with cream cheese is more of a luxury than it sounds.

A summer pudding of blackberries and currants

For years I have gorged myself on Christmas pudding in winter and summer pudding as soon as the currants and berries are ripe. They both have some magic attached to them that takes them far beyond the sum of their ingredients.

I make the classic summer pudding but generally stray off the beaten track (always a good idea with classics, since you may discover something you like even more) by adding black currants to the more regular mix of raspberries and red currants. I like their richness and breathtaking fruitiness.

As the summers have gone by, the red currants in my pudding get fewer, so that it is now virtually all black currants—too strong until the fruit meets the cream pitcher. Last year I introduced blackberries into the recipe. I suggest you start with half and half, then keep tweaking until the mix suits you.

enough for 6 to 8
mixed black currants and blackberries – a scant 2 pounds (850g)
white sugar – 3 tablespoons
firm, good-quality white bread – 7 or 8 slices,
    cut about as thick as your little finger
cream, to serve

Sort through the fruit tenderly, picking out any that are unripe or moldy. There's nearly always a few, especially if the weather is damp. Pull the currants from their stems, then put them, with the blackberries, in a stainless steel saucepan over low heat. Taste the fruit for sweetness and add sugar accordingly. For commercial, sweet blackberries and slightly tart currants, I add three tablespoons or so. Sometimes you may need slightly less if they are very ripe, or more if your blackberries were tart and from the hedge. Use your own judgment, bearing in mind that the finished pudding should have a bit of sharpness to it. Pour in a little water, a couple of tablespoons will do, then bring it to a boil. The currants will start to burst and give out their juice. They need no longer than three or four minutes at a cautious simmer. The fruit should be shiny and there should be much magenta juice in the pan. Turn off the heat.

Cut the crusts off the bread. Set one piece aside, then cut each of the rest of them into three long fingers. Push the reserved piece into the bottom of a 4-cup (1-liter) pudding basin or other deep, round dish, then line the inside of the basin with the strips of bread, pushing them together snugly so that no fruit can escape, keeping a few for the top. Fill the bread-lined basin with the fruit and its juice; it should come almost to the rim. Lay the remaining bread on top of the fruit, tearing and patching where necessary so that no fruit is showing.

Put the basin in a shallow dish or bowl to catch any juice, then lay a flat plate or small tray on top with a heavy weight to squash the fruit down. Some juice may escape, but most will soak into the bread. Leave overnight in the fridge (you may have to remove a shelf, depending on how deep your fridge shelves are).

Remove the weight and plate, then slide a thin spatula around the edge, pushing carefully down between bread and basin so as not to tear the bread. Put a plate on top, then, holding the plate in place, turn quickly upside down and shake firmly to dislodge the pudding. It should slide out and sit proud. Pass a pitcher of cream around—it is an essential part of the pudding.

A fabulous jam

I love jam. I love it more than molasses, much, much more than honey,
and only slightly less than marmalade. It is not just the preserve itself that
appeals but the tubby little pot on the table, its contents glistening as you
twist off the lid. The way the fruit and syrup fill the spoon as you push it
ever downward, and that sticky dribble that hangs, jewel-like, on the rim
of the jar.

The jam I use to measure all others was made by the late Dorothy
Carter—a glorious jam, the most memorable of which was her black
currant, a soft preserve that glistened on the spoon. When Miss Carter died,
the company survived briefly but the magic seemed to go with her. Miss
Carter's extraordinary preserve aside, there are some very good jams made
both commercially and by artisan cooks. Village fêtes and farm stands are
good hunting grounds.

Gooseberry, loganberry, and plum appeal to me more than the sweeter
preserves such as strawberry. But the pinnacle of jam-making for me is black
currant, and with good reason. The sharpness of the black currant makes it
one of the very few fruits that can cope with the copious amount of sugar in
the average jam recipe. That and the way it glistens as you spread it across
the rough furrows of a warm scone or a triangle of seedy brown toast.

Black currant slightly bucks the trend when it comes to sugar-to-fruit
ratios, because of the currant's supreme acidity. The recipe that follows is
for a softly set jam with a deep flavor of the fruit that glows deepest purple-
black on your spoon.

makes 2 jars
granulated or superfine sugar – 4½ cups (900g)
black currants – 1⅓ pounds (600g), about 5½ cups
water – 2⅓ cups (560ml)

Warm the sugar slightly in a low oven. Pull the currants from their stalks.
Put the fruit into a large saucepan with the water and bring to a boil. As the
mixture starts to bubble and the currants burst, tip in the sugar and let it
dissolve without stirring. Once the sugar is completely dissolved, turn the
heat down slightly so the jam simmers enthusiastically, stirring briefly. Leave
to cook for ten minutes, then switch off the heat.

Have two pint (500ml) preserving jars or four or five smaller jam jars
ready. They should be spotlessly clean, sterilized with boiling hot water and
dried. Spoon in the jam right to the top and seal.

A rice pudding to show off a fruit compote

I rarely sully the warm, ivory purity of a rice pudding. I make an exception for a compote of currants, though. I never stir, preferring to take a small amount of the glistening compote on the spoon with a larger amount of rice. Should you stir, you risk ending up with a pudding the color of a bruise.

enough for 4
short-grain white rice – ⅓ cup (70g)
whole milk – a quart (1 liter)
butter – 2 tablespoons (30g)
superfine sugar – 2 tablespoons
a vanilla pod

for the currant compote
black currants – 8 ounces (250g), about 2 cups
sugar – 2 tablespoons
water – 2 tablespoons

Preheat the oven to 275°F (140°C). Put the rice, half the milk, the butter, sugar, and vanilla pod into an ovenproof dish. Slide it into the oven and leave it to get on with things quietly for an hour. Lift the pudding out of the oven and pour in the remaining milk, stirring gently. Leave to cook for a further hour and a half.

Rinse the currants and pull them from their stalks. Drop them into a stainless steel or enameled cast-iron pan and add the sugar and water. Bring to a boil over low heat, taking care that the fruit does not burn. Lower the heat and allow to bubble gently for five minutes or so, until the currants have started to burst and you have a small quantity of deep purple juice. Switch off the heat.

Serve the rice pudding in all its simplicity or with a spoonful of the warm currant compote. A dessert to bring peace and calm to all who eat it.

A rose water meringue with black currants and cream

Meringue is always easier to make in large quantities (the same goes for mayonnaise, in my experience). You will find you have a few meringues left over for the next day. They will keep quite well in an airtight container. The idea of warming the sugar before adding it to the egg whites is new to me, a tip picked up from Yotam Ottolenghi, but I find it produces the stiff, glossy meringue that has previously evaded me.

enough for 8 to 10

for the meringues
superfine sugar – 1½ cups (300g)
egg whites – 5
a few drops of rose water

for the black currant sauce
black currants – 10 ounces (300g), about 2⅔ cups
superfine sugar – 3 tablespoons
water – 2 tablespoons

heavy cream – 1 cup plus 2 tablespoons (300ml)

Preheat the oven to 350°F (180°C). Make the meringues: scatter the sugar over a baking sheet, put it in the oven, then leave for ten minutes or so, until warm. Whip the egg whites with an electric beater until firm and fluffy, then fold in the warm sugar and the rose water. Keep beating with the electric beater for a good five minutes, until the meringue is shiny. Place large, heaped spoonfuls of the mixture on a baking sheet lined with parchment paper, leaving room for the meringues to spread and puff. Put it in the oven and immediately turn the heat down to 250°F (120°C). Bake for about an hour, turning down the heat if they are browning too much—you want them to be a pale honey color. When the meringues are crisp on top, let them cool. The ideal is for them to remain fudgy inside.

Pull the black currants from their stalks. Put them into a stainless steel saucepan with the sugar and water and bring to a boil. As soon as the berries start to burst and the juice turns a dramatic purple, remove from the heat and set aside. Leave to cool, then chill.

Whip the cream until it will just about keep its shape; it shouldn't be so thick that it will stand in peaks. Press the center of each meringue with the back of a spoon so that you make a hollow. Pile the cream inside. Serve the sauce in a pitcher to pour over as you eat.

Black currants under an oat and almond crust

A black currant purée, sorbet, even a compote, can be too highly flavored for some. It requires tempering. A dear friend, who died last year, got around the currants' overpowering strength by adding an oat crust—a sort of oaty, nutty rubble. This was one of his favorite puddings and I think of him, dear, lovely man that he was, every time I eat it.

enough for 4

for the filling
black currants – 1 pound (500g), about 4½ cups
superfine sugar – 3 heaping tablespoons

for the crumble
butter – 7 tablespoons (100g)
all-purpose flour – scant 1¼ cups (150g)
ground almonds – ⅔ cup (75g)
demerara sugar – ¼ cup (60g)
rolled oats (or barley) – ¾ cup (75g)
water – 2 to 3 tablespoons

Preheat the oven to 350°F (180°C). Top and tail the black currants. Rinse them under cold water and tip, still wet, into a 4-cup (1-liter) ovenproof dish. Scatter over the superfine sugar and toss gently. The sugar will stick to the berries like frost.

With your fingertips or using a food processor, rub the butter into the flour until it resembles coarse breadcrumbs. Stir in the almonds, demerara sugar, and rolled oats. Shake the water over the crumble mixture, then jiggle the bowl so that a few small, pebble-sized lumps are formed. This will give a delightful assortment of textures to the crumble.

Tip the crumble over the sugared fruit. I leave it just as it falls out of the bowl, to lend a looser texture to the crumble. I never pack it down. Bake for fifty minutes to an hour, until the fruit bubbles through the crust.

A quivering jelly

I find it slightly amusing that I am now the sort of person who makes jellies and jams. The process is relaxing and somehow good for my well-being. Twenty years ago I would have laughed at the idea of ever pouring cottage garden fruit through a jelly bag, let alone labeling my own jars of jam. Getting older isn't all bad.

It is useful to have a side-of-the-plate accompaniment for roast partridge, lamb, rabbit, or squab that will also add a mild sweetness when melted into their cooking juices in the roasting pan. Such a clear jelly will also make a discreet glaze for sweet tarts of raspberry, blackberry, or strawberry and is simple enough to make by simmering the fruit with an almost equal quantity of sugar, then sieving it to remove the skin and seeds.

I have always liked this shimmering jelly with roast meat, even at that early stage in my life when anything on the side of the plate—mint sauce, mustard, horseradish—was unwelcome. The homemade version has a sparkle to it, and is more lightly set than the stuff you buy in the store.

> red currants – 1 pound (450g), about 4 cups
> a small handful of black currants
> white sugar – 2¼ cups (450g)

Put the fruits, still clinging to their stalks, into a deep, stainless steel pan. Pour in the tiniest amount of water, barely enough to cover the bottom of the pot, then add the sugar. Stir from time to time and boil for eight minutes—no longer or the flavor will spoil—then pour through a fine sieve, or a jelly bag if you have such a thing, set over a bowl. Leave until all the juice has dripped through. It is a mistake to press the fruit in the hope of producing more juice. Ultimately, you will cloud the jelly.

Pour into clean jars you have sterilized with boiling water and dried, preferably in the oven or at least with a spotless kitchen towel. A lack of scrupulous cleanliness at this point will impair the jelly's keeping potential (it will be moldy within a month). Cut disks of wax paper to fit over the preserves. I think it is worth being neat, it will only take a minute, then cover tightly with a screw-top lid. Store in a cool, dry place.

Blueberries

The blueberry pie, its dusky berries and their purple juice held under a soft, sugar-dusted crust, is reason alone for the fruit's inclusion in this book. That and the botanical fact that the modern berry is a descendant of the diminutive and enchanting wild bilberry of British heath and moor—a forager's fruit—and one that deserves every bit of praise we can throw at it.

At first, I didn't "get" the cultivated blueberry. It lacked the sensual qualities I look for in a fruit—that rich, heady fragrance and the pinprick of sharpness that makes a berry interesting. Where, I wondered, was the gorgeous arterial juice of the logan; the winelike scent of the raspberry; the tempting gloss of the bramble or the charm of the wild strawberry? The fact that I first met it as part of a pavlova didn't help: the deep clouds of snow-white sugar-cake need a fruit with a sting in its tail (the Antipodeans are bang on with their inclusion of passion fruit) if the dessert isn't to cloy.

While I sometimes still find its flavor a little shallow, the fruit has slowly but surely grown on me. The powdery, violet-gray bloom, the neat little crown, its inky-blue skin and purple juice have gradually seduced me. Once you see the blueberry growing on its short bushes and witness the bell-shaped flowers in their shades of green and apple-blossom pink, it is difficult not to fall in love.

Its mild, dusky flavor, the gentle sweetness, and the way its skin bursts in the mouth to reveal its pale green flesh only add to its charm. If you eat it with thick yogurt or crème fraîche or add a squeeze of lemon juice, the flavor will sing a little louder than it does with sweet cream.

The modern blueberry, *Vaccinium corymbosum* (a cluster of fruits), is related to our smaller, native bilberry, the bush fruit that grows wild on moors, heaths, and oak woodland in southern England, Scotland, Lancashire, Yorkshire, Wales, and the southeast. The Scots know it as the blaeberry or whinberry for its habit of growing among "whin" or gorse.

In parts of the south, the berries are known as whorts. The wild fruit has not just the purple skin of the cultivated blueberry but purple flesh too. Its flavor is deeper, sharper, and more intense.

The blueberry is revered in North America—90 percent of the world's production comes from there—and it is to them we owe both our own blossoming blueberry industry and much of our year-round supply. The fruits we have now are the result of years of work by North American fruit breeders, who have given us a berry that is, unsurprisingly, bigger, sweeter, and with a longer shelf life—a berry more suited to big commerce. The search for a bigger berry that can be mechanically harvested, will sit on a supermarket shelf for days, and impress with its size is bound to result in a fruit very different from the charming, richly flavored berries I have occasionally picked from the wild, but it is an ingredient I would hate to be without. I admit to buying long-haul imports in a way I would never think of with a raspberry or strawberry. Once the American harvest is over, those of New Zealand, Poland, Mexico, and Chile come on line. Our own harvest appears in July and August, my favorite variety being Herbert.

The blueberry is rich in tradition and folklore. Just as the Scots gathered the wild fruit from the heaths, so the Native Americans picked it from their forests and bogs. The calyx forms a five-pointed star, which the elders believed was a sign that the fruit had been sent by the Great Spirit to halt famine. Tea was made from its leaves and used to strengthen the blood, while its juice was used as a cough medicine. All this before we knew of the blue pigments—anthocyanins—so rich in antioxidant properties. Most importantly, blueberries were dried and stored for winter food. The dried blueberry can be used in place of currants, if a little expensively. But it has a distinctive sharpness and I like it as part of a breakfast granola. I cannot remember a day when I did not eat at least a handful of these little blue berries.

Blueberries in the garden

Blueberries thrive on the acid soils also loved by other members of the Ericaceae family—heathers, azaleas, and rhododendrons. An alkaline soil will send them into a deep sulk. You can change the soil around them for an ericaceous (lime-free) one or add pine needles and sulfur to your existing soil, but they might do better in a pot, where you can easily control the pH levels.

The bushes demand not only a low pH soil (5.5 or below) but plenty of sunshine to ripen and more than a little water. And not just any old water either. Tap water is too alkaline for them; only rainwater will do. These needs met, the bushes will reward you handsomely throughout late summer. Deciduous and woody stemmed, the blueberry is generally one of the longer-lived fruit bushes.

The blossom, bell shaped and similar to that of heather, is often flushed with rose pink and appears in early spring. Like some apples and cherries, many varieties need a suitable mate and a good local bee population if they are to produce fruit. You can expect somewhere between 120 and 150 days from blossom to ripe fruit.

We have grown the fat blueberry in the UK since it was introduced from Canada in the 1930s, a "highbush" variety easier to harvest than the very hardy low bushes. A couple of bushes in pots outside the back door won't keep you in pies but are enough for a late-summer treat; at least that's what mine are.

Varieties

All need a wet, acidic soil of pH 4 to 5.5. You can check this with a little device available at most garden centers.

Berkeley* An early- to midseason berry with large fruits and plenty of flavor. The color is pale and rather elegant. You will need another variety to ensure pollination.

Bluecrop* Possibly the most popular variety in the world. A vigorous, upstanding bush producing light, medium-sized fruits for a total of five or six weeks.

Coville Moderate yields from a large bush. A favorite of blueberry specialist Jeremy Trehane, who describes its flavor as "perfumed."

Duke* Short bushes, large fruit, a little late, and great flavor. A very popular and vigorous variety with the supermarkets because of the firmness of its fruits, this one often does well in the north.

Early Blue One of the earliest to ripen, producing large, softly hued berries on upright bushes. Best in a protected site to reduce the risk of damage from early frosts.

Bluetta Compact bush with early blossom. Few varieties can be relied on for an earlier crop.

Chandler* A vigorous variety producing heroically large fruits.

Herbert An exceptional large, late berry and one of my favorites.

Nelson* Hardy and self-fertile. Well flavored.

Top Hat* A short, squat, late-cropping bush with glorious autumn color. Unusual in that it is self-fertile and doesn't need a mate.

Spartan* A useful variety that doesn't mind the cold, has large fruit of good flavor and attractive autumn foliage.

*Available from US sources.

Blueberries in the kitchen

To look across the undulating surface of a blueberry pie, its swollen mound, its edges oozing violet juice, is to witness one of the glories of home baking. I have used the fruit in a crumble too, where they make a lavish gesture though never quite hit the heights of one made with gooseberries or sharp plums.

This is the fruit with which to make a rib-sticking cobbler. The scone-like crust of sugar, flour, butter, and sour cream sits biscuitlike on the surface, while underneath collecting the vivid juice like a sponge. Less successful in fools and syllabubs because its mildness just cannot do battle with the cream, this diminutive fruit works admirably in the cosseting crumbs of a cake. I toss them into muffins too, and cupcakes, and make a thick sauce for cheesecake.

The little baubles tend to collapse in a pie, and a tender pastry crust, so fragile it crumbles with the merest pressure, seems more appropriate than a crisp one. That said, a flaky strudel pastry can be pleasing, even more so if you can keep the bottom layer crisp (getting your baking sheet hot in the oven before sliding the raw strudel onto it is a good start).

Blueberries take very little time to cook. In a pan with sugar and a spoonful of water they take less than ten minutes to reveal their treasure. Under a crust, they will be soft long before the pastry is the color of a biscuit. As soon as the skin bursts, you get a clearer understanding of what this once-wild berry is all about.

It is in those moments when my blood sugar drops that *Vaccinium corymbosum* truly comes into its own. A fat handful in the blender with a dollop of goat's milk yogurt, a scoopful of whey protein, and enough goat's milk or water to produce a result thin enough to find its way into a glass will produce a smoothie to save your life.

Blueberries and...

Yogurt Sharp dairy products such as natural yogurt and crème fraîche will bring out the flavor more successfully than sweet heavy cream.

Cream cheese and mascarpone Can be used as a base for blueberry cheesecakes or in a frosting for cupcakes.

Oats Oatmeal and rolled oats have an affinity with both the cultivated berry and, particularly, the sharper wild berries. A warm oatcake spread with cream cheese and a scattering of berries is a snack that works on many levels.

Lemon juice Even the smallest amount will make the berries' flavor shout a little louder.

Game Squab, pheasant, and partridge are appealing with a little puddle of blueberries that have been cooked with sugar and a dash of lemon juice. Or try adding them to the pan juices when you make the gravy.

* Avoid adding manure around the bushes as it may scorch their roots.
* Never let the plants dry out, especially when they are grown in pots.
* Blueberries often have a slight flash of olive green to them, and will darken and wrinkle as they age.
* This is one of the very few fruits I freeze. Whizzed with yogurt, the straight-from-the-freezer berry makes a glorious breakfast smoothie.
* In 2010, supermarket sales of the blueberry overtook those of the strawberry for the first time.
* Blueberries are just plain wrong with fish of any sort. Whatever anyone says.

Venison with blueberries

I like game birds and venison with berries. The addition is a mild one, yet entirely relevant. The birds may well have eaten wild blueberries, or blaeberries as they are sometimes known, and their dark, woodsy flesh works well with the sweetness of the berries. This is one of the few savory uses of the blueberry I have enjoyed.

enough for 2
black peppercorns – 12
thyme – the leaves of 3 small sprigs
a little olive oil
venison steaks – 4
port – 5 tablespoons (75ml; you could use Madeira or dry
    marsala instead)
blueberries – 5 ounces (150g), 1 cup
red currant jelly – 2 heaping tablespoons
butter – 2 tablespoons (30g)

Coarsely crush the peppercorns and thyme leaves with a mortar and pestle, add half a teaspoon of salt and just enough olive oil to form a rough paste, then rub into the venison. Get a shallow pan hot. Lay the oiled venison in the pan and leave for four or five minutes. Turn over and cook the other side. Ideally, the venison should be nicely browned on the surface and rare within. Remove to warm plates.

    Pour the port into the pan, stirring in any crusty or sticky bits left by the meat. Let it boil down by half, then add the blueberries and the red currant jelly. Continue boiling until the fruits start to burst and the pan juices turn purple. Stir in the butter, taste for seasoning, then spoon the sauce over the venison steaks.

Cassis jelly with blueberries and crème fraîche

Cassis has always been my favorite of the fruit liqueurs—uplifting, rejuvenating, a sort of adult Ribena. We make a good version in Britain, too. As with most of my jellies, this is designed to be soft, and tends to slouch rather than stand to attention on the spoon. Don't even think of putting it in a jelly mold.

enough for 4
leaf gelatin – a scant ½ ounce (12g)
fruity red wine – 1⅔ cups (400ml)
cassis liqueur – a generous ¾ cup (200ml)
sugar – 2 tablespoons
blueberries – 7 ounces (200g), about 1⅓ cups
crème fraîche and more blueberries, to serve

Put the gelatin, sheet by sheet (rather than in one solid block), into a bowl of cold water and leave to soften. It should be ready in about five minutes.

Pour the wine into a small stainless steel saucepan and stir in the cassis and sugar. Place over low heat and stir until the sugar has dissolved. Don't let it boil. Lift the gelatin from the water and drop it into the warm wine, stirring gently until it has totally dissolved. Put the blueberries into four small glasses, pour over the jelly, and set aside to cool, then refrigerate until set (about four hours).

Serve with a small bowl of crème fraîche and another of blueberries.

Blueberry pie

When you push the soft crust with your knife, the purple juice gushes to the surface like blood from a deep cut, staining the sugar-frost coating. I choose a soft pastry, too tender to transfer from tart pan to plate in one piece. More of a shortcake really.

enough to serve 6 generously

for the filling
blueberries – 1 pound (500g), about 3⅓ cups
lemon juice – 2 tablespoons
cornstarch – 1 generously heaping tablespoon
red currant jelly – 1 heaping tablespoon

for the crust
butter– 10 tablespoons (150g)
golden baker's sugar – ¾ cup (150g), plus a little more to scatter
    over the top
all-purpose flour – 2 cups (250g)
baking powder – 1 teaspoon
an egg, beaten
a little milk or beaten egg and milk, to finish

Preheat the oven to 350°F (180°C) and put a baking sheet in it (this will help keep the bottom of the pie crisp). Lightly butter a 9½-inch (24cm) shallow metal pie pan. Put the blueberries into a bowl with the lemon juice, cornstarch, and red currant jelly. Toss gently to mix, then set aside.

Cream the butter and sugar in a stand mixer until pale and fluffy, pushing the mixture down the sides of the bowl from time to time with a rubber spatula. Sift the flour and baking powder together. Incorporate the egg, a little at a time, into the butter and sugar mixture, adding a little flour if it starts to curdle. Mix in the flour and baking powder to form a soft dough.

Flour the work surface generously. Bring the dough together to form a ball, then knead lightly for a minute. Cut into two equal pieces and roll one out to fit the bottom and sides of the pie pan. Line the pan with the pastry, taking care to push the dough well into the corners and to leave some overhanging.

Add the filling. Roll out the remaining pastry. Brush the edge of the pastry lining the dish with a little milk or beaten egg and milk, then lower the pastry lid on top. Press the edges to seal, trim any overhanging pastry, and cut two small holes in the top (if you don't, the pastry may split). Brush with a little milk or beaten egg and milk and scatter lightly with sugar.

Bake on the hot baking sheet for forty minutes or so, until golden. Allow the pie to calm down a little before serving.

Blueberry batter pudding

Batter pudding, the French clafoutis, is one of the few hot puddings that is acceptable in high summer. Possibly because, like quiche, it is traditionally served warm rather than hot. Though cherries are more traditional, I find this pudding works exceptionally well with blueberries, their tart purple-blueness seeping into the quivering egg custard.

enough for 4 to 6
eggs – 4
all-purpose flour – a scant ⅔ cup (75g)
superfine sugar – a heaping ⅓ cup (80 to 90g)
light cream – 1 cup (250ml)
whole milk – a scant cup (225ml)
blueberries – 10 ounces (300g), about 2 cups
confectioners' sugar and cream, to serve

Preheat the oven to 400°F (200°C). Butter an ovenproof dish about 10 inches (25cm) in diameter.

Whiz the eggs, flour, superfine sugar, cream, and milk together in a blender or food processor, or beat them all together with a handheld whisk. Tip the fruit into the dish, pour over the batter, then bake for about forty minutes, until the batter is lightly risen, golden, and just firm to the touch. Dust with confectioners' sugar and serve with cream.

Blueberry yogurt smoothie

An alternative and slightly more substantial version of this can be had by adding a couple of scoops of whey protein in place of the banana.

enough for 1
blueberries – 3½ ounces (100g), about ⅔ cup
a medium banana
yogurt – 5 tablespoons
the juice of an orange

Drop everything into a blender and blitz until smooth. You can add ice cubes, if you like, to make a longer drink.

A quick blueberry fool

Sometimes fools can be almost as simple as stirring fruit into cream.

enough for 4
blueberries – 10 ounces (300g), 2 cups, plus some for decoration
superfine sugar – 3 tablespoons
heavy cream – a generous ¾ cup (200ml)
thick yogurt – about ⅔ cup (150g)

Put the berries in a small pan and add the sugar and 2 tablespoons of water. Put over low heat and simmer for five minutes. Crush the berries with a fork, then let them cool.

Whip the cream until thick, then gently fold it into the cold fruits with the yogurt. Leave to settle in the fridge for an hour or so, then serve decorated with blueberries.

Little blueberry pies

Again, the softest pastry, but this time for little pies. Crème fraîche or thick yogurt on the side would be appropriate.

makes 4

for the pastry
butter – 10 tablespoons (140g)
all-purpose flour – 2 cups minus 2 tablespoons (230g)
confectioners' sugar – a scant ½ cup (50g), plus a little more for dusting
a large egg yolk

for the filling
blueberries – 10 ounces (300g), about 2 cups
red currant jelly – 3 tablespoons
the juice of half a lemon
ground almonds – ½ cup (60g)

You will need four tartlet pans with removable bottoms, about 3 inches (8cm) in diameter.

Rub the butter into the flour with your fingertips, then mix in the confectioners' sugar and egg yolk. Bring the dough together and squeeze into a round, then roll into a short, fat log before putting it in the fridge for half an hour to chill. I find this pastry works well in the food processor too: first blitz the flour and butter, then mix briefly with the sugar and egg yolk.

Preheat the oven to 350°F (180°C). Rinse the fruit and toss it with the red currant jelly, lemon juice, and ground almonds.

Cut the pastry into four. Flatten each piece on a floured board and use to line the tart pans. Leave the surplus pastry overhanging the edges. Pile the filling into the tart shells, then loosely fold over the overhanging pastry.

Place the tarts on a baking sheet and bake for twenty-five minutes, until the pastry is biscuit colored and the fruit is bubbling. Dust with a little confectioners' sugar and eat warm or cool.

Blueberry pancakes

Thick, soft pancakes about the size of a digestive biscuit and mottled with the juice of the warm blueberries.

enough for 4
ricotta – 8 ounces (250g), about 1 cup
superfine sugar – 4 tablespoons
eggs – 3, separated
the finely grated zest of an orange
melted butter – 2 tablespoons, plus a little extra
all-purpose flour – 7 tablespoons (50g)
blueberries – 3½ ounces (100g), about ⅔ cup

In a large bowl, mix the ricotta, sugar, and egg yolks together. Grate the orange zest into the bowl and stir it in gently with the melted butter. Sift in the flour and carefully fold in.

Beat the egg whites with a balloon whisk in a large bowl until stiff, then fold them lightly into the ricotta mixture. It is important not to knock the air out. Carefully fold in the blueberries.

Warm a nonstick frying pan over medium heat, brush it with a little butter, then place a heaping tablespoon of the mixture in the pan, followed by another two or three depending on the size of your pan. Let them cook for a minute or two until they have risen somewhat and the underside has colored appetizingly, then, using a thin spatula, flip them over to cook the other side. Do this as if you mean it, otherwise they will collapse as you turn them. A further couple of minutes' cooking, then serve immediately, hot from the pan.

Meringue with warm berry compote

An extravagant dessert for a special occasion. The inclusion of black currants is to act as a contrast to the cream. I feel it is a necessary addition. Pour the fruits over at the very last minute before serving.

enough for 8 to 10
large egg whites – 5
golden baker's sugar – 1½ cups (300g)
white wine vinegar – a teaspoon
cornstarch – 2 heaping teaspoons
vanilla extract
heavy cream – 1⅔ cups (400ml)

for the fruit compote
a mixture of black currants, blueberries, and blackberries – 10 ounces
  (300g), about 2 cups
sugar – 2 tablespoons or so, depending on the sweetness of your fruit

Preheat the oven to 350°F (180°C). Lightly oil a nonstick, 8-inch (20 to 21cm) springform cake pan with almond oil, if you have it. If not, then use something similarly flavorless like peanut. Dust the pan lightly with flour.

Beat the egg whites with a metal whisk until they stand in billowing, shiny folds. The easiest way is to use a stand mixer with a whisk attachment. Beat in the sugar in two or three batches. Scatter over the vinegar and cornstarch, then add a couple of drops of vanilla extract and fold in gently with a large metal spoon. Don't overmix.

Scoop the lot into the prepared cake pan, smooth the top level, and put straight into the oven. Immediately turn the heat down to 300°F (150°C). Leave the meringue to cook, without opening the door, for a full hour and ten minutes. If the top is getting brown, turn the heat down a little further. It should be a pale honey color. Turn off the heat and let the meringue cool without opening the door. The marshmallow center will sink and leave high, crisp sides.

Check the fruit over, removing any leaves or stems, put it in a stainless steel saucepan with the sugar and bring slowly to the boil. You shouldn't need any liquid, but if the fruit looks as if it is starting to stick, then add a tablespoon or two of water. When the fruit starts to burst, remove from the heat and allow to cool a little.

Beat the cream in a cold stainless steel bowl until it sits in soft folds. Pile it on top of the meringue. At the last moment, just before serving, spoon the fruit compote over the top.

Spelt and blueberry "muffins"

Muffin makers will quickly spot that my blueberry muffin is a muffin only in looks, and bears little resemblance to the traditional recipe in either method or ingredients. In some ways, it is more like a cupcake (the butter and sugar are creamed together here, rather than the butter being melted and added at the end), and contains yogurt rather than the more usual milk or buttermilk. The result is softer and slightly richer, and without the taste of leavening agent that is a feature of many more traditional recipes. Enough pedantry. These are delightful little cakes, easily made and quick to bake.

makes 12
all-purpose flour – 1 cup (125g)
whole grain spelt flour – 1 cup (125g)
baking powder – 1½ teaspoons
baking soda – ½ teaspoon
salt – ½ teaspoon
butter – 4 tablespoons (55g)
golden baker's sugar – a scant ⅔ cup (125g)
large eggs – 2
vanilla extract – a teaspoon
yogurt – a scant ½ cup (110g)
blueberries – 7½ ounces (220g), about 1½ cups
demerara sugar, for sprinkling
rolled oats – a few spoonfuls

Preheat the oven to 375°F (190°C). Place twelve paper cup liners in a muffin pan. Sift together the flours, baking powder, baking soda, and salt.

Cream the butter and sugar together until pale in color, scraping down the sides of the bowl with a rubber spatula as you go. Lightly beat the eggs and add slowly to the butter and sugar mixture, beating thoroughly. Add the vanilla extract, then mix in the yogurt.

Gently add the sifted dry ingredients and continue mixing thoroughly. Fold in the berries. Drop the mixture into the paper cups, then scatter the tops with a little demerara sugar and a few rolled oats.

Bake for twenty to twenty-two minutes, until a metal skewer or knitting needle inserted in the center comes out clean. Let the muffins cool briefly in the pan, then place them on a cooling rack.

Cherries

Cherries bring with them a certain frivolity, a carefree joy like hearing the far-off laughter of a child at play. Their appearance, in deepest summer, comes when life is often at its most untroubled. A bag of cherries is a bag of happiness.

Britain has always had wild cherry trees, the "geans" and "mazzards" much loved by the birds, but it is only since the sixteenth century that we have enjoyed the rich, black-skinned cultivated fruits we have today. The British cherry season lasts for six weeks at the height of summer, the first appearing in the markets in late June with only the very late varieties still around in the second week of August. Before and after this, our supplies come from Turkey or the United States.

I often have a brown paper bag of cherries on my desk, picking at them absentmindedly as I type. They provide an accompaniment to my writing throughout July, like the slow ticking of a clock in the still heat of the day. My heart gently skips when I find a pair joined at the stalk, like a kid who has just been handed an ice cream. It is their crispness that makes them so full of joy—that and their brilliant carmine juices that stain their surroundings like blood splatter.

Cherries are perhaps at their most tempting when they come as a mixed bag: the hue of canary feathers with the pink of seaside rock; deepest saffron with cheeks of dark maroon; tarty scarlet; burgundy; inky purple-black. Yes, the flavor is more upfront in the darker fruits, but too many at once can cloy. The pale Rainier varieties have a more complex flavor, unmasked by the heavy sugar of the blackest varieties. They have a freshness to them and you are thankful for their lack of sweetness.

We probably have the Romans to thank for the cultivated cherry, though it was Henry VIII's fruiterer—one Richard Harris—who established the Kentish orchards and thus started the English cherry industry. At its height in the 1950s, there were 17,300 acres (7,000 hectares) of cherry orchards in the United Kingdom. Thirty years later, there were under 1,000 (400 hectares). But there is the occasional ray of sunshine: horticulturists have recently bred trees on smaller rootstock, allowing the tall, inaccessible trees of the past to be replaced by shorter, more easily managed stock with fruit less precarious (for which read expensive) to harvest. That, and a concentrated media campaign to restore our interest in locally grown fruit, may ensure a future for the industry yet.

The sudden sight of a cherry orchard in flower, perhaps as you turn a corner on a twisting country lane in Kent, can take your breath away. The delicate blossom, all marshmallow froth, with petals fluttering butterfly-like in the breeze, is one to awake the child in us, like seeing poppies in a field of corn. Fuller than that of plum and damson, and occasionally a little saccharine in quantity, cherry blossom is one of the glories of the English countryside in April.

A cherry tree in the garden

For all its soft, pink blossom, a cherry tree can be a brute in a small garden, hogging space and light. Neither is it the most characterful of trees, often having an uninteresting trunk and straight, spreading branches. Little will survive under its heavy canopy of tightly packed leaves. Unless you net the tree to protect the fruit, the birds will get more cherries than you.

A popular choice for a smaller garden is those cultivars that can be grown against a wall. If there was a single spare length of bricks in my garden, it would be home to an espaliered cherry, its branches tied to long cables so that they are encouraged to grow horizontally rather than upward. A long, low tree would be easier to net and the warmth from the wall would offer slight protection against frost and wind damage. Add to that the blossom and autumn leaf color and I would have a fine addition to the garden.

There are only a few specialist growers in the UK, but their stock lists are fascinating, featuring varieties you are unlikely to find in any garden center. They are the home of Napoleon and Montmorency, Guigne d'Annonay, and Old Black Heart, varieties more unusual than the ubiquitous, though juicy, Stella. Nurseries such as Keepers in Kent specialize in traditional varieties and will grow an exceptionally rare one especially for you if you have the patience.

If you are thinking of buying a cherry tree for your garden, it is worth checking if it is self fertile. Many, particularly the older varieties, need a mate if they are to produce fruit. Check with your nursery. The compact, almost dwarf trees from the new rootstocks are a possibility for the smaller garden.

A sour cherry such as a Morello will be happy grown in a little shade, but a sweet cherry is best planted in full sun. Shelter is essential: the blossom arrives early and is often hit by frost. Vigilant gardeners will drape a piece of row cover fabric over the branches on cold nights to protect the buds. What with frost and marauding birds, it is a wonder any cherries survive.

Varieties

The sour cherries

Morello* Ancient and revered cooking cherry that is ready for harvest in late summer and early autumn. The one to use in classic duck recipes. Self fertile, though the crop may be improved by having a pollinator.

Nabella Slightly earlier and more recently introduced than the Morello, but with similar acidic qualities.

Kentish Bush Late, red cooking cherry.

Montmorency* Midseason, acidic cherry that makes superb jam.

May Duke Red, midseason fruit for cooking.

The sweet red and black cherries

Lapins* Occasionally known as Cherokee, this late Canadian variety offers particularly sweet, dark red fruits. Self fertile.

Sunburst* Early July fruiting. Large and almost black when ripe. This tree is often used as a pollinator for others.

Summer Sun Purple-fleshed, exceptionally sweet fruit. This late variety, which originates from Norfolk, has good frost tolerance.

Stella* Sweet, prolific Canadian cherry that appears midseason. The most popular variety, often found in supermarkets. Self fertile.

Noir de Guben Medium-sized, dull, dark-skinned fruit of moderately interesting flavor.

Burcombe A Cornish cherry with much sweetness and freshness of flavor.

The "white" cherries

A more complex flavor.

Rainier* Exceptionally sweet (for a pale cherry), yellow flesh with a pink flush. A much sought-after modern cross between Bing and Van. Capricious and likes a mild climate.

Summit* Heart shaped, with sweet white flesh.

Merton Glory Early, yellow fruits with a pink tinge.

Napoleon* Often known as Naps or Royal Ann, a Kentish red-on-yellow variety, with plenty of sweetness and a fresh but complex flavor.

Whiteheart Sweet, late fruit. Needs a pollinator.

Also look out for:
Early Celeste, Early Rivers
Midseason Bradbourne Black, Hertford, Old Black Heart
Late Black Eagle, Tartarian,* Florence, Noble, Sweetheart,*
Turkish Black, Van*

*Available from US sources.

Cherries in the kitchen

Cherry jam can be glorious: the color of Beaujolais, glistening on the spoon, its texture barely firm enough to hold a shape. Good for breakfast with brown wheaty toast; on warm, diminutive scones; trapped between the layers of a Victoria sponge. A cherry pie can be worth the trouble too, especially with soft, sugar-dusted pastry and a river of unpasteurized cream running slowly over its warm crust. Even a duck leg, its skin roasted to a crisp, served with a sauce made from its roasting juices, sharp Morellos and red currant jelly is worth a thought. But there are few other reasons to cook with a cherry.

That duck needs cinnamon and nutmeg added to a stock made from its bones and giblets, a dash of port and a knob of butter whisked in at the end to give it body and a bit of gloss. Elizabeth David describes a dish of duck with cherries, where the pot-roasted duck has its cooking juices set in a terrine with stewed cherries, which is then served in squares with the duck. A terrible faff of a dish, which she describes as a simple version of the classic *canard à la Montmorency*.

Then there is the showy dessert, cherries Jubilee, invented by Escoffier in honor of Queen Victoria's jubilee, where the fruits are flambéed with kirsch and spooned over ice cream. A recipe now on the culinary scrap pile. Cherry clafoutis, the sweet batter pudding so beloved of French country restaurants (and even more so of French country cookbooks) often seems to look better than it tastes, and I feel is somehow one of those formulas that only succeed in French hands. Yet none of these classical recipes grabs me the way a bag of cherries on their stems does.

Cherries dull with age, keeping their lip-gloss looks for only a few days after picking. A glossy cherry is a fresh cherry. It is difficult to prolong the look, but they can be kept at their best by storing them in the fridge and spraying them with a fine mist sprayer every day. Once they have lost their shine, their crispness is next to go, but they will still be fit for jam.

The joy of cherries is their juice, but it can also be their downfall. Once they burst, or are split to remove their pits, the juice seeps out like blood from a cut. The purple juices can sabotage the crispest piecrust and turn a cake's crumbs to mush. I get around the pastry problem by giving my pie a top crust only, rather than one underneath as well. If you insist on a two-crust version, then scatter cornmeal over the bottom crust to protect it before you tip in the fruit. Even then, there will be some sogginess, as anyone knows who has been tempted by a cherry strudel in one of Vienna's swirls 'n' drapes cafés.

A handful of cherries can be a startling find in a salad. Halved and pitted, a few sweetly tart Sunburst or Lapins introduce a sharp contrast to the tarry notes of smoked ham or mackerel. Even better, I think, is a salad where they meet crisp lettuce and duck skin, the fruit slicing neatly through the rich, dark fibers of the duck.

Pie aside, the most famous recipe is probably cherry soup. I know that someone, somewhere makes a bowl worth supping but I have yet to bump into them. Most recipes are little more than cherry yogurt. The real thing—*meggyleves*—is Hungarian, made with sour rather than sweet cherries (a popular mistake) and sour cream, sweetly seasoned with cloves and cinnamon. I have always thought it sounded glorious. Curiously, in all my trips to Budapest I have yet to see it anywhere.

Cherries and...

Cinnamon Sweet, warm, and musky, the notes of finely ground cinnamon will add depth to a chocolate and cherry cake. Whole cinnamon sticks add a particularly subtle note when tucked into the syrup of a cherry compote.

Chocolate Something of a perfect marriage. Cherries have an affinity with chocolate like no other fruit. The arrangement can be as spare as the fruit being dipped into molten dark chocolate and left to set into a crisp shell or as sophisticated as an almost-liquid filling for a rich cake. Dried cherries go surprisingly well with white chocolate, their acidity slicing neatly through the intense sweetness of the candy.

Game Woodsy, dense meats contrast successfully with raw, bright-tasting cherries. I find they work best in a salad, though you could add the fruit to the roasting juices if the idea appealed. Squab, duck, and quail work well.

Ham Smoked meats can be cheered up by a few well-placed cherries. I bring them together in a salad, scattering the pitted fruits in among layers of thinly sliced smoked ham and salad leaves.

Tongue Of all meats, tongue has the most natural affinity with cherries. The sharp fruits lift the mild, almost creamy flavor of the meat and prevent it from cloying. A sauce or pickle made from the fruit, seasoned with cinnamon or juniper, is the most usual way to bring these two ingredients together, though a handful of the pitted fruits tucked among the leaves of tongue salad is a more straightforward approach.

Goat cheeses The raw fruit forms an exciting partnership with clean, chalk-white cheeses with a smack of acidity. A plate of chèvre and cherries is a beautifully understated way to bring a summer lunch to a close.

Almonds Most famously paired in a classic cherry and almond tart, the nut can also be toasted and scattered over a plate of poached cherries or ground and included in the crust of a crumble.

* When shopping for cherries, look for green stalks rather than brown ones. They are a sign of a young, recently picked crop.
* Pick the fruit by the stalks rather than risk bruising the flesh.
* Where strawberries and raspberries are best served at room temperature, or even slightly warm from the sun, cherries seem more interesting when chilled, or even served on a plate of crushed ice. The cold tightens their skins and makes them all the more crisp and refreshing.
* Cherries keep longer with their stalks intact.
* The fruit's skin dulls as it becomes overripe.
* Cherries cooked with their pits in often appear to have more flavor. The pits have subtle almond notes, which are particularly noticeable when the fruit is poached.
* The pits tend to polarize people. Some have no qualms about spitting a few out at the table, others can't be doing with it. I tend to pit them only as a last resort, and rather enjoy lining up the pits around the rim of my plate and playing "tinker, tailor, soldier, sailor" with them. My feeling is that the pits are acceptable in a pie, less so in an almond tart. A pie where someone has taken the time to pit the cherries is a great luxury and, despite the extra time involved, I always think, "I am so glad I did that."

A salad of summer leaves, cured pork, and cherries

The sweet-sharp notes of the cherries lift the smoky, herbal notes of cured ham in the same way small tomatoes will. Air-dried hams such as Parma, mildly cured ones like speck and coppa, or the paprika-spiced lomo or something exceptionally dark and woodsy will benefit from the uplifting quality of a handful of cherries. And yes, I think you must pit them for this.

enough for 2 as a light lunch
salad leaves – 4 generous handfuls
thinly sliced cured ham, such as lomo, speck, or coppa – 2½ to
    3½ ounces (75 to 100g)
cherries – 4 handfuls

for the dressing
Dijon mustard – a teaspoon
red wine vinegar – 2 teaspoons
olive oil – 3 tablespoons
heavy cream – 3 tablespoons
parsley – a little

Make the dressing: put the mustard in a small bowl with a pinch of salt, the red wine vinegar, olive oil, and a grinding of black pepper. Mix with a fork or small whisk, then introduce the cream. Finely chop the parsley leaves and add to the dressing.

Toss the salad leaves with the cured ham. Halve and pit the cherries and add them to the leaves. Drizzle over the dressing and serve.

Poached ham with a sharp cherry sauce

There is a common theme in my cooking of a large ham served with a fruit-based sauce. Sweet ham, sharp sauce, it works on several levels: something easy to cook and carve for a group; a dish as enjoyable cold as it is hot; a good-natured dish that will keep until you need it. The cherry version is one for early summer, the meat cooked in apple juice, the cherries only lightly sweetened. Creamed spinach is good with this.

enough for 6
boneless ham, rolled and tied – 5½ to 6½ pounds (2.5 to 3kg)
apple juice – 2 cups (500ml)
water – 2 cups (500ml)
black peppercorns – 12
an onion, halved but not peeled
bay leaves –2
cloves – 3

for the sauce
Morello cherries – 1 pound (500g)
sugar – ¼ cup (50g)
juniper berries – 8
a bay leaf

Put the ham in a large pan, pour over enough water to cover, and bring to a boil. Carefully tip away the water. Pour the apple juice and water over the meat, then add the peppercorns, the halved onion, the bay leaves and cloves, and bring to a boil. Turn down the heat so that the liquid simmers gently and cover with a lid. Leave until the meat is cooked—it will need about two and a half hours. The ham can remain in the cooking liquid until you need it.

To make the sauce, halve the cherries and remove their pits. Put them in a stainless steel or enameled pan with the sugar, the lightly squashed juniper berries, bay leaf, and 2 tablespoons of water. Bring to a boil, then lower the heat to a simmer. Leave for ten minutes or so, with the occasional stir. Turn off the heat and leave until needed.

To serve, slice the ham thinly and place on warm plates. Spoon the cherry sauce on the side.

A top-crust cherry pie

I have always had a soft spot for commercial cherry pie filling. Curiously, I prefer it to any pie made with fresh fruit, something I can only put down to nostalgia getting the better of good taste.

Fresh cherries need a little lemon juice if they are to shine under the crust of a pie. It also helps prevent them from browning as you pit them. Sometimes I pit the cherries, sometimes I don't. It adds fifteen minutes or so to the preparation time and it makes a refreshing change to have a mouthful of cherries unaccompanied by their pits. That said, if you take the pitting route, be very thorough—there is no shock greater than hitting a rock-hard pit you weren't expecting.

enough for 4

for the pastry
all-purpose flour – 2 cups minus 2 tablespoons (230g)
butter – 10 tablespoons (140g)
confectioners' sugar – a scant ½ cup (50g)
egg yolk – 1 large

for the filling
plump cherries –2¼ pounds (1kg)
a squeeze of lemon juice
superfine sugar – 3 heaping tablespoons, plus extra for sprinkling
cornstarch – 2 tablespoons

Put the flour into a bowl, rub in the butter with your fingertips, then mix in the confectioners' sugar and egg yolk. Bring the dough together and squeeze it into a round before putting it in the fridge for half an hour to chill. I find this pastry works well in the food processor too: first blitz the flour and butter, then mix briefly with the sugar and egg yolk.

Preheat the oven to 350°F (180°C). Pull the stalks from the cherries, dropping the fruit into a mixing bowl and squeezing over the lemon. Scatter the superfine sugar and cornstarch over the cherries and toss gently. Tip into a baking dish.

Roll or press out the pastry into a round. Lift it on the rolling pin and place it gently on top of the fruit. Cut two or three air holes in it, then bake for thirty minutes or so, until the pie is pale gold (start checking after twenty-five minutes). Remove from the oven, sprinkle with superfine sugar, and return to the oven for five or six minutes.

Leave the pie to cool a little before serving with a pitcher of heavy cream.

A cherry cheesecake

I am no stranger to the *Kaffee und Kuchen* tradition of Germany and Vienna. As much as I like the claggy cheesecake in *The Kitchen Diaries* and the soft, almost ice cream–like quality of the damson one in this collection, I have an interest, too, in the drier-textured cheesecakes you find in German cafés. The lightness appeals to me, as do the lack of sweetness and the clean, fresh note it leaves in the mouth. I take pleasure in pushing the open-textured crumbs together with the tines of my fork. This is that cake.

You could make a moist cherry topping by warming the pitted and halved fruit with a little sugar and water and thickening the resulting syrup with cornstarch or, for a less cloudy finish, arrowroot. I prefer to contrast the mild, milky quality of the cake with fresh, tart, and totally naked cherries.

enough for 8
ricotta – 1 pound (500g)
cream cheese or mascarpone – 7 ounces (200g)
heavy cream – ⅔ cup (150ml)
superfine sugar – ¾ cup (150g)
lemons – 2
vanilla extract – a drop
eggs – 4
an egg yolk
cornstarch – a heaping tablespoon
cherries – 1 pound (450g)

for the crumb crust
shortbread – 12 ounces (350g)
butter – 6 tablespoons (90g)

Preheat the oven to 350°F (180°C). Lightly butter an 8-inch (20cm) square cake pan.

Crush the shortbread to crumbs. I use the food processor for this, but it can be done in a plastic bag with a well-aimed rolling pin. Melt the butter, add the crushed shortbread, and mix well. Tip the buttered crumbs into the cake pan and pat down lightly. Refrigerate for half an hour, until the butter sets.

Put the ricotta, cream cheese or mascarpone, cream, and sugar in a stand mixer and blend briefly. Add the finely grated zest and juice of the lemons, the merest drop of vanilla extract, then the eggs and egg yolk. Lastly, blend in the cornstarch. Pour the mixture into the cake pan and slide into the oven. Bake for fifty minutes to an hour, covering the top with foil if it is coloring even slightly. Turn the heat off and leave the cake in the oven to cool. Refrigerate overnight.

Halve the cherries and remove their pits. Scatter them over the top of the cake and serve in small squares.

A clafoutis of cherries

Truth be told, I have never found this classic French dessert quite lives up to its lofty reputation. It is nice enough—in a bohemian, slightly-too-much-wine-at-lunch kind of a way—but the tart cherries in their overcoat of warm, soft batter always feel something of a letdown.

As a result I have spent a long time working on the recipe that follows. Straying only very slightly from the classic versions, it approaches what I have always wanted a clafoutis to be.

enough for 4
cherries – 14 ounces (400g)
butter – 5 tablespoons (70g)
superfine sugar – 6 ½ tablespoons (80g)
eggs – 2
all-purpose flour – ¾ cup (90g)
milk – ⅔ cup (150ml)
vanilla extract – a little
confectioners' sugar, for dusting

Preheat the oven to 350°F (180°C). Pit the cherries. It's a drag, but worth it. Lightly butter an 8-inch (20cm) diameter baking dish with a little of the butter, then dust with a couple of tablespoons of the sugar. Tip in the cherries.

Put the rest of the sugar in a mixing bowl and beat in the eggs, flour, milk, and a drop or two of vanilla extract with a large balloon whisk. Melt the rest of the butter in a small pan, then beat into the mixture.

Pour the batter over the cherries and bake for thirty-five minutes, until puffed and golden. Test by inserting a skewer into the center. If it comes out damp but clean, then the clafoutis is done. Remove from the oven and dust with confectioners' sugar.

Chestnuts

Just look at the chestnuts. Plump shells, flat on one side and as shiny as a mahogany banister, tucked up like sleeping dormice in the chestnut's prickly burr. No other food protects itself quite as effectively as the sweet chestnut, with spikes so long and piercingly sharp you need a leather glove to lift them into your basket.

Late afternoon in November, almost dusk, you suddenly catch the far-off smell of smoke. As you get closer to its source, it is joined by the warm scent of roasting nuts. But you pass by, hurrying home or to the store. The charcoal brazier, once a popular sight in city streets, is now rare, a quaint remainder of Dickensian times. The habit of eating warm roasted chestnuts from the bag has all but vanished here.

There are four species of chestnut, including the Japanese, the Chinese, and the American. The only one that concerns us at the table is the European or "sweet" chestnut, sometimes known as the Spanish chestnut. It is part of the beech family and its timber is as valuable as its fruits. The ancient name is *castanea*, a word that crops up in all manner of connections with chestnuts—in the Welsh name *Castan-wydden*, the Dutch *kastanje*, and the French *châtaigne*—and in recipes too, including the flat Tuscan cake known as *castagnaccio*.

The tree is rather beautiful, with its saw-edged leaves and gray bark. The honey-colored male catkins and the spiny green female ones are a familiar sight to anyone walking through the woods in late spring. The sweet odor is heavy and not to everyone's taste—indeed, the chestnut has fewer takers than our other native nuts, the walnut and hazel. I like them roasted, toasted, and puréed, but the honey made from chestnut blossom is a flavor too strong for me, with what I detect as distinct notes of cough syrup.

The fruits themselves are hidden inside a spiky shell similar to that of a conker or horse chestnut but with longer, thinner spines that genuinely hurt those who attempt to gather them. As the fruits inside mature, the burrs split open to reveal up to three polished nuts.

Free from their cases, the chestnuts are pleasing to roll over in your hand, like a particularly smooth pebble or the golden coin in a box of assorted sweets. I like the fact that each end has a name: the pointed tuft is known as the "flame," the dark, rectangular patch at the other end as the "hilum." (As a student, I remember being just as amused that even the sides of a house brick have their own names.)

The fruit has two skins, three if you count the green exterior. The first, called the "peel," is polished and dark, the second—the pellicle—directly underneath, is a thin, slightly furry coating that clings tightly to the grooves in the fruit. Easy to remove in the fresh fruit, it gets more fiddly with age and often needs the application of water or heat before it can be peeled off. I have less of a problem with its presence than most and in some cases leave it be, unless I am eating my chestnuts raw.

The sweet chestnut originates from Asia Minor and has at one point or another been a staple food in Italy, Spain, and Turkey. Even as late as the 1870s, it was almost the sole carbohydrate for short patches of the year in Tuscany. Pasta, polenta, and bread were made from its flour, particularly in mountainous areas where cereals could not be grown. Those grown around the Mugello region are considered by some to be the sweetest. The main production area in France is situated in the Ardèche, with its famous *appellation contrôlée*, Châtaigne d'Ardèche. Many of the exquisitely wrapped French *marrons glacés* are in fact made with Italian-grown fruits. Our own chestnut groves are due to the Romans, who planted them wherever they went.

The green cases first appear in early summer and start to ripen from September onward. As the nut ripens, the starch turns to sugar and the delicate notes of hazelnut and vanilla come into play. We eat them fresh and whole, either raw, steamed, or roasted, but most are bought ready prepared and either vacuum packed or frozen. More often than not, the nut creeps softly into our kitchen in the form of a ready-made purée. This comes in cans or tubes and is sometimes sweetened.

A chestnut in the garden

Planning for a small town garden can leave you frustrated. There are always trees (and indeed bushes, vines, and plants) that you simply don't have room for. The sweet chestnut was one that got "red penciled" at the planning stage. Despite the fact that you can keep the trees to a manageable size by coppicing, there just wasn't room. I include it here for those lucky enough to have a tree in their garden or nearby woodland.

Doubtless, my tree would never have reached the size of the famous "Great Chestnut of Tortworth" in Gloucestershire, which by 1720 measured over 50 feet in circumference. Wild chestnut trees can be spotted in warm lowland areas, particularly in the south of the country. There are extensive sweet chestnut coppices in Kent and the surrounding counties, many protected by preservation orders. Several are temptingly for sale. The trees often go hand in hand with bluebells, the piercing green of the unfurling saw-edged leaves, and the joyous singing blue of the wild hyacinth being a heart-lifting sight in May.

The trees fruit best where they are in good light, so they tend to produce a more prolific crop on a single open tree than in a crowded coppice. Perhaps this is why the Italian nuts, though no less sweet, are far larger than our own.

The mature nuts begin to fall in October, the spiky shells being picked up from the grass beneath the tree canopy rather than pulled from the tree—tricky even with gardening gloves on. Each case will contain up to three nuts, with their distinctive one flat side where they have been nestling up against one another.

Chestnuts in the kitchen

I sometimes toast a few chestnuts on a cold winter's day just for the smell that fills the kitchen. I don't have a chestnut roaster—the flat iron pan with holes and a long handle to keep you away from the heat that is traditionally used for chestnut toasting. I cook mine in a frying pan, their skins pierced with a sharp knife to prevent them exploding and ricocheting around the kitchen, constantly shaking the pan to keep them from scorching. They are ready when their shells crisp up, maybe a little scorched here and there—it's inevitable—and they have filled the kitchen with a deep, warm smell of roasted nuts.

Easy though it is to slit the skins with the point of a small, strong knife, you can soak them instead. Boil the kettle, pour the water into a heatproof bowl, and leave the chestnuts to soak for a good thirty minutes. By that time, their skins will have softened enough to be easily peeled by hand.

Chestnut flour has a distinctive and rather strong flavor. I have never taken to it, detecting an almost medicinal quality to everything I have baked with it. Bread made with this particularly soft flour (it is like putting your hand into talcum powder) will keep for a good couple of weeks, but it is a heavy flour and does not allow the bread to rise. The Tuscan chestnut cake, *castagnaccio*, is one of the few cakes that I never found a soft spot for, despite the traditional inclusion of pine nuts, raisins, and rosemary. Maybe I will learn to appreciate its many charms with age. Anyone with a food dehydrator may like to know that it is possible to dry the nuts, then grind them to flour in a food mill. The tawny flour is also used for pancakes and pasta (probably very good with a game stew) and was the original flour to use in polenta. The Corsicans make it into little doughnut-style fritters called *fritelli*, often made with sausage or with fresh cheese.

Chocolate cakes aside, the raison d'être of the chestnut is, for me, the plump, foil-wrapped *marron glacé*. To eat one after lunch on Christmas day, its tissue paper–thin sugar crust sparkling in the candlelight, is to truly understand the meaning of the word "sweetmeat." I have seen them being made in France—where they have been produced since the sixteenth century—and watched with awe as they were packed into boxes, each pleated wrapping being folded by the packer's nimble fingers in what appeared to be one long, poetic movement. You can make them yourself if you fancy simmering the peeled fruits in sugar syrup and letting them dry a little before dipping them in gossamer-thin icing. They are popular in Turkey too, where they are known as *kestane sekeri*.

The most famous chestnut-related recipe is Mont Blanc, the luxurious confection of meringue, sweetened chestnut purée, and whipped cream. I can't remember the last time I saw one on a menu. I have never understood how anyone could finish a meal with such a rich dessert, but it used to go down well with cups of dark, treacly coffee at the long-departed Swiss Centre in London's Leicester Square.

In the UK our only significant chestnut dish is that of stuffing for the Christmas bird. Usually a stir-up of day-old breadcrumbs, celery, chestnuts, bacon, and butter, it is seasoned with rosemary and sage. Sometimes it contains sausage meat, other times eggs, and it can be cooked in a flat pan or inside the bird. Traditionalists are likely to put sausage meat at one end and chestnut stuffing at the other. I tend to blow hot and cold about the idea of brussels sprouts and chestnuts. Sometimes I like it, other times I find it an odd match of textures.

Chestnuts and...

Mushrooms Nicely golden, a plump mushroom works well with this nut. Match them in a leafy salad or add a few chestnuts to a pan of sautéed fungi.

Bacon Sizzling bacon slices or cubes of pancetta have an affinity with the chestnut, as does thinly sliced air-cured ham with the roasted nuts.

Game and poultry The gamier meats such as pheasant, squab, and partridge appreciate a chestnut or two included in their stuffing or in a sauce in which they are presented. Turkey and strongly flavored free-range chicken, too.

Venison A stew of this lean, richly flavored meat is often the home for a few roasted chestnuts.

Grapes Just as they love a walnut, so sweet grapes of any sort are partial to a chestnut. In a salad perhaps, with bacon or smoked ham, or simply sharing a plate at the end of a meal.

Greens Sprouts and the darker members of the cabbage family such as lacinato kale can work splendidly with toasted chestnuts.

Chocolate The darkest chocolate, at least 80 percent cocoa solids, seems to work particularly well with a sweetened chestnut purée. Anything less becomes a little sickly.

Vanilla A heaven-sent combination, especially when the sweetened purée is lightly flavored with a few drops of the best extract.

* Two pounds (1kg) of chestnuts in their shells will yield approximately 1½ pounds (700g) of shelled nuts.
* This nut contains virtually no fat and its flour is free of gluten.
* A roasting chestnut whose skin has not been slashed will inevitably explode as the fruit inside expands, resulting in a hot nut ricocheting around the kitchen, sending little bits of shrapnel flying.
* The Portuguese have a chestnut liqueur that I have never tried.

To roast chestnuts

Score the fruits with a sharp knife, piercing through the skin but stopping before you reach the kernel. One shallow incision on the flat side is usually easiest. The skin is less tight here than on the other side. Drop them into a dry frying pan, and leave until the shells have darkened, shaking occasionally. The nuts are ready when they are soft and fudgy inside.

To peel chestnuts

Use a short, sharp knife (or better still a utility knife) to cut a small slit in the flat side of the shell of each chestnut. Put them into a heatproof bowl. Pour over a kettleful of boiling water and leave for thirty minutes. Remove the chestnuts from the water and peel away the outer shell and as much of the brown skin as you can. The chestnuts are now ready to add to a casserole.

Chestnut purée

You may feel that life is too short to purée your own chestnuts, a task that involves piercing the shells, roasting, peeling, then poaching the nuts in sugar syrup before pushing them through the fine screen of a food mill or a potato ricer. I have to say I would agree with those whose think this is a lot of work for even the most committed of cooks, compared with unscrewing the top of a tube of the ready-made stuff.

> chestnuts – 2 pounds (1kg)
> golden baker's sugar – ½ cup (100g)
> water – 1 cup (250ml)
> a vanilla pod, split in half

Make a small slit in each chestnut with the point of a sharp knife. Roast them at about 400°F (200°C) for fifteen minutes, then cool slightly before peeling.

Make a light syrup by dissolving the sugar in the water over heat, adding the vanilla, then using it to poach the chestnuts for thirty minutes until tender. Drain the chestnuts and pass them through a food mill—the endlessly useful *mouli-légumes* is the one, or if not, a potato ricer. A food processor is likely to turn them to glue. Cool and sweeten to taste.

A casserole of parsnips, chestnuts, and mushrooms

Some good stock is called for here. If it is close to Christmas, the turkey bones simmered with bay and onion will give a suitably rich liquor. If you want to keep meat out of it altogether, then a vegetable stock will work admirably as long as it has plenty of flavor. This is also the recipe in which to use up your ends of Christmas marsala, Madeira, or sherry when you add the stock.

Some brown basmati rice, steamed with a cinnamon stick, a clove or two, and some black peppercorns, would be good here to soak up the juices. Couscous is another possibility.

enough for 4, with rice
onions – 2
butter – a thick slice
rosemary needles – 2 teaspoons, finely chopped
juniper berries – a teaspoon, lightly bashed
small carrots – 4
large parsnips – 4
celery stalks – 2
button mushrooms – 4 ounces (125g)
peeled chestnuts – 5 ounces (150g)
all-purpose flour – 2 tablespoons
good hot stock (vegetable, chicken, or turkey) – 3 cups (750ml)
bay leaves – 2
red currant jelly – 2 tablespoons

Peel the onions, then cut them in half from root to tip and slice each half into six segments. Put them in a deep, heavy-bottomed saucepan with the butter, rosemary, and juniper berries and leave over medium heat until the onions are deep gold and soft enough to crush between finger and thumb. It is important to let them become golden and sticky; much flavor will come from this. They will need an occasional stir.

Scrub the carrots and parsnips and chop into pieces roughly the size of a wine cork, then add them to the pan. Thinly slice the celery and halve the mushrooms. Stir them into the other vegetables together with the chestnuts and leave to color very lightly. You may need to add a little more butter or some oil at this point. When the parsnips' edges are starting to turn a deep gold, scatter the flour over and continue cooking for a few minutes, then pour in the hot stock. Season with salt and black pepper, add the bay leaves and bring to a boil. Lower the heat and leave to simmer for twenty minutes.

Stir in the red currant jelly and taste for seasoning. Simmer briefly until the jelly has melted, then serve with brown rice.

Chestnut, sausage, and marsala stuffing

There is a moment, usually on Boxing Day, when I stand and eat a doorstop sandwich. It is often the best sandwich of the year. Made with white bread, layers of thinly sliced, generously salted roast turkey, crisp bacon, and thinly sliced stuffing. Coarse-textured and thoroughly seasoned stuffing is essential to what I regard as one of the glories of Christmas.

onions – 2
butter – a thick slice
thyme – a large sprig or two
rosemary – a large sprig
sausage meat – 14 ounces (400g)
fresh breadcrumbs – 3 handfuls
cooked peeled chestnuts (boiled or roasted) – about 2 ounces (50g),
     coarsely chopped
Madeira or dry marsala – a wineglass

Peel and cut up the onions just short of finely chopped (this is a coarse-textured stuffing, but you don't want the pieces so big that the mixture falls apart). Melt the butter in a saucepan, add the onions, and let them soften and color lightly, stirring from time to time. While they are cooking, strip the leaves from the thyme and stir them in. Remove the needles from the rosemary twig and chop them finely. Stir them into the onions.

Preheat the oven to 350°F (180°C). When the onions are soft enough to crush between finger and thumb, add the sausage meat, breadcrumbs, chestnuts, and the Madeira or marsala. Season generously with salt and black pepper. Shape the stuffing into balls slightly larger than a golf ball and set them in a buttered or foil-lined baking dish (they can remain here for a day or so, refrigerated, until you need them). Bake for about thirty minutes, until sizzling.

Mushrooms, chestnuts, and bacon

A light, late-autumn salad of hot bacon, mushrooms, and chestnuts. I have made this with curly frisée and young spinach and both worked well. The spinach leaves tend to soften deliciously under the heat of the mushrooms, the frisée stays crisp. The choice is ours.

enough for 4
bacon – 8 slices
peanut or vegetable oil – 4 tablespoons
butter – a thin slice
medium-sized mushrooms – 12 ounces (350g)
garlic – a juicy clove, peeled and crushed
peeled chestnuts – 8 ounces (250g)
salad leaves – 4 handfuls

Cut the bacon into pieces about the size of a large postage stamp. Warm the oil in a large frying pan, add the butter and then the bacon. Once the bacon fat is golden, lift out and set aside on paper towels. Cut the mushrooms in half and add to the pan together with the garlic and chestnuts. Let them cook over medium heat, soaking up the bacon-flavored fat, until pale gold.

Divide the salad leaves between four plates and tip the bacon, chestnuts, and mushrooms over them, together with any cooking juices from the pan.

Brussels sprouts and chestnuts

You either feel this classic use for the chestnut is an abomination or consider it an essential and unmissable part of the Christmas feast. Whichever way you lean, here is a really good version with bacon fat and masses of butter.

enough for 4
peeled chestnuts – 3½ ounces (100g)
milk – ¾ cup plus 2 tablespoons (200ml)
butter – 5 tablespoons (75g)
bacon – 2 slices, or even a little bacon rind
brussels sprouts – 1 pound (500g)

Put the peeled chestnuts into a pan with the milk, simmer for fifteen to twenty minutes, until tender, then drain. Melt the butter in a shallow pan, add the bacon or bacon rind and the drained chestnuts, and leave to cook over low heat. The butter must not color.

Cook the sprouts in deep, very lightly salted, ferociously boiling water until just tender—a matter of three or four minutes, depending on the size of your sprouts. Drain them thoroughly, then toss gently in the bacon-flavored butter. I like to add a little black pepper at this point, coarsely ground.

Red cabbage with chestnuts and sherry

The list of vegetables appropriate for Christmas lunch is not long. Red cabbage is one of them and I usually make a dish of it, often cooked with apple and cider, to pass around with the goose. Chestnuts have an affinity with any of the brassica family and especially, I think, with red cabbage.

enough for 4 to 6 as a side dish
half a good-sized red cabbage – about 1½ pounds (750g)
a little peanut oil
pancetta or bacon in one piece – 7 ounces (200g)
peeled chestnuts – 5 ounces (150g)
medium-dry sherry – a glass

Shred the cabbage finely, then rinse and drain. Heat a couple of tablespoons of oil in a large saucepan, coarsely dice the pancetta, and add it to the pan, letting it color lightly. Add the chestnuts, continue cooking for a few minutes, then add the drained red cabbage. Expect it to hiss and pop. Turn the cabbage in the fat and cover with a lid. Continue cooking over medium heat for seven or eight minutes, until the cabbage has wilted slightly. Add the sherry, a little salt (depending on how salty the bacon is), and leave until almost evaporated. Serve immediately.

A chocolate and chestnut terrine

A seriously rich recipe to be enjoyed in thin slices. You will get a good eight or even ten portions from this cake.

enough for 8 to 10

for the cake
butter – 1 cup plus 2 tablespoons (250g)
golden baker's sugar – 1 cup plus 2 tablespoons (225g)
self-rising flour – 1¾ cups (225g)
baking powder – 2 teaspoons
cocoa powder – 5½ tablespoons (30g)
eggs – 4
milk – ⅓ cup (80ml)
hot espresso coffee – 3 tablespoons

for the chestnut and chocolate filling
dark chocolate, 79 percent cocoa solids – 8 ounces (250g)
butter – ½ cup plus 1 tablespoon (125g)
chestnut purée (page 192) – 14 ounces (400g)
superfine sugar – 2 tablespoons

to finish
10 to 12 cooked or candied chestnuts
dark chocolate – 8 ounces (250g)

You will need an 8-inch (20cm) square cake pan lined with parchment paper and an 8 by 3½-inch (20 by 9cm) loaf pan or similar for shaping the cake (measurements are taken across the bottoms of the pans).

Preheat the oven to 325°F (160°C). Cut the butter into small dice and put into a stand mixer with the golden baker's sugar. Beat until light and fluffy. Sift together the flour, baking powder, and cocoa powder (don't miss this step; it is really important that the dry ingredients are well mixed). Crack the eggs into a small bowl, beat them briefly to mix, then stir in the milk.

Introduce the flour mixture and the eggs and milk to the butter and sugar, adding a little of each at a time, with the mixer going constantly, until you have a smooth mixture. Finally mix in the coffee.

Spoon the mixture into the lined square cake pan and smooth the top, then bake for forty-five to fifty minutes, until risen and firm to the touch. Test with a metal skewer. If it comes out moist but clean, without any raw cake mixture stuck to it, then it is ready. Remove from the oven, leave to settle for fifteen minutes, then run a thin spatula around the edges and gently turn out onto a cooling rack. Peel off the parchment.

Make the chestnut and chocolate filling. Break the chocolate into small pieces and melt it in a glass or china bowl set over a pan of simmering water. Do not stir, other than to push any unmelted chocolate down into the liquid chocolate. Turn the heat off as soon as the chocolate is melted. Cut the butter into small pieces and stir it gently into the chocolate until it has melted.

Beat the chestnut purée with the sugar until well mixed, then fold gently into the melted chocolate and butter. Try not to overmix. Set aside.

Cut the cake in half to make two long pieces. Slice each half in two horizontally and trim to fit the loaf pan. Place a piece of cake in the base of the pan, add half the chocolate chestnut cream, and smooth the top. Place a second piece of cake on top, followed by the rest of the chestnut cream. Place a third and final piece of cake on top. (You will be left with one remaining piece, which I suggest you freeze for later or nibble at will.)

Wrap the entire loaf pan in plastic wrap, pressing down firmly to encourage the layers to stick together. Refrigerate for at least two hours.

Remove the plastic wrap, loosen the cake from the sides of the pan with a thin spatula, and turn it out onto a wire rack. Place the chestnuts along the top if you are using them. Melt the chocolate as before, then pour it over the top of the cake, smoothing it over the sides. Leave to set before serving.

Chestnut meringue

Monte Bianco, Mont Blanc, call it what you will. Named after the mountain that stands over the Aosta Valley in Italy and the Haute-Savoie region of France, this is a sweet mountain of meringue, chestnut purée, and cream, and is still the signature dish of the Angelina café in Paris where it was, reputedly, invented (some prefer the location as Jiyugaoka in Japan). I cannot think of a more long-winded ending to a meal—meringue shells to be baked, chestnuts to be roasted and then laboriously puréed, cream to be whipped, and finally the whole thing assembled to resemble the eponymous mountain. Shortcuts have been known to involve store-bought meringue shells, cans of sweetened chestnut purée, and squirty cream.

I would sit on the fence, insisting on homemade meringue, but using ready puréed chestnuts. At the risk of getting my wrists well and truly slapped by traditionalists, I coat mine with a crisp web of melted chocolate. A snowfall of confectioners' sugar, to represent the mountain peaks, is de rigueur.

enough for 6 to 8

for the meringue
egg whites – 4
a pinch of salt
superfine sugar – 1¼ cups (250g)

for the filling
heavy cream – 1 cup (250ml)
sweetened chestnut purée (or the chestnut purée on page 192) – 1 pound
    (500g)
confectioners' sugar
dark, bitter chocolate – 5 ounces (150g)

Preheat the oven to 275°F (140°C). Put the egg whites and salt into a bowl and whisk until soft peaks form. Beat in half the sugar, in short stages, until glossy and thick. Fold in the remaining sugar with a large metal spoon (a wooden one tends to knock the air out). Spoon the mixture onto a baking sheet lined with parchment paper, making rounds approximately ¾ inch (2cm) high and 4 inches (10cm) in diameter. Flatten the tops slightly. Bake in the preheated oven for roughly an hour, until they are crisp but still chewy within.

To assemble, whisk the cream until thick. It should just form soft, rolling peaks. Spoon it onto the meringues. Place the chestnut purée in a bowl with a tablespoon of confectioners' sugar and beat until smooth (it will inevitably be a little grainy; that is the nature of the beast). Mound the purée on top of the cream, or more correctly push it through a food mill to achieve a lighter, open mass. Melt the chocolate in a bowl over simmering water, then drizzle in thin stripes over the chestnut and meringue. Dust with confectioners' sugar.

Damsons

Few trees offer such delicate blossom or as charming a fruit, dangling from the tree's fine twigs in early autumn like dusty, violet-black bonbons. In late September, as their short season draws to a close, you may still find a handful of bloom-covered damsons among the turning yellow leaves—a particularly poetic moment for any gardener or cook. The trees are self fertile, so you can stick one in a far corner of the garden and in a year or two it will give you enough fruit for a crumble. I planted one almost as soon as I had signed the deeds.

Damsons are ripe in early September, at a time when the garden paths are festooned with spiderwebs and the leaves start their slow journey toward gold and bronze. A time of faint melancholy and mellow scents, of early winter squash, fat pears, and late, spiky dahlias. At no point in the calendar am I happier. Damsons mark the point in the year when I start to relax, my shoulders unhunch, I can begin to feel the safety of dark nights and damp mornings, the supreme comfort of a favorite, holey sweater. Just as so many are saddened at the end of the summer, I feel curiously rejuvenated, my sap rising as others' does in the spring. Different strokes for different folks.

I value the damson principally for its glorious, inky juice. The sort that seeps into the crust of a crumble or leaves swirls of darkest indigo in custard or cream. The trees you come across in old gardens and hedgerows are laden with nostalgia for me, their crop—in pies, jam, and tender-crusted tarts—being the single best thing about my country adolescence. To run my fingers through a box of tiny, dusty damsons, the occasional stray leaf among them, is as much a marker of the year's passing as the summer solstice or the Midnight Mass on Christmas Eve.

The damson is named after Damascus in Syria, where it is suspected to have originated. In Britain it has been in decline since the Second World War. The lack of sugar available during rationing wreaked havoc on the damson industry—it is one the few fruits almost useless without the addition of sugar—and many ancient orchards were torn up. But there is still a white froth of blossom to be seen in April, covering the hedges of what used to be known as Westmorland, now part of Cumbria.

The Westmorland damson is probably the best known of all these marble-sized plums (the fruit has been grown there commercially since at least the 1700s), though it grows well in Shropshire too, where its presence is said to be a legacy of the nearby wool and cotton mills. The royal purple pigment in its skins had been used for dye since Roman times. Often planted as windbreaks for other crops, the "wild" trees that survive can be found in hedgerows or tucked at the corners of fields. The crop is still sold at farm gates and roadside stands during September.

Much effort has been spent on reviving the damson's fortunes. There are once again Damson Days in the Lyth Valley, complete with Morris dancers and wandering fiddlers, when the blossom is toasted by its many fans. When people tell me they don't like this fruit I find they generally mean they are bothered by its pits, or aren't prepared to look for it. More often than not, they are suspicious of any fruit you cannot eat without cooking.

There is no cooking fruit I hold in greater regard, none whose arrival in the markets I wait for more impatiently. The arrival of the little violet-black Damascene plum is without question the high point of my fruit-cooking year.

A damson tree in the garden

Wild damson trees can still be found in old hedgerows, their sweet rot a characteristic smell of the countryside in late autumn. Many turn out to be the smaller, shudderingly sour bullace or even the sloe, the ancestor of the damson and the fruit you can use for a glistening crimson gin.

The damson tree shares many of the characteristics of the plum family with the exception of, perhaps, a smoother trunk. A slightly damp clay soil will keep it happy, but it is less than fussy about altitude. Only very sandy or waterlogged soil or serious amounts of shade will cause problems. It can remain productive for at least fifty years.

If you are choosing a tree from scratch, then I suggest going for one with the more modest-sized fruits, such as Farleigh. Their flavor is richer and truer than the large, more maroon-skinned fruits, which are apt to have a prunelike note about them. If I appear to be urging you to plant a tree, it is simply that I want this fruit more than any other to survive the march of time.

Commercial orchards are few, but to witness the tree's rare beauty you might like to take a trip through Shropshire in late March or the Lyth Valley a couple of weeks later, when sudden gusts of wind take the tissue-paper blossom off the trees like snowflakes against a clear gray sky. Or join the small but loyal band of customers waiting patiently each September, jam jars in hand (and none more loyal than this one).

The earliness of the damson's blossom, appearing while there is still a risk of hard frosts, is a constant worry to anyone who has a tree in their garden. There is little we can do other than plant in a sheltered position that gets as much sun as possible. A covering of row cover fabric for short trees on cold nights might help more than just crossing your fingers, but larger trees are pretty much at the mercy of the elements.

One rarely considers feeding an established tree but it can be of sustenance to one that has previously fruited heavily. Some manure in spring will be welcomed, especially for its moisture-retaining properties. Younger trees will benefit from a scattering of potash in winter.

My damson tree fruited from its third year. Hidden in the farthest west corner of the garden, it shelters the compost heaps and provides enough fruit for a couple of crumbles. I live for the day it produces enough for a decent batch of jam.

Young damson trees are available from specialty nurseries. They will arrive probably on the coldest day of the year when you least feel like getting the spade out. Their roots will probably be bound in burlap and your hoped-for tree will look distinctly unpromising. Worry not. Plant as per your nursery's instructions and, come spring, the odd leaf opening here and there along its spindly branches, it will look more hopeful. Within a couple of years you should have a lovely little garden tree, with enough fruit on it for at least one good pie.

Varieties

By mid-September the path between the vegetable beds is almost overgrown. Dahlias so dark red as to be nearly black; sagging, tobacco-brown stems of Jerusalem artichokes; a wild lemon verbena and tangled clouds of Mutabilis roses block your route to the little damson tree at the back of the garden. Every few feet means doing battle with a spiderweb. I'm willing to bet few know the variety of their own damson tree, so it is worth recording the name somewhere if you put a new one in, so that future generations may know.

Farleigh Damson Introduced in about 1820, large leafed and something of a copious cropper, the Farleigh has small, rich, bloomy purple fruit that appear in September. Makes superb crumbles.

Merryweather Large, late fruits from a variety found in 1907.

Shropshire Prune Regarded by growers such as Keepers Nursery as the classic damson. Around in early September.

Blue Violet A true Westmorland variety, small and early. You may even see it around in early August.

Bradley's King You will find this particularly sweet Nottinghamshire variety from mid-September. To my knowledge, I have never tasted this one.

Blue Damson* Large clusters of deep purple-black fruits with tart, spicy flesh; bears in midsummer.

*Available from US sources.

Damsons in the kitchen

Damsons are a cook's fruit. None has a deeper, more powerful flavor or such penetrating juice. They will need sugar, probably more than you might wish in these days of healthy eating, and patience with the pits— only a masochist would attempt to remove them before cooking. The intense flavor is unmistakable, and embellished with sugar and a very little water they will produce copious amounts of highly flavored syrup. Their strident flavor needs tempering with a soft pastry crust or a drizzle of cream. Crumbles or fools are the most acceptable, but a soft suet dough such as that of a roly-poly pudding would work too.

The simplest way to treat them is to bring them to a simmer with sugar and a little water. I use about 4 tablespoons of sugar for each pound (500g) of fruit. As the fruit bursts, its skin colors the juices and the flesh turns from a dull greeny yellow to deep apricot amber. The juice will usually curdle when added to custard or to cream or yogurt, but no matter. The ensuing flavor, poised somewhere between plums and black currants, will generally win the squeamish eater over.

They will need a good sorting through before cooking, to remove any twigs, leaves, and the odd mushy or shriveled specimen. Stalks should be removed but pits can be left in, adding a faint almond note and providing the necessary details for a game of tinker, tailor, soldier, sailor.

Damsons make the most gorgeous jam. I am not fond of the commercial versions I have tried (too firmly set and too sweet by far) and tend either to make it myself or to seek out homemade versions at village fêtes, farm stands, and charity events. The artisan variety found in delicatessens is often worth picking up. It is an easy preserve to make, less of a diva than, say, strawberry, and often sets softly like a good jam should. The pits will sometimes rise to the surface during cooking and can be scooped off with a slotted spoon.

The savory applications are few but outstanding. A few damsons allowed to soften in the gravy of a game bird can produce rewards, as can a pickle made with the whole fruit, vinegar, and spices. I also add them to the Christmas ham, using some of my precious store from the freezer.

Damsons and...

Red wine vinegar A good way to brighten up a damson compote that you wish to serve with cold roast meats.
Ginger Both the dried and fresh versions are appropriate.
Almonds A spot-on addition to a damson cake.
Duck The perfect fruit for slicing through a quacker's copious fat.
Pork and ham A nice change from applesauce.
Cream cheeses Soft, sweet cheeses such as mascarpone and cream cheese will soften the fruit's sharpness. An excellent topping for a cheesecake.
Aniseed and star anise Use the spice in pickles and savory sauces.
Cinnamon The plum spice. The earthy sweetness seems very much at home with the knife-sharp, fruity quality of this little plum.
Allspice So says Mrs. Beeton.

* The blossom is among the earliest and the most fragile. A sheltered spot will help reduce frost damage.
* Damson Sunday was the point in April when tourists thronged the country lanes of Westmorland admiring the damson blossom.
* Damson Saturday was the day in September when many tons were taken to the market in Kendal and then off to be jammed.
* Damson Day is the new celebration of all things Damascene, from blossom and beer to jam and gin. Set up by the Westmorland Damson Association in 1996, it has become the fruit's answer to Apple Day.
* Damson cheese is a preserve similar to *membrillo*, the Spanish quince paste.

Twice-cooked ham with damson gin sauce

Damsons are one of the few fruits I freeze. Their season is so fleeting that I pack them into plastic freezer boxes to ensure there is enough for winter crumbles and the occasional sauce for a piece of ham. Damson is often my preferred sauce at Christmas too, made with frozen fruit and a spiking of damson gin. The sweetness seems entirely in tune with the festivities, but this works for a large autumnal gathering too. If you substitute sloe gin for damson, please only use a homemade or (all natural) British one.

enough for 12
smoked boneless ham, rolled and tied – 5½ to 6½ pounds (2.5 to 3kg)
pear or hard apple cider – two pint (500ml) bottles
black peppercorns – 12
an onion, halved but not peeled
bay leaves – 3
cloves – 3

for the damson gin sauce
damsons – 12 ounces (350g)
sugar – 2 tablespoons
red currant jelly – 1¾ cups (400g)
sloe (page 578) or damson gin – ⅔ cup (150ml)
cloves – 6

for the quince glaze
quince jelly – 1¾ cups (400g)
Dijon mustard – 2 heaping tablespoons
fresh white breadcrumbs – a handful

Put the ham in a very large pan. Pour over enough water to cover and bring to a boil. Carefully tip away the water. Pour the cider over the meat and top up with water to cover if necessary. Add the peppercorns, the halved onion, the bay leaves, and cloves and bring to a boil. Lower the heat so that the liquid is simmering gently and cover with a lid or a dome of foil. Leave to cook until the meat is cooked right through—about two and a half hours. You can leave the ham in the cooking liquid until you need it.

To make the sauce, put the damsons in a stainless steel saucepan with the sugar and 2 tablespoons of water. Bring to a boil and simmer for ten minutes or so, until the fruit starts to burst its skins. Stir in the red currant jelly, pour in the gin, then add the cloves and let it return to a boil. Simmer for five minutes, then turn off the heat and leave to cool. The jelly will thicken or maybe even set very softly.

Remove the ham carefully from the liquid and put it in a roasting pan. Peel off and discard the thick dark skin and the string without removing the fat. (The cooking liquid has served its purpose, but it is worth using as a stock for soup. Just check that it isn't too salty first.)

To make the glaze, put the quince jelly into a mixing bowl and stir in the mustard and breadcrumbs. Spread the glaze over the outside of the ham and bake at 350°F (180°C) for twenty to twenty-five minutes, until the ham is glossy and just starting to color. Leave for a few minutes before carving into thin slices and serving with the sauce. If there is any sauce left over, pour it into clean jars, cover tightly, and store in the fridge.

Roast duck with damson ginger sauce

The damson's sharp kick is a useful contrast to rich meats such as duck (which is why duck is so often teamed with Seville oranges). The spicing works well with the sauce that accompanies the Chinese-style pork roast in the plum chapter (see page 414) but is too good not to repeat here with damsons.

enough for 2, with leftovers

a duck – 4½ to 6½ pounds (2 to 3kg)
Szechwan peppercorns – 2 tablespoons
sea salt – 3 tablespoons
ground anise – a teaspoon

for the sauce
damsons or sharp plums – 2 pounds (900g)
sugar – 3 tablespoons
water – ½ cup (120ml)
fresh ginger – a large knob, about the size of a walnut,
    peeled and cut into matchsticks
star anise – 4
salt – ½ teaspoon
smooth red wine vinegar – 2 tablespoons

Wipe the duck with paper towels and sit it in a plate or shallow dish. Warm the Szechwan peppercorns in a nonstick saucepan until they smell aromatic and start to crackle a bit, then remove them from the heat. Grind together the salt, toasted peppercorns, and ground anise. Easiest with a mortar and pestle, but you can also do it with a plastic bag and a rolling pin. You want a fine beige powder. Rub the seasoned salt over the duck, taking care to get into the tight corners under and around the legs and all over the breasts.

Cover with wax paper and set aside for at least eight hours, preferably overnight, in the fridge.

To make the sauce, put the damsons or plums into a colander and give them a good rinse under cold running water, pulling off any stalks and leaves as you go. Tip the fruit into a stainless steel saucepan (aluminum will taint sour fruits such as plums), then add the sugar, water, ginger, star anise, and salt and bring to a boil. Leave to simmer for about ten to fifteen minutes, until the fruit has burst and the sauce has thickened to a deep purple-red. Stir in the vinegar and simmer for five minutes more. Watch that it doesn't get too thick or catch on the bottom; it is inclined to become a bit jammy at this stage.

Now, depending on whether you can cope with the pits or not, either put the sauce somewhere to cool or, if spitting out pits at the table really isn't your thing, sieve it. Tip it into a large sieve set over a bowl and push the fruit through the sieve with a wooden spoon. Keep going until all you have left is a few pits. Set aside; you can warm it up just before you serve the duck.

To roast the duck, preheat the oven to 400°F (200°C). Prick the skin lightly all over with a fork. The idea is to go through the skin but not the flesh. You want the fat to escape, not the meat juices. Roast for one to one and a half hours, basting occasionally (if your duck is very fatty, then pour off the excess during cooking). Leave to rest for ten minutes before carving.

A hot compote

Remove the little stalks from the damsons, discarding any squashed fruit. Put the fruit in a stainless steel saucepan and add a small amount of water to come no further than a third of the way up the fruit. Sweeten generously to taste, then bring to a boil, turn the heat down, and simmer gently until the fruits have burst their skins and the juices have worked with the sugar to produce a rich purple sauce. Serve warm, with cream or ice cream.

Creamy cheesecake, sharp sauce

Of the several cheesecakes in this book, this is the one for lovers of those with a deeply creamy texture, the sort that sticks to your knife. This is not the cheesecake to partner strawberries or even raspberries; it needs the knife-edge sharpness of damsons or passion fruit.

enough for 10

for the crust
butter – 6 tablespoons (90g)
shortbread – 7 ounces (200g)
Scottish-style oatcakes – 5 ounces (150g)

for the filling
heavy cream – 1½ cups (350ml)
superfine sugar – ¾ cup (150g)
cream cheese – about 1½ pounds (650g)
grated zest of a lemon
a drop of vanilla extract

for the damson sauce
damsons – 1 pound (500g)
superfine sugar – ¾ cup (150g)
water – 4 tablespoons

Line the bottom of an 8-inch (20cm) springform cake pan with parchment or strong wax paper. Melt the butter in a small pan. Crush the shortbread and oatcakes to fine crumbs and stir them into the melted butter. Tip them into the cake pan and smooth them flat. Refrigerate for half an hour or so, until firm. You can speed the process by putting it in the freezer, if you wish.

Put the cream and sugar in a stand mixer and whisk until thick. Keep an eye on the mixture all the time, stopping once it starts to thicken. Stir in the cream cheese, grated lemon zest, and vanilla. Tip the mixture into the crumb-lined cake pan, cover with plastic wrap, and put in the fridge for at least four hours.

To make the damson sauce, remove the stalks, tip the fruit into a stainless steel pan with the sugar and water, and bring to a boil. Leave to simmer gently for ten to fifteen minutes, until the skins have split and the fruits have softened. Leave to cool, then transfer to a dish, cover, and refrigerate for a couple of hours.

Run a thin spatula around the sides of the cheesecake, then release it from its pan. Slide it carefully onto a serving plate. Serve in thick slices, spooning over the damson sauce as you go.

A soft-textured crumble for stone fruits

Should plum crumble be on my lips when I die, then I will go a happy man (damson or gooseberry would be appreciated even more, but let's not push it). Plums suit a crumble crust not because of their juice alone but because of their inherent acidity, which contrasts neatly with the sugary crust.

I offer a crumble recipe without apology. Each tweak to the ratio of flour and butter, every additional ingredient (in this case almonds) produces a slightly different result. My signature crusts tend to be of the soft, buttery, melting kind rather than the fine, tightly packed sand variety that one comes across when people have been parsimonious with the butter.

enough for 6
damsons or plums – 1½ to 1¾ pounds (700 to 800g)
superfine sugar – 4 tablespoons, or more to taste
a thick slice of butter

for the crumble
butter – 7 tablespoons (100g)
all-purpose flour – a scant 1¼ cups (150g)
ground almonds – ½ cup (50g)
superfine or light brown sugar – ⅓ cup (75g)

Preheat the oven to 400°F (200°C). Put whichever fruit you are using in a shallow pan with the sugar, butter, and a tablespoon or two of water. Cook over medium heat until the juices start to flow—a matter of five minutes, depending on the ripeness of your fruit. Tip the fruit and its juice into a deep pie plate.

Rub the butter, which should ideally be cold from the fridge, into the flour with your fingertips. When the mixture resembles coarse fresh breadcrumbs, stir in the ground almonds and sugar. Sprinkle a tablespoon or two of water over the mixture and stir lightly with a fork. Some of the crumbs should stick together in small lumps—this gives a more interesting crumble.

Scatter the crumble over the fruit, then bake for about thirty-five minutes. The crumble is done when the crust is pale gold, smudged with juices. Serve with thick, golden cream.

An ice cream for early autumn

Flavor is numbed by cold. An ice cream mixture must have a clear and strident flavor before it goes in the freezer, otherwise it will lack any character when it is served. Damsons, whose flavor rings out like a bell, produce the most flavorful of all ice creams (save possibly black currant), instantly recognizable and barely diminished by a night in the freezer.

That said, my first damson ice cream was a little too creamy and lacked the clarity I was after. So I cut the custard-to-fruit ratio and swapped half the custard for sheep's yogurt in order to bring the fruit to the fore. The result is an ice cream that tastes of autumn.

enough for 4
damsons – 1 pound (500g)
water – 4 tablespoons
egg yolks – 4
superfine sugar – 1 cup (200g)
heavy cream – 1 cup (250ml)
natural yogurt – 1 cup (250g)

Rinse the damsons, then bring them to a boil with the water in a stainless steel pan. It won't seem like enough water but trust me. Lower the heat so the fruit simmers gently and cook for ten minutes, until their skins have burst and you have a good quantity of deep purple juice. Push the fruit through a fine sieve with a wooden spoon, pressing and stirring until you have nothing left but the pits. Leave the resulting purée, including that rescued from the underside of the sieve, to cool.

Beat the egg yolks and superfine sugar until pale and creamy. Bring the cream almost to the boiling point in a medium-sized saucepan, then pour it over the egg and sugar, stirring. Rinse the pan, then return the custard to it, putting it over a gentle heat and stirring until you have custard the thickness of heavy cream. It is essential that the mixture doesn't get too hot. I stir continuously with a wooden spoon, right into the corners of the pan, until it is just thick enough, then immediately transfer it to a cool bowl set in a sink of shallow, cold water. The sudden cooling helps keep the custard from curdling, as does a damn good whisking. Let the custard cool.

Mix the damson purée with the custard and the yogurt. Pour into an ice cream machine and churn until almost frozen. Remove to a freezer-safe plastic box and freeze until needed.

If you don't have a machine, you can still make the ice cream. Just pour the mixture into a freezer-safe box and place in the freezer, removing it every hour and giving it a good beating with a small whisk, bringing the frozen outer edges into the middle. The result will be less light and creamy than if made in a machine. It will need a good four hours or so to freeze.

A quick damson ice cream

Of all the commercial food products available, I regard ready-made custard—the sort made with cream and eggs and available in the refrigerated section—as possibly the most useful of all. I love making custard but I can't pretend I always have time for it, especially when I have to cool it to make ice cream. You could make your own for this recipe, warily stirring the mixture of cream and eggs until it thickens—there's a recipe on page 493. But I have to tell you that once it meets the intense flavor of the cooked damsons, you might as well have used ready-made. This, incidentally, is the one in the photograph.

enough for 6
damsons – 1 pound (450g)
superfine sugar – 4 tablespoons
custard – 1 cup (250ml)

Wash the damsons, tip them into a stainless steel or enameled pan, then pour over the sugar and 3 tablespoons of water. Bring to a boil and turn the heat down to a simmer. Continue cooking until the fruit starts to soften, its skin splits, and deep purple juice has formed in the pan—about ten minutes.

Pour the juice into a mixing bowl, suspend a sieve over the top, and push the fruit through the sieve until only the pits are left. Scrape any purée from the bottom of the sieve (it tends to collect there in large amounts) and stir it into the juice. Leave it to cool.

Slowly stir the custard into the damson purée. Pour into your ice cream machine and churn until frozen—or freeze by hand as in the preceding recipe.

A damson trifle

Damsons are one of the few fruits I think it is worth freezing, because their season is exceptionally short. I deliberately keep the sugar on the low side for this recipe so that some of the fruit's characteristic sharpness shines through the billowing cream.

Note: It is not worth doing this if you can't be bothered to remove the pits. If you are feeling lazy, then make something else.

enough for 6
ladyfingers – 7 ounces (200g)
large eggs – 2, separated
superfine sugar – 4 tablespoons
mascarpone cheese – 1 pound (500g)
heavy cream – 1¼ cups (300ml)
a little vanilla extract
a few candied violets and chopped pistachio nuts, to decorate

for the fruit layer
damsons – about 1½ pounds (750g)
water – 1⅔ cups (400ml)
superfine sugar – 4 tablespoons

Put the damsons, water, and sugar into a stainless steel saucepan and bring to a boil. Turn the heat down to a simmer and leave for fifteen to twenty minutes, until the fruit is starting to burst. Remove from the heat and set aside. Some of the pits will come to the surface. Use a slotted spoon to remove as many pits as you can (the fewer that end up in the trifle, the better), then extract the rest by squishing the fruit between thumb and fingers. It won't take long (about ten minutes) and is pleasant enough if the fruit is still warm and you are not in a hurry.

Put the ladyfingers in a shallow dish. Spoon the damsons and all their juice over and set aside to cool.

Put the egg yolks and sugar in a bowl and mix well, then stir in the mascarpone. Whip the cream with a few drops of vanilla extract until soft and thick—it should lie in soft, undulating folds rather than stiff peaks—then fold into the mixture. In a clean bowl, and with a clean whisk, beat the egg whites until stiff and frothy. Fold them into the mascarpone mixture.

Spread the mixture over the ladyfingers and damsons, cover with plastic wrap, and refrigerate for at least two or three hours, adding any decoration such as violets and nuts before serving.

A moist cake of damsons and spelt

A shallow cake, almost puddinglike at the bottom, with flashes of purple-pink through its soft crumbs. Spelt flour, made from an ancient form of wheat, has a gentle whole grain note that gives a pleasingly tender and open crumb to the cake. It is not essential. All-purpose flour will do, but the texture will be firmer. The wetness at the bottom, where the damsons lie, is entirely deliberate.

I have made plum cakes before, usually incorporating ground almonds or occasionally pine nuts, and eaten them both as dessert and as a cake for tea. Cream seems unnecessary—they carry enough moisture in the fruit. Damson, with its rich flavor and sudden sour note, seems a perfect contrast to the sweet cake crumbs. I just spit the pits out as I go.

enough for 6 to 8
butter – 10 tablespoons (150g)
golden baker's sugar – ¾ cup (150g), plus an extra tablespoon
large eggs – 3
spelt flour – a generous ¾ cup (110g)
baking powder – 1½ teaspoons
ground almonds – ⅔ cup (75g)
damsons, stalks removed – 14 ounces (400g)
confectioners' sugar, to finish

You will need a square cake pan measuring 8 to 8½ inches (20 to 22cm) across the bottom. Line the bottom of the pan with a piece of parchment paper. Preheat the oven to 350°F (180°C).

Cream the butter and the ¾ cup (150g) of sugar until light and fluffy. It is so much easier to do this with an electric mixer, but I have met others who prefer the wooden spoon method. Whatever, don't stop until the mixture is almost white in color. Crack the eggs and beat them gently, then add to the mixture a little at a time, beating thoroughly between each batch.

Mix the flour and baking powder and add to the ground almonds. Fold into the cake mixture gently but firmly. If you overmix, the cake will be heavy. Transfer the mixture to the lined cake pan with a rubber spatula, then lay the damsons on top and shake over the tablespoon of sugar (the damsons will sink during cooking, leaving only one or two peeping through the surface).

Bake for forty-five minutes, covering with foil for the last ten minutes if it looks to be browning too quickly. Remove from the oven, leave to settle, then, when almost cool, remove from its pan. Dust lightly with confectioners' sugar and serve.

A glorious, lightly set jam

In autumn I haunt the farmers' markets and village fêtes looking for jam people. One could say "stalk." From time to time I find a jar of damson, a wondrous jam when the fruit's sharpness is allowed to shine through the sugar. I make my own too, leaving it slightly less firmly set than most cottage-garden jam makers, so that it drips off my morning toast and down the sleeves of my dressing gown. More to the point, it makes a good sauce for vanilla ice cream or almond sponge cake.

enough for about four 14-ounce (400g) jars
damsons – 2 pounds (1kg)
water – 1 cup (250ml)
granulated or superfine sugar – 2¼ pounds (1kg), 5½ cups

Rinse the damsons, removing any stray leaves, stalks, and twigs as you go. Tip them into a deep stainless steel saucepan with the water and bring to a boil. Turn the heat down so that the fruit simmers to tenderness. You can expect this to take about twenty-five minutes or so, depending on its ripeness. Stir in the sugar, then bring to a boil and continue to let the fruit and dissolved sugar bubble away for about twenty minutes, until it has thickened a little. To test whether the jam is set enough, dip a wooden spoon into it and lift it clear. Hold it level over the jam. It is ready when the jam that runs down forms a large droplet that falls slowly from the spoon. If it pours off in a steady stream, you need to boil it a little longer. If you have a candy thermometer, it is ready when the temperature reaches 220°F (105°C).

Remove from the heat and leave for ten minutes to let the skins settle throughout the jam, during which time you can scoop off any froth and remove some of the floating skins and pits. It will still have more pits than you may like but removing them all would be an endless task. Ladle the jam into warm, sterilized jars and seal.

A damson fool

The fool came to us as a use for the gooseberry but it makes a pretty good end for a bag of damsons, too. Care is needed here if your cream and fruit are not to curdle. Introduce the softly whipped cream into the fruit a little at a time and stop either when the flavor is as you like it or at the first sign of a grainy quality appearing. I like to keep back a little of the fruit juice to trickle over the fool as I bring it to the table.

enough for 4
damsons – 1 pound (500g)
superfine sugar – 4 to 5 tablespoons
heavy cream – 1¼ cups (300ml)

Rinse the damsons, removing any stems or leaves as you go. Put the fruit in a stainless steel pan with the sugar and 3 tablespoons of water. Bring to a boil, lower the heat, and leave to bubble gently until the fruit has split and you have a copious amount of juice.

Push the fruit through a sieve suspended over a bowl. Keep going until all you are left with is dry pits (wash the sieve before the fruit dries or you will never get it off). Leave to cool.

When the fruit is entirely cool, pour the cream into a cold bowl and whip gently until soft and thick (I put the cream, bowl, and whisk into the fridge first; it makes for better whipping, with less fear of curdling). You want the whipped cream to barely hold its own shape rather than stand in stiff peaks. Slowly, gently, fold some of the cold fruit purée into the cream and keep going until you have a deep purple cream. It should be soft and sweet-sharp. If the consistency has become sloppy, you can give it a brief whisking until it thickens again. Spoon into glasses or little pots and leave in the fridge for an hour to settle before serving.

A sharp damson pickle for cold meats

The effect of pickles on cold meats, pâtés, and the like is extraordinary.
Even the most mild-mannered of terrines or workaday slices of cold roast
beef come alive the second they rub shoulders with a sharp and spicy pickle.
Think pork pie with a pickled onion; coarse pâté with tiny, comma-shaped
cornichons; cold roast pork with a dark and sinister pickled walnut or two.
Damsons, sour cherries, and plums pickle well, offering a fruity sharpness
that cuts through a plate of cold meat like a warm knife through mozzarella.
This is the sort of preserve I plan to dress neatly with a burlap mobcap
and a ribbon and hand out to friends, Martha Stewart style, at Christmas.
I never do.

damsons – 2 pounds (1kg)
superfine or granulated sugar – 3¼ cups (650g)
a cinnamon stick
black peppercorns – 18
bay leaves – 6
white wine vinegar – 2 cups (500ml)
green cardamom pods – 8
cloves – 6

Check the damsons over thoroughly. Put the sugar, cinnamon stick,
peppercorns, bay leaves, vinegar, whole cardamom pods, and cloves into
a stainless steel or enameled pan and bring to a boil. Tip in the whole
damsons and bring back to a boil. Simmer for five minutes, then remove
from the heat, ladle into sterilized preserving jars, and seal. Leave for a
couple of months before eating.

Elderflowers
and elderberries

Early June, the seventh to be precise, and next door's elder tree is a vast cloud of creamy-white blossom, as delicate as Honiton lace. It is not a handsome tree, they rarely are, but I feel honored that the branches have chosen to hang over my garden, the froth of flowers dancing in the breeze with the same delicate movement as cow parsley or sweet cicely. Those I fail to pick are followed, in early autumn, by clusters of dark and glossy edible berries.

The smell of the blossom is, like that of spreading lavender honey on hot toast, the essence of the English summer Miss Marple might have known. Of cricket matches and policemen on bikes, village greens and shady, leafy lanes. On a less romantic note, I detect a hint of fresh yeast and tomcats.

Last year I cut most of the flowers—flat and open like lace parasols—dipped them into a light batter of egg white, flour, and sparkling mineral water, and fried them until golden. We dipped each one into a saucer of superfine sugar and ate the fritters still crackling from the pan. This year the blossoms made their way into bottles of thick, sweet cordial. And all this from a tree I had no intention of having in the garden. Better still, a tree that appears wild in cities and countryside alike—sweets for the asking.

The berries, purple-black and the size of the lead shot you find in your game bird casserole, appear in early September. I try to get to them before the fat birds, who will otherwise leave their bright purple calling cards splattered over the garden furniture. These are the tartest of all edible berries, and their copious juice will stain everything in its path. Pick them in your oldest clothes.

It has to be said that *Sambucus nigra*, the common elder, does not produce the most versatile of fruits. A crumble or pie made purely of elderberries is often too potent to be enjoyable (and it will turn your guests' teeth a fetching shade of violet). Mixed with apple, however, the flavor is altogether softer and more palatable. The quandary in our house is whether to eat the clotted cream–colored flowers or the glossy black fruit. Sadly, you cannot have both, unless the tree is a particularly large one, or you limit yourselves to just a handful of crisp, sugar-dusted fritters each June.

An elder tree in the garden

Most streets, commons, and wasteland support a *Sambucus nigra* or two. Untended gardens are often good hunting grounds. At last, something for the urban forager.

They are easily recognized by their flat-topped umbrellas of cream flowers in June and their pointed, somewhat saw-edged leaves. Beware that you identify them correctly. Other trees, such as the rowan, are not dissimilar from a distance but lack the distinctive tomcat smell of the elder.

As a tree, the elder is a bit of a brute—unattractive, untidily formed, and generally considered something of a weed. I have never known anyone actually choose to plant one. I spend too much time in spring pulling up the young "treelets" that have seeded themselves in my garden.

When I first made this garden, I used to prune the tree drastically, usually in a temper. Then I found a use for its blossoms, and then its berries. Now I welcome it, even though it shades my hollyhocks and phlox, making them bend forward in an attempt to see the sun. For all its uses, I really cannot recommend you plant an elder. There are too many better things to put in its place.

Elder blossoms and berries in the kitchen

Make the fritters; they are light and crisp and have an ethereal Muscat whiff to them. But should you have a glut of elderflowers, then perhaps you might like to make a bottle or two of cordial or a jelly, or dip the heads into a pan of simmering gooseberries. I have read, too, of their use in custard, though I have yet to try it.

The elderflower has been popular since Victorian times, though its use as an ingredient for cordial goes back much further. The Romans are said to have made it. The aromatic flavor of the fruit is held by the sugar syrup, which is then diluted with spring water. The large quantity of sugar is balanced by a heavy dose of citric acid or lemons to give a truly refreshing drink.

The cordial can be added in place of the flowers to gooseberry fool or poached fruit, and is often used as the base for a sorbet. I like it as a sticky syrup with which to soak an almond cake.

The berries are not widely used in the kitchen. I have added them to a casserole of pheasant with reasonable success and once, memorably, to a crumble, whose extraordinary purple color didn't confine itself to the dish. A small handful will give an inky color and flavor to a gravy, and I have mashed them into the pan juices of a roast game bird before now.

Both the flowers and berries are a favorite of home winemakers. The flowers produce a straw-colored drink with soft Muscat notes, the berries a rich and majestically colored drink of which the makers invariably seem rather proud.

Elderflowers and berries and...

Gooseberries Elderflowers and gooseberries are one of those perfect culinary marriages that feel right in so many ways. Not only do they look beautiful together but both are at their peak at the same time. Use the two together in fools, compotes, crumbles, ices, and drinks.

Lemon Citrus flavors bring out the sweetness of the flowers.

Vinegar A softly spoken vinegar such as white wine or cider can be used with the flower heads to make a slightly sweet dressing. Very good with young green lettuces.

Cinnamon A light dusting of sugar and the ground spice on the finished fritters can be pleasing.

Game birds Lean flesh with deep flavors, such as pheasant, squab, and wild duck, goes well with the tartness of the berries. Add the berries to game casseroles.

Venison The rich, dark meat of venison is flattered by any berry sauce. Elderberries add tart richness to the pan juices.

* Pick the flowers in the morning when the air is cool and the blossoms are at their most fragrant. The sun makes them weary.
* The flowers should not be eaten raw in any quantity, as they are mildly poisonous. Berries, too, must be fully ripe before eating.
* Steer clear of the leaves, bark, and twigs. They are poisonous if consumed.
* Tests consistently show that patients who are given elderberry juice recover more quickly from flu than those who are not.
* Make an elderberry vinegar by steeping 14 ounces (400g) of fruit in 2 cups (500ml) of white wine vinegar for two or three days before straining, sweetening with 1¾ cups (350g) of sugar and bringing to a boil, straining again, and bottling.
* A few flowers tied in a cheesecloth bag can be pushed into a pan of stewed apple where they will discreetly flavor it.

Elderflower fritters

You need a really light batter for these to flatter the delicate nature of the blossoms. My batter barely covers the flowers and cooks particularly quickly, leaving the fritters frail and crisp. For a more robust batter, you should add a little more flour to the mixture. When the flowers emerge from the oil, I usually dip them into superfine sugar, but sometimes a very faint dusting of cinnamon can be pleasing.

enough for 4
large elderflower heads – 16
oil for deep-frying
a plate thickly dusted with superfine sugar

for the batter
all-purpose flour – ¾ cup plus 1 tablespoon (100g)
sunflower oil – 2 tablespoons
sparkling mineral water – ¾ cup (175ml)
superfine sugar – a tablespoon
an egg white

Sift the flour into a large bowl, then add the oil and water, beating slowly to make a thick paste. Stir in the sugar and set aside for thirty minutes. Don't be tempted to skip the resting time; this is essential for a light batter. Just before you plan to fry the elderflowers, beat the egg white until almost stiff and fold it gently into the batter.

Wash the elderflowers with great tenderness in a bowl of water. Just dipping them briefly in and out of the water should do it. This will not affect their flavor and they are easy to shake dry. Make certain that there are no little aphids hiding among the flowers. When you are sure that they are clean, get the oil on to heat up. Snip the flower heads into small stems.

Test the oil to make sure it is hot enough—it should fry a cube of bread golden in a few seconds—then dip the elderflowers into the batter and lower them into the hot oil. Push them down, holding them under the oil by pushing down on the stem. The batter will bubble up around the flowers like little pearls. Fry until the batter is pale gold and crisp, then lift out of the oil and dip straight into the sugar. Eat the fritters while they are hot and crisp.

Gooseberry and elderflower fool

There is another gooseberry fool in the chapter dedicated to that fruit, but this one relies more on the essence of the flower, so I feel it belongs here.

enough for 6
gooseberries – 1 pound (450g)
superfine sugar, to taste
heavy cream – 1¼ cups (300ml)
elderflower cordial

Top and tail the gooseberries, put them into a stainless steel pan with a very little water, and cook over low heat until they are soft and squashy—a matter of ten minutes. Drain off any extra liquid and crush the berries with a fork. I never do this very thoroughly, believing that the texture is more interesting with a bit of fruit in it, but go as far as you want. Stir in the sugar; the amount you will need depends on how sharp the gooseberries are, but take care not to take the sharpness out. I like a tart fool, so I add no more than 2 or 3 tablespoons. Leave to cool, then refrigerate.

Whip the cream to soft folds. You really should do this slowly toward the end so that you can stop at the exact moment the cream starts to feel heavy on the whisk. Gently fold the gooseberries into the cream, taking care not to whip the cream further. Spoon the fool into chilled glasses or pretty cups and leave to settle a while in the fridge. Drizzle a teaspoon of elderflower cordial over each as you serve.

Gooseberry elderflower trifle

In summer there is often a bottle of elderflower cordial in my fridge. The Muscat scent as you drop in the ice cubes and pour in the mineral water is one of summer's most potent aromas, like that of honeysuckle, mown grass, or sliced cucumber. It adds a note of summer to all it touches, including the sponge cake for a gooseberry trifle.

enough for 6
gooseberries – 1 pound (500g)
golden baker's sugar – 2 tablespoons
a couple of elderflower heads, if you have them
ladyfingers – 7 ounces (200g)
elderflower cordial
custard (page 493) – 2 cups (500ml)
heavy cream – 1¼ cups (300ml)
a handful of shelled pistachio nuts

Top and tail the gooseberries and rinse them thoroughly. Tip them into a stainless steel pan with the sugar, 2 tablespoons of water, and, if you have them, a couple of heads of elderflowers. Bring to a boil, then cover with a lid and turn the heat down so that the gooseberries bubble very gently. You don't want the liquid to evaporate. Shake the pan every few minutes to keep the fruit from sticking. It should be soft after seven minutes or so. Check for sweetness; the gooseberries should be tart but not sour. Remove the elderflowers, leave the fruit to cool, then cover and chill thoroughly.

Line the bottom of a shallow china or glass dish, about 12 by 8 inches (30 by 20cm), with the ladyfingers, breaking them to fit where you need to. Drain the juice from the gooseberries and mix it with a little elderflower cordial to make it up to 7 tablespoons (100ml). Pour the liquid over the ladyfingers, then spoon the gooseberries on top.

Cover the gooseberries with the cold custard, smoothing it flat with the back of a spoon. Pour the cream into a chilled bowl and whip it until it starts to thicken. The cream should be firm enough for the whisk to leave a trail but not stiff enough to stand in peaks. Smooth the whipped cream over the custard, cover tightly with plastic wrap, and place in the fridge. It should stay there for a good two hours for all the flavors to marry.

Chop the pistachios coarsely and scatter them over the top of the trifle.

Elderflower cordial

My version is only slightly different from most classic versions of this ancient drink in that I include a lime or two. I find they make it even more refreshing.

makes 2 medium-sized bottles
elderflower heads – 20, about 8 ounces (225g)
superfine sugar – 2¼ pounds (1kg), 5½ cups
water – 5 cups (1.25 liters)
lemons – 2, cut into quarters
limes – 2, cut into quarters
citric acid – 1¾ ounces (50g)

Inspect the flowers for insects and dust. Shake or quickly rinse, but don't wash them. Remove the toughest stalks with scissors; they are likely to be bitter.

Warm the sugar and water together in a large saucepan until the sugar has dissolved, then remove from the heat. Dunk the flowers and the quartered fruit into the syrup, stir in the citric acid, and set aside to cool. When the liquid is cold, cover and refrigerate for at least twenty-four hours. Strain through cheesecloth or a fine sieve and decant into sterilized bottles.

Raspberries in elderflower jelly

A summer delight. Use strawberries and red currants too, if you fancy. It is probably best to stick to one or two fruits, otherwise the effect can become cluttered.

enough for 4
leaf gelatin – ⅓ to ½ ounce (12g)
elderflower cordial – 5 tablespoons (70ml)
superfine sugar – 1 heaping tablespoon
sparkling mineral water – 1 cup (250ml)
white wine – 1 cup (250ml)
raspberries – 14 ounces (400g)

Soak the leaves of gelatin in cold water. They will start to soften after five minutes or so. Pour the elderflower cordial into a small saucepan and add the sugar, mineral water, and half the white wine. Lift the softened gelatin out of the water and drop it into the cordial and wine. Place over low heat and stir until the gelatin and sugar have dissolved. Remove from the heat and add the remaining white wine.

Divide the raspberries among four large glasses. Pour the jelly over the raspberries and leave to cool before refrigerating. The jellies should be set within an hour or two.

An elderflower and gooseberry syrup

This is the syrup to dilute with mineral water on a hot summer's day. A glass with ice, approximately six parts water to cordial, will make you think you have walked into a Merchant Ivory film. The recipe is my version of Constance Spry's, from her charming, long out of print book, *Come Into the Garden, Cook.*

makes 2 medium-sized bottles
gooseberries – 2¼ pounds (1kg)
water – 1¼ cups (300ml)
granulated sugar – 3¼ cups (650g)
elderflowers – 8 large heads

Put the gooseberries in a large, deep pan with the water and sugar and bring to a boil. Simmer until the fruit is ready to pop, but stop before it does. While the gooseberries are simmering, check the elderflowers, snipped from their stems, for dust and insects. Lay them on a piece of cheesecloth and tie them up in it. When the gooseberries are done, turn the heat off and lower the bag of flowers into the pan. Leave it to steep in the syrup for ten minutes or so (taste it; you may want a stronger flavor, in which case leave the flowers in a while longer), then remove and discard them.

Pour the syrup through a piece of clean cheesecloth or a fine sieve into a large pitcher and then into a sterilized glass bottle. Store in the fridge.

Roast venison with elderberry sauce

enough for 4
black peppercorns – 10
juniper berries – 12
sea salt – half a teaspoon
thyme – 2 or 3 sprigs
olive oil – 2 tablespoons
venison fillets or leg, boned and rolled – 1¾ pounds (800g)
white wine – a generous ¾ cup (200ml)
red currant or rowan jelly – 3 heaping tablespoons
elderberries – 6 tablespoons

Preheat the oven to 400°F (200°C). Coarsely crush the black peppercorns, juniper berries, sea salt flakes, and thyme leaves, using a mortar and pestle. Rub the oil over the venison, then massage in the crushed aromatics.

Warm a roasting pan or shallow, nonstick pan over medium heat and add the venison. Brown lightly on both sides, then transfer to the oven and roast for twenty minutes, until rose pink inside. Remove the meat from the roasting pan and set aside in a warm place. Add the wine to the pan and bring to a boil over high heat. As soon as it starts to bubble, add the rowan or red currant jelly and the elderberries, then crush the berries lightly with the back of a spoon. Let the pan juices and seasonings bubble until you have a rich, purple-red sauce.

Slice the venison into thick rounds and serve with the sauce.

Elderberry jelly-jam

I hadn't thought to make a jam with elderberries until I met Linden Monck, whose beautiful garden with its comfortable shed and lovely old pear tree has a prolific elder bush. Her gorgeous gift of homemade jam, glowing darkly in its pot, inspired me to make my own. Linden's was better than mine.

A jam chock-full of elderberries is almost too much of a good thing (though very good for stuffing a roly-poly pudding—see page 243), so I now make a soft elderberry and apple jelly instead, and stir in a few of the reserved, cooked berries. The result is a jelly but with some of the berries' texture, so it sits nicely between jelly and jam. Because elderberries have a low pectin content, they generally need to be mixed with crab apples or tart green apples in order to set. On their own, they will produce a jam that may refuse to set.

> ripe elderberries – 2¼ pounds (1kg)
> sharp apples or crab apples – about 1 pound (500g)
> water – 3½ cups (800ml)
> granulated sugar – 2¼ pounds (1kg), 5½ cups

Pull the elderberries from their stems and place in a deep stainless steel pan. Halve the apples, but don't peel them, then add to the elderberries with the water. Bring to a boil. Turn the heat down and simmer gently for twenty minutes or until the apples are soft. Remove from the heat, allow to cool slightly, then pour through a clean jelly bag. Leave overnight to drip through slowly. Don't push the fruit pulp through, otherwise the jelly will be cloudy. Retain some of the berries if you want to put them in your jelly.

The next day, add the sugar to the juice (with the reserved berries if you are using them) and bring back to a boil, then boil hard for a full ten minutes or so, until the jelly tests positively for setting (a spoonful on a fridge-cold saucer should quickly form a skin and barely move when the saucer is tipped on its side). Pour into sterilized jars, seal, and leave to set.

Black jam roly-poly pudding

It is the sumptuously dark jams—damson, black currant, and loganberry—that are best in a suet crust. Their deep hue stands out in a richly colored spiral; their intense flavor acts as a perfect balance for the bland laundry-colored dough. The one I made last autumn with elderberry jam was perhaps the jolliest of all.

You can steam a roly-poly, but I much prefer them baked. Yes, the jam leaks a little, but to a certain extent you can prevent it by pushing the roll to one edge of the baking sheet and tipping it at a slight angle in the oven to keep it from spreading. I don't really mind if it flattens a bit as it bakes—it is what it is. Enough jam generally stays inside the pudding to keep it interesting.

What we put with such a rib-sticking pudding is up to us. Custard sounds a bit extravagant, but it works superbly here, surrounding the golden dough in a vanilla-scented pool. Cream is another thought, served by the generous jugful.

enough for 4
self-rising flour – 1⅓ cups (175g)
shredded suet – 3 ounces (85g)
superfine sugar – a tablespoon
cold water – ⅔ to ¾ cup (160 to 175ml)
jam, elderberry for instance – a good 1 cup (250g)

Preheat the oven to 425°F (220°C). Sift the flour into a mixing bowl, tip in the shredded suet and the sugar, then mix to a sticky but workable dough with the water. At this point you can add a little more flour or water as necessary in order to achieve a rollable dough that doesn't stick to your rolling pin.

Roll the dough out on a well-floured board into a rectangle approximately 12 by 8 inches (30 by 20cm). Spread the jam over it, then wet one long edge and roll up into a thick sausage. Press the wet edge firmly to seal.

Lift onto a nonstick or parchment paper–lined baking sheet and bake for thirty-five minutes or so, until golden. Serve in thick slices.

Figs

Tender as bruised flesh, a ripe fig is at its most seductive eaten warm from the sun. Jade, amber, purple, or almost black, figs need the utmost care to get them from branch to plate in perfect condition. Small wonder, then, that so many are sold underripe. Even then, they need a safe pair of hands to carry them home from the store without piercing their delicate skin (for once there is an excuse for supermarket-style overpackaging).

Like an apricot, the fig loses all point if it is not perfectly ripe. You might as well eat cardboard. Firm specimens can be ushered into a state of ripeness in a warm room, the fruit set well apart on a plate. They have a tendency to mold when they are stored touching one another. I take pleasure in "bringing on" fruits like this, fondling them respectfully every day—a sniff, a caress, a watchful eye—to check on their progress.

The fragility of the fruit is also part of its attraction. Stroke the ripest fig and it is as if you are touching flesh. Sniff it and not only is it summer but the hottest day, the air heavy and still, the earth beneath your bare feet cracked and dry. Sink your teeth in and you meet no resistance. Just soft, sumptuous flesh and tiny pearlescent seeds, little crimson beads that dissolve on your tongue.

The skin of most figs is edible, though some insist on its removal. The perfect fruit should probably be eaten in a quiet, respectful moment, but they tend to come in a glut (mine often ripen within the space of a fortnight) and it is then that their potential as the filling for a tart or as a syrupy preserve can be exploited.

Botanically, the fig is not a fruit as such but an "inflorescence," where flowers and seeds have grown together to form one mass. Tear one apart and it feels like a flower opening in spring.

There is something ancient, almost biblical, about the fig, in much the same way as there is about the olive (it is one of the oldest plants in civilization). It would be difficult to overestimate its importance as a food. Remains have been discovered that predate wheat or barley by a thousand years, making it possibly the earliest crop in cultivation. Ancient Egyptians regarded it as the tree of life. To the Greeks it was a symbol of fertility (what wasn't? I hear you ask), and it is even now the National Tree of India. The Romans planted them too: Cato the Elder lists five varieties, including the Mariscan and the black Tellanian.

Mentioned in both the Bible and the Quran, the fig tree is often a sign of prosperity. "Each man under his own vine and fig tree" (1 Kings 4:25) still conjures up a certain sense of peace, fortune, and well-being. It is a favorite fruit of artists and has been painted throughout history. Prudish collectors often added a fig leaf to nude portraits long after the original painting was completed.

This fruit almost defines the Mediterranean. Match it to the warmth of thyme or mint and there is no doubting the provenance of your recipe. The fig's friends, anchovy, pomegranate, almonds, prosciutto, honey, goat cheeses, and lavender, tell us much about where it feels at home. This is an ingredient that will also take being baked or simmered in red wine or squashed into jam or chutney and will happily end its days in a simple almond tart. But any attempt to get it into contrived "haute cuisine" and its magic will generally desert you.

The fig's laxative properties are well known but it also carries favorable levels of calcium, potassium, and trace minerals. Add this to its high fiber content and the picture of the historical importance of the fig becomes even clearer. Nowadays a fresh or dried fig is a treat, but for a long time it verged on being a staple food, and was particularly important to early travelers as it could be dried with ease, was light to carry, and could be used as sustenance along the way. Now, the principal producers are Turkey—particularly the Aydin and Izmir regions, which send out over a million tons each year—and Egypt.

My own fig trees give me untold pleasure. Their naked, ashen branches, pointed and witchy against a Nordic winter sky, are as beautiful as when they are in full summer flush. The first green shoots unfold in earliest spring like tiny, waving hands. The excitement of spotting the first hard fruits and then, at last, the honey-sweet scent of the tree laden with ripening riches. Most of all, it is the lush shade that I appreciate, the heavy leaf growth protecting the garden table as successfully as any parasol.

Given a long, baking summer, the fig tree will reward us with two crops. Last year would have been a bumper crop for me, the weight of the fruit pulling the brittle branches almost to the ground, only for the tree to fall prey to a fierce and unprecedented hailstorm (honestly, as big as ice cubes) that snapped its heaviest branches and dashed many of its ripe fruits to jam on the stone terrace.

I should mention that I knew the dried fig long before I had ever seen the fresh. First as the brown crystallized fig, a sweetmeat passed around after

Christmas lunch in its black and gold box, oval brown jellies glistening with a hoarfrost of sugar. Then came the faintly sinister mahogany rectangles of squashed figs at the early health-food stores, sticky and almost impossible to pry apart. Lastly, the wicker baskets of dried fruit covered in chocolate that appeared in the local Italian grocer's for a few weeks in early winter. The delectably chewy, parchment-colored dried figs I now munch in lieu of sweets came much, much later.

A fig tree in the garden

When I moved into this house, there was a thriving young Ficus in the lawn that bore as many fruits as we could eat. Tragically, it didn't survive the redesign of the garden (it was in the wrong place and had a root system too sprawling to move). It was quite clearly a happy tree and I have felt uncomfortable about its demise ever since. I have attempted to assuage my guilt by replacing it with two more.

The two new trees, a Rouge de Bordeaux (which should ideally be in a greenhouse) and a Brown Turkey, were joined four years ago by a third, a fan-trained Petite Negri from Reads Nursery in Norfolk (a garden can never have too many figs). This latest addition now spans much of the north-facing wall of the "courtyard" area outside the kitchen and is exceedingly generous with its small, dark fruit.

Ficus carica is not even remotely fussy about the soil in which it finds itself, but the trees do like to be in a sunny spot. It reminds them of home. Mine get very little water and even after a rainstorm the soil around their feet is rarely damp, but the general rule is to give them plenty. I put their generous fruiting down to the fact that their root growth is contained. This is simple enough to do. We dug a deep pit, barely 28 inches (70cm) square, which was then lined with a sheet of zinc. Broken pottery was placed in the bottom for drainage (we could have used coarse gravel), then the young tree was lowered into the hole and backfilled with ordinary garden soil. Equally we could have used paving slabs or planted the tree in a large pot. The point is simply to contain the roots. This single act of restriction encourages prolific fruiting.

Fig trees can become very large. My red fig has grown to thirteen feet (four meters) in seven years, its slender, brittle branches snapping off during bad weather. You can train them to cover a wall, as I have done with the Petite Negri. The young, whippy branches are supple for the first year of growth and can be tied along wires to form a dense covering for a wall or even the side of the house. As each new branch appears, you need to tie it to wires or a strong trellis. Smaller varieties will survive in good-sized pots too, but you will need to be generous with the water.

A happy tree will often reward you with two crops a year. The first, called *breba*, appears on last year's growth. The second, generally a smaller crop, appears mostly, though not exclusively, on new growth. With their smooth gray bark and dinner-plate leaves, the trees love a long, hot summer and without it, the second crop is unlikely to have the chance to ripen.

Varieties

It is the self-pollinating figs that do best in Britain, notably the Black Mission, Brown Turkey, and Brunswick, but with a greenhouse or sheltered spot the possibilities get a little more interesting. Most have two crops in a long summer, though if the second fails to ripen, the hard, green infants should be picked off at the end of the season. A jam can be made with the unripe figs but I am honestly not sure it is worth it. Yes, it's jam, but where is the heart and soul of the fruit?

Purple or black figs
Violette Solleis A greenhouse variety with flattish, dark purple fruits on a rose-colored stalk. A pink-fleshed fruit with dark violet skin.
Violette de Bordeaux* Small, dark purple fig with strawberry-colored flesh.
Rouge de Bordeaux Sweet, dark-skinned fruit that needs a warm, sheltered spot. Revered for the flavor of its raspberry-red flesh.
Petite Negri (sometimes Negra) A neat bush with rich-tasting, almost black fruits. Good for pots or for training up a wall. Mine has done well on a north-facing wall, the fruit ripening in late September and October.
Fig Grise de St. Jean One for a conservatory or large greenhouse. First recorded in 1702, this is a very beautiful violet fig with a dusty, gray bloom and pale pink, fragrant flesh.
Black Mission* Deep purple skin, reddish brown flesh, and honey-sweet flavor—a versatile classic.

Green, yellow, and brown figs
Panachee* Striped green and yellow fruit from a vigorous tree that I have seen yet sadly never tasted.
White Marseilles Also known as Figue Blanche, an early to midseason variety with pale, translucent flesh that is particularly sweet. Grows well in British gardens and in pots.
White Ischia* Heavy crops of small, pale-skinned fruit with a faint brown blush and sweet pink, honey-scented flesh. Best indoors.
Italian Honey Also known as Peter's Honey. Sweet, crimson flesh under a beautiful golden skin. Much prefers a greenhouse.

Angelique These charming yellow figs with a distinctive perfume turn red where they face the sun. White flesh with a slightly pink tinge to it.

Brunswick* Yellowish-bronze, pear-shaped fruit with a distinct brown blush. This is the one that is meant when people refer to the Madonna fig. Survives our climate well but dislikes rain. Pale red flesh and enormous leaves.

Drap d'Or A late, pale, almost golden fruit with a reddish blush and very fine flavor. The tree needs a warm site, preferably a greenhouse.

Brown Turkey* The most popular fig in British gardens. Plump and of fairly good flavor, the Brown Turkey produces green, pear-shaped fruits with a good purple-brown blush and deep red, seedy flesh. One of the most reliably prolific and good natured.

*Available from US sources.

A fig in the kitchen

A fig is ready when it has a bead of nectar at its eye and the skin is bulging. It may even show a little crack, as if the pressure of the ripe flesh within is too much for the skin. Most of the velvet-skinned figs that come my way during the summer and autumn are eaten at the table and almost always with a certain hushed reverence. These are fruits that deserve more than to be chomped from the hand like an apple.

Often there will be a piece of cheese involved in my "fig-fests" too, and for that I can recommend the blues—Cashel, Gorgonzola, Stilton, and Stichelton—and almost any soft goat cheese, especially if you mix a little chopped fresh thyme in too.

None of this means I am not also prepared to bake a fig or two. Though the heat will give a fulsome silkiness to the texture, the real bliss point is when you reach the seeds within. Together, the warm flesh and crunchy seeds are as sensuous a mouthful of fruit as you could ever wish for. Even more so when the juices mix with fudge-colored brown sugar, marsala, or a glass of Beaujolais. Eaten warm, the flesh, seeds, and juice present a whole package of gorgeousness.

While they don't take well to a pie, a crumble, a crisp, or a cobbler, figs can work in place of apples in a tarte Tatin or as thin slices in a puff pastry *tarte fine*. They bake beautifully in red wine and honey, taking on the color of deepest claret, and I like them sunk into the frangipane filling of an almond tart. Just spoon a classic almond filling (butter, sugar, flour, eggs, and ground almonds) into the tart shell, then push the quartered fruits down so they are almost, but not quite, submerged, and bake.

Raw, the ripe fig is a masterful partner to smoked and air-dried meats. The classic Italian plate of figs with Parma ham is just a start. Speck, San

Daniele, heavily marbled coppa, and any coarse-grained salumi are all possibilities, as are slices of bacon draped around the fruits and grilled or baked.

The fig delights in hiding beneath the leaves of a salad just as the fruit likes to snuggle under the leaves on the tree. I use it with crisp greens as a contrast to its soft flesh—so Belgian endive, perky spinach, frisée, and florets of mâche. Often there will be nuts in my salad too, such as walnuts and chopped hazelnuts, and occasionally a few shards of crisp bacon.

As one expects from its provenance, the fig enjoys the company of olive oil, but you may also appreciate it with a cream-based dressing of blue cheese. A mixture of olive oil, egg yolks, and finely grated Parmesan given a little spark with lemon juice is a perennial favorite dressing of mine. As is a spoonful of moist ricotta eaten with each fat, ripe fruit.

Fig preserves are among some of the most luscious to be had, especially as the fig is less inclined to set firmly than many other fruits. Fig jams and conserves are often the sort that fall lazily from the spoon, making them too soft for the average British jam maker with their love of jams that bounce. Turkish fig jam is often sublime and can be used as an impromptu sauce with vanilla ice cream or, my own choice, a sauce of pale and milky fromage frais scattered with toasted walnuts.

Dried figs

Dried figs are not in any way meant to replace the fresh variety. They are an entity in themselves, sharing little in terms of texture, flavor, or sensuality with the fresh. I eat them from the packet as others eat sweets. The crunch of their myriad seeds between the teeth is as much one of the sounds of my day as the ping of the oven timer or the low Zen gong of my cell phone ring tone. The ancient, parchment-colored fruit is my favorite form. I find pleasure in its chewy quality, but the soft so-called ready to eat variety is more user-friendly in the kitchen and can be used straight from the packet in cakes and other bits of baking. The downside is its initial slimy texture and its depressing dun color. Never mind, it's a pleasure to have in the kitchen and I include it here only for those moments when it is more suitable than the fresh article—never as an attempt at a substitute.

Figs and...

Ham Any sort of ham has an affinity for the fig, from pink, soft-textured York ham on the bone to the firmer-textured air-dried treatments such as Parma and coppa.

Bacon Whether they meet up in a salad or as one wrapped around the other, bacon and the fig are a delectable combination.

Venison One of the best fruits for partnering this lean and surprisingly mild meat. A few halved figs added to the pan when sautéing a venison steak will provide glorious pan juices.

Duck Roast duck likes to be joined by a few figs toward the end of roasting, and they are welcome in a duck casserole too.

Blue cheeses Rarely can fruit and cheese form such a perfect combination.

Mozzarella The cool, milky quality of buffalo mozzarella and the sweetness of the fig make a gentle lunch dish; the texture of the quivery cheese and crunchy seeds is a quiet joy.

Spinach Whether as a textural or flavor combination, the partnership works brilliantly.

Brown sugars Demerara and soft light muscovado are an excellent way to sweeten a fig. They beef up the flavor without intruding.

Marsala and Madeira Rich, sweet alcohols that add much to the fruit. The mellow flavors work in perfect harmony.

Nuts Almonds and walnuts work well with the fruit in recipes but also raw to form a simple dessert. A few cracked walnuts and almonds scattered over a platter of figs has to be one of the most superbly understated ways to end a meal. Ground almonds are pleasing as the base for an open tart of figs.

Chocolate Although fresh figs and chocolate work well enough as a pairing, I prefer chocolate with dried figs.

Orange Elizabeth David used oranges to lift the sweetness of a plate of fresh figs.

Thyme With the exception of basil, there are few herbs that add anything much to the pleasure of eating a fig. However, the resinous flavor of thyme is a different matter entirely. Used together, figs and thyme conjure up scorched hillsides in the baking sun. Try adding a sprig or two to baked figs, then eat them with the goat cheese below.

Goat cheeses Fresh, slightly acidic goat cheeses form the happiest of all fig and cheese marriages. A gentler pairing than the blue cheeses with which figs are more usually married, the effect of the fig's crunchy seeds with the soft, slightly sharp notes of the cheese is a delight.

Honey Especially that sourced from clover and wildflowers, often feels a more appropriate sweetener for fig dishes than sugar. Try it trickled over torn figs and a sharp, young goat cheese.

* The sap from the tree and leaves is an irritant to the skin. Something I found out the hard way.

* The term "I don't care a fig" is generally thought to originate from the fig's abundance. Personally I tend to use "I couldn't give a fig" as a polite alternative to what I really wanted to say.

Figs and Cashel Blue

On a late summer's evening, I will occasionally put a plate of purple figs on the zinc table in the garden together with a lump of blue cheese from Ireland or Italy. We help ourselves, cutting the fruits in half and placing a piece of Cashel Blue or Gorgonzola on their deep maroon flesh.

Figs with creamed Gorgonzola

Gorgonzola is often the softest of the blue cheeses. Mixed with cream or oil, it will form a less grainy dressing than the firmer varieties such as Stilton. Ideally, the cheese should be excessively ripe, almost to the point of liquidity.

enough for 4
figs – 8
spicy leaves, such as arugula, watercress, and mizuna – 4 handfuls

for the Gorgonzola cream
ripe Gorgonzola – 8 ounces (250g)
heavy cream – ½ to ⅔ cup (100 to 150ml)
a teaspoon of white wine vinegar

Put the cheese in a mixing bowl and stir in enough of the cream to give a creamy, slightly lumpy sauce. It should be thick enough to spread. Add the vinegar.

Cut the figs in halves or quarters, depending on their size. Divide the salad leaves among four plates, then add the figs and a spoonful or two of the Gorgonzola cream to each plate.

Baked feta, figs, and flatbread

Warm feta, salty, herbal, and nicely sharp, is something I eat in high summer, baking it in the oven or warming it wrapped in foil on the grill. Its appearance with figs was an accident, but one that has been repeated several times. The warm, slightly salty cheese and its notes of thyme and rosemary work very well with the lusciousness of the figs.

Middle Eastern flatbreads, soft and warm as a baby's skin, are well known for scooping up dips of eggplant and cod roe, but you can use them for so much more. I have been known to eat an entire stew with them, and often serve them with roast vegetables. Whether you have pita, lavash, or even Italian focaccia doesn't really matter, they all perform the same task. Unwrap the hot cheese at the table so that everyone gets to smell its lactic, deeply herbal scent. Some cold beers would be good here, too.

enough for 2 as part of a mezze platter
olive oil – 3 to 4 tablespoons
thyme – several sprigs
rosemary – a few short sprigs
green peppercorns – a tablespoon
a clove of garlic
a small fresh red chile
feta – 7 ounces (200g)

to serve
warm flatbread, such as Iranian lavash or Turkish pita
figs – 6 ripe

Preheat the oven to 400°F (200°C). Pour the olive oil into a mixing bowl. Hold the herbs over the bowl and strip off the leaves, letting them fall into the oil. Stir in the green peppercorns and a coarse grinding of black pepper. Peel the garlic and crush it so that it resembles a thick paste, then stir that in too.

Cut the chile in half, scrape out the seeds, and chop the flesh finely. Stir it into the oil and herbs. Place a piece of foil on a baking sheet, lay the cheese on top, then spoon over the oil and herbs. Fold into a loose parcel and bake for fifteen minutes.

Warm the breads, then serve them with the figs, halved, and the hot feta.

Marinated goat cheese for a fig and cheese lunch

The fruit and cheese lunch takes many forms in my house: a Russet apple
and a lump of orange-fleshed Cheshire; a pear with a mild goat cheese;
melon with snow-white feta. Figs can take the strongest of cheeses, from
the saltiest of blues to the most strident of washed-rind varieties. I like them
with goat cheeses that have been marinated in oil and aromatics so that they
take on a more pungent note. They are often brought to the table with slices
of coppa or speck, too.

enough for 3
small goat cheeses – 6
thyme – 6 small sprigs
bay leaves – 3
small dried chiles – 2
black peppercorns – 8
olive oil to cover
figs – 6 or 8 ripe

Cut the goat cheeses in half horizontally. Put into a large bowl and tuck the
herbs and chiles around them. Crack the peppercorns with a heavy object
such as a pestle or even a can of something—you just want to split each one
into two or three rather than crush them—and add them to the bowl.

Pour enough olive oil over the cheeses to just cover them, then cover
the bowl tightly with plastic wrap and set aside somewhere cool overnight.
The refrigerator will do, but you should bring them out and back to room
temperature for a good hour before serving with ripe figs.

Duck with figs and Barolo

The rich flesh of a roasted duck—sumptuous, fatty, glorious—needs something in the way of contrast if it is not to cloy. A single piece of fruit, orange say, or plum, generally fits the bill. For a midweek supper, I often roast a leg or two (more interesting meat than the breast), then make a thin, simple gravy with a glass of wine. The addition of figs, cut in half and allowed to soften in the wine, works very well as a contrast of texture. Any fruity red wine will do.

enough for 2
duck legs – 2
a few sprigs of thyme
figs – 4
a wineglass of red wine, such as Barolo

Preheat the oven to 400°F (200°C). Season the duck legs with salt and black pepper, tuck in the thyme sprigs, then roast in the oven until golden and crisp-skinned—a matter of twenty-five to thirty minutes or so. Holding the duck in place with a spatula, pour off the fat and reserve for another day. It will be wonderful for potatoes. Cut the figs in half and tuck them, cut side down, around the duck. Pour in the red wine and place over medium heat until the wine has evaporated by half and the figs have softened, scraping any crusty bits from the pan into the wine.

Pot-roasted guinea fowl with figs

A simple pot-roasted bird takes five or ten minutes to prepare, followed by an hour or so of unattended cooking. The result is meat that is both tender and flavorsome, cooking juices instilled with the essence of the meat, and only one pan to wash up. The figs here offer a certain harmony to an autumn dish of gentle flavors.

> *enough to serve 2 generously*
> a guinea fowl
> an onion
> rosemary – a small sprig
> white vermouth, such as Noilly Prat – a wineglass
> half a lemon
> figs – 4

Preheat the oven to 400°F (200°C). Season the guinea fowl with salt and pepper. Peel and coarsely chop the onion and put it into a large, deep Dutch oven. Add the rosemary, vermouth, guinea fowl, and the lemon half, cut in two. Cover with a lid and roast in the oven for an hour, until tender. Halfway through cooking, add the figs, cut in half. Check for doneness by inserting a skewer in the thickest part of the thigh. If the juices run clear, then the bird is cooked. Serve in thick slices with the onion, figs, and cooking juices.

Baked figs, red wine, and vanilla

enough for 4
fruity red wine – 2 cups (500ml)
golden baker's sugar – 3 tablespoons
thick honey – a tablespoon, or more to taste
a short length of orange peel
a vanilla pod, split
cloves – 2
figs – 12

Preheat the oven to 400°F (200°C). Place the wine, sugar, honey, orange peel, split vanilla pod, and cloves in a stainless steel saucepan and bring almost to a boil. Gently wipe the figs and place them snugly in a shallow ovenproof serving dish (they look wonderful in earthenware). Pour the hot wine over the figs, then bake them until they are soft and full of juice—this will take thirty to forty-five minutes. Turn the figs over and baste them during cooking.

Pour the juice through a sieve back into the original saucepan, bring to a boil, turn down the heat, and simmer until the liquid starts to thicken. It should end up the consistency of thin syrup. Pour the syrup over the figs and chill thoroughly before serving.

Roast figs with marsala and muscovado

Dark-skinned figs, warm from the oven with a drizzle of cream, are one of the most sensuous of late-summer desserts. Effortless to make and to eat, they are best served straight from the oven. Lucky are those with their own fig tree. I have used both sweet and dry marsala for this before now. If you have the latter, add a further tablespoon of sugar.

enough for 4
figs – 8 (maybe more if they are small)
sweet marsala – a small wineglass
light muscovado sugar
cream, to serve

Preheat the oven to 400°F (200°C). Cut the stalks from the figs and slice a deep cross into each fruit, going about halfway down. Press each fruit around its middle so that it opens up like a flower (or a baby bird in its nest yelling for food). You can cut them in half, if you prefer. Place the figs in a baking dish, then sprinkle over the wine and a couple of tablespoons of sugar. Bake for about twenty to twenty-five minutes, until the fruit is meltingly tender and the edges have started to caramelize. If they haven't browned nicely, then pop them under a hot broiler for a minute.

Serve the fruit, pouring over a little of the pan juices (there won't be much) as you go, and a drizzle of cream.

Fig, orange, and polenta cake

This cake, scented with cardamom and sweetened with honey, works both as something to eat with glasses of mint tea and as a dessert, in which case you might like to serve it with yogurt.

enough for 8
butter – 1 cup (220g)
golden baker's sugar – 1 cup plus 2 tablespoons (220g)
almonds – 5 ounces (150g), 1 cup
ground almonds – 5 ounces (150g), 1⅓ cups
large eggs – 3
polenta – a scant 1 cup (150g)
baking powder – a level teaspoon
finely grated zest and juice of a large orange
green cardamom pods – 12
figs – 6

for the syrup
the juice of 2 oranges
the juice of 2 lemons
honey – 4 tablespoons

Line the bottom of a nonstick 8-inch (20cm) springform cake pan with a piece of parchment paper. Preheat the oven to 350°F (180°C).

Beat the butter and sugar in a stand mixer until light and fluffy. Put the almonds in a heatproof bowl and pour boiling water over them. Remove them a few at a time with a slotted spoon and pop them from their skins. Blitz the almonds in a food processor until they are finely chopped (or chop them by hand if you prefer), then add them, together with the ground almonds, to the cake mixture.

Break the eggs into a small bowl, beat them lightly with a fork, and stir them into the mixture. Mix the polenta and baking powder together, then fold them into the mixture together with the grated orange zest and juice. Crush the cardamom pods and extract the little black seeds, then grind them to a fine powder. I use a mortar and pestle for this, but you can do it in a coffee grinder if you want. Add the spice to the cake mixture.

Cut the figs in half. Transfer half the cake mixture to the lined pan, add the figs, then add the remaining cake mixture and smooth the top level. The figs will appear as a moist layer at the bottom of the cake. Bake for thirty minutes, then turn the heat down to 325°F (160°C) and bake for a further twenty-five to thirty minutes, until the cake is firm to the touch. Test it for doneness with a metal skewer—it should come out clean, without wet cake mixture sticking to it.

To make the syrup, squeeze the orange and lemon juices into a stainless steel saucepan, bring to a boil, and dissolve the honey in it. Keep the liquid boiling for four or five minutes, until it has formed a thin syrup.

Spike holes into the top of the cake (still warm and in its pan) with a skewer, then spoon over the hot citrus syrup. Leave until almost cool, then lift out of the pan. Serve in thick slices, with thinly sliced fresh oranges and, if you wish for something more decadent, a little natural yogurt.

A crumbly, upside-down tart of figs

I like my tarts to be warm, crumbly, messy, and sweet. To this end, I use a very short pastry with a high proportion of butter and treat the raw pastry very gently, patching it where it crumbles. To deliver perfection, I add a tart cream such as crème fraîche or a ball of ice-cold vanilla or cinammon ice cream.

enough for 8

for the pastry
cold butter – ¾ cup (175g)
all-purpose flour – 1¾ cups (225g)
large egg yolks – 2
golden baker's sugar – 2 level tablespoons

for the filling
butter – 5 tablespoons (75g)
golden baker's sugar – ⅓ cup (75g)
figs – 10, halved and tough stems removed

vanilla or cinnamon ice cream or crème fraîche, to serve

You will need a tarte Tatin mold or a metal-handled frying pan or sauté pan about 8- to 9-inches (20 to 23cm) in diameter.

To make the pastry, cut the butter into cubes, then rub it into the flour until the mixture resembles fine fresh breadcrumbs. Sometimes I do it by hand, other times the speed of the food processor beckons. Mix in the egg yolks and sugar, then bring the mixture together into a ball with your hands. Wrap in wax paper and refrigerate for twenty minutes.

Preheat the oven to 425°F (220°C). Melt the butter and sugar in the Tatin mold or frying pan over medium heat, stirring from time to time. When the mixture looks syrupy and is starting to color, add the figs, cut side down. Let them cook for three to five minutes, until they are soft and starting to darken. Remove the pan from the heat.

Roll out the pastry to make a circle about ¾ inch (2cm) larger than the frying pan. Fold the extra pastry over to make a double "rim" around the edge. Place the pastry rim-side down on top of the figs (the best way to move this very short and crumbly pastry is to wrap it lightly around the rolling pin, then carefully lift it onto the pan). Place in the oven and bake for about forty minutes, until the pastry is a deep biscuit color. Take it out of the oven and leave it to calm down a bit. Cut into slices and serve straight from the pan (the slices will crumble a bit), with ice cream or crème fraîche.

Baked figs, red wine, fruit jelly

The fruit jelly I suggest here gives body to the cooking liquid.

enough for 4
small, plump figs – 12
red wine or port – 1 cup (250ml)
a vanilla pod
runny honey – 2 tablespoons
red currant jelly – 2 heaping tablespoons

Put the fruit into a stainless steel pan. Pour the red wine over the fruit together with ½ cup (125ml) of water, then tuck the vanilla pod underneath and drizzle over the honey and red currant jelly. Simmer gently for thirty minutes or so, until the fruit is tender.

Lift the figs into a serving dish, then bring the juices to a boil and keep an eye on them until about half has evaporated. They will have thickened into a dark red, glossy syrup that will thicken even further, almost to the consistency of liquid honey, as it cools. Strain the syrup over the figs and put them aside to cool. I serve these at room temperature.

Dried figs

Slow-baked figs with orange and Vin Santo

I much prefer the old-fashioned, hard, and intensely chewy lumps of beige fruit to the new squidgy, soft-dried version. The pale, fudge-colored dried figs from Turkey have a deep flavor and a moreish crunchiness and are better suited to long, slow cooking than the soft variety.

enough for 4
whole dried figs – 1 pound (450g)
Vin Santo – 1 cup (250ml)
water – 1 cup (250ml)
an orange
cloves – 2
red currant jelly – a heaping tablespoon

Preheat the oven to 375°F (190°C). Tip the figs into a casserole dish with a lid and pour over the wine and water. Remove three wide strips of zest from the orange with a vegetable peeler, then add it to the figs, along with the cloves and the red currant jelly.

Cover with a lid and bake for one hour, by which time the figs will have plumped up into fat, wine-laden bundles. Eat warm or chilled.

Baked figs with red wine and black currant jelly

I used a glass or two of Madiran for this because that is what happened
to be open, but any heavy red wine would have done. This is an occasion,
perhaps, to use one of those oak-and-vanilla red wines from California.
A very light wine will give a correspondingly thinner syrup.

enough for 4
small, whole dried figs – 7 ounces (200g)
red wine – 1 cup (250ml)
a vanilla pod
runny honey – 2 tablespoons
black currant jelly – 1 heaping tablespoon

Find a baking dish into which the figs will fit comfortably, then pour in
enough warm water to barely conceal them. Set them aside for several hours
so that the fruit softens; if you can leave them overnight they will be even
better, the water thickening to a light amber syrup.

Preheat the oven to 350°F (180°C). Pour the red wine over the fruit and
its soaking liquid, then tuck the vanilla pod underneath and drizzle over the
honey and black currant jelly. Bake for a good hour, until some of the syrup
has evaporated and the figs are plump.

Lift the figs into a serving dish, then pour the baking juices into a
stainless steel pan. Bring the syrup to a boil and keep an eye on it until about
half has evaporated. It will have thickened into a claret-colored, glossy syrup
that will thicken even further, almost to the consistency of liquid honey,
as it cools. Strain the syrup over the figs and put them aside to cool. I serve
these at room temperature, with a somewhat unnecessary pitcher of pouring
cream for those who wish.

Steamed fig pudding

An old-fashioned steamed pudding, a recipe that I am continually asked for, so here it is again.

> *enough for 4*
> dried figs – 1 pound (450g)
> port – ⅔ cup (150ml)
> a cinnamon stick
> a bay leaf
> runny honey – 2 tablespoons
>
> **for the sponge cake**
> butter – 7 tablespoons (100g), room temperature
> golden baker's sugar – ½ cup (100g)
> large eggs – 2
> fresh breadcrumbs – about 1 cup (50g)
> self-rising flour – ¾ cup plus 1 tablespoon (100g)
> ground ginger and cinnamon – ½ teaspoon each

Cut all but six of the figs into quarters, then place them all in a small, heavy pan with the port, cinnamon stick, bay leaf, and honey. Bring to a boil, then turn down the heat and simmer for about ten minutes. Lift the figs out with a slotted spoon and then reduce the syrup to about 5 tablespoons by boiling rapidly. Butter a 4-cup (900ml) pudding basin or deep stoneware dish. Place the whole figs (only) and syrup in the bottom.

Beat the butter and sugar with an electric mixer until pale and fluffy. Add the eggs one at a time and beat in. If the mixture curdles, and it probably will, it will come to no harm. Just fold in the breadcrumbs, chopped figs, and sifted flour and spices.

Spoon the mixture into the basin, on top of the whole figs and syrup, and smooth the surface flat. Place a piece of wax paper over the top of the basin, folding a pleat down the center as you do so, and secure with string. Cover with cheesecloth or foil and secure that also. Place the basin on a trivet in a large saucepan with enough water to come two-thirds up the sides of the basin. Steam, covered with a lid, for an hour, topping up the water from time to time.

Carefully remove the pudding from the water, leave for a few minutes, then remove the covers and turn it out onto a serving plate. Serve with cold cream or hot custard.

Dried fig and pumpkin seed bars

Chewy, oaty, buttery bars.

makes 12
walnut halves – 2 ounces (60g), about ½ cup
soft dried figs – 2½ ounces (70g)
dried sour cherries – 1½ ounces (40g), about ¼ cup
pumpkin seeds – 1 ounce (30g), about ¼ cup
rolled oats – 1⅓ cups (200g)
ground almonds – ⅓ cup (35g)
butter – 7 tablespoons (100g)
maple syrup – 7 tablespoons (100ml)
superfine sugar – scant ½ cup (90g)

Preheat the oven to 325°F (160°C). Roughly chop the walnuts, figs, cherries, and pumpkin seeds. This is done in seconds in a food processor but will take a bit longer by hand. The coarser your mix, the more crumbly the bars will be. The bars will hold together better the finer the mixture.

Tip in the oats and ground almonds. Melt the butter in a large saucepan, pour in the maple syrup, and add the sugar. When it all comes to a rolling boil, add the dry ingredients, stir thoroughly, and tip into a nonstick baking pan, about 9½ inches (24cm) square. Press the mixture down firmly again and bake for twenty to twenty-five minutes.

Press the mixture down firmly as it cools. Cut into 12 small bars while warm and leave to cool completely.

Gooseberries

This garden fizzes in spring. The infant leaves of the hornbeam, fig, crocosmia, and red currants sparkle in shades of lime and gold against the somber black-green of the yew hedges. In particular, I like the way the light shines through the tiny leaves of the three Hinnomaki gooseberry bushes. Among the very first to burst in March, they smack of freshness and change, of the excitement of a new gardening year.

I like the way you can see through a gooseberry on the bush, the transparency of it. Despite the angry thorns that have so regularly drawn my blood, I have a soft spot for this small and splendidly sour fruit. Especially its part in the dreamy, creamy gooseberry fool that so perfectly sums up our careless, buttercup-meadow summers.

The gooseberry's short season and lack of friends (it is rarely exploited commercially like the strawberry or blueberry) means that this is not the easiest ingredient to track down in mainstream shops. But come June and July, farmers' markets, farm stands, produce stores, and street markets have a few in cardboard baskets, usually among the sea of strawberries. They are one of the few fruits I buy in quantity and freeze (the other being the damson). Not normally a fan of the freezer, I challenge anyone to tell frozen gooseberries from fresh once they are hidden in the sweet rubble of a crumble.

British cooks are among the most prolific users of *Ribes uva-crispa*, yet the genus is indigenous throughout Europe and Western Asia. No cuisine seems to have quite as many gooseberry recipes devoted to it as we have. Wild bushes are rare—I have certainly never seen one—and any surviving ones may well be those that have made a bid for freedom near backyard gardens and vegetable patches.

As with red currants and blackberries, cool weather is more favorable for the gooseberry's cultivation. They are found right up to the Arctic

Circle. The bushes do particularly well in Lancashire and Yorkshire (the flavor is said to improve the farther north you go), where there are societies and clubs devoted to growing, showing, and celebrating the fruit. The oldest, dating from 1800, is at Egton Bridge near Whitby, and has an annual show on the first Tuesday in August. Plenty of time for the fruit to plump up to a size suitable for winning prizes—like vegetable shows, flavor barely comes into it.

In the south, the gooseberry needs a bit of shade. My bushes live on the cool side of the garden, under the spreading arms of the medlar tree. It is not just shady here but cool, and the soil rarely dries out. My previous bushes often produced barely enough for a single fool or crumble, yet somehow that was enough to justify their existence. That was all I asked of them.

I rank the green gooseberry, with its piercing sharpness, as one of the finest kitchen fruits we have. In my book it comes only just behind the damson and the black currant as a bringer of fresh, piquant flavors to our desserts. The fruit's astringency is bracing, and is why it is one of the few fruits that work in place of lemon in a meringue pie. It is also surely in the running for a pavlova.

Victorian cookbooks offer more possibilities than contemporary ones, and their recipes for ice cream, fools, jellies, and compotes are still in use by fans. Yes, the fruit is a celebration of nostalgia, but also one for fresh thinking: in my kitchen it is included not only in its well-known forms of fool and compote but also in cakes for tea and sauces for fish and roast pork.

I still rate the soft-crusted gooseberry pie made by the cooks at my Worcestershire school as one of the most memorable desserts of my life. To this day I can taste the softly-softly pastry with its fine sugar crust and the gray-green filling, slightly sweet and bracingly sharp. This is not the fruit of instant appeal to the masses like the strawberry, but a fruit of quiet pleasure, something for the few who understand and appreciate its charms.

A gooseberry in the garden

Three Careless gooseberry bushes were among the first plants to go into this garden. Within a fortnight of the lawn being uprooted and the ground being turned I had dug them in, and within a year they were fruiting well enough for an early-summer crumble and a pie. As the years went on, and despite careful pruning and generous feeding, they bore fewer and fewer fruits and sadly had to go (you can normally expect a decade or more out of a healthy bush).

A vegetable patch needs a gooseberry bush like it needs a crown of rhubarb, so it wasn't long before three replacements went in. I chose Hinnomaki, a variety known for its flavor and disease resistance; one of each color, green, yellow, and red. They now live in light shade in the medlar bed, a few feet away from the rhubarb crowns.

Gooseberries are not the fussiest of bushes and are one of the few fruits to tolerate shade or soil that is less than perfect. Hardy bushes, they will cope with cold and even frosts, despite their early flowering. Rhubarb aside, they are among the first fruits to ripen in the garden, with some varieties giving tart fruit suitable for cooking as early as late May. Be ready with the sugar bowl.

New plants may arrive in pots at any time of year, or from November to April as bare root plants. They can be grown as low bushes or as standards, if you have a feel for the pruning knife, and the latter's long stem will give better air circulation. Dig plenty of manure into the soil before planting your young bushes. Ideally put them in during late autumn to give them a chance to get their feet down before the sap starts rising in spring. If you can't plant until spring, no worries, they will almost certainly forgive you. At least, mine have.

Whatever the variety, the plants need at least a yard (1m) between one another. They love good air circulation. Very little upkeep is required other than keeping the base of the plant free of weeds (a prickly, skin-tearing task) and giving the odd early-winter feed of well-rotted manure. Large quantities of manure can increase the size of the fruit, if that is something that interests you.

Pruning is straightforward. In winter, cut the previous year's growth back to two buds. In summer, trim new growth back to five or six leaves along each branch. Snip out any crossing branches in the center of the bush to allow the air to get in there.

There are two harvesting possibilities. The first is to remove the acid green fruit in early summer and use it in cooking, while the second is to leave it on the stem to ripen fully. Even the sharpest of varieties can often sweeten up enough to eat raw if given plenty of sun and patience.

Varieties

Green "white" gooseberries
White Eagle An old variety that has recently been reintroduced. Long, pale fruits that are almost transparent.
White Lion Large, sweet, white fruits from large bushes. This old variety is a late but vigorous cropper.
Whitesmith* Large, white berries of good flavor that appear early in the season.
Invicta* A prolific modern cultivar from East Malling that is particularly resistant to mildew. Pick in July. Very thorny.
Careless* This is the variety I grew for ten years. A good, sharp berry that

is perfect for pies, although I sometimes let it ripen on the bush for dessert eating. Less hairy than most, it appears in midseason.

Greenfinch Very resistant to disease, this new compact variety is a prolific cropper.

Pixwell* The berries, excellent in pies and preserves, grow abundantly on almost thorn-free bushes. A pink Pixwell is also available.

Yellow gooseberries

Leveller Oval, yellowish, midseason fruit of excellent flavor. Not as generous a cropper as some, but it did well enough in my garden.

Early Sulphur Early, medium-sized fruit with a good golden color. The plants are vigorous and spreading, the fruit long rather than round.

Hinnomaki* Large, green to gold fruit with good disease resistance. The plants can grow to quite a size, so allow a good yard between them.

Howard's Lancer* A middle-to-late-season, medium-sized berry. Round and gold, with a thin skin, this spreading variety is one of our oldest. Wonderful for jam.

Golden Drop A much-liked midseason berry with a deep gold color. An upright bush, suitable for a small garden.

Red gooseberries

May Duke* Possibly the earliest fruiting berry I have come across, this is the one for that first, lip-puckering crumble of early summer.

Whinham's Industry* One of the dark red varieties well suited to eating as a dessert fruit as well as in a crumble. Large, oval berries appear midseason.

Lancashire Lad A long-established red variety, found on many an allotment.

Hedgehog Great name for a favorite old dessert variety. The fruits are large and crop well on an upstanding bush.

Achilles* A large, red berry good for both cooking and eating as a dessert fruit. Left on the bush, its flavor will soften.

Hinnomaki Red* Large berries, good flavor, and a strong resistance to disease.

*Available from US sources.

Gooseberries in the kitchen

Considering this little green fruit is far from the country's favorite, it has managed to secure everlasting fame in both a classic and a hot dessert. Gooseberry crumble is one of Britain's most celebrated hot desserts, as well known as treacle tart or roly-poly pudding. Its enduring popularity is in part due to the contrast between the sharp, soft fruit and sweet, crisp crust.

The fruit is also known for its role in the quintessential summer dessert, gooseberry fool.

Once it meets the heat, the gooseberry loses its translucency and turns opaque. Its skin collapses and the fruit slides toward a delicious mush. While this quality excludes it from open tarts, it means it can be used in fools and creams with little more than a mild crushing from a fork. On the down side, it is almost impossible to make a jam where the whole fruits are visible.

Some form of sweetening is almost always necessary. The butterscotch notes of the unrefined sugars work particularly well, especially golden superfine. Honey too, has something of an affinity. The herb sweet cicely can be used to sweeten if you want to cut down on the amount of sugar (first find your sweet cicely). The amount of sugar or honey you need will obviously depend on the variety of your fruit, but more importantly on its ripeness. Early in the season, even red gooseberries can be extremely tart. A June crumble will generally need more sugar than one baked in late July. I often mix sugar and honey.

Savory applications are few and far between. The best known is that of serving gooseberry purée with mackerel, but I also like a slithering dollop on the side with a pork chop. It works in the same way as applesauce or poached rhubarb, slicing through the fat with its inherent acidity. Be parsimonious with the sugar if you use this fruit in a savory way.

Gooseberries and...

Elderflowers The white flowers appear at the same time as the first of the gooseberries and have an extraordinary affinity with them. Simmer whole flower heads with the fruit and a generous amount of sugar.

Honey A small amount will lend warmth to poached gooseberries.

Pork The fruit has the effect of removing the fatty quality from roast pork or pork chops, slicing through it like a sharp knife. I sometimes throw a few berries in with the pan juices when making gravy for a roast.

Mackerel Although gooseberry sauce can be served with cold salmon, I find it most successful with mackerel, especially when the fish has been grilled or broiled and its edges lightly charred.

Cream Few fruits have quite the same affinity with cream as this one. It is as if they are inseparable. Gooseberry pie or pudding without cream seems almost pointless. Where the flavor of most fruits is diminished slightly once cream comes into the picture, in this instance its presence is of great value in bringing out the fruit's best qualities.

Ginger One of the few spices that have a rapport. Added to a gooseberry jam or a sauce, the sweet heat of ginger works well.

* The sawfly is the bush's main attacker. It can be kept at bay—to a certain extent—by opening the bush to get good air circulation. Cutting out any crossing branches in the center of the bush will help, as will opening up the middle to create a goblet shape.
* "Topping and tailing" means removing both the dead flower head and the gooseberry's tiny stalk. It is not a difficult job, though mildly irritating if you are in a hurry. I try to choose a day when I am not too busy and, if possible, do it outside, sitting on the back step, when the peaceful repetition can be strangely relaxing.
* This fruit is high in pectin, making for a firm jam set. A few gooseberries added to a strawberry or other low-pectin fruit jam can help the setting.
* Carol Klein recommends removing half the crop in early summer and using it in the kitchen, then leaving the rest in place to ripen enough for eating raw. Best of both worlds, I would have thought.
* The quantity of sugar needed will depend on the variety; less sugar is needed as the season progresses.

A gooseberry sauce for grilled mackerel or roast pork

Makes enough to accompany grilled mackerel or roast pork for six.

gooseberries – 1 pound (500g)
sugar – ¼ cup (50g)
water – 3 to 4 tablespoons

Top and tail the gooseberries, tip them into a stainless steel pan, then add the sugar and water. Bring to a boil, lower the heat, and simmer for ten minutes. Use warm or at room temperature.

A hot gooseberry and ginger sauce

The pairing of the berries with elderflower is used primarily in sweet treatments, such as compotes and jams, but rarely have I seen the two brought together in a savory context. The idea is that of Yotam Ottolenghi, whose food I find exciting, original, and extraordinary.

enough for 6
gooseberries – 14 ounces (400g)
superfine sugar – ½ cup (100g)
elderflower cordial – 4 tablespoons
fresh ginger – a large lump about the size of your thumb

Top and tail the gooseberries and tip them into a pan with the sugar and cordial. Peel and coarsely grate the ginger and add to the pot. Bring to a boil, turn down the heat, and simmer for ten minutes. Serve with pork or oily fish.

Gooseberry, apple, and elderflower pie

Slightly different from the one on page 288, this pie has the age-old pairing of elderflowers and a marginally crisper crust.

enough for 8

for the pastry
butter – 10 tablespoons (150g)
golden baker's sugar – ¾ cup (150g), plus extra for sprinkling
a large egg yolk (reserve the white)

all-purpose flour – 2 cups (250g)
baking powder – a level teaspoon

for the filling
gooseberries – 1 pound (500g)
cooking apples – 1¾ pounds (800g)
golden baker's sugar – ⅔ cup (125g)
elderflower cordial – 3 tablespoons

You will need a 9½-inch (24cm) (7-inch [18cm] across the bottom) metal tart pan with a shallow rim.

Cream the butter and sugar together until soft and pale, in a stand mixer or with a wooden spoon. Mix in the egg yolk. Mix the flour and baking powder, then add to the creamed butter and sugar. Bring the dough together and squeeze into a ball. Cut the pastry in two, putting half in the fridge, wrapped loosely in wax paper. Flour the work surface and roll out the first piece of pastry to fit the tart pan, smoothing it up the sides and over the rim—I tend to roll this particular pastry a little thicker than usual. Leave any overhang in place for the time being. Refrigerate for thirty minutes.

Preheat the oven to 350°F (180°C). Top and tail the gooseberries. Peel the apples, quarter them, and remove their cores, then slice them thickly (I usually cut each quarter into about three pieces). Put the apples, gooseberries, sugar, and elderflower cordial into a stainless steel pan (aluminium will taint the gooseberries) and cook over low to medium heat for about ten to fifteen minutes, until the apples are showing some signs of tenderness and the gooseberries are starting to soften. Remove the fruit from the pan with a slotted spoon and set aside in a bowl, leaving the juice behind.

Turn up the heat under the juice and let it boil for five to ten minutes, until it has started to turn a little jammy, stopping before it turns brown and caramelizes. Let it cool (it may set; no matter).

Put a baking sheet into the oven. Roll out the second piece of pastry. Put the fruit into the pastry-lined tart pan, again using a slotted spoon. Spoon over the concentrated fruit syrup. Brush the rim of the pastry with egg white, then place the second piece of pastry over the top, pressing it down onto the rim to seal the edges. Trim any overhanging pastry with a sharp knife. Cut three small slits in the center of the pastry to let out the steam, then, if you wish, decorate the pastry with leaves made from the trimmings. Bake the pie on the hot baking sheet for thirty-five minutes. Gently beat the egg white until bubbles appear on the surface, then remove the pie from the oven, brush with egg white, scatter a thin layer of sugar over the surface, and return to the oven for five minutes. Leave for twenty to thirty minutes to settle down before serving with heavy cream.

Gooseberry pie

A soft, fragile pastry crust the color of old linen is sometimes more appropriate than something crisp and honey colored. I have worked at such a crust for some time now, and feel that this is the one for a gooseberry pie. Tender and pale, this is pastry that collapses beneath the fork, as gentle as a whisper.

enough for 6

for the pastry
butter – 10 tablespoons (140g)
all-purpose flour – 1¾ cups (230g)
confectioners' sugar – a scant ½ cup (50g)
a large egg yolk

for the filling
gooseberries – a scant 2 pounds (850g)
sugar – ¾ cup (160g)
water – 4 tablespoons

Rub the butter into the flour with your fingertips, then mix in the confectioners' sugar and egg yolk. Bring the dough together and squeeze it into a round, then put it in the fridge for half an hour to chill. I find this pastry works well in the food processor too; first blitz the flour and butter, then mix briefly with the sugar and egg yolk.

Top and tail the gooseberries, then put them into a nonreactive saucepan with the sugar and water and simmer until the fruit has softened slightly— it will go paler in color too. But stop before the gooseberries collapse. Lift the fruit into a bowl with a slotted spoon, then turn up the heat and boil the liquid down to a thick syrup, stopping before it caramelizes.

Preheat the oven to 400°F (200°C). Roll out half the pastry and use to line an 8-inch (20cm) tart pan, pushing it up the sides. I use a crinkle-edged tart ring with a removable bottom or an old-fashioned metal tart pan. Chill thoroughly, or freeze for fifteen minutes, then bake for fifteen minutes, baking blind, if you wish, until the pastry is dry and pale-biscuit colored. Transfer the drained berries to the pie shell, pour over the thickened syrup, and leave to cool a little.

Roll or press out the remaining pastry into a round. Lift it on the rolling pin and place it gently on top of the pie, pressing the edges down to meet the bottom crust. Cut two air holes in the top crust, then bake for twenty minutes until the pie is pale gold. Remove from the oven, sprinkle with superfine sugar, and return for a further five or six minutes.

Leave the pie to cool a little before serving with a pitcher of heavy cream.

Gooseberry pudding

A twist on the usual summer pudding made with raspberries and red currants. Whether it will stand up when you turn it out is up to the fruit itself. I feel the pudding is inclined to be more delicious if it doesn't, when the fruit and bread are too soft and silky to stand up. A pitcher of cream is not an embellishment here, it is essential. Preferably thick, yellow, and unpasteurized.

enough for 3
gooseberries – 1½ pounds (750g)
superfine sugar – 3 to 4 tablespoons
water – 1 cup (250ml)
brioche or bread – 8 or 9 thickish slices
heavy cream, to serve

Top and tail the gooseberries, then drop them into a stainless steel pan with the sugar and water. Bring to a boil, reduce the heat, and simmer gently for seven to ten minutes, until the sugar has dissolved and the berries are soft enough to crush. Remove the crusts from the brioche or bread and use these to line the bottom and sides of a medium-sized pudding basin or deep baking dish. Spoon the filling into the basin, then pour over the juice, pressing down gently so that the bread is thoroughly soaked in juice. This is really quite important if the pudding is to be truly luscious and juicy.

Put a small plate and a heavy weight on top and set aside in the fridge overnight. Serve from the dish, or turn it out onto a serving dish if you are feeling confident (it may well collapse), and accompany with cream.

Gooseberry fool

I like my fools to have a slightly rough texture, with crushed fruit in among the cream. This is easy to do if you crush the berries with a fork rather than sieving them. The seeds add important contrast to the general creaminess, and the streaks of greeny-gold are pleasing to see through the glass. Add a tablespoon of elderflower cordial to the berries as they cook, if you wish.

enough for 6
gooseberries – 1 pound (450g)
sugar
heavy cream – 1¼ cups (300ml)

Top and tail the gooseberries, put them in a stainless steel pan, and sprinkle over a little sugar. How much you use will depend on the sourness of your fruit. I use about 3 tablespoons for this quantity of gooseberries, but you can always add more after the fruit has softened.

Put the fruit over gentle heat and leave to soften. Take care that the berries do not catch on the bottom of the pan—you can add a tablespoon of water if you wish, but I don't find it necessary if you keep the temperature low. When the fruit is pale and swollen, squash it gently with a fork, leaving a rough mash rather than a smooth purée, and set aside to cool.

Whip the cream softly, so that it rests in folds rather than stiff peaks. Fold the fruit into the cream, leaving trails of unblended fruit throughout. Spoon into glasses and rest for a while in the fridge before serving.

Honey polenta cake with elderflower and gooseberries

A moist, honey-scented cake with a slightly crunchy texture, which works both as a cake for tea and as a dessert to serve with poached gooseberries and thick yogurt. Incidentally, it is gluten-free.

enough for 8
butter – 1 cup (220g)
golden baker's sugar – 1 cup plus 2 tablespoons (220g)
unblanched almonds – ⅓ cup (50g)
ground almonds – 1⅓ cups (150g)
large eggs – 3
polenta – 1¼ cups (200g)
baking powder – a slightly heaping teaspoon
finely grated zest and juice of a large lemon
thick, cold yogurt, to serve

for the syrup
the juice of 2 lemons
elderflower cordial – ⅔ cup (150ml)
honey – 4 tablespoons

for the gooseberries
gooseberries – 1 pound (450g)
superfine sugar – 4 tablespoons

You will need a nonstick springform cake pan about 8 inches (20cm) in diameter, the bottom lined with a piece of parchment paper.

Preheat the oven to 350°F (180°C). Beat the butter and sugar in a stand mixer until light and fluffy. Put the almonds in a heatproof bowl and pour boiling water over them. Remove them a few at a time with a slotted spoon and pop them from their skins. This will seem an endless task at first but in practice it actually takes about ten to fifteen minutes. Discard the skins. Blitz the almonds in a food processor until they are finely chopped (or chop them by hand, if you prefer), then add them, together with the ground almonds, to the butter and sugar mixture.

Break the eggs into a small bowl and beat them lightly with a fork, then stir them into the mixture. Mix the polenta and baking powder and fold them into the mixture together with the grated lemon zest and juice.

Transfer the cake mixture to the lined pan and smooth the top level. Bake for thirty minutes, then turn the heat down to 325°F (160°C) and bake for a further twenty-five to thirty minutes, until the cake is firm to the touch. Test it for doneness with a metal skewer—it should come out clean and without wet cake mixture sticking to it.

To make the syrup, squeeze the lemon juice into a stainless steel saucepan, add the elderflower cordial, and bring to a boil. Dissolve the honey in it and keep boiling until it has formed a thin syrup (about four or five minutes).

Spike holes into the top of the cake (still warm and in its pan) with a skewer and spoon over the hot syrup. Leave until almost cool, then remove it from the pan.

Top and tail the gooseberries, put them into a baking dish or small roasting pan, and scatter with the sugar. Bake at 400°F (200°C) until the fruit has burst and the juices are starting to caramelize in the pan. Serve with the cake and some thick yogurt.

Gooseberries with honey and elderflower

My first bushes were of the Careless variety, whose name makes me wonder if it wasn't exactly these fruits that inspired Elizabeth David to refer to a fruit fool as "untroubled." Gooseberries need sugar—its popularity was at its height in the late 1800s with the abolition of the sugar tax—but honey works well too, as in this recipe for baked gooseberries with elderflower. If the flowers have finished but you still have gooseberries, then stir in two or three tablespoons of elderflower cordial and cut down a bit on the honey.

enough for 4
gooseberries – 14 ounces (400g)
mild honey or sugar – 2 to 3 tablespoons
water – 4 tablespoons
a single head of elderflowers or 2 tablespoons of elderflower cordial

Top and tail the gooseberries, put them in a heavy-bottomed nonreactive pan with the honey or sugar, water, and the sprig of elderflowers, then bring to a boil. Turn the heat down so that they simmer gently. They will take about ten to fifteen minutes to soften. When they have started to burst and have produced much sticky syrup, turn off the heat. Remove the elderflowers. If you are using cordial instead, add it now.

Serve warm or cold, as they are or with a pitcher of cream.

Grapes

Climbing the wall either side of the kitchen doors is a vine, planted about six years ago in the hope of the occasional grape to pick at as I cook. That is all I asked of it. A few grapes for a mellow autumn afternoon, to be picked when the garden is damp with autumn mist and there is a pall of woodsmoke in the air. But it has given me so much more. Eighty small bunches last year, fifty or so this, of quite the most handsome clusters of fruit this side of Fauchon. I'm surprised, amused, and a wee bit proud.

The ripening grapes are a part of this garden's slow descent into winter sleep. A time that, if I am honest, I look forward to as much as the first buds of spring. Those grapes that live in direct sunlight, perhaps where I have purposefully snipped off a leaf or two, are sweet enough to attract the blackbirds by late October. Weather permitting, they will stay on the vine in good condition for a further month. As the leaves fall onto the gravel paths and the garden starts its annual collapse, the bunches continue to swell until the hoarfrost. I eat some of the last few frozen, when they taste like a glass of chilled Beaumes de Venise. Those that remain are my gift for the blackbirds, who swallow them whole, like a pelican wolfing a fish.

I have always delighted in the juicy pop of a grape in my mouth. With their tight skin and spurt of cold, sweet juice, they are refreshing fruits to eat, especially if you have remembered to put them in the freezer for a few minutes beforehand. You can sugar them too, dipping hand-snipped bunches first into fork-beaten egg white, then into superfine sugar. The effect under candlelight is like sugar-snow on the rose hips in the garden on a winter's evening.

There are a few homegrown bunches about in the markets, smaller, sharper, and often more interesting than the characterless grapes of commerce. There are good grapes elsewhere, too, with some shops stocking the pale, winelike Muscats with their heavy juice and almost alcoholic sweetness. The major supermarkets often have these, sold as specialty grapes. There is more than a hint of the golden pleasures of Beaumes de Venise to them, and I can barely sleep knowing there is a bunch in the fridge.

My own vines arrived, bare rooted, as two bent and sorry-looking sticks, and I had little hope for their survival. They did fairly well those first few years, annually sending out a few leafy shoots and the odd grapes that barely ripened; until the autumn they suffered a ruthless pruning at the hands of the painters who needed to get at the wall behind them. From then on they have produced more grapes than I can handle—festoons of bloomy, deep purple fruits literally dripping from the vines.

I will occasionally take a bunch of grapes of some sort into the kitchen, either to bake alongside a partridge or pheasant once the price has come down a bit, or perhaps to fold into the undulating yeast dough of a foccacia or *schiacciata*. I have put them into a batch of muffins but wouldn't do it again, and I rather like the plump black ones in a white cabbage salad, especially when I have included toasted walnuts, apples, and a dark cured meat such as speck or bresaola.

The leaves come in useful when they are young and pliable and can be roped in to wrap bundles of long-grain rice flecked with sweet raisins, softened onions, dill, and pine nuts. I have used them to wrap a partridge for roasting. A romantic use—the leaves turn gold, then tobacco-colored in the oven's heat—but a useful one too, keeping the breasts moist during the early part of cooking just like a few slices of bacon. Very young leaves, if you can bear to pick them, can apparently be shredded and used in a sauce for fish, though I have never tried it.

The prunings have their use too, the twigs making aromatic kindling for a barbecued fish. They add nothing in terms of flavor, but the act has an aesthetic significance and a certain French country charm.

Of course, there is another application of the grape, or rather its juice, in the kitchen, the nectar that is sweet-sour verjuice. It is not easy to find here, and is far from cheap when you do. I pick it up occasionally as a treat, and use its mellow sourness to work a certain magic with rabbit or chicken. A dish to celebrate the return of sparkling, frosty mornings.

Grapes in the garden

Grapevines often seem to do best where they have to struggle, growing in stony ground in direct, baking heat. I see them surviving in otherwise inhospitable places, often scrambling up greenhouses and lean-tos, seemingly happy with their feet in thin soil. My own are never fed and only occasionally watered. Generally, they are not fond of particularly fertile soil that is inclined to encourage leaf growth at the expense of fruit.

Many dessert grapes need a greenhouse if they are to ripen fully, unlike wine grapes (with which we are not concerned here) that will happily grow outside in our climate. Those varieties that will grow outside need a warm wall and plenty of sunshine, especially in late summer and autumn when the fruit is ripening.

You will need some way of keeping the birds at bay. I use plastic netting, pulling it over the vines as the fruits start to ripen. The downside is that the grapes and netting can get in a bit of a tangle.

Prune your vines in late winter. Any later than the end of February and they will bleed sap. I do mine round about St. Valentine's Day, trimming each stem right back to the first or second visible bud with the secateurs. I have found that the more severely I prune my vines, the better they fruit.

Varieties

The varieties here are sweet dessert grapes that will work in the garden or in a greenhouse.

Boskoop Glory A well-flavored black grape for mid- to late autumn.
Black Hamburg You will need a greenhouse for this one, but it can be excellent given the right conditions, cropping in October.
Buckland Sweetwater Sweet and easy to grow. Not the most prolific of vines, so suitable for the smaller greenhouse.
New York Muscat* Given a warm wall, this white grape will provide sweet fruit in midautumn.
Muscat of Alexandria* Usually known simply as Muscat, this golden-pink grape prefers a warm wall and, given the right conditions, should produce fruit of an excellent flavor. Rich and spicy.
Fragola Small, thick-skinned grapes with flavors of hazelnut and strawberry. The flesh is particularly soft and juicy. This grape literally pops in the mouth. I can pick eighty or more bunches from one vine.
Concord* Hardy, vigorous grower that yields blue-black, richly flavored grapes for the table, jelly, and juice.

*Available from US sources.

Grapes in the kitchen

Rarely do grapes make it to the stove, the majority being eaten straight from the vine. Yet they are really rather good when tossed into a salad of pointed spinach leaves and crisp bacon, providing a sweet freshness to contrast with the salty meat. They are also good with game, duck, and thick shards of smoked ham.

Grapes can be cooked, too, though they tend to lose any subtlety of flavor. When the skin of a black grape bursts, the juices delightfully stain whatever sauce or crust they come into contact with. Grapes added to a focaccia dough will send purple streaks throughout it. A few added to the pan juices of a roast game bird will add a sweet-sharpness to the gravy. Small dark grapes can be used in a baked puff pastry tart in the style of a *tarte fine*.

The leaves of the grapevine have been used for centuries to wrap food, whether it is a ripening cheese such as Oregon's Rogue River Blue or the little parcels of seasoned rice we know as dolmades.

A word about verjuice

Verjuice is a rare and fascinating ingredient—the juice of unripe green grapes (they are picked about halfway through ripening) that was at one time used in lieu of lemon juice. Verjuice has a complexity far greater than lemon juice or vinegar and is at once both sour and sweet, mellow and warm. It is produced by only one or two artisan companies and is easier to buy in southwest France and Australia than here in the UK. Were it not so difficult to track down, I would use it more than I do. I appreciate it in salad dressings and for sharpening cream sauces, but this is a deeply intriguing ingredient that is currently underexploited and deserves to be better known.

* The tiny Corinth grape is the variety most often used for the dried "currants" we put in Christmas cakes and mincemeat. The word *currant* is a corruption of Corinth.
* When shopping for green grapes, those with a slight hint of amber to them will be sweeter than those of an acid green.
* Could I also take this opportunity to remind you of the pork with grapes recipe in *The Kitchen Diaries.*

Chicken with verjuice, celery, and cream

This is a rich dish, but stops short of cloying thanks to the grapey-apple sharpness of the verjuice. Greens of some sort are essential here, and spinach would be my choice. I used the tiniest black grapes I could find for this, tart and deeply flavored at the same time.

enough for 6
olive oil
chicken thighs – 8 large
celery – 4 thinnish stalks
verjuice – a generous ¾ cup (200ml)
bay leaves – 3
heavy cream – ⅔ cup (150ml)
capers, rinsed – 2 heaping teaspoons, or more if you wish
black grapes – a handful, seeded if large

to serve
large starchy potatoes
greens

Preheat the oven to 400°F (200°C). Warm a casserole or Dutch oven—a heavy one, perhaps of enameled cast iron or stainless steel—over medium heat with enough olive oil to cover the bottom. Rub the chicken pieces generously with oil and salt and pepper, then lay them skin-side down in the hot oil and let the skin color appetizingly.

In the five or so minutes it takes the chicken to color, wash and chop the celery. You need it to be in short pieces the length of a cork. Turn the chicken over and, as you do so, add the celery to the pan. Leave for a couple of minutes, tucking the celery in around the meat, then add the verjuice and bay leaves. As the steam rises, cover tightly with a lid, then put the whole thing in the oven. Bake for forty minutes.

At this point you can peel and cut the potatoes and get a pot of water boiling for them. Get the greens ready, too, washing them thoroughly and removing any tatty bits of leaf or tough-looking stems. Drop the potatoes into the boiling water and salt them.

Put the greens on. I just put a steamer pan over the boiling potatoes, but you could cook the (still wet) greens in a pan with a lid, if you prefer. Remove the chicken from the oven and switch it off. Lift the meat out onto a serving dish and return it to the oven, then pour off the fat from the pan, leaving any interesting-looking juices in place. Put the pan over medium heat. Once the juices start bubbling and reducing a little, pour in the cream, stirring at the bottom of the pan to dislodge any tasty bits. Season with salt and black pepper, then let the liquid bubble until it starts to thicken a wee bit and turns deep ivory in color. Add the capers and grapes and correct the seasoning.

Spoon the creamy juices over the chicken and serve with the greens and potatoes.

Celery root and grape salad

An ice-white salad for a crisp day. Perhaps when there is a roast loin of pork with crackling singing in the oven, or some fatty chops in the pan, their flesh freckled here and there with crushed juniper berries.

enough for 4
red cabbage – a quarter
celery root – a medium-sized one
half a bulb of fennel
a Russet apple
a little lemon juice
grapes – 2 large handfuls
walnuts – a handful

for the dressing
parsley leaves – a large handful
crème fraîche – 1 cup (250ml)
the juice of half a lemon
smooth Dijon or whole-grain mustard – 2 tablespoons

Shred the cabbage, celery root, and fennel finely. Cut the apple into quarters, discard the core, then slice very finely. Toss the apple slices immediately in a little lemon juice to keep them from discoloring. Cut each grape in half and remove and discard the seeds. Toast the walnuts in a nonstick pan until they smell warm and nutty.

Make the dressing. Coarsely chop the parsley. Mix the parsley, crème fraîche, lemon juice, and mustard together and stir in a little salt and black pepper. Toss with all the salad ingredients and serve.

Black grape focaccia

I have previously added blackberries to my sweet focaccia, but black grapes are more traditional. This is excellent with a fresh, mild cheese.

enough for 8
white bread flour – 3¼ cups (450g)
quick-rise yeast – 1 package (7g), about 2 teaspoons
sea salt – 1 teaspoon
superfine sugar – 1 tablespoon
warm water – 1½ cups (350ml)

for the topping
sweet black grapes – 14 ounces (400g)
olive oil – 2 tablespoons
superfine sugar – 2 tablespoons
a little confectioners' sugar

Put the flour in a large bowl, add the yeast, the sea salt (if you are using coarse salt, crush it finely first), then the sugar and warm water. Mix with a wooden spoon, then turn the dough out onto a generously floured board and knead lightly for five minutes or so. You need not be too enthusiastic. A gentle pummeling will suffice.

Once the dough feels elastic and "alive," put it into a floured bowl, cover with a clean cloth or plastic wrap, and leave it somewhere warm to rise. It will take approximately an hour to double in size. Once it has, punch it down again, knocking some of the air out. Tip it into a shallow baking pan about 12 inches (30cm) in diameter. Gently knead half of the grapes into the dough, scattering the remaining ones on top. Cover the dough once more and return it to a warm place to rise.

Preheat the oven to 425°F (220°C). Once the dough has expanded to almost twice its size, drizzle over the olive oil, scatter with the superfine sugar, and bake for thirty-five to forty minutes, until well risen, golden brown, and crisp on top. It should feel springy when pressed. Leave to cool slightly before dusting with confectioners' sugar. Cut into thick wedges and eat while it is still warm. It will not keep for more than a few hours.

Roasted grapes

Snip bunches of dark grapes into small sprigs, place them in a baking dish or roasting pan, and cover them lightly with olive oil. Roast in a hot oven for fifteen minutes or so, until the skins have started to wrinkle and the fruits are bleeding juice. Serve with roast pork, steak, or game birds.

A salad of game, grapes, and verjuice

At the butcher's counter I often pause, wallet in hand, to double up on what I am buying (a chicken or a pair of duck breasts, partridge or quail) for eating cold. They will be roasted at the same time as those intended for supper, saving time and cash, but then they will be removed, left to cool, and wrapped in plastic wrap for the following day. Nine times out of ten, the cold roast birds have their flesh stripped from the bones in large pieces, which is then tossed with salad leaves, a simple dressing, and perhaps some fruit. Duck with pomegranates is good, as are quail with spinach leaves and slices of blood orange.

> *enough for 2*
> cold roast game or chicken – 14 ounces (400g) boned weight
> grapes – 2 handfuls
> celery – a large stalk
> walnut halves – 2 tablespoons
> radicchio or other slightly bitter leaves – a couple of handfuls
>
> **for the dressing**
> verjuice – 5 tablespoons (70ml)
> lemon thyme – 3 or 4 little sprigs
> smooth, mild mustard – 1 teaspoon
> olive oil – 5 tablespoons (70ml)

To make the dressing, pour the verjuice into a small mixing bowl. Pull the thyme leaves from their stalks and chop them finely, then add them to the verjuice, together with a good pinch of salt, a little black pepper, and the mustard. Pour in the olive oil, beating with a fork or tiny whisk.

Keeping the meat in large strips and chunks, stir it into the dressing. Halve the grapes and flick out their seeds with the point of a knife. Finely slice the celery. Add the grapes and celery to the meat and dressing.

Toast the walnut halves for a couple of minutes in a shallow pan. Rinse the salad leaves. Toss gently with the rest of the ingredients and divide between two plates.

Hazelnuts

I catch my breath and stand quite motionless; a moment of quiet excitement. I feel as if there is a butterfly in my chest. There, two feet away, is the first catkin of spring, already heavy with yellow pollen and dangling like a lamb's tail from a bare, brittle twig. Then another, and as I crane my neck to get a closer look I spot the first tuft of female flowers on the same tree, like tiny crimson stars. The ground is still icy, dry leaves crackle underfoot, but slowly I start to notice everything else that is happening: the leaf buds already on the gooseberries; the snowdrops suddenly visible through the trailing ivy; the crocuses waking up beneath my feet.

The hazelnuts were among the first trees to go into this garden, taking their place close, too close as it turned out, to the mulberry, the medlar, the mirabelle, and the quince. The nut trees grew faster than the others, unfettered by my timid attempts at pruning. They grew to almost fifteen feet (five meters), their whippy branches swaying each autumn under the weight of the local gray squirrels.

In early spring the hazel family, including the cultivated cob and filbert, produces a canopy of piercingly green leaves bright enough to lift even the darkest of winter spirits. Mine were, until I dug them out in a desperate quest for more space, a refreshing dapple of brightest lime against the black-green of the ivy walls behind. The one a Cosford Cob, the other a slightly shorter and more delicate Purple Filbert, fruited well enough, but trying to catch the nuts before the squirrels got to them became increasingly frustrating. As much as I valued their charming catkins, their flash of verdant green and the coolness under their canopy on a summer's day, they had to go. One late-spring day, I took a saw to them, then wrenched up their eight-year-old roots.

The young cobnut marks the change of season as clearly as turning the page of a calendar. The last week of August and the first two of September are our only chance to catch sight of the new season's nuts, pale, sweet, almost milky. Easily spotted at the produce market by their frilly-edged husks, their freshness is astonishing, almost springlike, and shakes you by its immaturity when all else seems to be crisping to gold and bronze.

The protective husk of a little cobnut seems too big for the sweet nut within, like a child's blazer at the start of a new school term. You can peel away the husks and rub your thumb over the downy covering of the shell, which is soft enough to crack with your back teeth. Inside, a plump kernel of mild-flavored nut.

At this point in the year there is a milky quality to the nuts, a gentle sweetness and a faint hint of fresh coconut about them. Those that aren't munched from the hand could end up in a salad. As September wears on, their pale green husks crisp up and turn a dusty brown. The fluff on their chins disappears and their shells harden. This was the moment when children, impatient for autumn, would use them as makeshift conkers.

The cultivated hazel is generally separated into cobnuts and filberts, though the difference is minimal in terms of flavor and appearance. The filbert has the longer husk, the papery frill almost completely covering the little nut within. The cobnut husk is shorter, leaving a clearly peeping nut. Since the nineteenth century the most cultivated has been the Kentish Cob, a particularly plump and juicy variety of hazelnut. But others are planted too. Kent is the cobnut's commercial home. Yes, new orchards, known as plats, are being planted, but we are still far from the 7,000 acres that the Victorians had. And if they seem a little expensive when they first appear, then it is simply because they are handpicked.

As September starts to curl in on itself, the nuts ripen. By the end of the month, most of those for sale will have the rich brown shell we know from Christmas stockings and Beatrix Potter watercolors. Throughout the autumn, the nuts continue to ripen, the husks crisp up, and the starches in the kernel turn to sugar. The golden brown nuts are sweeter than when in the green, but their flavor is richer. Toast them a little in a dry, shallow pan and you will have the deepest flavor of all.

A hazelnut in the garden

A hazelnut grown on richly fertile soil is likely to produce leaves at the expense of nuts. I know mine did. Ideally they like a light topsoil with a well-drained subsoil. Most are not fussy about the acid levels and will grow happily in partial shade and woodland, but they are not keen on wet feet. The trees will grow from one end of the country to the other, but seem happiest in the warm orchards of Kent.

It is the female flower, like a tiny red star on the bare stems, that produces the nut and only if it is fertilized by the pollen from a male flower. The male flowers are the long yellow catkin and cannot pollinate the female flowers of the same variety. Most of their pollen is distributed by the wind, though I have probably done enough pollinating myself, walking through the woods with streaks of yellow pollen on my fleece. The male and female flowers are out at different times on different varieties, hence the need for each tree to grow near a pollinator of an alternative variety.

I failed to prune my trees, which resulted in them reaching a good fifteen feet in height. An act of sloth for which the squirrels were doubtless exceedingly grateful. Anyone who intends to pick their nuts green rather than waiting for the ripe ones to fall will need to keep their trees at six feet. Cut them back in late winter (a wonderfully bracing job on an icy day that leaves you curiously satisfied and ready for toasted muffins); this will encourage flower production. This is also the time to snip away any thin, whippy shoots from the base.

If you are mulching the garden and have a little to spare, then chuck a spade or two in the direction of your nut tree. It will thank you for your generosity.

Varieties

Kentish Cob So many qualities. The trees will stand up to any amount of cold, they crop abundantly and produce fat, juicy nuts possessing a good flavor. The trees are sometimes known as Longue d'Espagne. They will need to be pollinated by a nearby Gunslebert, Cosford, or Merveille de Bollwiller.
Cosford Cob A little less prolific than some, Cosford is not as widely grown as it could be. But this is a deeply flavored nut with a thin, easily crackable shell. You will need a neighboring Gunslebert or Kentish Cob to serve as pollinator. Unpruned, they can get to a great height. Mine did.
Purple Filbert The deep-maroon-leaved filbert, Purpurea, brought a wave of melancholy to the top end of the garden but I managed barely a handful of nuts, which is not unusual for what is essentially an ornamental variety. The sight of a cluster of nuts with their purple-edged husks is quite poetic.
Gunslebert You will need Cosford or a Kentish Cob to pollinate this prolific bush.
Merveille de Bollwiller Sometimes known as Hall's Giant, this producer of particularly large nuts needs another such as Cosford or Butler to pollinate it.
Butler This large and vigorous nut is a classic filbert. You will need Ennis, Cosford, or Merveille de Bollwiller as a pollinator.
Ennis There are claims that the flavor of this one is better than the rest, but it is hardly prolific and is rarely grown commercially. A nearby Butler will be necessary.
Jefferson* A hardy, late bloomer, the Jefferson produces abundant harvests of good-sized nuts with relatively little maintenance. Will pollinate with a nearby Yamhill.

Yamhill* A productive, disease-resistant small tree that yields pretty, round, sweet nuts. Pair with a Jefferson for pollination.

*Available from US sources.

Hazelnuts in the kitchen

We shouldn't let ourselves get bogged down with the differences between wild nuts, cobnuts, and filberts. They are all hazelnuts and once they have lost the greenness of youth they are interchangeable for cooking with. It seems only polite to bring some green nuts into the kitchen on August 20, the feast of St. Philibert of Jumièges (*c.* 608–684), for whom the filbert was named. In a good summer, the nuts should be just about ready to pick by then.

Once the green nuts have been celebrated (for themselves; in a salad with early apples and young spinach; or toasted, chopped, and rolled around goat cheese), then you can use them in any number of baking recipes, in both chopped and ground form. Whether you are using them ground to moisten the crumb of a cake, as you might ground almonds, or as nuggets in a chocolate chip cookie, the flavor will be richer if the nuts are toasted first. They will be less moist but their flavor will be deeper. To toast them, I usually scatter the shelled whole nuts in a frying pan, let them toast over medium heat, then tip them into a kitchen towel. Rub the nuts in the towel to loosen their skins, then pick the naked nuts out and return them to the pan. Inevitably there will be some skins that refuse to peel away, no matter. Toast the skinned nuts until pale gold, watching them carefully, as they burn in the blink of an eye. Grind them in a food processor.

Ready-ground nuts are a temptation but in my experience they have a mealy quality to them, and toasting them when they're already ground has a tendency to dry them out.

A pastry to which the ground nuts have been added makes a flattering crust for a blackberry or fig tart. One of the classic uses for hazelnuts in the kitchen is for a meringue that is to be filled with peaches or apricots. A recipe that screeches Cordon Bleu Cookery School as loudly as Constance Spry screams Coronation Chicken. The effect is sublime, but I like it even better when used with a coffee buttercream instead of fruit.

We shouldn't forget the beauty of a dish of whole cobnuts, complete with their parchment-crisp hulls. Nutcrackers and a glass of something rich and deliberately out of fashion, like an amber Madeira or a glass of bone-dry sherry, turn a handful of nuts into something rather special.

Hazelnuts and...

Chocolate In many ways a perfect marriage, this well-known partnership seems to work best with chocolate that is on the creamy side.

Cinnamon The most appropriate spice with these nuts. Add a dusting to hazelnut cookies or use it in the buttercream for a hazelnut cake.

Oranges Really juicy, sweet-sharp oranges appreciate the warm, crisp qualities of a scattering of toasted nuts. There are few finer ways to end a January lunch than slices of meticulously peeled blood oranges with a dressing of coarsely broken hazels and a flick of ground cinnamon.

Pork One of the few meats that work with this nut (pheasant and squab are other possible candidates). Use the nut in a stuffing to accompany a roast loin or added to a pan of pork steaks sizzling in butter and sage.

Coffee Try filling a hazelnut cake with coffee buttercream or trickling coffee icing over it.

Raspberry Austrian Linzertorte is at its best with warm hazelnut pastry filled with raspberry jam.

Pear Include young nuts in a salad of pear and spinach or scatter toasted nuts over slices of ripe pear.

* You can buy fat, juicy cobnuts by mail order. It is hardly the cheapest way to do it but the nuts are carefully sorted and you tend to get the pick of the crop.
* Hazelnuts are about 17 percent protein.
* Pick the nuts as soon as the green leaves show signs of turning gold, in an attempt to beat the squirrels.
* You can store cobnuts in their shells and husks until Christmas if you put them in an airtight can.
* Don't worry if the cobnuts you store in a can take on a slight musty smell. They are fine inside. However, once husked and shelled, they should be stored somewhere dark, airtight, and cool.
* Someone who tends a nut orchard is known as a "nutter."

Hazelnut and breadcrumb ice cream

A rather wonderful little recipe, this. It has an innate simplicity that appeals to me but it would be very good with the merest trickle of melted bitter chocolate.

enough for 4
soft, fresh breadcrumbs – 2 ounces (60g), about 1⅓ cups
light muscovado sugar – ⅓ cup, packed (80g)
golden baker's sugar – ⅓ cup (80g)
skinned hazelnuts – 3½ ounces (100g), ⅔ cup
heavy cream – 1 cup (250ml)
pourable yogurt – 1 cup (250ml)

Put the breadcrumbs on a baking sheet and scatter over the sugars. Blitz the hazelnuts to coarse gravel in a food processor or chop by hand, then add to the baking sheet. Place under a hot broiler and leave until the sugar, nuts, and crumbs are deep golden. You will need to keep your eye on the job, as the sugar can burn very easily. Leave to cool, then break up into small pieces.

Add the sugared crumbs to the cream and yogurt, pour into an ice cream machine, and churn until frozen. Put into a freezer-safe box and store in the freezer until needed. If you have no ice cream machine, you can freeze the mixture once you have mixed the cream and crumbs, stirring every hour or so until frozen.

Toasted hazelnut cookies

A chunky, rather crumbly cookie, best eaten warm.

makes 8 to 10
butter – ¾ cup (170g)
golden baker's sugar – ½ cup (100g)
skinned hazelnuts – 2 ounces (60g), ⅓ cup
ground almonds – ⅓ cup (40g)
all-purpose flour – generous 1½ cups (200g)
confectioners' sugar

Preheat the oven to 325°F (160°C). Cream the butter and sugar together until light and fluffy (I recommend a stand mixer with a paddle attachment). Toast the hazelnuts in a dry pan until golden, then reduce them to a coarse powder in a food processor and mix them with the ground almonds. Add the nuts and flour to the butter and sugar mixture and stir until thoroughly mixed. I sometimes knead the mixture a little to mix it fully.

Take generously heaping tablespoons of the mixture and shape them into large, unruly balls. Place them on a nonstick baking sheet and bake for twenty-five minutes, until the cookies are barely colored. The insides should be slightly soft. Remove from the oven and leave to cool for five minutes before attempting to lift them from the tray with a thin spatula. Roll them in confectioners' sugar. Eat the cookies slightly warm, or certainly within twenty-four hours.

Hazelnut cookies

Sweet, soft, and tender, these fragile cookies are made with both hazelnuts and nut butter, which is available from health-food shops, near the peanut butter. Although they are very much meant to be eaten the day they are made, they will keep for a few days in an airtight container. They are extraordinary with vanilla ice cream. Serve them on the side, or maybe crumble them over the top.

makes about 12
butter, at room temperature – 7 tablespoons (100g)
light muscovado sugar – 3 packed tablespoons (50g)
golden baker's sugar – ¼ cup (50g)
toasted hazelnuts – 2 ounces (60g), ⅓ cup
hazelnut butter – a generous ⅓ cup (100g)
all-purpose flour – ¾ cup plus 1 tablespoon (100g)
baking soda – ½ teaspoon
baking powder – ½ teaspoon

Preheat the oven to 375°F (190°C). Cut the butter into chunks and put it in the bowl of a stand mixer. Add the sugars and beat for several minutes at moderate speed until very pale and smooth. Coarsely chop the toasted hazelnuts. Mix in the nut butter and most of the nuts.

Mix the flour, baking soda, and baking powder and stir gently into the butter and sugar mixture to form a soft dough. Spoon heaping tablespoons of the dough onto a nonstick baking sheet lined with parchment paper (you can push them down a bit with a fork if you like, but the chunkier they are the more moist they will be). Scatter over the remaining hazelnuts and bake for twelve to fourteen minutes, until the cookies are pale gold and just dry on top. Inside, they should be slightly moist. Remove them from the oven and let them cool slightly before transferring them to a cooling rack (you won't be able to move them when they are warm).

Soft hazelnut chocolate cookies

Softly textured, fragile cookies. Lightly crisp outside, soft inside.

makes 9 large cookies
dark chocolate, at least 70 percent cocoa solids – 7 ounces (200g)
butter – 5 tablespoons (75g)
light muscovado sugar – 1 cup, packed (225g)
eggs – 2
vanilla extract
skinned hazelnuts – 2 ounces (50g), ⅓ cup
self-rising flour – 1¼ cups (150g)

Preheat the oven to 350°F (180°C). Snap the chocolate into pieces and put them in a small heatproof china or glass bowl. Place the bowl over a small pan of simmering water, with the bottom of the bowl not quite touching the water. Allow the chocolate to melt. Don't be tempted to stir other than to occasionally push any unmelted chocolate down into the liquid chocolate to encourage it to melt. Turn off the heat as soon as the chocolate has melted.

Beat the butter and sugar together in a stand mixer until smooth and creamy. Break the eggs into a small bowl or pitcher with a drop or two of vanilla extract, whisk them just enough to break them up, then add gradually to the butter and sugar, beating constantly. It is worth scraping down the sides of the bowl with a rubber spatula from time to time to ensure a thorough mixing. Add the melted chocolate.

Toast the hazelnuts in a shallow pan until golden, shaking regularly so they color evenly. Grind the nuts coarsely to the texture of gravel, then remove half and continue grinding the other half until it resembles fine breadcrumbs. Add the flour and both textures of nut to the mixture. Stop beating as soon as everything is combined.

Place large heaping tablespoons of the mixture on a baking sheet lined with parchment paper. You should get nine large cookies. The mixture is fine to wait for a few minutes if you are doing them in two batches. Don't be tempted to flatten the cookies, they will do so in the oven anyway.

Bake for ten minutes. The cookies will have spread and be very soft to the touch. Remove them from the oven and set aside to cool a little. As soon as they are cool enough to move without breaking, slide a thin spatula underneath and carefully lift them to a cooling rack. They will keep in good condition in an airtight container for a few days.

A cake of roasted hazelnuts, muscovado, and coffee

The point of introducing hazelnuts into a cake is often twofold: the oil in the ground nuts will help to keep the cake moist, while the toasted nuts will add much in terms of flavor. A nutty cake is something for an autumn afternoon, and even more so once the leaves have fallen. Eat it to the scent of wood smoke.

> *enough for 8 to 10*
> butter – 1 cup plus 2 tablespoons (250g), at room temperature
> golden baker's sugar – ⅔ cup (125g)
> light muscovado sugar – ½ cup, packed (125g)
> shelled hazelnuts – 7 ounces (200g), 1⅓ cups
> eggs – 3
> self-rising flour – ½ cup (65g)
>
> **for the coffee icing (optional)**
> confectioners' sugar – 2 cups (250g)
> espresso – 1 to 2 tablespoons

Cut the butter into small pieces and beat together with the baker's and muscovado sugars until light and fluffy. Even with a stand mixer, this will take quite a while—you want to end up with a mixture that is smooth and latte colored.

While the sugar and butter are creaming, preheat the oven to 325°F (160°C) and line the bottom of a deep 8½-inch (22 to 23cm) cake pan with parchment paper. Tip the nuts into a dry frying pan and toast over medium heat until golden and lightly flecked with brown on all sides. Grind half of them to a fine powder and the other half rather less so, so they retain a certain nubbly quality, like very fine gravel.

Break the eggs into a small bowl and beat them lightly with a fork, then introduce them a little at a time to the creamed butter and sugar, beating thoroughly between each addition. Tip in both batches of ground hazelnuts and mix lightly.

Gently add the flour to the creamed mixture, incorporating it thoroughly but carefully, then scrape into the lined cake pan using a rubber spatula. Smooth the top gently so that it doesn't peak during cooking. Bake for forty-five to fifty minutes, covering the top lightly with foil for the last ten. Remove from the oven and leave to settle for fifteen minutes or so before turning out onto a cooling rack. Gently peel away the paper from the bottom and leave the cake to cool. Mix the confectioners' sugar and coffee together until smooth, then drizzle over the cake and leave for an hour or so to set.

Praline tiramisu

One Sunday in late autumn, the day after a serious storm that had wrecked my television aerial and blown all the ripe medlars off the tree, I felt the need to drown my sorrows in dessert. A classic tiramisu, like trifle, with its layers of soft, damp sponge cake and alcoholic creaminess, is something I tend to think of as the food of angels. The hazelnut liqueur is only a suggestion. The idea of incorporating a hazelnut praline came out of the blue.

enough for 6

for the praline
skinned hazelnuts – 7 ounces (200g), 1⅓ cups
superfine sugar – ½ cup (100g)

for the sponge layer
ladyfingers – 7 ounces (200g)
hot espresso coffee – ⅔ cup (150ml)
Frangelico hazelnut liqueur – 4 tablespoons

for the mascarpone cream layer
large eggs – 3, separated
superfine sugar – ¼ cup (50g)
mascarpone cheese – 1 pound (500g)
Frangelico hazelnut liqueur – 3 tablespoons

Put the skinned hazelnuts in a nonstick frying pan and let them toast gently over medium heat until they are pale gold. Toss the pan occasionally and keep a close eye on them. Lightly oil a nonstick baking sheet.

Scatter the sugar over the nuts, lower the heat, and let it melt. Do not stir. Just watch the sugar melt and become pale gold in color. Gently move the hazelnuts occasionally with a spoon to check the progress of the sugar, but avoid too much movement in the pan. When the caramel is deep golden (and well before it starts to smoke), stir the nuts gently and tip them onto the oiled tray. Leave to cool.

Put the ladyfingers in a large serving dish, preferably in one tight layer, squeezing them in to fill the gaps wherever you can. Pour over the coffee and, if you are using it, the hazelnut liqueur.

Make the mascarpone layer by creaming the egg yolks and sugar together until they are pale, then mixing in the mascarpone and, if you are using it, the hazelnut liqueur. Beat the egg whites until stiff and fluffy, then fold them into the mixture.

Remove slightly less than half of the sugared hazelnuts from the baking sheet and blitz them in a food processor until they look like coarse crumbs.

Fold them into the mascarpone mixture, then tip it on top of the coffee-soaked ladyfingers. Smooth the top, cover with plastic wrap, and refrigerate for a good five hours, preferably overnight.

Set the remaining sugared hazelnuts aside. About an hour before you want to eat the dessert, roughly crush the nuts—a texture akin to coarse gravel is about right—and scatter them over the top.

Chocolate praline truffle cake

A cake for serious chocolate fans only—I serve this in extremely thin slices. It needs something to offset its extraordinary richness. Raspberries work beautifully, as do poached pears.

enough for 10 to 12

for the praline
skinned hazelnuts – 3½ ounces (100g), ⅔ cup
superfine sugar – ⅓ cup (80g)

for the truffle
dark chocolate, about 70 percent cocoa solids – 12 ounces (350g)
heavy cream – ¾ cup (170ml)
butter – 6 tablespoons (85g)
a little cognac, rum, or Frangelico hazelnut liqueur

Line an 8 by 4-inch (20 by 10cm) loaf pan with parchment paper or plastic wrap.

Make the praline. Put the nuts in a shallow pan and toast over medium heat until they are fragrant and a deep, golden brown (if your hazelnuts still have their brown skins on, rub them vigorously in a kitchen towel until the skins flake off, then toast the nuts once more).

Put the sugar in a small, heavy-bottomed saucepan (it will burn in a thin one), place over low to medium heat, and allow it to melt and slowly turn toffee colored. This is not the time to be distracted. An occasional stir or shake is useful, but too much will prevent it from melting and cause the caramel to crystallize. Stir in the toasted nuts, leaving them to cook in the caramel for one minute. Lightly oil a baking sheet. You can use peanut oil but I prefer hazelnut oil if there is some around. Tip the praline mixture onto the tray and leave to cool. Should any of the caramel have stuck stubbornly to the pan, it can be removed with a little boiling water.

To make the truffle mixture, snap the chocolate into pieces and melt in a bowl resting on top of a pan of simmering water. The bottom of the bowl should not be low enough to touch the water. Stir just once or twice, no more. As soon as the chocolate has melted, switch off the heat. Gently stir in 2 tablespoons of hot water and leave be.

Scrape the cold praline off the baking sheet, put it in a plastic bag, and bash with a rolling pin. You could use a food processor if you prefer, but take care not to crush it too finely. It should be the size of coarse gravel rather than fine grit. Uneven-sized lumps add to the interest.

Whip the cream until it will stand in soft folds rather than stiff peaks. Beat the butter with a wooden spoon until soft and light, then stir into the melted chocolate until the butter is melted. Fold in the crushed praline and the cream. Now is the time to add the cognac, rum, or Frangelico if you are using it. Spoon the mixture into the lined pan and smooth flat. Leave overnight in the fridge to set (if you are impatient, you can probably get away with three or four hours).

When the cake has set, slide a warm knife down the sides of the pan and unmold onto a serving dish. Serve in thin slices, with raspberries or, even better, a dish of poached pears.

Chocolate chip hazelnut cake with chocolate cinnamon buttercream

I like birthday cake. I love making them and, if truth be told, I rather enjoy receiving them too. This is my first choice for such an occasion, a nutty sponge cake rich with chocolate nibs and a dark chocolate and cinnamon frosting. I serve it in appropriately thin slices.

enough for 10 to 12
butter – 1 cup plus 2 tablespoons (250g)
golden baker's sugar – 1¼ cups (250g)
shelled hazelnuts – 3 ounces (75g), a generous ½ cup
dark chocolate – 4 ounces (120g)
large eggs – 4
self-rising flour – 1 cup (125g)
ground cinnamon – ½ teaspoon
strong espresso – 4 teaspoons

for the spiced chocolate buttercream
dark chocolate, 70 percent cocoa solids – 8 ounces (250g)
butter – ½ cup (125g)
ground cinnamon – a knifepoint

Preheat the oven to 350°F (180°C). Line the bottom of an 8-inch (20 to 21cm) deep springform cake pan with parchment paper. Cut the butter into small chunks and put it with the sugar into the bowl of an electric mixer, then beat until white and fluffy. Toast the hazelnuts in a dry pan over medium heat, then rub them in a kitchen towel until most of the skins have flaked off. There is really no need to be too pernickety about this, you just want most of the skins removed. Grind the nuts to a coarse powder, less fine than ground almonds but finer than they would be if you chopped them by hand. Chop the chocolate into what looks like coarse gravel.

Break the eggs into a small bowl and beat them gently. Slowly add them to the butter and sugar mixture, beating all the time—it may curdle slightly but it doesn't matter. Stop the machine. Tip in half the ground nuts and half the flour, beat briefly and at a slow speed, stop the machine again, then add the rest, together with the chopped chocolate and cinnamon, and mix briefly. Gently fold in the espresso, taking care not to knock the air from the mixture, then scoop into the lined cake pan. Smooth the top and bake for thirty-five to forty-five minutes, covering the cake with foil for the last ten minutes if it is coloring too quickly. Remove the cake from the oven and test with a skewer—you want it to come out moist but clean, without any uncooked cake batter clinging to it. Leave the cake to cool a little in its pan before turning out onto a cooling rack and peeling off the paper from its bottom.

To make the chocolate buttercream, snap the chocolate into small pieces and let it melt in a small bowl balanced over a pan of simmering water (the water should not touch the bottom of the bowl). Leave to melt, with little or no stirring, then add the butter, cut into small pieces, and the spice. Stir until the butter has melted. Leave to cool until the mixture is thick enough to spread. (I sometimes impatiently put mine in the fridge for about fifteen minutes.) Spread the chocolate cream over the top of the cake, decorate as the whim takes you, and leave for an hour or so before cutting.

Peaches
and nectarines

There is a solitary peach on my desk, picked up at the local farmers' market. Diminutive compared to the Italian- and French-grown varieties, a little flat on one side where it has snuggled against a sibling on the twig. Grown on a tree older than its owner, its skin is covered in fine gray down. And that for me is the point of the peach and why I hold its qualities above those of the nectarine— the feel of the peach's soft fuzz on first my upper and then my lower lip, the way the skin puckers as I bite, a teasing prelude to the sweet flesh that will follow. And all this before the juice—sweet, cool, sensuous—even touches my tongue.

When a peach is at its most sublime, it needs a plate to catch the juice, though I invariably forget. Or is it that I can never quite believe I will need one? Either way, it is usually followed by that embarrassing little noise that comes from the corner of your mouth as you try to catch the escaping trickle of juice.

For all its intimate pleasure, the skin that covers those blood-red cheeks is usually removed after cooking, when it is easy to slide off with your thumb, revealing the golden flesh beneath. Removing it before cooking is an almost impossible task.

The peach and the bald, bright nectarine are available in our shops all year, imported from Spain, Italy, and France in summer and Egypt, the United States, or South Africa during winter. The farther they travel, the more disappointing they generally are. There is something depressing about these fruits in winter, pointless even. I usually wait until early summer for my first taste.

Thousands of trees fruit regularly in this country too, but the crop rarely makes it to market. Most ripen in private gardens and allotments in too small a quantity to be offered for sale. Local farmers' markets have them sometimes, in varying stages of quality, in July, August, and early September. We grew them in our Worcestershire garden when I was a child, at the top of the little orchard, the long, gray branches trained along the wall that separated us from the damp buttercup meadow beyond. The tree got the dreaded leaf curl, of course—they always did in those days, before new, disease-resistant varieties were developed and everyone learned to protect the vulnerable early buds with row cover fabric.

The single factor that deems a peach or nectarine worth eating is not so much its variety or color or even where it is grown, but its ripeness. An unripe peach is crunchy, dry, and flavorless. An unripe nectarine is barely distinguishable from munching a rubber ball. Few fruits are quite so reliant on "the moment" as these two. We must catch them where and when we can.

It is rare to find a perfectly ripe peach in the store, with good reason. A peach that is truly ready to eat is too fragile to get home without bruising. The supermarket "ripe and ready to eat" sticker is only partly true (some things we must learn the hard way). What it means is that the fruit within is indeed edible, but far from being at the moment of perfection. To reach that point, the fruit will need some tender, loving care from us. Take your nectarines and peaches home, remove the plastic so they don't sweat, but leave them in the soft, protective cradle the supermarkets have so sensibly provided us with. Keep the fruits in a warm room, turning them each morning until they are ready (I do it while I am waiting for my first espresso of the day to drip through, as I do with Indian mangoes in June or pears at Christmas).

Check their progress daily. Poking them with your thumb will almost certainly lead to disaster. There are few more easily damaged fruits. Picking them up, cradling them in the palm of your cupped hand, and sniffing them is a more reliable and respectful test. Peaches tend to announce their ripeness with a scent that is almost roselike. The white varieties often seem even more fragrant, their perfume a Jean-Baptiste Grenouille–like blend of raspberries, rose, and honey. Though of course, that could just be my imagination.

Prunus persica is native to China. The flowers are pink or occasionally pink and white and appear in early spring, before the frosts are over. (Stay in a Japanese hotel, or *ryokan*, in February and March and you may find sprigs of tight peach blossom on display.) This goes some way toward explaining how precious a ripe peach is when grown in this climate. They need to be in the hands of someone who will rush out at the first hint of frost and wrap the tree in row cover fabric. In France, I have seen farmers light fires at the end of the rows to stop entire orchards being decimated by a late and sudden frost. None of which should put us off planting a tree—they survive well enough.

The name peach may come from the belief that the fruit originally came from Persia, now Iran (it was the Persians who brought the peach to the attention of the Romans and from them to us). Yellow peaches, depending on their variety, can have a pit that is either loose or impossible to extricate without mashing the flesh. Neatly halving a ripe clingstone peach is one of those kitchen tasks that defeats me. These latter "clingstones" are generally used for canning, although a few have ended up, usually as a squashed mess, on my cutting boards. Use in a salsa.

The peach promises much. Cradled in tissue paper or packed into cartons, it tempts as few other fruits can. But the peach can disappoint, so much so that for a while I stopped buying them, burned one time too many by those that failed to ripen.

A single fruit was to change everything. I bought my first white peach out of curiosity, intrigued by its floral scent and gentle color and mesmerized by its beauty on a simple jade-green plate. It was that first white-fleshed peach that I held against my face, felt its down brush against my lips, breathed in its rose water scent. This was the fruit that made me fall in love with the peach again. This is the variety so beloved of Japan and China, and which, on a good day, stands second only to the Alphonso mango as the fruit I hold in the highest esteem.

The nectarine has become more popular of late. It has a smooth "plum skin," removing much of the peach's quality even before we are through the threshold. The nectarine's appearance is not due to any crossbreeding with a variety of plum but to a recessive gene, and can sometimes appear unexpectedly as a "sport" of a fuzzy peach. So, your peach tree may suddenly send out seedlings that produce fruit as bald as a coot. The skin of a nectarine, though its sunset hues appear stronger than those of the peach, is in fact no different. It is the fine gray down that gives the peach a more sophisticated appearance.

The nectarine is a newer fruit altogether, and where the peach is mentioned in Chinese literature from 10 BC, its smooth mate is first noted around the early seventeenth century. The two fruits share a flavor. You would be hard-pressed to tell the difference between them once they are cooked.

In China the peach has long been held as a symbol for immortality. The Jade Emperor and his mother fed them to the gods to ensure their eternal presence. I eat them all summer, sometimes with a piece of torn mozzarella or even a wedge of Roquefort—the salty character of the latter bringing out the sweetness of the juice.

I like the fact that the pit of the peach contains a little cyanide, though not as much as its sister, the bitter almond. The far-off hint of danger seems only to add to the peach's exotic and sensual qualities.

A peach in the garden

I have known three or four peach trees over the years. Only one suffered with the dreaded leaf curl that tends to put off even the most enthusiastic gardeners. All were trained against walls, their branches bound to wires or strings nailed into the wall, rather than grown as an orchard tree. Every one of them fruited, albeit intermittently, causing much excitement. Perfectly edible as they were, none quite reached the rich, juice-soaked heights of those grown in France and Italy.

Last year I picked up quite a few grown here. Not quite the perfect looking specimens I buy from the supermarket, but their flavor was impressive. The rash of pockmarks on their skins was the only telltale sign that they had not come from a warmer place. The juice and flesh were everything you expect of a peach.

There is no doubt that the trees enjoy our warming climate, but they still need to be watched carefully at blossom time and covered with row cover fabric if necessary. Most of my peach-growing friends say they often forget about this, and regularly lose a few buds to the frost.

If I ever find myself with a larger garden, then a peach will be planted, maybe even two. I will dig them in somewhere where they have as much protection as possible, a south- or southwest-facing wall, perhaps close to the house. The *Prunus* genus loves rich soil. I recently saw a stunning tree on an estate where they feed the soil annually with organic matter. The tree was in hog heaven.

In many ways the peach tree is perfect for the smaller urban garden. They can be bought ready trained into a fan shape so you are spared the intimidating task of early pruning; rarely grow very large (the rootstock onto which they are grafted prevents this); and they are self fertile too, so don't need a mate to produce fruit. You can even grow them successfully in pots, though I have only seen those growing in conservatories, not outside. Get your new tree in the ground in the autumn, preferably in deep, rich soil, and water it copiously in its early growing stages.

Peach blossom appears early, often in March, long before the insects necessary for pollination are around. My father used a paintbrush to transfer pollen from one piece of blossom to the next. Others swear by a rabbit's tail. He very gently took pollen from the stamens of one pink blossom on his brush, then gently brushed them onto another. It was something he looked forward to enormously, one of the more intimate moments of an old gardener's life.

However tempting it is to leave all the young fruit in place, a bit of careful thinning, removing any small, crowded fruits, will encourage larger peaches. The generally accepted rule is a final thinning to leave 7 inches (18cm) or so between fruits, but none of the proud growers I have spoken to can bring themselves to be quite that ruthless. It's not like thinning radishes,

Peaches

340

where you still eat the unlucky ones whose lives are cut short. Try to keep the birds off. Toward the day of harvest, increase the supply of water.

Ideally, we should let our fruit ripen on the tree, but with that comes the risk of something pinching the prized fruit at its peak. It happens with my strawberries and apples, so it is an idea to harvest just before the fruits ripen and bring them on using a warm indoor windowsill.

Varieties

Peaches

Avalon A new variety with a high resistance to leaf curl. I have only eaten commercially grown fruits of this yellow-fleshed variety, but was impressed with their flavor and juice.

Babcock* White-fleshed, juicy fruits with minimal fuzz and sweet, aromatic, low-acid flavor.

Blood Peach I would dearly like to grow this dark-fleshed peach with its streaks of ruby, like a blood orange. Unfortunately, you need a greenhouse for this one. Reads Nursery, from where I have bought several fruit trees over the years, says that this is "collector's" fruit.

Dixired* Deep-colored skin with rich, yellow flesh. The pits do cling to the flesh.

Duke of York* Well-known, heavy-cropping variety that ripens a little earlier than most. Give it a warm, south-facing wall and by all accounts it should do well.

Dymond An old variety from the 1800s. Rarely colors well, being on the green side, but with a fine flavor and soft, white flesh.

Early Alexander Small to medium fruit. One from the Rivers Nursery that brought us so many excellent plums. Known for its juice.

Kestrel A long-established cross between the Early Rivers nectarine and Hales Early Peach. Dark skinned and as sweet as they come.

Peregrine* Reliable white-fleshed peach of great repute. In the north of the country it will need a greenhouse, though it does well outside in the south.

Red Wing Named for its red skin without the usual yellow or white flashes, the fruits are almost completely dark red. Suits a cooler climate.

Rochester A dependable, late-flowering variety. Needs protection from heavy rains during winter.

Saturn* Fashionable, flat-topped fruit that can disappoint when purchased commercially. Its pale flesh is sweeter and more interesting when allowed to ripen on the tree.

Nectarines

Lord Napier A popular old variety of deep color and dependable white-fleshed fruit.

Early Gem Likes a warm wall, but can produce deep-colored fruits with well-flavored yellow flesh.

Firegold Orange skin, yellow flesh. I have yet to taste this one.

Fantasia* Larger fruits than is usual, with yellow flesh. Should be ripe by mid-August.

Mericrest* Performs well in cooler climes. Large fruits with red skin, yellow flesh, and pleasantly tangy flavor.

Snow Queen* A late, white-fleshed variety that is considered to be the best flavored of the nectarines.

*Available from US sources.

A peach in the kitchen

I rarely cook a peach. They are seen in my kitchen nestling next to the crisp skin of a roast chicken salad or perhaps cold ham or hot roast guinea fowl; stuffed with mascarpone or ricotta or amaretti; or simply nudging a few slices of Parma ham and a fistful of spiky-leaved arugula. I will broil them, stuffed with cream cheese and glazed with molten sugar, bake them with almonds and honey, and poach them with honey and a drop of rose water. Occasionally (very occasionally), I will tuck them into the cream filling of a meringue with passion fruit or raspberries or add them to a salad of wine-dark cherries.

The idea of cooking a peach under a pastry crust can work, though its sweetness can cloy. Better, to my mind at least, eaten cold with a jug of unpasteurized cream. Hot, it can tempt with a slowly melting ball of vanilla ice cream, mostly because of the contrast of temperatures between the sugary crust and the freezer-cold ice cream.

Lacking the acidity present in even the ripest apricot, peaches and nectarines are difficult to marry with savory ingredients. As a knife-sharp salsa with roast duck; in a cilantro-speckled couscous; layered in a salad of white crabmeat maybe. But generally, I keep my peaches and nectarines as they are, fragile globes of sweet flesh and sticky juice.

Peaches and...

Pork and bacon Roast pork, particularly when spices are involved, and salty smoked bacon bring out the sweetness of the peaches.

Cream Despite the roll-off-the-tongue term "peaches 'n' cream," I have never felt the two do each other many favors. Two sweet, mild things stirred together do not make for interesting eating. A fool or an ice cream made with the fruit is always bland. Warm, a peach pie can be good with ice cream or very softly whipped cream.

Lemon juice Even the smallest squeeze of citrus will lift the flavor of a peach to great heights. I tend to use lemon rather than vinegar in salads where peaches make an appearance.

Honey A little in a dressing for a fresh peach and Little Gem lettuce salad can be a good thing, as can a drizzle of liquid honey over baked peaches.

Mozzarella Soft, milky cheeses make nice bedfellows for a ripe peach.

Almonds Use a frangipane base for an open peach tart; a few ground almonds in the pastry for a peach shortcake; scatter chopped almonds over a dish of peaches and honey before baking.

Duck Crisply roasted duck and a gravy made from the pan juices, sliced peaches, and a drop of Grand Marnier can certainly be worth the trouble.

Blue cheese All the blue cheeses such as Roquefort, Beenleigh Blue, Gorgonzola, and Fourme d'Ambert go well with excessively ripe peaches.

Fresh soft cheeses Ones such as caprini freschi, the sort that come in a shallow paper wrapper, are heavenly with nectarines that are heavy with juice.

Basil The slight peppery heat of sun-baked basil leaves is extraordinary with a fridge-cold, juicy peach.

Mint Chopped mint added to a lemon juice dressing will make a ripe peach really sing.

* When ripening peaches at home, make sure they don't touch one another. They will mold where they butt up against one another.

* Peaches are particularly low in pectin. They make an extraordinarily beautiful preserve, soft and difficult to keep on your toast. A good shot of lemon juice is essential if the jam is to thicken even slightly.

* Few will ripen before August in our climate, though on a good warm wall in a clement season, an established tree should give us something in late July.

* Early peaches tend to be of the clingstone variety and the flesh can be the very devil to get off the pit in one piece. Later in the season you can easily halve a peach with a knife and cleanly twist one half away from the other.

* Adding a peach pit or two to a dish of poached peaches may enhance the flavor.

* Nectarines can be substituted for peaches in all of the recipes that follow.

A salad of peaches, mozzarella, and basil

enough for 4
splendidly ripe peaches – 4
Parma ham – 16 thin slices
mozzarella – 2 large balls
salad leaves – 4 handfuls

for the dressing
white or tarragon wine vinegar – a tablespoon
olive oil – 4 tablespoons
crème fraîche – 2 tablespoons
basil leaves – about 20

Slice the peaches in half, pull out the pits, and slice each half into three. Divide the Parma ham among four plates, tear the balls of mozzarella in half, and place a half on each plate.

Make the dressing by putting the vinegar in a small bowl and stirring in a pinch of sea salt. Gently beat in the olive oil and crème fraîche to give a creamy dressing. Tear the basil leaves and stir them in, then season with coarsely ground black pepper. Toss the salad leaves in the dressing and add to the plates, tuck in the peaches, and serve.

A mint and peach tabbouleh

enough for 4
bulgur – 5 ounces (150g)
slim green onions – 6
ripe peaches – 4
a hot red chile
mint – 6 bushy sprigs
cilantro leaves – 2 large handfuls
parsley leaves– 2 large handfuls
juice of a lemon
olive oil – 2 tablespoons

Pour the bulgur into a bowl and just cover with boiling water, then set aside.

Cut the green onions into small pieces and put them in a mixing bowl. Slice the peaches in half, remove their pits and cut the flesh into small dice, then add to the onions. Seed and finely chop the chile, then coarsely chop the mint, cilantro, and parsley and add to the onions. Add the juice of the lemon, the olive oil, and a good grinding of salt and black pepper.

Fluff the bulgur up with a fork. Crumble into the peaches and onions, then serve.

A salad of chicken, mint, and peaches

Warm roast chicken and its golden skin, ripe peaches, the sting of watercress, chiles, and basil. A light lunch, crisp, bright, invigorating. And one of the very few times I use peppers raw.

enough for 4, as a light main course
chicken breasts – 1⅓ pounds (600g), bone in, skin on
a little olive oil
mint leaves – a large handful
basil leaves – about 30
watercress – 4 handfuls
red or orange bell peppers – 2
peaches – 4

for the dressing
lime juice – 3 tablespoons
fish sauce – 3 tablespoons
palm or superfine sugar – 2 teaspoons
small, hot red chiles – 2
green onions – 4

Preheat the oven to 400°F (200°C). Put the chicken breasts in a small roasting pan, rub with olive oil, and season generously with salt and ground black pepper. Roast for twenty minutes, until golden and lightly cooked right through. Remove from the oven and leave to rest for ten minutes.

Make the dressing: put the lime juice and fish sauce in a small bowl and stir in the sugar. Finely chop the chiles and add to the bowl. Trim and finely chop the green onions, add them to the dressing, and set aside.

Keep the mint and basil leaves whole. Put them in a bowl with the watercress, minus its toughest stems. Halve the peppers, remove and discard the seeds, then slice the flesh into long, very fine strips. Slice the peaches in half, remove the pits, and slice the peaches into thick pieces. Add to the herbs with the peppers.

Shred the chicken and its crisp skin finely. Toss all of the ingredients together with the dressing, leave for five minutes, then serve.

Crisp pork belly, sweet peach salsa

Ask your butcher to score the skin finely for this, as the crackling is essential. The first brief roasting at the higher temperature sets the crackling on the route to crispness. These ribs are not sweet and sticky like the ones in *The Kitchen Diaries*, but lightly crisp and lip tingling.

enough for 4
pork belly – 2 to 3 pounds (1 to 1.5kg), boned, skin intact and finely scored

for the rub
garlic – 3 cloves
light soy sauce – 2 tablespoons
peanut oil – a tablespoon
salt – 2 teaspoons
dried chile flakes – half a teaspoon
Chinese five-spice powder – a slightly heaping teaspoon

for the peach salsa
green onions – 2
a small red chile
peaches – 3
cherry tomatoes – 8
cilantro – a small bunch
juice of 2 limes
olive oil – 3 tablespoons

Put the pork in a china or glass dish. Peel and crush the garlic to a paste, stirring in the soy, oil, salt, chile flakes, and five-spice powder. Spread this paste over the skin and underside of the pork and leave it to marinate for a good four hours, if not overnight.

Preheat the oven to 425°F (220°C). Place the pork in a roasting pan, then cook, skin-side up, for about twenty minutes. Lower the heat to 400°F (200°C) and continue cooking for a further forty to fifty minutes, until the skin is dark and crisp. Leave to rest for ten minutes before carving.

Make the salsa. Trim and finely chop the green onions. Finely chop the chile. Peel, pit, and finely chop the peaches and tomatoes and chop the cilantro. Toss gently, then dress with the lime juice and olive oil. Serve the pork with the salsa.

Peaches with lemon verbena

Something to serve alongside cups of green tea in the afternoon. You can use dried verbena leaves too, but they lack a little of the magic of the fresh herb.

serves 3
small peaches – 6
water – 1 cup (250ml)
lemon verbena – 10 large leaves
sugar – 3 tablespoons

Put the peaches in a small saucepan with the water, verbena leaves, and sugar and bring to a boil. Turn the heat down and leave to simmer for seven to ten minutes, until the peaches are soft. Leave to cool, then chill thoroughly before serving.

Peaches with kaffir lime leaves and lemongrass

A refreshing recipe for the dog days of summer.

enough for 4
sugar – 1½ cups (300g)
water – 2½ cups (600ml)
kaffir lime leaves – 6
a stalk of lemongrass
peaches – 4

Put the sugar and water in a saucepan and bring to a boil. Once the sugar has dissolved, turn down the heat so that the syrup is quietly simmering and add the lime leaves, crushing them slightly as you go. Bash the lemongrass so that the stalk splits into fibers, then add it to the syrup.

Lower the peaches, their skins intact, into the syrup. Let them poach to total tenderness—the point of a small knife or skewer should glide effortlessly into the flesh. Turn off the heat and let the fruit cool in the syrup.

Slide the skin off the peaches with your thumbs, halve and pit the fruit carefully, and place in a shallow dish. Strain the syrup through a sieve and pour over the fruit, then chill until ready to serve.

Baked peaches with maple syrup and vanilla

Like honey, maple syrup is a more interesting way to sweeten a peach than sugar, adding subtle notes of walnuts and caramel.

enough for 4
ripe peaches – 4
maple syrup – 4 tablespoons
vanilla seeds – a pinch (the contents of a single pod)
juice of a lime

Preheat the oven to 400°F (200°C). Wipe the peaches and slice them in half. Discard the pits and place the fruit, cut side up, in a shallow baking dish.

Put the maple syrup in a bowl with the vanilla seeds and the lime juice. Mix well, then pour over the peaches. Bake for approximately thirty-five minutes, until the peaches are thoroughly tender. It is a good idea to baste the fruit from time to time as it cooks.

Baked peaches with an almond crust

This rough, buttery almond crust works with nectarines and apricots too.
Just scatter it over the halved and pitted fruit before baking. Good though
this is on its own, I can see every reason for cream here.

enough for 4
ripe peaches or nectarines – 4
almonds – 2 ounces (50g), ⅓ cup
golden baker's sugar – ¼ cup (50g)
butter – 3 tablespoons (45g)

Preheat the oven to 350°F (180°C). Wipe the peaches or nectarines and cut
them in half. Tug out the pits, then place the halved fruits cut side up in a
shallow baking dish.

Put the almonds in a food processor—there is no need to skin them
first—and blitz them to a coarse texture. They should be somewhere
between gravel and traditional ground almonds (you just want them to
lend a crunch to the soft fruit). Add the sugar and butter and briefly
continue to mix.

Spoon the almond mixture on top of the peaches and bake for forty-
five to fifty minutes, until the fruit is meltingly soft and the top is crisp. An
occasional basting with the buttery juices in the dish can only help.

Grilled peaches, mascarpone vanilla cream

Stone fruits grill well. Whether you use peaches or nectarines—or, later in the year, plums—the fruit needs to be really ripe in order to soften. Unripe fruit will simply dry out. It is probably worth making sure the bars of the grill have no savory residue on them.

enough for 4
peaches – 4
lemon juice

for the cream
eggs – 2, separated
superfine sugar – 2 slightly heaping tablespoons
mascarpone – 8 ounces (250g)
a knifepoint of vanilla seeds or a few drops of vanilla extract
a little grated orange zest

Whisk the egg yolks and sugar until they are pale and creamy in color. Add the mascarpone and beat until mixed, but take care not to overmix. Beat the egg whites until stiff and fold in gently, together with the vanilla and orange zest. Leave to firm up a little in the fridge.

Cut the peaches in half and twist gently to separate the halves, then tug out the pits. Rub them with lemon juice and put them cut side down on the bars of a preheated grill. Leave to soften, turning them once. They will take a good ten minutes or so—a bit longer than you might expect. When they are hot and thoroughly tender, serve them with the mascarpone cream.

Peaches with rose petals

Fried zucchini blossoms and elderflower jelly aside, I have barely begun to explore the virtues of flowers in cooking. Scatter a fistful of dill flowers on cooked sea bass; fold dandelions into the egg-and-milk batter for pancakes; toss vermilion nasturtium petals into a spinach salad, and you begin to get their visual worth. Let a handful of rose petals fall onto a peach salad and your heart will melt.

A fragrant and very gentle dessert here—one to follow a salmon and cucumber salad on a calm summer day.

enough for 4
large, ripe peaches – 4
water – 4 cups (a liter)
elderflower cordial – 3 tablespoons
sugar, to taste
rose petals, to serve

Wipe the peaches and put them in a stainless steel pan. Pour in the water, then stir in the elderflower cordial and at least 2 tablespoons of sugar. Bring to a boil, turn down the heat, and leave to simmer gently until the peaches are completely tender. Turn off the heat and leave the peaches in their syrup to cool. When they are cold, chill thoroughly.

Serve a peach per person, skinned if you wish, with some of the chilled syrup and a few scattered rose petals.

Warm peaches and blueberries

enough for 2
peaches – 2
blueberries – 7 ounces (200g), 1⅓ cups
superfine sugar – 2 tablespoons
water – 3 tablespoons
cream, crème fraîche, or vanilla ice cream, to serve

Cut the peaches in half and discard the pits. Rinse the blueberries and tip them into a medium saucepan together with the sugar and water. Nestle the halved peaches among the berries and place over low to medium heat. Leave to simmer gently for ten to fifteen minutes, spooning the sauce over the peaches as you go, until the berries have started to burst and the juice has mixed with the sugar and water to make a thick sauce.

Transfer to warm bowls and serve with cream or ice cream.

Peach and blueberry cobbler

A further thought on the marriage of peaches and blueberries, but this time with a scone crust. Something for when the late-September evenings start to get a bit nippy.

enough for 6

for the cobbler crust
all-purpose flour – 1¼ cups (150g)
baking powder – 2 teaspoons
superfine sugar – 1 tablespoon
butter – 5 tablespoons (80g)
sour cream – about ⅔ cup (142ml)

for the filling
large, ripe peaches – 3
blueberries – 12 ounces (350g)
juice of a lemon
superfine sugar – a tablespoon, plus extra for dusting
all-purpose flour – a tablespoon

Preheat the oven to 400°F (200°C). Put the flour, a pinch of salt, the baking powder, sugar, and butter in a food processor and blitz for a few seconds, until the mixture resembles soft, fresh breadcrumbs. Tip into a bowl.
Slice the peaches, pulling the pits out as you go and dropping the fruit into an ovenproof dish. Toss the sliced peaches with the blueberries, lemon juice, sugar, and flour. At this point it will look less than inviting, but worry not.

Mix the sour cream into the crumb mixture; you will have a soft dough. Break off walnut-sized pieces, flatten them slightly, and lay them on top of the fruit. Dust the rounds of dough with sugar, then bake in the preheated oven for twenty-five minutes, until the cobbler is golden and the fruit is bubbling.

Pears

Like a snowflake, the perfectly ripe pear is a fleeting thing. Something to be caught, held tenderly, briefly marveled at, before it is gone forever.

Ripeness is all. Pears have a tendency to turn gritty in texture if left to ripen on the tree (that is the sugar crystals turning to starch). The dessert varieties are generally picked when approaching softness and brought to perfection indoors. Summer and autumn pears are gathered before they are fully ripe, while they are still green, but snap from their branches easily when twisted.

This is a fruit whose progress you must watch if you are not to miss it at its peak. I ripen mine on a plate, taking care their skins do not touch, and check them each morning, usually while waiting for the coffee to drip through. The window of perfection is indeed brief, a day or two at most, then a slow descent toward soft shapelessness.

The pear was domesticated long after dates, the fig, and the pomegranate, around 1000 BC. Though wild trees have been recorded here since Anglo-Saxon times, it appears most likely that the domestic pear was introduced by the Romans. From the family Rosaceae, which includes meadowsweet, brambles, hawthorn, and quince, members of the *Pyrus* genus possess a sophistication that can only be dreamed of by the apple, with extraordinarily subtle hints of wine, rose, honey, and nuts. Occasionally you might detect a note of musk or a distant breath of aniseed. The apple has these too, but more obvious and upfront.

Unless we are very lucky, there are few varieties of pear available to us. I get my first taste as late as October, with perhaps a Beurre Hardy, a crisp, lightly flavored fruit with a distinct grain to it. I like it. But there are many earlier varieties that can be found from late July onward, such as Beth and the tiny Doyenne d'Eté with its fresh, lemony notes.

We talk of apples and pears in the same breath, as we might salt and pepper, yet they are as different as you can imagine. An apple is about a loud crunch, a quick hit, a fruit to be enjoyed on the run. The pear is of a more gentle nature, something to take our time over. At its point of perfection, an apple shouts, a pear whispers.

If a pear does speak in a quieter voice, it is partly because of its texture: melting, luscious, sensual. The flesh of a ripe pear is giving and its effect on the eater calming. It is the most serene of fruits and often brings about a certain thoughtfulness.

We have eaten this fruit since prehistoric times and the word appears in all Celtic languages. It probably comes from the Germanic *pera*, a variation of the Latin *pira*. Anything pyriform indicates that something is pear shaped.

It is a long way from the Tian Shan mountains to Birmingham, but the genus is thought to have originated in the Central Asian mountain range, while Perry Barr, a neat suburb of the West Midlands, is one of the few places named after the fruit. It is mentioned in the Domesday book as Pirio and, curiously, is where I spent much of my childhood, at my aunt's house in Perry Avenue. No sign of the ancient tree for which the area was named now, of course. Even the produce market closed down a while ago.

Like roses, many varieties of this fruit carry a French name. Christopher Stocks, in his book *Forgotten Fruits* (Random House, 2008), points out that this is because it was French breeders who "took the initiative in pear breeding from the seventeenth century on." But then, they have the climate for it, this fruit liking just that bit more warmth than the apple.

As I write, there is a thrush on the Winter Nelis pear outside the window, pecking at a small, overripe fruit almost hidden by the reddening leaves. Each sharp peck is preceded by a long, bright-eyed look around, then in he goes again.

A pear in the garden

If you went to the top of our sloping Worcestershire garden, past the bent and lichen-encrusted plum tree, the tallest golden gages, and the rhubarb patch, there were two aged and rather splendid pear trees. Pear trees tend to grow taller and more upright than apples, their branches less spreading. My father balanced a long, wooden ladder against the trunk to collect the lowest hanging fruit, while I watched from below, giddy with the vertigo that dogs me to this day. Too high to reach, the remaining fruits were left to ripen until they dropped, in sweet, canary-yellow splashes, on the ground below.

I have two pear trees in my garden now. A weeping Winter Nelis, whose blossom is used as a pollinator and whose hard, bauble-sized fruits are good for poaching with vanilla and honey. The second, of which I am rather proud, is an espaliered Doyenne du Comice that I have trained along a south-facing wall outside the kitchen. The blossom is large and less fine than the Nelis, and its fruit generous in size and prolific in quantity. I feel honored.

The foliage of both trees is distinct and glorious. The leaves of the Winter Nelis become crimson in November, the Doyenne basks in shades of shiny green, tangerine, and ocher. A yard away from each other, they got off to a good start ten years ago and have become excellent and happy roommates. I recommend them to anyone with a small garden like mine.

The blossom, almost snow white, occasionally blushed with the softest pink, is less fragrant than the sweet apple. You could almost say it's fetid. Not that that stops me inhaling it in March, when it is among the first to appear. Along with black currant, it is a scent I appreciate and others shun. A good show in spring is less reliant on a cold snap than the apple.

The dense wood of the pear tree has long been used for the manufacture of high-end woodwind instruments and is often employed for pipes now that briarwood has become expensive. In the United States it is much used as a smoking wood for barbecues, supplied in chips or short logs. As a wood for furniture making, it is particularly revered. Hard and flesh pink, it requires sharp tools to work it and is considered to be a joy to handle. Furniture maker David Savage describes it as a "well-mannered wood. Pleasant to be with. One of the most pleasant things about it is the way it works. The way fine silky shavings will come off with a well-sharpened bench plane. The way new hues and colors are exposed with each shaving. Working with pear wood is a genuine sensuous experience, and one that should be cherished."

Plant a pear tree in a warm corner and it will be happier than one left to fierce winter winds. An alternative is to train them low, to make a thick fence to edge a path or even a vegetable bed. Care and a little expertise are needed to train the branches along low wires or hurdles, but it is certainly an option. Trees trained in this way can often bear heavy crops because all the plant's strength is put into the fruit rather than the tree.

Varieties

There are something like 460-odd varieties of dessert pear and many cider varieties, too. Although commerce tends to concentrate on just a handful, farm stands and farmers' markets are a sensible hunting ground for more unusual types. The names are as much a joy to read as the fruit is to eat. Who could resist the short, fat Bishop's Thumb or a Christmas-ripening variety called Santa Claus?

Early pears (ripening August to September)

Chalk A Scottish pear that dates from the 1790s, now quite rare, this is often the first dessert pear to ripen in August. Straightforward, simple flavor.

Beth A small, pale-green Kentish fruit from the 1930s, this little pear has much charm and a surprising amount of flavor for an early-ripening fruit. Ripens in September.

Moonglow* I have never seen, let alone tasted, this small, yellow-skinned variety but who could resist such a beautiful fruit with its flash of crimson?

Doyenne d'Eté Also known as Doyenne de Juillet or Roi Jolimont, the summer Doyenne is small and sweet with yellowish flesh that offers a hint of lemon. It has been around since the 1700s, for which some say we must thank Capuchin monks. Look for it in late August.

Beurre Hardy A sweet, well-flavored pear, yellow-green, with a coppery russet. The trees have glorious scarlet autumn foliage. The fruit is large, its creamy, perfumed flesh often melting. I detect a hint of rose water.

Merton Pride An English pear from the 1940s. Large, green, and with pale flesh and plenty of juice. Many unnamed garden pears are actually this variety.

Marguerite de Marillat An exceptionally large dessert variety, dating from 1872 and still around in many French gardens. Look for it in mid-September.

Triomphe de Vienne Of French origin, this large fruit has green-bronze skin and juicy flesh. Around until October.

Williams Bon Chrétien* Often simply called Williams or Bartlett and the world's most planted pear, this is a very beautiful fruit, with pale, clear yellow skin and scarlet streaks from where it has been in the sun. Originally found in a schoolmaster's garden in Aldermaston in the late 1700s, it has very white and buttery flesh, with little of the grainy quality that one either likes or not. With its heavy, musky aroma, this is a pear you can smell the minute you walk into the room. Its name comes from the Williams fruit nursery in Turnham Green, which bred and distributed it. It is called Bartlett in the States, after Enoch Bartlett, who imported it there. This is the universal canning pear. Although it is revered by many (some even say it is the finest pear), I have to say I find it rather sweet and sickly.

Midseason pears (ripening September to October)

Bergamotte d'Automne Dating from the time of Julius Caesar, this rough-skinned variety is one of the oldest pears in existence. The Bergamotte family—Heimbourg, Marbré, d'Eté, Précoce, d'Hiver, etc.—are French in origin. The Autumn Bergamot is small, roundish, and perhaps a little dull, but it can be heavily perfumed with exceptionally juicy, tender flesh.

Beurre d'Amanlis A warm corner is needed for this old variety. I have yet to try this pear, whose skin starts green, then slowly forms patches of russet and reddish brown as it ripens. The flesh of this long and slender French pear can apparently become exceptionally sugary and perfumed.

Beurre Superfin A new variety of utmost beauty. At the Royal Horticultural Society's autumn shows, it takes everyone by surprise with a scarlet-blushed cinnamon and russet skin that seems to glow from within. The flavor is of the best, and the tree is a useful size for a small garden. September cropping.

Concorde A recent variety from East Malling, a cross between Conference and Doyenne du Comice, with large pale fruit and melting, sweet flesh. I am not fond of this rather sweet fruit.

Robin Some consider this Norfolk pear to be one of the finest of all. Needless to say, the fruits are small and have a scarlet blush.

Swan's Egg Who could resist a fine old pear called Swan's Egg? A roundish fruit, yellow-green on the shaded side, slightly red on the other, and with a handsome russeting.

Durondeau A large, cinnamon-colored fruit, its skin shiny and slightly russeted and streaked here and there with crimson. A very fine pear of which the original tree is said still to exist at the home of the late M. Durondeau, at the village of Tongre-Notre-Dame in Belgium. Ripens at the end of October.

Conference* With its elongated fruit, green, freckled skin, and grainy texture, this is one of our most popular and easily recognizable pears. It keeps well under refrigeration. It is a variety I am not fond of when ripe, and I prefer to eat it as a crisp, ice-cold pear with cheese, ideally on a chilly October or November day.

Doyenne du Comice* Exquisitely perfumed, this large, lemony-yellow fruit has patches of russet speckling. With its very fine flavor and juicy, almost buttery flesh, there is something voluptuous about this fruit. In perfect condition, when you may need a cloth to cope with the juice, it can be memorable. Ripening in October, it can keep through to April. Pears don't come sexier than this one. France, 1849.

Pitmaston Duchesse An excellent old English fruit as good for cooking as it is for dessert. I have seen enormous examples of this beautifully russeted pear, the size of a clenched fist. Originally recorded in 1841 in Worcestershire, where it was raised in the same nursery as the Worcester Pearmain apple. Look for it in October and November.

Fertility (Improved) A late-nineteenth-century variety, and a heavy cropper, but a slightly underwhelming dessert fruit.

Beurre Hardy One of the finest dessert pears, this is tender, juicy, and sweet with a hint of rose water. It was first named in 1820, in France.

Glou Morceau A pea-green Belgian dessert fruit from the 1750s, with a melting texture and good flavor—I would say excellent, on occasions. Best planted in a warm place.

Late-season pears (ripening November onward)

Forelle* Charming, scarlet-orange fruit with freckled skin, like the trout after which it is named. A German variety from the 1670s, it is eye-catching in the garden but needs a sheltered position.

Black Worcester An ancient variety from the 1570s that is generally used for cooking. I knew it as the pear on my school badge and from the wild trees dotted through the local hedgerows. Like most wardens, it makes a very fine winter compote. A good keeper, around until March.

Double de Guerre A handsome, red-skinned fruit that is at its best when poached. Appearing late and with its nutmeg and crimson skin, it makes a good pear to have around at Christmas.

Easter Beurre One of the latest fruits of all, the Easter Beurre—good until the early spring—is a Belgian pear with a distinctive musk flavor.

Joséphine de Malines A very rich, almost buttery modern pear (1993) to have around at Christmas. Grown in a warm location, it will be a reliable cropper, but the fruit is delicate and easily bruised.

Uvedale's St Germain A large, very old English cooking pear. It can be around until March.

Winter Nelis* A small and rather hard Belgian variety, best for cooking. The tree itself is untidy, the branches thin and tending to weep like a willow, but it has profuse and delicate spring blossom. The autumn foliage is simply gorgeous, showing maroon, crimson, and tangerine leaves throughout October and early November.

Jargonelle The old pear whose name was used for the pear-shaped boiled sweets known as Jargonelle pears. The fruits are generally left on the tree and picked as you need them. The autumn Jargonelle is small, with pale green skin that ripens to pale yellow, dotted and streaked with dark crimson on the side next to the sun. Sugary, a little perfumed, it doesn't keep for long once off the tree. Leave it be until you need it.

*Available from US sources.

A pear in the kitchen

The pear is often the first fruit we eat. Its mild flavor and soft texture appeal to a baby's palate, but more importantly, it is rare that it produces an allergic reaction. The pear is perhaps the gentlest of fruits. At the other end of our lives, it can help lower blood pressure and cholesterol and is one of the few fruits allowed on exclusion diets. The large amount of insoluble fiber gifts the fruit with gentle laxative effects.

My first pear was from a can, sitting in a pool of thin, sweet syrup (always wonderful when generously chilled), the violin-shaped hollows of the fruit filled with evaporated milk, which would float off into the syrup like oil paint poured into water. If I am honest, I still rather like canned pears in syrup, the agony being whether to eat them with or without cream. Sometimes I add it just to watch the cream following the hollows of the halved pear.

The pear behaves differently from the apple in the heat. As ripe as a Comice may be, it doesn't always translate as such once under the crust of a crumble or a pie. The flesh seems to dry out in the oven rather than forming juice, as might an apple (I get around this with the addition of that liquid amber of the kitchen, maple syrup). But for the most part, the pear is cooked less often than the apple because it tends to lose its subtlety when heat is applied. The flavor can appear elusive.

That said, I like a baked pear, perhaps with a stream of honey to caramelize on the dish, or hollowed out and stuffed with mincemeat, when it is a thoroughly good thing. Poaching in a light sugar syrup is often the most successful way to enjoy them. The flesh keeps its flavor, stays juicy, and takes on a glowing transparency. As a breakfast dish, it is pure and clean; as a dessert, its hollows can be stuffed with whipped cream, crushed florentines, or gingersnaps and trickled, Jackson Pollock style, with dark and piercingly bitter chocolate.

In a savory sense, the old cream cheese and herb option, stuffed into the hollows left when the core is removed, is still relevant. The thick, fresh cheese and chopped herbs work in more than a tongue-in-cheek retro way.

Pears can be cooked around a roast in much the same way as a parsnip. Their edges catch in the roasting juices and take on appetizing flecks of gold and bronze. Pork is without doubt the best choice here, but a guinea fowl or a pheasant might appreciate their company too. A spoonful of rowan jelly, shimmering like an uncut ruby, might be good when dissolved in the roasting juices.

Sautéing a pear, cut into thick segments, produces something mellow and buttery to go with a jagged lump of Cheshire cheese, or perhaps a coleslaw salad with toasted hazelnuts or salted almonds. They can be slipped onto a slice of toast and covered with a modest amount of grated cheese, or served alongside a thick slice of warm ham.

I find you need a good squeeze of lemon when peeling a pear to keep the exposed flesh from browning. Rub the cut side of the lemon over the pared pear. Even so, they still discolor more quickly than apples. Stewed pear, which can be wonderful for breakfast with sheep's or goat's milk yogurt, or even cream, can be difficult to accomplish without it turning the color of old pantyhose. I tuck half a lemon into the peeled and sliced fruit and sugar as it simmers.

There are some varieties that are exclusively for the kitchen. I include the Winter Nelis and Beth in this. A cooking pear is one that refuses to soften without the application of heat, or whose flavor has little interest until warm. A cooking pear used to be known as a warden—(warden pies are mentioned in Shakespeare's *A Winter's Tale*). Their name comes from Warden Abbey in

Bedfordshire, one of the senior Cistercian monasteries in the country, founded about 1135. It is now leased by the Landmark Trust and can be rented for holidays. I would imagine there's a waiting list in autumn. Some varieties are simply stubborn and never come to ripeness. I see these fruits hanging forlornly in gardens all over the country. But then I see uncollected fruit all over the place. They would make a good pickle or a chutney but may well be glorious when brought to tenderness in sugar syrup.

Pears and...

Ham and bacon The more herbal or salty, the better the marriage. Air-dried hams, such as Parma, excel at bringing out the sweetness of the fruit and its juice. The two probably work most successfully in a salad with spinach or pale winter leaves such as frisée or Belgian endive. I often add a pear to the pan when I am cooking a ham steak. But it needs to be very ripe.

Pork A few pears tucked around a roasting loin is a great autumn and winter favorite in this house, as are a few slices sautéed in the same pan as a pork chop. I sometimes include slices of crisp, grainy pear with a plate of cold pork and homemade pickles.

Game Pheasant, duck, partridge, and squab enjoy a pear or two, particularly when the pears are pushed around the birds as they roast.

Chocolate While a raw pear and a sliver of chocolate is a simple enough way to end a supper, the marriage takes on a more luxurious note once the pear is cooked and the chocolate melted. The poached fruit served with a thick, dark chocolate sauce is the classic interpretation, but it can be extended to a chocolate mousse served alongside poached pears; a chocolate cake filled with pears and cream; a pear and chocolate trifle; and nuggets of chocolate tucked into a pear crumble or betty. Even milk chocolate, not normally associated with the kitchen, can work here.

Caramel Toffee-style sauces such as butterscotch and caramel send shivers of joy down this writer's spine. The ice-cold juice of the pear neatly contrasts with the smooth and buttery notes of the sauce.

Cinnamon Sticks of this sweet, musky spice can be added to the syrup used for poaching pears or in a sauce to accompany them.

Almonds An almond frangipane mixture is the classic support for pears in a French-style *tarte aux poires* or a more homely pear Bakewell. A careless scattering of toasted sliced nuts provides a crisp contrast to a cooked pear. Pistachios and walnuts are natural bedfellows too.

Aniseed flavors Star anise, aniseed, tarragon, chervil, and fennel all work with the pear in different ways (Conference and fennel being a crisp, refreshing autumn salad). I assume licorice would work too, though I can't say I have ever tried it.

Vanilla While it is difficult to think of a fruit that vanilla does not complement (only melon and oranges spring to mind), it is particularly welcome here.

Greens Watercress, spinach, and the bitter salad leaves are a masterful addition to a salad that contains pears. Throw in some air-dried ham or crisp snippets of fried bacon.

Wine Both red and white wine can be used as the cooking liquid for pears. A fair bit of sugar is needed too, plus orange peel, cloves, a cinnamon stick, and maybe a spoonful of honey. The sweet wines such as a Muscat or a treacly Sauternes are more suitable than the drier whites. A good, fruity red such as a Beaujolais or Zinfandel gets my vote for the red. I tend to serve the latter on cold winter nights. A drop of medium-sweet sherry is no bad thing in a pear trifle.

Black currants A tart, purple-black purée of the sieved and sweetened fruit is a gorgeous sauce to trickle over a melting poached pear.

Raspberries Not so much as partners in a salad, more as a sauce for the cooked fruit or as a purée to serve with a pear sorbet.

Honey A spoonful or two added to the simmering water in which you are bringing the fruits to tenderness is worth trying, as is using it to baste pears you are baking in the oven.

Ginger Either as a ground spice to season a pear cake or in its fresh form as coins dropped into a sugar syrup for cooking the pears.

Cheese A jagged lump of Parmesan and a ripe pear have been lunch for me on many a winter's day. The cold juice and salty cheese form a tantalizing partnership. Cheeses with a salty note, such as Parmesan, pecorino, and many of the blues, will tease out the sweetness of the pear's juice in much the same way that Parma ham does for a ripe melon.

The punchy blues, such as Picos, Roquefort, and Stichelton, seem particularly at home with the melting flesh of a bulging Comice, but crisp pears, the sort that makes your gums ache, their flesh hard and white as snow, can be strangely addictive too—a heavily blued Roquefort and a slender, underripe Conference being a particular favorite.

In a salad, the two ingredients will benefit from some toasted hazelnuts or almonds, or fresh, pale walnuts. White winter salad leaves, with their blush of maroon and scarlet freckles, work better with a pear than soft leaves, though a crisp pear and spinach salad is an exception worth trying.

The softer, milder cheeses are pleasing, too, for when I want something altogether gentler. Perfectly fine but less interesting than those that have a pungency to contrast with the pear's sweet juice.

* Perry is fermented pear juice—pear cider.
* Pears will ripen faster if placed next to bananas in a fruit bowl. They stay fresh longer if kept in the fridge.

A pork pot roast

Perry is an astonishing drink—refreshing, dry, and fruity. A small bottle upended into a pot roast will ensure a moist result and leave you with a decent amount of fruity pot juices to spoon over.

> *enough for 4, with some left for cold*
> olive or peanut oil – 2 tablespoons
> a piece of pork on the bone – about 3 pounds (1.5kg)
> a large onion
> large pears – 4
> bay leaves – a couple
> pear or apple cider – 1⅔ cups (400ml)
> mild honey or maple syrup – 3 tablespoons

Preheat the oven to 400°F (200°C). In a deep, heavy pan, warm the oil over a lively heat and add the pork, generously salted and peppered. Let the meat color a little—it should be pale gold here and there—then turn it so the other sides take on a little color too.

Peel the onion, slice it fairly thinly, then add it to the pot. While it softens, slice the pears thickly, removing the cores as you go. I see no reason to peel them. Add the pears, bay leaves, perry or cider, and honey or maple syrup to the pot with a little salt and black pepper. Cover with a lid and bake for fifty minutes to an hour.

Serve in thin slices, with the pears and the thin, delicious juices, some mashed potato, and perhaps a little braised red cabbage.

A weekday supper of pork and pears

enough for 2
pork chops – 2
peanut oil – 2 tablespoons
garlic – 2 large cloves, crushed flat
pears – 2
dry white wine or vermouth – a wineglass
stock – 5 tablespoons (75ml)

Season the chops with salt and pepper. Heat the peanut oil in a shallow pan with the crushed garlic cloves. When the oil is hot, slide in the pork chops—take care, they will spit at you. Seal on both sides. Meanwhile, cut the pears into eighths and core them.

Turn down the heat, add the pears to the pan, and cook for about ten minutes, until tender and browned lightly. Remove the chops and pears to warm plates. Pour most of the fat from the pan and return to the heat. Pour in the wine or vermouth and scrape away the bits of pork and pear stuck to the pan. Add the stock and simmer until reduced by half. Pour over the chops and pears.

Eat with
* A salad of bitter leaves such as arugula or frisée.
* Belgian endive leaves dressed with lemon and chopped walnuts.
* Spinach leaves, cooked for a few seconds with some drops of water until they wilt, black pepper, no butter.

A Sunday roast of pork, perry, and pears

Slow-maturing, hardy varieties of pig, particularly Tamworth and Gloucester Old Spot, make an extraordinarily succulent roast. I like to rub their skin with a salt and rosemary paste to encourage it to turn into good crackling. Perry, the cider made from pears, has been made in the south of the country for 200 years and is undergoing a renaissance. I use dry apple cider—and apples instead of pears—when perry proves evasive.

Pork will produce more reliable crackling if the meat is dry before roasting. Leaving it unwrapped and in open air for an hour will help.

enough to serve 4 to 6
rosemary needles – 2 tablespoons
sea salt – 1 tablespoon
black peppercorns – 1 teaspoon
olive oil – 5 tablespoons
a rolled leg or loin of pork – about 3 pounds (1.5kg), scored
onions – 2
pears – 4
pear cider – 1 cup (250ml)

Preheat the oven to 425°F (220°C). Finely chop the rosemary leaves and crush them with the sea salt and peppercorns, using a mortar and pestle. When you have a sandlike mixture, pour in 3 tablespoons of the olive oil to make a paste.

Put the meat in a roasting pan and massage the rosemary paste into its skin and cut edges. Roast for twenty minutes, then reduce the temperature to 400°F (200°C) and continue to roast for twenty-five minutes per pound (500g).

While the pork is roasting, peel the onions and chop them coarsely. Let them cook with the remaining oil in a shallow pan over medium heat until soft and palest gold. Peel and quarter the pears (I keep them from browning with a little lemon juice). Add the onions and pears to the roasting pan after the pork has been cooking at the lower temperature for twenty-five minutes, basting the pears with any available pan juices.

When the pork is ready, remove it from the oven and let it rest in a warm place with the pears, lightly covered with foil (a tight covering will make the crackling soften).

Put the roasting pan over medium heat, add the cider, and boil the juices until reduced to a generous ¾ cup (200ml) or so. They won't thicken, but you just want to concentrate the flavor a little. Adjust the seasoning.

Serve the pork in thin slices, together with chunks of its crackling, pears, and oniony pan juices.

Roast partridge, juniper, and pears

enough for 4
young, plump partridges – 4
thyme – 6 bushy little sprigs
juniper berries – 12
butter – 7 tablespoons (100g)
unsmoked bacon – 8 thin slices
pears – 2
a squeeze of lemon juice
white bread – 4 small, thick slices
red currant, rowan, or quince jelly – 2 tablespoons
vermouth or white wine – a glass

Before I start, I always check the birds all over for any stray feathers or bits of shattered bone. Preheat the oven to 425°F (220°C).

Pull the leaves from the thyme branches and mash them with the juniper berries, butter, and a hefty pinch of sea salt and black pepper, using a mortar and pestle. Reserve a tablespoon for cooking the pears, then spread the butter all over the birds, but particularly on their breasts.

Lay each slice of bacon flat on a cutting board, then stretch with the flat of a knife blade to give a longer, thinner slice. Wrap the slices around the birds and place in a roasting pan.

Cut the pears into thick slices, core them, toss them in a little lemon juice, and cook briefly in the reserved herb butter in a shallow, nonstick pan. When both sides are pale gold, transfer them to the roasting pan.

Roast for twenty minutes, then peel off the bacon, setting it aside if it is crisp enough or leaving it in the roasting pan if not. Return the birds to the oven for a further ten minutes' roasting.

If you want to fry the bread, warm a little butter or oil in a shallow pan (I use the same one I used for the pears), then fry the bread until crisp. Drain on paper towels.

Remove the pan from the oven, set the birds on the fried bread, with the bacon and pear beside them, then leave to rest (I use a warm plate for this with an upturned bowl on top). Put the roasting pan over medium heat, drop in the jelly, and let it melt into the pan juices. Add a small glass of vermouth or wine and stir to dissolve the pan-stickings. Bring to a boil, put the birds and their bits and pieces onto warm plates, then spoon over the "gravy."

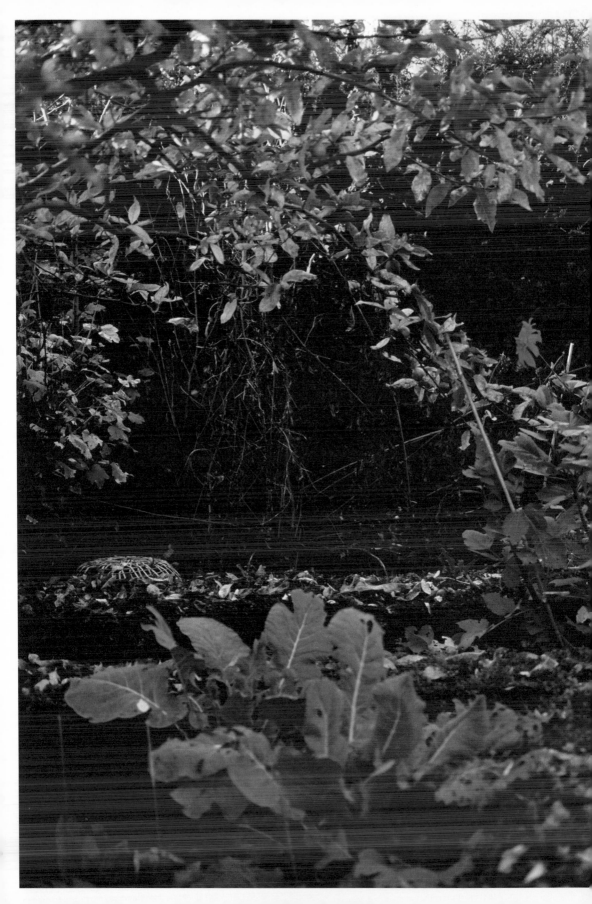

Pears with maple syrup and vanilla

The double cooking of these pears, first in a light syrup and then baked, ensures that they are truly soft and tender. You could use honey if maple syrup proves elusive.

enough for 4
large pears – 4
sugar – 4 tablespoons
water – 3 cups (750ml)
maple syrup – 4 tablespoons
vanilla extract – 2 to 3 drops
cream, to serve

Peel the pears, cut them in half, and scoop out their cores. Bring the sugar and water to a boil, slip in the pears, and let them simmer for ten to fifteen minutes, until approaching tenderness. Drain and discard the syrup; it has done its work. Preheat the oven to 350°F (180°C).

Place the pears in a shallow baking dish. Drizzle with the maple syrup and the vanilla extract. Bake for about an hour, until the pears are meltingly soft and pale gold here and there. Serve with a pitcher of cream, though they are quite pleasing as they come.

A crisp salad of red cabbage and pears

The variations on cheese and pears are almost endless. The one I exploit the most is that of blue cheese with ripe pears—here, in a salad of crisp cabbage, soft and powerful blue cheese, and pears. I suggest Picos, but Cashel Blue would work well here, as would Roquefort.

enough for 4
red cabbage – 14 ounces (400g)
crisp white cabbage – 7 ounces (200g)
pears, crisp rather than ripe – 2
Picos or other blue cheese – 5 to 7 ounces (150 to 200g)
poppyseeds – a tablespoon

for the dressing
tarragon vinegar – 1 tablespoon
crème fraîche – 1¼ cups (300ml)
whole-grain mustard – 1 tablespoon

Discard any less than crisp outer leaves from the cabbages and shred the heart leaves finely. I use a large knife for this, though others may prefer to find a suitable disk in their food processor's box of gadgets. Soak briefly in cold water and drain. Cut the pears into thin slices, removing the core as you go. Mix the pears and cabbage together. Cut the cheese into thick slices, break each slice into large, flat crumbs, then add to the cabbage and pears.

Make the dressing by dissolving a large pinch of salt in the tarragon vinegar, then stirring in the crème fraîche and whole-grain mustard, together with a little black pepper. Taste for sharpness, adding more mustard or vinegar as you wish. Scrape the dressing into the salad and toss gently, taking care to coat all the cabbage and pears. Pile into a serving dish or divide among four plates, then sprinkle over the poppyseeds.

A winter salad of pears and blue cheese

Slightly underripe pears with a little crispness to them are better for this than truly ripe ones—the contrast works well with the cheese. Salad leaves such as frisée and maybe some red-leaf chard would be good here. You might like to continue the pomegranate theme or use golden or regular raisins instead.

enough for 2
a plump pear, ripe but still slightly crisp
lemon juice
small, crisp salad leaves – a couple of handfuls
Stilton, Stichelton, or other firm blue cheese – 4 thick slices
walnut halves – a handful
half a pomegranate

for the dressing
cider vinegar or white wine vinegar – a tablespoon
peanut oil – a tablespoon
walnut or hazelnut oil – 2 tablespoons
heavy cream – a tablespoon

Slice the pear into quarters, remove the core, then cut the fruit into thin slices. Brush each piece with lemon juice.

Make the dressing. Pour the vinegar into a small mixing bowl and dissolve a pinch of sea salt in it. Stir in the oils, then the cream, and whisk well. Divide the salad leaves, pear, and cheese between two plates and pour over the dressing. Toast the walnuts, break the pomegranate into separate seeds, then scatter both nuts and seeds over the salad.

Pear, pecan, and maple syrup betty

enough for 4
pears – about 2 pounds (850g)
a little butter
golden baker's sugar – 2 tablespoons
a pinch of ground cinnamon
a handful of pecans or shelled walnut pieces

for the crumb layer
butter – 5 tablespoons (75g)
maple syrup – 3 tablespoons
soft white breadcrumbs – 2 ounces (65g), about 1½ cups
rolled oats – 2 ounces (65g), a generous ½ cup
light muscovado sugar – a generous ⅓ cup, packed (90g)

Preheat the oven to 350°F (180°C). Peel the pears, remove and discard their cores, and chop the flesh into large chunks. Melt the butter in a small casserole over medium heat and add the pears. Let the fruit cook until it starts to color appetizingly around the edges. It should be tender but not soft. Add the sugar, cinnamon, and nuts and turn off the heat.

To make the topping, put the butter and maple syrup into a saucepan and let it melt slowly over medium heat. Mix the breadcrumbs, oats, and muscovado sugar together and tip them over the pears. Spoon the melted butter and maple syrup over the top, then bake in the preheated oven for thirty-five minutes, until the crust is lightly crisp and the fruit is fully tender. There will be crisp crust, juicy pears, and a layer of delicious syrup at the bottom.

Baked pears with cranberries and orange

There is something about an ice-white winter sky that makes me abandon my usual breakfast of yogurt and fruit for a chilled fruit compote. Most times it's stewed apple but occasionally there are pears to use up.

enough for 4 as breakfast or dessert
pears – about 2 pounds (1kg)
a pinch of ground cinnamon
the juice of half a lemon
cloves – 4

for the compote
dates – 7 ounces (200g)
dried cranberries (or cherries) – 2 ounces (50g), about ⅓ cup
a stick of cinnamon
honey – 3 tablespoons
the finely grated zest and juice of a large orange

Preheat the oven to 400°F (200°C). Peel, quarter, and core the pears and coarsely chop them. Put them in a baking dish, then toss with the cinnamon and lemon juice and tuck in the cloves. Bake the pears until they are soft. Depending on your choice of pear, this will take anything from thirty to forty-five minutes.

While the fruit is cooking, remove the pits from the dates and toss them in a small saucepan with the dried cranberries, cinnamon, honey, and the orange zest and juice. Bring to a boil, turn the heat down to a gentle simmer, and leave to bubble very gently for about ten minutes, until the fruit has plumped and softened.

To serve, spoon the pears and their juice into dishes, then top with the hot dried fruit. Both will keep well in the fridge for several days.

A dish of baked pears with marsala

When the oven has been on for a roast, I sometimes sneak in a dish of baked fruit.

enough for 4
large pears – 4
a lemon
sweet marsala – 4 tablespoons
superfine sugar – 3 tablespoons
butter – 3½ tablespoons (50g)

Preheat the oven to 400°F (200°C). Peel the pears but leave them whole, dropping them into cold water with a squeeze of lemon juice in it as you go to keep them from browning.

Put the marsala, sugar, and butter into a baking dish, then add the whole pears. Bake for about an hour, until the pears are butter-soft. It is essential to baste them once or twice, turning them over in the juices. Serve them warm, spooning over the sweet, buttery juices.

Pears with a brandy snap cream

Simmered in juice or water and sugar, pears can end up as soft as butter. A crisp element such as a cookie or wafer offers a welcome contrast. Little chocolate florentines or brandy snaps are an alternative. Brandy snaps are buttery, tubular cookies available in North America by mail order and in specialty and British import shops.

enough for 4
superfine sugar – ½ cup (100g)
water – 4 cups (a liter)
a lemon
a vanilla pod
small pears – 8
heavy cream – a generous ¾ cup (200ml)
a little vanilla extract
small brandy snaps – 3½ ounces (100g)
dark chocolate – 3½ ounces (100g)

Dissolve the sugar in the water over low heat with a good squeeze of lemon juice and the vanilla pod. You are making a light, mildly flavored syrup. Peel the pears, rubbing with the lemon as you go, then cut them in half and remove their cores. Slide the fruit into the syrup. With the pan covered, bring the syrup to a boil, then turn the heat down immediately. Let the pears simmer very gently until translucent and tender to the point of a knife. Depending on the ripeness of the fruit, this will take about fifteen minutes, maybe longer. They really must be butter-soft if they are to be good.

Let the pears cool in the syrup for a good hour, then lift them out and put them in a shallow dish in the fridge. Whip the cream softly—it should not be too stiff—then fold in a couple of drops of vanilla extract and the coarsely crushed brandy snaps.

Break the chocolate into small squares and melt it in a small bowl set over a pan of simmering water. Just let it melt—don't stir it. As soon as the chocolate has melted, turn off the heat, then fill the pears with the brandy snap cream. Drizzle over the chocolate in thin zigzag lines, then leave in the fridge for a few minutes to crisp.

Poached pears with pomegranate sorbet

I adore a feast as much as anyone, but I do find those at Christmas can be just too rich. I constantly look around for something light and refreshing with which to end my meal. A dish of cool, luscious pears full of mildly spicy juice slithers down easily after a rich meal. The accompanying ice, rose pink and as refreshing as a waterfall, is a deeply fruity accompaniment to the softness of the pear.

It is essential to use unsweetened pomegranate juice here. That means either using fresh fruit and squeezing it yourself or checking the labels of your juice carefully. Pom brand is the one I use.

enough for 4
superfine sugar – ½ cup (100g)
water – 4 cups (a liter)
a lemon
a cinnamon stick
star anise – 4
a vanilla pod
a small orange
large pears – 4

for the pomegranate sorbet
superfine sugar – a scant ⅔ cup (120g)
pomegranate juice – 4 cups (900ml)

Dissolve the sugar in the water over low heat. Add a good squeeze of lemon juice, the cinnamon stick, star anise, and vanilla pod. Remove 2 or 3 long strips of peel from the orange with a vegetable peeler and add them to the pan. You are making a light, mildly flavored syrup.

Peel the pears, rubbing with the lemon as you go. If you wish, you can cut them in half and remove their cores. But I tend to cook mine whole. Slide the fruit into the syrup. With the pan covered, bring the syrup to a boil, then turn the heat down immediately. Let the pears simmer very gently until translucent and tender to the point of a knife. Depending on the ripeness of the fruit, this will take about thirty minutes, maybe longer. Continue cooking until they are butter-soft.

Let the pears cool in the syrup for a good hour, then lift them out and put them in a shallow dish in the fridge. Chill until you need them.

For the sorbet, stir the sugar into the pomegranate juice until dissolved. If it isn't disappearing, then warm the mixture slightly until it does. Don't let it boil though, as this will affect the flavor and color. Pour the mixture into an ice cream maker and churn until almost frozen. Remove and transfer to a freezer-safe plastic box.

continued

No machine? Then you are probably better off making a granita. Pour the mixture into a shallow plastic freezer-safe tray and freeze for about an hour. Stir with a fork, bringing the ice crystals that have formed around the edge into the middle. Return to the freezer. Leave for a further hour or so, then repeat. Do this until the mixture is almost frozen solid. It will freeze quite hard, but when shattered with a fork or knife will break into a quite granular ice. If it is frozen solid, allow it a good twenty minutes to come to room temperature, then break up with a fork into deep pink snow.

A water ice of pear and lemon

There is much elegance in this delicately flavored, ivory-colored sorbet. Depending on the time of year, I sometimes eat it with apricots that have been poached in a little light sugar syrup, or perhaps with a handful of velvet raspberries. The texture is smoother if the sorbet is made in a machine. If you are making it by hand, then it is probably best to treat it as a crystalline granita instead.

> *enough for 4 to 6*
> water – 2 cups (500ml)
> superfine sugar – 1¼ cups (250g)
> pears – 6
> a lemon

Bring the water and sugar to a boil in a stainless steel saucepan. Peel the pears, cut them in half, and scoop out the seeds and tough core with a teaspoon. Rub each piece of pear with a cut half of the lemon. Slide the pears and the lemon halves into the hot syrup and let them cook at a low simmer until the pears are truly tender. They should take the point of a sharp knife without you having to exert any pressure. Switch off the heat and leave them in the syrup until completely cool.

Put the pears and their cooking syrup—but not the lemons—into a blender and blitz until smooth and white. Now either pour into an electric ice cream maker and churn until almost frozen or pour the mixture into a shallow freezer-safe plastic box and place in the freezer. If you are making it without a machine, leave the sorbet for a couple of hours until ice crystals are forming around the edge. Stir them into the center with a whisk, then return to the freezer for another couple of hours. Remove and whisk again, continually bringing the frozen edges into the middle, then freeze once more. Just as the sorbet is almost frozen, give it one final beating with the whisk and leave it to freeze. Once frozen, it is a good idea to take it out of the freezer twenty minutes or so before serving, leaving it in the fridge.

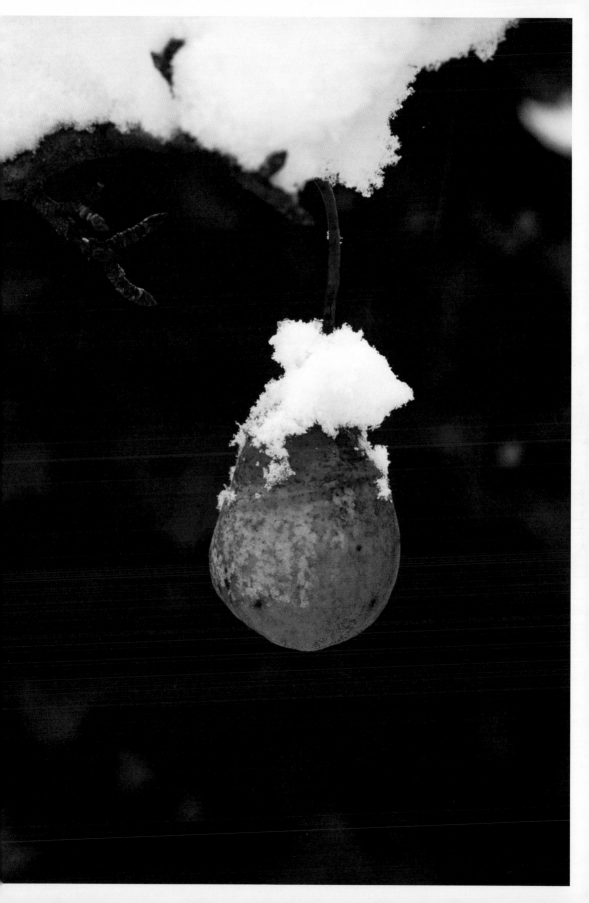

Pears in sweet wine

Sweet wines—Sauternes, Tokay, Beaumes de Venise, and the occasional orange Muscat—tend to accumulate in the cupboard. Often received as gifts, they are wines I have to be in the mood for and, frankly, rarely drink. This recipe is a good end for those you might be wondering what to do with.

> *enough for 4*
> hard pears – 4
> juice of half a lemon
> sugar – 1¼ cups (250g)
> a vanilla pod
> half a bottle of sweet white wine, Sauternes, or orange Muscat

Wipe the pears and cut each one in half lengthwise. Put into a deep saucepan with the juice of the half lemon, the sugar, vanilla, wine, and 1⅔ cups (400ml) of water. Bring to a boil, then turn the heat down to a simmer. Let the pears cook gently until they are completely tender to the point of a knife. This will take a good forty-five minutes, maybe longer. Don't even think of undercooking them.

    Lift the tender fruit out with a slotted spoon and remove the vanilla pod. Now remove any bits of froth with a slotted spoon, put the liquid over high heat, and let it reduce to a thin syrup, taking care not to let it boil to jam. Pour it over the pears and leave it to cool, then refrigerate. Serve cold.

Pears with praline ice cream and chocolate sauce

Another example of the marriage of pears and chocolate, but this time with a nutty ice cream. It is a seductive contrast of texture. Silky pears, heavy with syrup, cold, nubbly ice cream, and warm, velvety chocolate sauce.

enough for 4
golden baker's sugar – 2 tablespoons
a vanilla pod
juice of half a lemon
pears – 4
praline ice cream
fine dark chocolate – 7 ounces (200g)

Pour a good quart (liter) of water into a deep, wide pan, then add the sugar, vanilla pod, and lemon juice and bring to a boil. Peel the pears and tug out their stalks, then halve the fruit and scoop out the cores with a teaspoon. Drop the fruit into the sugar syrup and let them simmer for about fifteen minutes, until translucent and tender. Leave them in the syrup to cool. During this time they will become silkily soft and soaked through with syrup.

Get the ice cream out of the freezer. Chop the chocolate. Bring ¾ cup (200ml) of water to a boil, then whisk in the chocolate, removing the pan from the heat as soon as it has melted—a matter of seconds. Place two pear halves on each of four dishes, add the praline ice cream—one ball per person should be ample—then pour over the warm chocolate sauce.

Poached pears with warm chocolate sauce

The marriage of pears and chocolate is extraordinary. It is as if they were made for each other (curiously, apples and chocolate have little affinity with each other). The effect is possibly at its most sumptuous when the pears are poached in a light sugar syrup until almost translucent and the chocolate comes in the form of a warm, flowing sauce.

enough for 4
golden baker's sugar – ½ cup (100g)
water – 4 cups (a liter)
a vanilla pod
a little lemon juice
plump pears – 4

for the chocolate sauce
fine dark chocolate – 7 ounces (200g)
strong black coffee – 2 tablespoons
heavy cream – ¾ cup (180ml)
butter – a tablespoon

Bring the sugar, water, vanilla, and lemon juice to a boil, then turn down the heat and leave to simmer gently. Meanwhile, peel the pears, cut them in half lengthwise, and remove the cores with a sharp knife and a teaspoon. Slide them into the syrup and let them simmer gently until they are tender to the point of a knife. You can expect this to take anything up to thirty-five minutes, depending on the ripeness of the pears. I think they should be really tender and full of juice. Leave them to cool in the syrup.

Break the chocolate into small pieces and put it into a heavy-bottomed saucepan with the coffee and cream. Heat slowly, stirring from time to time, until the chocolate has melted. It is essential that the heat is kept low. Once the chocolate has softened, stir until smooth, then stir in the butter and pour the sauce into a warm pitcher.

Drain the pears and put them on a dish. Pour over the warm chocolate sauce.

A cake of pears, muscovado, and maple syrup

Cakes like these, where the sugar and butter are creamed first before the other ingredients are added, are so much easier to make when the butter is at room temperature rather than straight from the fridge. It's a small and perhaps obvious point but one that I continually forget. It will make life much easier.

enough for 8
butter – 6 tablespoons (100g), softened
golden baker's sugar – ¼ cup (50g)
light muscovado sugar – a scant ¼ cup, packed (50g)
all-purpose flour – 1¼ cups (150g)
baking powder – a teaspoon
ground almonds – ½ cup (50g)
large eggs – 3
milk – 2 tablespoons
vanilla extract – a couple of drops

for the pears
ripe pears – 1 pound (450g)
butter – 4 teaspoons (20g)
ground cinnamon – a couple of pinches
maple syrup – 3 tablespoons, plus a little more to serve

Line the bottom of a deep 8-inch (20cm) baking pan with parchment paper. Peel, core, and chop the pears. The pieces should be quite small, about ⅓ inch (1cm) square. Put them into a shallow pan with the butter and cinnamon and let them soften for ten to twelve minutes over medium heat, stirring from time to time so they do not burn. Pour in the maple syrup, let the mixture bubble up briefly, then remove from the heat. The pears should be sticky and deep golden.

Preheat the oven to 350°F (180°C). Put the butter and sugars into a stand mixer and beat until pale and thick. They should be the color of milky coffee. Sift the flour and baking powder together (I don't normally suggest sifting flour but it is essential when you are incorporating baking powder to ensure it is evenly distributed). Add the almonds to the flour. Beat the eggs and milk in a small bowl with a fork, then add to the butter and sugar mixture a little at a time, alternating with the flour and almonds. Stir in the vanilla extract.

Tip the mixture into the cake pan and smooth the top. Spoon the pears and any remaining syrup over the mixture. They will gradually sink on cooking to make a sticky layer further down.

Bake for forty minutes, or until golden and lightly firm. Serve warm, in thick slices, with cream and a little more maple syrup.

Mulled perry with pears and spices

Soft pears, crisp cookies. Every year I make a trip, you could call it a pilgrimage, to one of Europe's Christmas markets: Berlin, Brussels, and Vienna all get a visit. While there is an element of tattiness about some of the stalls, there are good things too: old-fashioned decorations for the tree, gingerbread cookies with sugar frosting, and glasses of mulled cider. There is something quite magical about these frosty evenings, holding mugs of hot cider in mittened hands.

Back home, with a gray Christmas rather than a frosty white one, the magic somewhat disappears, but the warm, fruity drink is still more interesting than our own mulled wine. I use perry, or pear cider, which glows in the glass, spiked with cloves and pieces of pear that soften in the heat. A wonderfully refreshing drink, even when warmed with sugar and spice. The smell as it fizzes on the stove is pure Christmas. I serve it with crisp spice cookies, their ginger notes just right for the pear.

enough for 6 to 8 glasses
large pears – 2
butter – a thick slice
pear cider – 4 cups (a liter)
soft brown sugar – 2 tablespoons
cloves – 12
cinnamon sticks – 3
a nutmeg
the juice of a small orange

Peel and core the pears and cut them into large dice. Melt the butter in a shallow pan, add the pears, and leave them to soften for ten minutes or so. They should be tender but still retain some shape.

Pour the pear cider into a stainless steel saucepan, tip in the sugar, then add the cloves, cinnamon sticks, and a fine grating of nutmeg. Squeeze the orange into the cider and let the mixture warm slowly, allowing it to come almost to a boil. Lower the heat to keep it warm.

Divide the softened pears among the glasses, then pour in the spiced cider. Have some spoons around for the pears.

Brown sugar spice cookies

The simplest of Christmas cookies. Dark, mildly spiced, and the sort of crisp cookies you find hanging from Christmas trees all over Europe. If by any chance you are ever looking for the ideal mixture to make gingerbread men, this is it. Serve these with the mulled perry on the preceding page.

> butter – 5 tablespoons (70g)
> light muscovado sugar – ⅓ cup, packed (80g)
> black treacle or dark molasses – 2 heaping tablespoons
> cardamom pods – 8
> all-purpose flour – 2 cups (250g)
> baking soda – half a teaspoon
> ground cinnamon – 2 teaspoons
> ground ginger – a teaspoon
> an egg yolk
> milk – 3 to 4 tablespoons
> confectioners' sugar

Preheat the oven to 350°F (180°C). Cream the butter and sugar together in a stand mixer until light and fluffy, then add the treacle or molasses. Break the cardamom pods open and crush the seeds finely. Add them to the mixture with the flour, baking soda, cinnamon, ginger, and egg yolk. Beat in a couple of tablespoons of milk, then slowly add more until you reach a point where the dough is soft enough to roll. Bring the ingredients together, then roll out on a floured board like pastry. Cut out into rounds, moons, and stars. I sometimes do a few Christmas trees too. Lay them on a lightly buttered baking sheet and bake for twelve to fourteen minutes. Remove and cool on a wire rack, then toss in confectioners' sugar.

Pear and pecan tart

I am honestly not sure if this is a tart or a cake, I only know that it is delicious when served warm, with cream.

enough for 6
butter – ¾ cup (180g)
golden baker's sugar – a scant cup (180g)
large pears – 2
a little lemon juice
large eggs – 3
all-purpose flour – 1 cup (120g)
baking powder – 1 teaspoon
ground almonds – ⅔ cup (70g)
milk – 5 tablespoons (80ml)
vanilla extract – a few drops
pecan halves – 2 ounces (60g), ½ cup
half-and-half, to serve

Preheat the oven to 350°F (180°C). Line a shallow baking pan, approximately 8½ inches (22cm) square, with parchment paper.

Cut the butter into small chunks and put it into a stand mixer with the sugar. Beat until pale and creamy. Meanwhile, cut the pears into thick slices, coring and tossing them in lemon juice as you go. You can peel them or not as you wish, but I rather like the contrasting texture of the unpeeled ones.

Beat the eggs into the butter and sugar one at a time. Fold in the flour, baking powder, and almonds, then the milk and vanilla. Scrape into the lined pan, press the pecans and pear slices lightly on top, and bake for an hour, until pale gold and risen.

Leave to cool slightly, then cut into thick slices and serve warm, with cream.

Cinnamon pear cake with vanilla fudge sauce

This is the most gorgeous fudge sauce imaginable, tasting like melted, creamy vanilla toffee. The pear cake isn't bad either.

enough for 8 to 10
butter – 1 cup minus 2 tablespoons (200g)
golden baker's sugar – 1 cup (200g)
large eggs – 3, lightly beaten
self-rising flour – generous 1½ cups (200g)
baking powder – half a teaspoon
vanilla ice cream, to serve

for the pears
ripe pears – 1½ pounds (750g)
half a lemon
butter – 3 tablespoons (40g)
light muscovado sugar – 3 tablespoons
ground cinnamon – a heaping half teaspoon

for the fudge sauce
light muscovado sugar – a scant ½ cup (100g)
maple syrup or golden syrup – ⅓ cup (100g)
butter – 3½ tablespoons (50g)
heavy cream – ⅔ cup (150ml)
vanilla extract – a couple of drops

You will need a 9½-inch (24cm) nonstick springform cake pan, very lightly buttered. Preheat the oven to 325°F (160°C).

Peel the pears, then halve, core, and coarsely chop them, dropping them into cold water acidulated with a good few squeezes of the lemon. It will keep them from turning brown. Melt the butter and muscovado sugar in a shallow pan over medium heat, stirring occasionally. Drain the pears and add them to the pan, taking care that they don't spit at you. Let them cook in the melted butter and sugar until they are tender and the sauce is thick and coats the pears. Stop before the sugar turns dark and bitter. Set aside to cool.

To make the cake, put the butter and sugar in a stand mixer and beat until light and creamy. It should be almost white. Add the eggs and a little of the flour alternately, so that the mixture doesn't curdle. Fold in the remaining flour and the baking powder, followed by the cooked pears and their syrup. Scoop the mixture into the buttered baking pan and smooth the top lightly. Bake for forty-five minutes, until risen and golden, then check for doneness with a metal skewer; it should come out clean. Remove the cake from the oven and leave to cool before taking it out of the pan.

continued

To make the sauce, put the sugar, golden syrup, and butter in a small, heavy-bottomed saucepan and bring to a boil, stirring only enough to stop it sticking. Stir in the cream and the vanilla and leave to cool. The sauce will thicken as the temperature drops.

To serve, put a slice of cake on each plate with two balls of ice cream, then pour over the fudge sauce.

And to go with the perfect pear

Sometimes you want to eat your perfect pear alone; its flesh and juice may demand a plate all to itself. But there are several good things to consider eating alongside your pear: a slice of melting Reblochon; a moussy-fresh goat cheese; something more mature and fudgelike; or perhaps a herb-speckled scone straight from the oven or a slice of fruit-flecked whole grain loaf.

Goat cheese and thyme scones to eat with pears

enough for 4 to 8, as a snack or part of a light lunch
all-purpose flour – 3½ cups (450g)
baking powder – 2 tablespoons
cold butter – 6 tablespoons (85g)
strong Cheddar cheese – 3½ ounces (100g)
strong, firm goat cheese – 8 ounces (250g)
chopped thyme leaves – 2 teaspoons
buttermilk – 1½ cups (350ml)
a little more grated cheese and a few sprigs of thyme, to finish

Preheat the oven to 400°F (200°C). Sift the flour into a large mixing bowl with the baking powder. Cut the butter into small cubes and rub it into the flour using your fingertips or a food processor. You are after fine crumbs. Grate the Cheddar into the flour, crumble or cut the goat cheese into small cubes, and add to the mixture with the thyme leaves.

Pour in the buttermilk and bring the ingredients together to form a firmish dough. Turn onto a well-floured work surface and pat gently into a large round, about 8 inches (20cm) in diameter. Lift onto a lightly floured baking sheet. Score deeply (though not through to the baking sheet) with a large knife to divide the scone into eight wedges. Grate a little more cheese on the surface and scatter with a few remaining herbs.

Bake in the preheated oven for forty to forty-five minutes, until golden and firm to the touch. Allow to cool for a few minutes, then slide carefully onto a wire cooling rack. Serve warm (rather than hot from the oven).

Plums

When I find the perfect plum, jelly-fleshed and incandescently ripe, its golden skin flashed with crimson freckles, I make a great fuss of it. I have even been known to get out a small plate and a napkin. I eat slowly, imagining time stopped. More usually, I come across such a fruit without warning, having little alternative but to eat it from the hand, spitting the pit into the long grass below.

The British plum season runs for about six weeks, from the Pershore Yellow Egg and Early Rivers in late July to the sultry Marjorie's Seedling that I have found in good condition as late as mid-October. August and early September is greengage time, when we also see some of our 350 varieties, though only the luckiest of us will ever taste more than a handful. From the small, round wild plum of the country hedgerow to the rare Kea plum of Cornwall, they vary in shape, sweetness, and color, but all have one thing in common—luscious, honeyed flesh that tastes of the very essence of summer turning to autumn.

It breaks my heart to think of the plum orchards we have lost in the last two decades, but what else can a farmer do when the crop is no longer profitable, consumers have more interest in peaches and nectarines, and the stores continue to sell imports even during our own brief season? I salute the British plum grower.

The flavor of a plum is somewhat reliant on the amount of sugar it contains—the higher the percentage, the richer the flavor. But more importantly, as with any fruit, much also depends on the soil and climate in which it finds itself. Old Transparent has long been revered for its flavor. It is the plum I grew up with, and I cannot help measuring everything else by the memory of its honeyed notes and golden, almost liquid flesh. Early and Late Transparent, Denniston's Superb, and the Jefferson are consistently discussed as the finest of the bunch and I would certainly agree.

The single most important point in finding the perfect plum is to catch it at its ripest—that brief moment just before it starts to soften that little bit too much. When its flesh has almost, but not quite, turned to jelly and the fruit appears to be glowing from within. It is a moment worth waiting for.

The gages

There is no real difference between plums and gages, though we use the latter name to describe the smaller and more prized members of *Prunus domestica*. They are named for Sir William Gage, who first imported the tiny, chartreuse-colored Reine Claude variety from France. The name stuck, and now any small, green plum is called a gage. They are interchangeable in cooking with our own larger Pershore varieties, but when left to ripen can excel in terms of flavor.

I grow Oullins Gage, an early cropper with green-gold flesh that needs a good summer to show itself at its subtle best. If I were to choose again, it would be an Early Transparent, a fruit so sweet and honeyed the word nectar springs to mind as you eat. This is the plum, along with perhaps an Old Greengage and a few Mirabelles, that I regard as some the finest fruit on earth.

A plum tree in the garden

I like to think everyone has a special tree. A tree they may be lucky enough to see every day, or pass on a regular journey. Perhaps it is one they remember from their childhood. A tree whose trunk is memorably gnarled or whose exposed, twisting roots run like serpents through the grass. Perhaps the memory is of a particular branch they used to sit on in more carefree days. A tree can welcome you as one might an old friend.

My "special" tree was an ancient plum, its trunk covered with dusky gray lichen. Barely taller than a man, its bent and craggy trunk had to be held up by a pile of old bricks. And once the fruit had fallen, its shape became almost sinister, its brittle twigs pointing like witches' fingers against a cold winter sky. I knew it through most of my childhood and can recall almost every branch.

The plums, typically as it turns out, could be few and far between or so prolific we thought the branches would snap under their weight. The variety, like many of the best fruit trees, had been lost in time; the fruits were almost translucent, a deep saffron yellow flashed with rusty crimson. Large, too; at least that is how I remember them.

On a brief trip back to my childhood cottage, a little saddened by the state of the once-immaculate garden, I dared not look at the top end of the paddock, the bit we referred to as the orchard, in case my tree had vanished. What worried me more, I suspect, was finding that my tree never existed.

Those plums are now tainted with the rose-pink glow of nostalgia, but I like to think they were as sweet and luscious as I remember them. My guess is that they were some form of the much-maligned Victoria that the late Alan Davidson sniffily dismissed as "good marketing rather than inherent distinction." Perhaps he didn't know it as I did, when left to ripen properly, until each fruit looks as if there is a candle burning inside it and you have to shoo the wasps away.

There are now five plum trees in my tiny garden, all of which I have planted in the last decade (I must admit to a slight obsession with this fruit). A golden Mirabelle, whose marble-sized fruits as sweet as maple syrup come in their hundreds; a Crimson Drop that has only recently started to show its hand; an Oullins Gage, whose fruits glow deep gold though their dusky skin; a damson for crumbles; and a wild plum, whose seed may have come from a careless bird or maybe from my habit of hurling plum pits and apple cores out of the window. Either way it is welcome. I recommend a semidwarfing St. Julian "A" rootstock for a smallish garden. Otherwise it will take over the entire space, like a carelessly purchased greengage once did here.

The plum tree is a member of the same family as the apricot and the cherry but has a slightly mistier history. What is clear is its presence in monastery gardens. I sometimes think if I had to limit myself to just one tree it would be some sort of plum.

Planted and staked, they require little in the way of pruning, although I do cut out crossing branches at the start of the growing season. The blossom is some of the earliest and can be lost to frost but, God willing, there will be fruit turning gold by early July and truly ripe by mid-August or September.

Varieties

We will never know the names of many of the old trees in our gardens. We just eat their fruits and say thank you. Anyone planting a tree now would be lucky to come across the Cox's Emperor, with its majestic growth and dark red, yellow-spotted fruits, or the apricot-fleshed Manaccan, so prized for its jam. Specialty nurseries still have many time-honored varieties suitable for a small garden, such as the purple Angelina Burdett, the sugary Reine Claude de Bavay, and the yellow- and red-mottled Golden Bullace. Many are self fertile. Some, such as Opal, require a friend.

Pershore Yellow Egg One for the pot. Not the juiciest or most flavorsome when eaten raw but makes jolly good jam. It was discovered in the wild, at Tiddesley Wood near Pershore, some time between 1827 and 1833 (accounts vary). As a kid, I saw more of this canary-colored plum in my local Worcestershire farm stands than any other. They were even sold in the post office.

Early Laxton A yellow fruit with flashes of pink and a faint lavender bloom, introduced in 1916. The trees are long leaved, with graceful, drooping branches. An early variety for kitchen or table.

Old Greengage Known in France as Reine Claude and named after the wife of François I, who died in 1547, so we are talking about a variety of great antiquity. Rich, sugary fruits of a deep yellow green. Superb flavor. Perfect for the larger garden. Mine shades most of my vegetable patch.

Czar A dark purple and green plum, often rather large, named after the Russian emperor, Czar Alexander II. Grown since 1874, with large, primrose-flecked blossom, its yellowish flesh is probably at its best in a crumble. I see a lot of these at farmers' markets.

Blue Tit Small, sweet, bright blue plum. A good flavor and useful both in the kitchen and for eating from the tree.

Kirke's Blue A large, heavy plum with plenty of juice when truly ripe. Likes a warm spot.

Warwickshire Drooper Orange-yellow flesh, often used for jam but can be good at the table if left long enough. A plums-and-custard plum.

Kea A rare variety from a chance seedling grown only near the Fal estuary in Cornwall. Sweet, with a deliciously acid note, this highly sought-after plum has been grown since about 1635. Available locally from mid-August to late September. This small, round, blue-red fruit is my favorite kitchen plum. Usefully, you can buy them frozen via the Internet. But it makes a very costly crumble.

Victoria Variable, ubiquitous crimson and gold all-arounder, found in July and August.

Excalibur Burgundy-red flesh, a little russeting.

Marjorie's Seedling A vigorous grower with bloomy, purple-maroon fruit that can be found in late September and October. I get less than excited about this one, but others disagree.

Oullins Gage* Often the first of the gages to ripen; needs a good, hot summer to be at its best.

Elephant Heart* Heart-shaped fruit with mottled purple skin and sweet, deep red flesh. Requires pollenizer; Santa Rosa is a good choice.

Italian Prune* Quite sweet when fully ripened, fruits have amber flesh and dusky purple skin.

Santa Rosa* Large, tangy fruits with red-purple skin and red-streaked golden flesh. Adapts to wide variety of environments.

*Available from US sources.

The plum season

Blink and you risk missing your favorite member of the plum family. I include a list of their approximate seasons, purely as an *aide-mémoire*.

July Pershore Yellow Egg, Victoria, Opal, Santa Rosa (early)
August Jubilee, Avalon, Excalibur, Kea (late), Victoria, Oullins Gage, Cambridge Gage, Transparent Gage
September Marjorie's Seedling (late), Warwickshire Drooper, Kea, Kirke's Blue, Reine Claude de Bavay (late), Elephant Heart, Italian Prune

Plums in the kitchen

There has been a plum of one hue or another in my kitchen every day of July, August, and September for as long as I can remember (except 2008, when there was a national shortage due to bad weather at blossom time). Any plum is suitable for cooking but some more so than others, often because they need a little heat and sugar to tease out their character. The most widely used in the kitchen are the Laxtons, Rivers, Pershore Yellow Egg, and Czar, with Marjorie's Seedling and all members of the damson family calling time in late September and early October. Victorias are fine too, but prone to collapse and with a tendency to produce a surfeit of rather pale juice. Leave the skins on to retain the fruit's characteristic sharpness. The Cornish Kea is my number-one kitchen plum but, rarely available outside its manor, it is not exactly the easiest for those of us north of the Tamar to get our hands on. The fragrant, tangy Santa Rosa is a kitchen workhorse, too.

Most varieties will need sweetening, for which you can use sugar or a subtle honey such as clover (avoid the strongly flavored chestnut). Vanilla is a wise seasoning, though probably not if you used honey as the sweetener. Together they can be overpowering. Ground ginger has an affinity with all plums, as do the warm-bun spices, particularly cinnamon. For savory use, juniper berries, coriander seeds, and fresh ginger all bring something worthwhile to the party.

I cannot join in with Enid Blyton or even Jane Grigson's disdain for stewed plums. In our house, finding a crock of soft, silk-textured stewed fruit in the fridge, with juice the color of a semiprecious jewel, is one of the delights of early autumn mornings. When the fruits and their pits have been cooked with sugar, the juice is sweet-sharp, almost cough-syrup thick, and will glisten in the early morning light. It is difficult to think of a more uplifting start to the day. Though I probably could if pushed. Sometimes I stir in a spoonful of sheep's milk yogurt. It always curdles, but no worse than custard, stewed plums' knee-jerk accompaniment. Baked, the plums' flavor is possibly even richer.

The plum family is perhaps the perfect crumble fruit, having the correct amount of juice and tartness to balance the dry, butter-sugar-flour crust. The inherent sharpness comes from the mouth-puckering hedgerow blackthorn, or sloe, that is part of the ancestry of our modern plum. The "undercrust," my word for that damp, almost magical place where crumble meets fruit, can be particularly blissful when plums are involved. It is a question of balancing the sweet layer with the slightly sour fruit. Which is why most of us hold the plum, damson, or gooseberry in higher esteem than the apple or peach as a crumble contender. A handful of rolled oats, sesame seeds, or sliced almonds added to the crumble topping can be a pleasing note that shouldn't offend the purist. Walnuts have a tendency to burn.

As a pie fruit, the plum can produce too much juice for a double crust. More successful, I find, is to have only an upper crust—the downside being that you never get a neat slice the way you do with the fruit trapped between the two pieces of pastry. I make up for this by using a chunky, almost shortcakelike pastry as the top crust (you can never have too much pastry as far as I'm concerned).

Jam seems like a cop-out to a writer who tries to offer at least a modicum of fresh thinking, but is there a more wonderful jam than plum? (Black currant, possibly.) It is the one jam we make that most resembles the sumptuous, soft preserves of the Middle East. I pick mine up from market stalls. Despite plums having high levels of pectin, the natural jelling agent found in ripe fruits, plum jam is often to be found gently set rather than in true bouncy British style (you might like to see my note about the British obsession with heavily set jams in *Eating for England*).

Plum pudding, incidentally, was made with raisins, the word *plum* meaning any old dried fruit, so we can quickly dispense with that one. It was often known as Sussex plum duff and was very comforting on a December night. But true plum recipes abound, particularly those from the Victorian era, which was probably the golden age for the kitchen plum. Look out for traditional crumble and recipes such as the lighter American "crisp," made with breadcrumbs (there's a good one in my book *The Kitchen Diaries*); plums and custard; plum pie; and preserves such as plum and ginger jam. I also offer here a seriously crumbly tart, a single-crust pie, a sweet-hot chutney, and a sharp, ginger-spiked sauce for a crisp pork roast.

This fruit will take a savory treatment too. I am not big on fruit with meat, other than gooseberries or apples with pork and bitter oranges with duck, but game birds, especially wild duck, pigeon, and partridge, have the sort of smoky, woodsy flesh that works well with a plum sauce. As does roast pork, especially the fatter breeds such as Gloucester Old Spot and Tamworth. I keep the sharper, less ripe fruit for this. There's usually plenty around. A sticky pulp of stewed Victorias, sugar, and a splash of red wine vinegar will make a piece of smoked pork and shredded cabbage happy. Cinnamon is the spice you want.

I have tried using greengages and larger varieties in a stuffing, but the result was too wet, even when mixed with blotterlike breadcrumbs. It is worth making a salad with them though. Pit them, then chop and toss with soaked bulgur wheat, lemon juice, and masses of chopped parsley and cilantro. The result is sensational. We ate it one autumn with cold roast duck, another with grilled squab. As birds are so fond of picnicking on my Mirabelles, I find the marriage particularly apt.

Plums and...

Almonds A few ground almonds introduced into a sponge cake or crumble mixture or a tart filling is appropriate with any member of the plum family. A scattering of sliced almonds on an open plum tart or the surface of a crumble can be good too.

Hazelnuts Stir ground hazelnuts into the flour, butter, and sugar crust of a crumble. Throw a few toasted and chopped hazelnuts over a dish of poached plums.

Game birds Most richly fleshed game birds appreciate a few poached plums on the side, seasoned with ginger and perhaps juniper. A plum chutney or relish is a sound partner for cold roast game birds.

Pork and duck The fattier the meat, the more appropriate a side relish of plums.

Ginger Ground, fresh, preserved. It all works.

Honey Often works better than sugar when you are looking for something with which to sweeten your fruits.

Spices Almost any spice, from cinnamon to cardamom and chile to coriander seeds, works with the plum family. Use them in cakes, puddings, and pickles.

A Chinese-style pork roast with plum ginger sauce

The rule is that a sharp sauce is needed with pork to cut its fattiness. More important, I think, is the fact that the sauce should flatter the gamey notes of the meat. Apples do this well enough but gooseberries do it better, having more natural sharpness than any cooking apple. Plums and damsons flatter the flesh of the pork as well as the fat, and their fruity notes blend harmoniously with the pan juices.

The Chinese flavors here demand something other than potatoes as an accompaniment, so I go for some dark green cabbage, coarsely shredded the width of pappardelle and cooked in a very little water until bright emerald green. No butter, just vital, earthy greens to contrast with the richness of the meat and its sauce.

enough for 4 to 6
a piece of pork belly – about 3 pounds (1.5kg)
Szechwan peppercorns – 2 tablespoons
sea salt – 3 tablespoons
ground anise – 1 teaspoon

for the sauce
sharp plums or damsons – 2 pounds (900g)
sugar – 3 tablespoons
water – ½ cup (120ml)
fresh ginger – a large knob about the size of a walnut, peeled
        and cut into matchsticks
star anise – 4
salt – ½ teaspoon
smooth red wine vinegar – 2 tablespoons

Put the pork in a shallow dish. Warm the Szechwan peppercorns in a nonstick pan until they start to crackle a bit, then remove from the heat. Grind together the salt, toasted peppercorns, and ground anise. Easiest with a mortar and pestle, but you can also do it with a plastic bag and a rolling pin. You want a fine, beige powder. Rub the spice mixture over the pork and its skin, cover lightly with wax paper and set aside for at least 8 hours, preferably overnight in the fridge. This is for the dry marinade to work its magic.

To make the sauce, put the plums or damsons into a colander and give them a good rinse under cold running water, pulling off any stalks and leaves as you go. Tip the fruit into a stainless steel saucepan (aluminum will taint sour fruits such as plums), add the sugar, water, ginger, anise, and salt, and bring to a boil. Leave to simmer for about ten to fifteen minutes, until the fruit has burst and the sauce has thickened to a deep purple-red. Stir in the vinegar and simmer for five minutes more. Watch that it doesn't become too thick or catch on the pan's bottom; it is inclined to get a bit jammy at this stage.

Put the sauce somewhere to cool or, if spitting out pits at the table really isn't your thing, sieve it first: tip it into a large sieve set over a bowl and push the fruit through with a wooden spoon. Keep going until all you have left is a few pits. Set aside; you can warm it up just before you serve the pork.

Roast the pork in an oven heated to 400°F (200°C) for about an hour, basting occasionally. Leave to rest for ten, or even fifteen, minutes before carving, and pass the sauce around at the table.

A plum tabbouleh

Ripe fruits live happily with the nutty texture and flavor of bulgur, the cracked, steamed, and crushed wheat grains used in many versions of tabbouleh. They need soaking in hot water rather than cooking, making them a quickly assembled base for a starchy salad. I have tossed bulgur with everything from red currants to mangoes as an accompaniment to grilled or cold meats.

enough for 4 as a side dish
bulgur – 1 cup (150g)
slim green onions – 6
large, juicy plums – 6
a small, hot red chile
mint – 8 bushy sprigs
flat-leaf parsley – 8 bushy sprigs
juice of a lemon
olive oil

Put the bulgur into a bowl and just cover with boiling water, then set aside.

Finely slice the green onions, discarding the toughest of their leaves, then put into a mixing bowl. Halve, pit, and coarsely chop the plums. Seed and finely chop the chile, then coarsely chop the mint and parsley leaves and add everything to the onions. Pour in the lemon juice, a couple of tablespoons of olive oil, and a generous seasoning of salt and black pepper.

Rough the bulgur up with a fork, making sure it has absorbed all the water. Crumble it into the plum and onion mixture, stir in another glug or two of olive oil—the grain should not be wet—then serve.

A pudding cake of honey, cinnamon, and plums

The plum harvest of 2009 was legendary for its quality. I probably ate the most luscious fruits I had had since childhood. I brought them back from the market by the bagful. Avalon and Jubilee from Witney market near Oxford, Excalibur and Old Greengage from my local farmers' stands, Black Kea from Tregothnan in Cornwall.

Plums were poached for breakfast, pickled for Christmas ham, and simmered for jam. They also found their way into cakes, such as the almond-based teacake in *The Kitchen Diaries*. One Sunday afternoon, late—swathes of golden light had already hit the back garden—I started work on a plum cake that had the faintest stickiness of a gingerbread but the mellow qualities of a spice cake. Spongelike on top, moist (almost soggy) with warm, jammy Victoria sponge cake underneath, it was the sort of cake you could serve as a dessert with a pitcher of cream or cut into squares to tuck into the week's lunch boxes.

enough for 8
all-purpose flour – 2 cups (250g)
baking powder – a slightly heaping teaspoon
baking soda – a level teaspoon
ground cinnamon – a slightly heaping teaspoon
golden syrup – ⅔ cup (200g)
thick honey – 2 heaping tablespoons
butter – ½ cup (125g)
light muscovado sugar – ½ cup, packed (125g)
plums – 12 ounces (350g)
large eggs – 2
milk – 1 cup (240ml)

Preheat the oven to 350°F (180°C). Use parchment paper to line a cake pan or baking dish about 9½ inches (24cm) square. Sift the flour, baking powder, baking soda, and cinnamon into a bowl.

Warm the golden syrup, honey, and butter in a pan until the butter melts. Stir in the muscovado sugar. Halve the plums, or cut them into quarters if they are very large, then pull out their pits.

Break the eggs into a bowl, pour in the milk, and whisk lightly to mix. Pour the golden syrup mixture into the flour and mix with a large, metal spoon. Pour in the eggs and milk and continue stirring until you have a loose, almost sloppy batter without any traces of flour.

Tip the mixture into the lined cake pan, drop in the plums, and bake for thirty-five minutes. Place a piece of foil loosely over the top of the cake and leave to cook for ten to fifteen minutes longer. Switch off the oven, but leave the cake in for a further fifteen minutes, then remove and leave to cool.

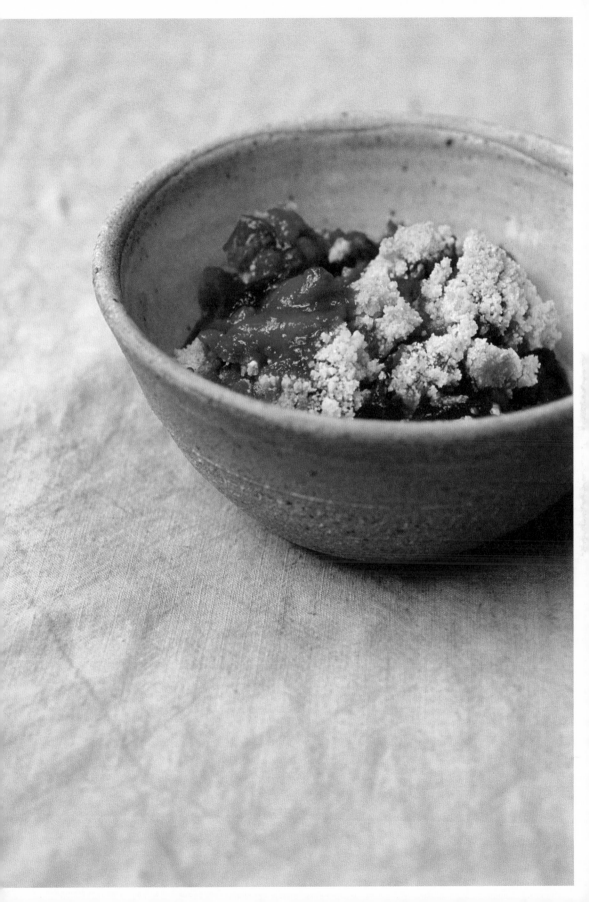

Plum crumble tart

Is this a tart or a cake? I'm not sure it really matters what you call something as moist and tender as this.

> *enough for 6 to 8*
> all-purpose flour – 2 cups plus 1 tablespoon (260g)
> soft brown sugar – ½ cup, packed (125g)
> ground almonds – a scant cup (100g)
> fridge-cold butter – 1 cup (220g)
> plums, greengages, or damsons – 1⅓ pounds (600g)
> pine nuts – 2 ounces (50g), a generous ⅓ cup

Preheat the oven to 350°F (180°C). Line the bottom of a 9- to 9½-inch (22 to 24cm) square baking pan with a single piece of parchment paper, bringing it up two opposite sides of the pan so you can use it to lift the tart out easily.

Put the flour, sugar, and almonds into a mixing bowl, cut the butter into small chunks, and rub it into the flour mixture with your fingertips. Stop when what you have resembles coarse fresh breadcrumbs. Tip two-thirds of the crumb mixture into the baking pan and gently flatten it to form a thin base, pushing it well into the corners. Firm it gently, but don't compact it.

Cut the plums in half, unless they are huge, in which case quarter them. Remove the pits and lay the pieces of fruit on the crumb base. Mix the pine nuts into the remaining crumbs and scatter them loosely over the plums. Let some of the fruit show through.

Bake for forty-five to fifty minutes, when the fruit should be gently bubbling, the crust golden. Leave to settle before lifting out of the baking pan and onto a cooling rack.

Poached plums, spices, and ginger

The British have long had a love of ginger: gingerbread, gingernuts, ginger beer, and ginger wine are all part of our culinary history. I sometimes include its sweet, sticky heat in the syrup for poaching fruit such as pears (wonderful) and large plums, especially on a cold day. The syrup from a jar of preserved ginger is worth using too, and the glistening orbs themselves can make comfortable bedfellows for any of the plum family.

enough for 4
plums – 12 large ones, or more if small
superfine sugar – a scant ½ cup (90g)
water – 1 cup (250ml)
star anise – 2 whole flowers
cloves – 6
lumps of preserved ginger in syrup – 3, chopped
syrup from the preserved ginger – 4 tablespoons

Wipe the plums and remove their stalks. Stir the sugar and water together in a heavy-bottomed saucepan. Bring to a boil, then add the star anise, cloves, chopped ginger, and ginger syrup. Lower in the plums and turn down to a gentle simmer, then partially cover with a lid. Let the fruit poach in the scented syrup for twenty minutes or so, until it is truly soft and melting.

Serve warm, three fruits per person, in little dishes or glasses, with some of the glowing syrup spooned over.

Note: Poached fruits such as these can also be served with roast pork. Add a little of the sweet cooking liquid to the pan juices of the roast, then serve the fruit on the side. Plums work well with pork and duck and with baked ham.

A hot, sweet plum chutney

Just as curry, stew, or trifle left for a day or two in the fridge will often taste more interesting (rounded, deeper) than when freshly made, the character of a chutney can change over time. My first taste of a homemade plum preserve appeared to have a jamlike sweetness. Two weeks later, the same chutney had taken on a mellowness, the underlying heat from the chiles coming forward, the initial hit of sugar taking a step back.

It is into this recipe I dip for something to go with a few slices of cold roast pork, beef, or the remains of a roasted game bird. Its autumnal sweetness flatters a lump of cheese too—an orange-fleshed Cheshire or a Wensleydale.

makes a couple of jam jars' worth
plums – 1½ pounds (750g)
onions – 12 ounces (350g)
raisins – a generous ¾ cup (125g)
light muscovado sugar – 1 cup, packed (250g)
crushed dried chile – ½ teaspoon
salt – a teaspoon
yellow mustard seeds – 2 teaspoons
cider vinegar – ⅔ cup (150ml)
malt vinegar – ⅔ cup (150ml)
a cinnamon stick

Halve the plums and discard the pits. Peel and coarsely chop the onions. Put the fruit and onions into a large stainless steel or enameled pan with the raisins, sugar, chile, salt, mustard seeds, vinegars, and cinnamon stick. Bring to a boil, turn down the heat, and leave to simmer for an hour, giving the occasional stir to reduce the risk of the chutney sticking.

Spoon into sterilized jars and seal.

Cinnamon and anise plums

Wipe the fruit, remove its stalks, and bring to a boil with 4 tablespoons of water and 2 tablespoons of sugar per pound (500g) of fruit. Tuck a cinnamon stick and 2 stars of anise among the plums and turn the heat down to a gentle simmer. Leave the fruit to bubble slowly to tenderness— a matter of ten to twenty minutes, depending on its ripeness. Eat warm or cool, for breakfast.

Plums for breakfast

A pot with a sturdy bottom, a pound (500g) of plums, or damsons, maybe greengages, ½ cup (100g) of golden baker's sugar, a vanilla pod split down its length, its seeds exposed, and just enough water to leave a wet film on the bottom of the pan. Place over gentle heat, let the sugar melt and the plums burst, their juices mingling with the sugar. Keep the heat low, your eyes on the job. After ten minutes, maybe fifteen, the plums will have collapsed, their juices taken up some of the warm vanilla notes, and you will have a dish of plums to cool, then thoroughly chill, and eat for breakfast.

A single-crust pie for particularly juicy plums

Asked to define the "bliss point" in a culinary sense, I would venture to suggest the underside of a pastry crust where it meets the fruit. Still crisp and sugary on top, it is moist, almost sodden underneath with sweet-sharp, scarlet juice. But some fruits can produce so much juice that the bottom crust collapses. Plums are particular culprits. The answer: a single crust on top of the pie. Fine in dispensing with a soggy bottom, but as a pastry lover I feel robbed. My version uses a top crust of shortcake thickness. Intensely crumbly, this solves the riddle of how to get enough crust when using a particularly juice-producing fruit. The pastry crust here is thick but very tender, and will crumble as you serve it.

Occasionally cream is called for with a pie, and this is just one of those occasions.

enough for 4

for the pastry
butter – 7 tablespoons (100g)
golden baker's sugar – ½ cup (100g)
an egg, lightly beaten
all-purpose flour – 1⅓ cups (175g)
baking powder – ½ teaspoon
a little milk, for brushing

for the filling
ripe plums or greengages – about 2 pounds (800g to 1kg)
superfine sugar – 2 to 3 tablespoons
ground cinnamon – a knifepoint

Cream the butter and sugar in a stand mixer until light and fluffy. Mix in the lightly beaten egg, then gently add the flour and baking powder. Remove from the bowl and roll into a ball on a heavily floured work surface. Knead the dough for a minute or two until smooth and soft. Wrap in wax paper and refrigerate for about twenty minutes.

Preheat the oven to 350°F (180°C). Cut the plums in half and remove their pits. Cut the fruit into large pieces, toss with the sugar and cinnamon, and put into a lightly buttered 8- to 8½-inch (20 to 22cm) baking dish. Roll out the pastry on a floured board, then lift carefully onto the pie. There will be a little left over. The crust is very short and it really doesn't matter if it tears as you lower it over the fruit. Some of the juice will probably erupt through it as it cooks anyway. At least I hope so.

Brush lightly with milk and bake for forty minutes. The pastry should be pale biscuit colored. Dust with superfine sugar and serve warm.

A plum feast

July 2, 2007, a wet summer's evening and we had finished our steaks, the smokers among us had lit up, and the rain poured torrentially against the glass roof. Suddenly, my hosts put a vast branch on the table, its end apparently ripped from the tree, still in leaf and covered with wild red plums.

A memorable way to end a meal, but somehow brutal too; it was the tree's last stand. The branch had been rescued from an elderly plum tree in a century-old East End allotment near the River Lea in Hackney. A much-loved site that was to be bulldozed for an Olympic walkway and its tenants evicted. Grown almost certainly from a wild seedling, its small, bright-red Myrobalan fruit had been as much a part of the allotment as the beds, sheds, and fava beans. We pulled at the tiny crimson fruits, breaking off laden twigs and passing them around the table, sucking at the sweet-tart fruits while my hosts told the story of the community of allotment holders, their fig trees and fertile land, and their futile fight to stop the march of the bulldozers.

I now kick myself for not planting one of the many pits that lay sucked on my plate. But their house is not far from mine, and I often wonder about the ancestry of the wild cherry plum that has appeared in my vegetable patch.

Quinces

There is a quince on the kitchen table. Plump, golden, curvaceous. A fat cherub of a fruit, with waxy skin and, here and there, patches of soft, pubescent down. Leaf attached, it has an extraordinary scent that you catch in occasional wafts like blossom on a breeze, part floral, yet a little sickly too.

I sometimes buy a paper bag of quinces simply for their presence in the house. Their arrival marks the start of winter as surely as a tomcat marks his territory. They live in a shallow Chinese dish in the hall, welcoming me home. I cook them eventually, just as the odd blemish appears on their deep, imperial-yellow skin. A fruit that, once cooked, has an incomparable subtlety, whispering in low notes of honey and rose.

The spreading, deciduous tree has the most elegant blossom in late April, each loose bud opening to reveal a milk-white flower of mothlike fragility, its edges brushed a pale and watery pink. A flower so gentle it could be shattered by a shower of rain or blown apart by a sharp gust of wind. It is hard to believe that a bloom so soft will eventually produce a fruit impenetrable to all but the sharpest of cook's knives.

Native to Iran and Armenia, the quince—*Cydonia oblonga*—was introduced to Europe via Serbia, Albania, Greece, and Turkey, the latter of which now produces almost a quarter of the world's output. The quince is the most ancient of fruits, predating the apple and the pear, and is considered in many cultures to be a symbol of love, fertility, and happiness. Sacred to Aphrodite, the fruit was offered by the Greeks at their weddings, where, it is said, the bride would nibble a quince to sweeten her breath before "entering the bridal chamber." It is the fruit of Edward Lear's poem, "The Owl and the Pussycat," where they "dined on mince and slices of quince, which they ate with a runcible spoon." Runcible being one of the poet's favorite nonsense words.

There is a certain abandon in a bowl of large quinces, like the women in a Beryl Cook painting. But for all its gorgeous looks, most varieties of quince are virtually inedible raw. Like damsons, rhubarb, and the gooseberry, this is one for the kitchen rather than the fruit bowl. A cook's fruit, if you like. It can be baked or simmered in syrup or used to fill a shallow puff pastry tart. After a long, slow cooking with sugar, the flesh of the quince often turns a majestic crimson. I sometimes pot roast them with sugar and a little water, leaving them to putter away until they are glowing red and almost transparent.

The quince is most often seen in the form of a jam or paste such as the Spanish *membrillo*. The fruits are peeled and cored, chopped, then boiled with the pectin-rich trimmings tied up in cheesecloth until you have a thick purée, sometimes referred to as a fruit cheese. Sugar is then added and the mixture cooked once again until thick and smooth. On cooling, the paste sets to the point where it can be sliced.

Quince paste is most often served with sharp cheeses such as Manchego, the sheep's milk cheese from La Mancha in Spain. It works well with many of our artisan-made cheeses. I eat it with both Caerphilly and Wensleydale. On winter afternoons I sometimes put a slice of quince paste and a smidgen of crème fraîche on a water cracker and eat it as the light outside fades to gray.

Despite its Rubenesque quality and heavenly fragrance, the quince will never be the most popular of fruits, as is the case with any fruit you cannot simply bite into. But for this cook it will always hold a certain mystery and intrigue and, with its ample curves and sensual fragrance, a sense of both the exotic and the erotic.

A quince in the garden

It is one of those mellow afternoons in autumn, the garden a scene of peaceful rot. Mauve stars of Michaelmas daisies twinkle through the tangle of brown stems and dew-covered cobwebs that stick to your face as you walk through them. Nature is taking the garden back from me once again. At the far end, past the compost and the yew hedge, is a handful of awkward, misshapen fruit trees: a damson, a young mulberry, and a quince that has fruited every year since it was planted.

Amid the dark green leaves, a single fruit—a downy, golden orb—hangs from a black branch too weak and pliable for any thieving squirrel to climb. The only sign of life in a garden slowly falling asleep, like a pensioner in a much loved but threadbare chair. It is late and time for tea, but tomorrow I will pull the branch down and take a closer look.

Even before this garden was dug, I knew the first trees to plant: damson, medlar, mulberry, and quince. Quince is frost hardy and requires a cold period below 45°F (7°C) to flower properly. It is suited to the small domestic garden, rarely growing larger than sixteen feet (five meters), although it can become wide unless pruned. Small and deciduous, it is often used as rootstock on which to graft apple trees.

The trees like moisture, particularly during the summer. Like clematis, they prefer their roots to be cool (the most prolific I have ever seen were growing beside a waterfall in a Croatian nature reserve). They need a long growing season and fare best in a warm, secluded spot. It is worth watering them well if the weather has been dry for any length of time.

The immature fruit are charming, covered by a thick, gray down that wears away as they grow and ripen. By late summer they will be the size of a small pear and turning from green to canary yellow. The hue darkens as they ripen. Though ripening quinces can be left on the tree, they tend to become heavy as the season develops and have a habit of dropping off. I pick them as their skins turn from green to yellow and bring them on indoors. Unripe and full of pectin, they make a heavier-set preserve.

The fruits will keep for months, but need air around them. Slatted shelves are good, especially if the fruits aren't touching. With luck and a modicum of care, they will stay in fine condition until after Christmas.

Varieties

It is unlikely you will be offered anything but the most popular varieties, though there are many grown elsewhere in Europe, including such romantically named ones as Le Bourgeaut, Lescovacz, Perfume, Pineapple, and Van Deman.

Champion Rather round, perfectly formed fruits, which grow quite prolifically.
Meech's Prolific* Pear-shaped fruits of good flavor. Historic American variety.
Portugal* Works in a warm spot, but keep away from frost. Good flavor, some suggest the best.
Vranja Large, popular, pear-shaped, and heavily perfumed variety that I have much success with.
Smyrna* Large, pear-shaped fruits with lemon-yellow skin and highly aromatic flesh. An established Turkey variety.
Orange* Traditional variety with round, large fruits, orange-yellow flesh, sunny yellow skin, and a perfumed flavor.

*Available from US sources.

A quince in the kitchen

The quince is the fruit of frosty mornings and blackened leaves, keeping in sound condition through the cold months. I sometimes bake a few in a low oven with a glass of marsala or quince liqueur and a thick drizzle of maple syrup or honey. They emerge, a good couple of hours after you put them in, a transluscent, glowing amber. They rarely fluff up like an apple, but take on the texture of melting fudge.

We cannot hurry a cooking quince. They are ready when they feel like it. I have known the most stubborn to take forty minutes or more to poach to tenderness in sugar syrup. The really large ones, the weight of a small pineapple, can take even more of our precious gas. But the scent of them cooking fills the house with a rich, mellow sweetness, especially if I have used a glass or two of wine in the poaching liquid.

The Romans were fond of this fruit, and the cookbook of Apicius gives recipes for them stewed with honey and even combined with leeks. (Better you than me.)

Quinces love to end their days with a glass or two of something alcoholic and sugary, such as Muscat de Beaumes de Venise or a cheap Tokay. Even so, a little extra sugar is needed, too, and some water, and more than a little patience. Once cooked, they will keep in the syrup for a few days. Eat them in all their purity, or lower one into a dish of baked rice pudding, or eat with thick yogurt for a hedonistic breakfast.

You cannot eat the skin, so it should be pared before poaching, but you can happily bake them whole or halved in their skins. Once the peel is removed the flesh browns almost instantly—certainly faster than a pear or apple. I brush them with lemon juice and drop them into acidulated water. A little lemon juice on the peeler blade can help too.

The old notion of tucking a few cubes of the fruit into an apple pie works. The small amount of quince flesh is enough to send its mild, floral notes throughout the whole pie. I have used this trick with a crumble, too. Quinces are rarely used in open tarts, which is a shame, but a jelly of them is often used to glaze French-style pastries. The color is flattering to all manner of fruits and the flavor mild and complementary.

The quince contains a very generous amount of pectin. It is almost impossible to make a quince jelly that doesn't set. The pectin levels are higher in unripe fruit and diminish as it turns yellow. Quince jelly sometimes sets heavily enough to slice. In Malta, a jam—*gamm ta l-isfargal*—is produced, rather like the Lebanese *sfarjel*, Portugal's *marmelada*, and Pakistan's glowing, orange-red *muraba*. Thick and fragrant, this conserve is wonderful as a breakfast jam but also, served in elegant spoonfuls, with a soft cheese or crème fraîche. The word marmalade, incidentally, was originally used to describe quince jam rather than the conserve of bitter oranges we know now.

Drinks are made from *Cydonia oblonga*, too: a brandy in the Balkans, a digestive known as *liqueur de coing* in Alsace, and in Britain a glowing liqueur by Bramley and Gage, whose fig and date notes make it a smooth and moreish after-dinner drink.

Quinces and...

Honey More than just a sweetener, honey offers a subtle warmth to baked or poached quinces without intruding on their flavor.
Apples A large quince gives an extraordinary perfume to an apple pie. The two fruits manage to coexist without one canceling the other out.
Lemon A sharp seasoning that works to enhance the quince's flavor.
Verjuice Somewhat elusive, this mellow juice of unfermented grapes makes a pleasing cooking liquid for the fruit. Whenever I see it, I buy several bottles, as it keeps almost indefinitely.
Lamb A useful stuffing ingredient for the fruit, especially when seasoned with golden raisins, cumin, onion, and pine nuts.
Vinegar The marriage of sour liquid and fragrant fruit works very well. Hence the inclusion of the pickle recipe on page 454.
Cinnamon A stick dunked into the sugar syrup for a compote will lend a warmth to the finished dish. Works especially well with honey.

* Quinces are especially high in pectin. It is just unfortunate that they are rarely around in summer, when they would be exceptionally useful for setting strawberry and other low-pectin jams.
* The fruit's lasting properties were particularly useful before the advent of refrigeration, when it was one of the few that would keep the family in pies all winter.
* The strong aroma of a ripe quince will permeate all the other food in the fridge, especially the milk, so best store it in another cool place.

Lamb with quinces

Rather than painstakingly designed, much of my daily cooking is made up on the spot. It was very much the case with this lamb stew. I had planned a slow-cooked casserole of lamb shoulder, adding sweet spices and honey as it cooked to serve with a simple rice pilaf (white rice, steamed with a couple of cloves, a few peppercorns, and a bay leaf). The addition of quinces was very much a last-minute decision, as was the final flourish of bright-tasting herbs. Later, while writing this book, I discovered that my idea was far from original and the combination is well known in parts of the Middle East. This is a rich, slightly sweet dish, fragrant and gently spiced.

enough for 4
olive oil
butter – a thick slice
lamb shoulder – 1¾ pounds (800g), cut into large cubes
onions – 2
a cinnamon stick
fresh ginger – a thumb-sized lump, peeled and finely shredded
saffron threads – a good pinch
honey – 2 tablespoons
quinces – 1¾ pounds (800g)
the juice of a lemon
cilantro – a small bunch
mint – 4 bushy sprigs

Warm a little olive oil in a deep, heavy-bottomed pan. Add the butter and as soon as it melts add the lamb, seasoned with a little salt and black pepper. Let it color nicely on all sides, but avoid moving the pieces around the pan too much. While the lamb colors, peel and thickly slice the onions. Lift the meat out with a draining spoon and set aside.

Put the onions in the pan and leave over medium heat to soften and color lightly. Stir from time to time. As the onions cook, they will pick up some of the caramelized pan-stickings left by the lamb. Add the cinnamon stick, ginger, saffron threads, and a generous seasoning of salt. Return the lamb to the pan and drizzle in the honey.

Pour enough water over the lamb to just cover the surface—about 3 cups (750ml)—then bring to a boil. Lower the heat so the lamb simmers gently. Partially cover with a lid and leave to cook for an hour and ten minutes, checking the liquid level and giving the occasional stir until the meat is tender.

While the lamb is cooking, peel the quinces and remove the cores. Tie the peelings in a cheesecloth bag and put it in the stew as it cooks; this will add flavor to the sauce. Cut the quince flesh into cubes or thick slices and keep in a bowl of water to which you have added the lemon juice until needed.

When the lamb is tender, add the pieces of quince and continue to simmer for twenty minutes, until the fruit is almost soft. Chop the cilantro and mint leaves and mix together. Stir into the lamb stew, check the seasoning, and serve with a simple rice pilaf.

Slow-roasted loin of pork with quinces and marsala

Roasting the pork on the bone will give you more succulent meat. The downside is that meat on the bone is harder to carve. I get around this by asking my butcher to "chine" the meat for me, a neat little technique that results in leaving the bone intact but cutting it almost through, making it a cinch to carve. Best ask your butcher the day before (ask him for a few bones for stock, too). I find a piece of scored, bone-in loin with eight to ten bones will serve six, plus enough for seconds the next day.

It is worth getting the bottle of dry or semidry "cooking marsala" as soon as you can. The more easily found sweet version isn't really suitable.

enough for 6 with leftovers
an 8- to 10-bone pork loin – about 6½ pounds (3kg), on the bone
olive oil
garlic – 8 cloves
quinces – 6
dry marsala – ½ cup (125ml)
chicken stock – 1 cup (250ml)

Preheat the oven to 400°F (200°C). Unwrap the pork and make sure that the fat is dry to the touch. Wet fat won't crisp. Rub the meat generously all over with olive oil, then season it with salt. Lay the meat in a roasting pan so that the fat is facing upward. Roast for 30 minutes, then reduce the heat to 350°F (180°C) and continue to cook for thirty minutes per pound (450g).

Put a small pan of water on to boil. Add the garlic cloves and cook for fifteen minutes. Drain and pop the cloves from their skins.

An hour before the meat is due out of the oven, wipe the quinces, then tuck them in around the roast, together with the garlic cloves. Wet them with a little oil and continue roasting.

Test the roast for doneness. The fat should be golden and crisp. Pierce the skin with a metal skewer and check that the juices contain no sign of blood. Lift the meat out onto a warm serving dish. Cover with foil and leave in a warm place to rest. Lift out the quinces and put them in a warm dish. If they are not quite tender and fluffy, then return them to the oven.

Tip the layer of oil from the roasting pan into a heatproof pitcher; you can use it for roasting potatoes another day. Place the roasting pan over low heat and pour in the marsala and the chicken stock. Bring to a boil, scraping at the sticky sediment in the pan as you go, stirring it into the gravy. Crush the garlic cloves with the back of a wooden spoon, then leave the gravy to bubble slowly for three or four minutes. It should be thin, glossy, and deeply flavored. Taste for seasoning, adding salt and pepper as you think fit.

To serve, slice the meat thinly, pulling the bones away as you go—though no one should mind if they get one. As your knife reaches the backbone, the meat should come away quite easily. Place a quince on each plate, then drizzle over the marsala gravy.

Buttered quinces—a bowl of glowing, tender fruit

Quinces tend to give up less juice than an apple or pear. I find they also benefit from a little sugar. Their flavor, which can be ethereal and roselike, is best appreciated when they are lightly cooked with butter and golden superfine sugar. This can be in the oven or, if you want to experience them with a little more juice, in a pan on the stove top. In the final moments before they are tender, the quinces will be incandescently beautiful, the thick syrup that has formed in the pan the color of a winter sunset.

enough for 4
quinces – 3 pounds (1.5kg)
the juice of 2 lemons
butter – 3½ tablespoons (50g)
golden baker's sugar – a scant ½ cup (90g)

Peel and quarter the quinces, then core and cut them into thick slices, dropping them into a bowl of cold water into which you have squeezed half a lemon.

Melt the butter and sugar in a shallow pan, then add the quinces and the remaining lemon juice. Leave the fruits to soften, stirring occasionally, until they are pale gold, translucent, and tender enough to require only the merest squeeze to crush them (if they are not thoroughly tender, they won't be worth eating).

Lift the slices carefully into a bowl with a large spoon, leaving the juices behind. Turn up the heat and bring the liquid to a boil, letting it thicken slightly, then pour it over the warm fruit.

Roast quinces

You can cut a quince in half and bake it like an apple, but I prefer to poach them first so that their flesh becomes melting and almost transparent. Maple syrup offers a deep, almost caramel-like autumnal warmth, but you could use honey if you prefer. Cream would be no bad thing here.

This is a dessert to me, but I wouldn't mind trying it with some slices of broiled ham; a contemporary take on the 1960s ham and pineapple idea.

enough for 4
sugar – 4 heaping tablespoons
water – 2 cups (500ml)
cloves – 4
star anise – 2
smallish quinces – 4
half a lemon
maple syrup – 4 tablespoons

Put the sugar and water into a saucepan and bring to a boil. Add the cloves and star anise. Peel and halve the quinces, scoop out the cores, and rub them with the lemon to keep them from browning. Lower the quinces into the sugar syrup and let them simmer until tender. They may be ready in twenty-five minutes or perhaps take a little longer, depending on their size and ripeness.

Preheat the oven to 350°F (180°C). When the quinces are tender to the point of a knife, lift them out and put them in a shallow baking dish or roasting pan. Measure out ⅔ cup (150ml) of the cooking liquid, add the maple syrup, and, together with the aromatics, pour them over the quinces. Bake for thirty minutes or so, until very soft and tender. Serve with the cooking juices.

Soft quinces under a crisp crust

My guess is that this recipe would also work well with pears, which could be useful when quinces elude you. As well as at farmers' markets and the occasional produce market, quinces tend to turn up in Turkish and Cypriot stores in autumn. Farm stands are a good hunting ground too. I always buy more than I need, simply because they are rarely around when you want them and they have a good shelf life (I have kept them for weeks in the pantry).

enough for 4
lemons – 2
quinces – 4 pounds (1.75kg)
butter – 3 tablespoons (40g)
superfine sugar – ½ cup (100g)

for the crumble topping
all-purpose flour – a scant ⅔ cup (75g)
cold butter – 5 tablespoons (70g), diced
large, soft, fresh breadcrumbs – 1½ ounces (40g), about 1 cup
light muscovado sugar – 3 packed tablespoons (40g)
ground almonds – ⅓ cup (40g)
water – 2 tablespoons

Preheat the oven to 375°F (190°C). Fill a bowl with cold water and the juice of one of the lemons. This will help to keep the quinces from browning. Peel, core, and thickly slice the quinces, dropping each piece into the bowl of water. They brown quickly, so I try to get them in the water as soon as possible. Heat the butter in a large frying pan over medium heat, add the sugar and the juice of the remaining lemon, and toss the fruit in gently. Cook for twenty-five to thirty minutes, keeping the heat fairly high, until the fruit is tender, deep gold, and juicy. Tip into a shallow baking dish.

To make the crust, put the flour in a bowl, then add the cold diced butter. Rub the butter into the flour with your fingertips (or, of course, use a food processor, if you prefer) until the mixture resembles coarse breadcrumbs. Stir in the fresh breadcrumbs, sugar, and ground almonds. Drizzle over the water, then stir it lightly into the crumble with your fingertips. It should make tiny "pebbles" among the crumbs. Tip the mixture over the quinces and bake for twenty-five to thirty minutes, until the top is golden and the fruit is bubbling.

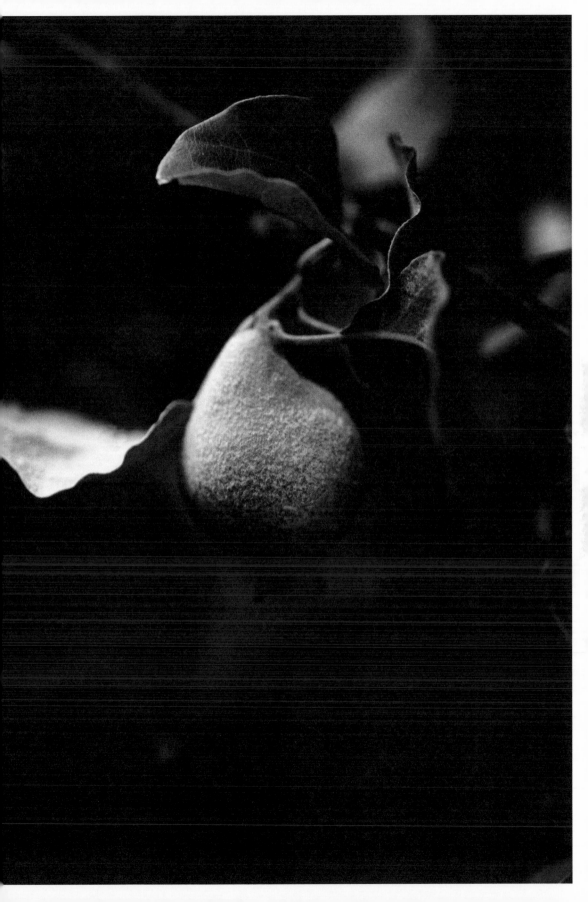

Apples and quinces baked in cream

A soothing, warm dessert for a cool autumn evening.

enough for 4
a large quince
sweet medium apples – 4
a little butter
golden baker's sugar – 3 tablespoons
a little all-purpose flour
grated nutmeg
heavy cream – 1⅔ cups (400ml)

Wipe the quince and rub the fluff from its skin, then put the whole, unpeeled fruit into a small, deep saucepan and cover it with water. Bring the water to a boil, then turn down the heat, so that it simmers gently. Lift the fruit with a slotted spoon after twenty minutes or so and squeeze it gently. If you can feel the quince flesh give a little, then lift it out and leave it to cool. If the fruit is still firm, let it simmer a little longer. It needs to be really quite soft.

Preheat the oven to 325°F (160°C). Peel and core the apples, slicing them thickly. Peel the quince too, remove its core, and cut it into slices a little thinner than the apples. Butter a medium-sized baking dish—it should hold the fruit comfortably in a single layer—then scatter over the sugar. Toss the fruit in a little flour, just a dusting really, and grate over some nutmeg. Pile the floured fruit into the sugared and buttered dish, then pour over the cream. You will find some of the fruit stands proud of the cream—no matter. Bake for forty-five to fifty minutes, until the cream is thick and scented and the fruit is thoroughly tender. Serve warm rather than hot.

Slow-cooked quinces with cassis

The combination sounds a little unlikely, yet it works rather well.
The color, too, is glorious.

> *enough for 6*
> golden baker's sugar – ¾ cup plus 2 tablespoons (175g)
> water – 4 cups (a liter)
> large quinces – 3
> a vanilla pod
> crème de cassis or other black currant liqueur – 1 cup (250ml)

Put the sugar and water in a deep pan and bring to a boil. Meanwhile, peel
the quinces, cut them in half, and scoop out the cores. I use a large, heavy
kitchen knife to halve the fruit, which is sometimes so hard as to be almost
impenetrable. The peeled fruits brown quickly too, so I like a halved lemon
on hand to rub over the surface as I proceed.

Slide the halved fruits into the sugar syrup and add the vanilla pod
and liqueur. Bring back to a boil, turn down the heat to a gentle simmer,
and leave to cook for a good forty to sixty minutes, until the fruit is totally
soft and full of juice, like a canned pear. I test mine with a metal skewer,
and don't switch off the heat until the skewer will slide effortlessly through
the fruit.

Take to one side and leave to cool a little. I tend to serve this dish warm
or at warm room temperature, when all the heady black currant scent is at
its strongest.

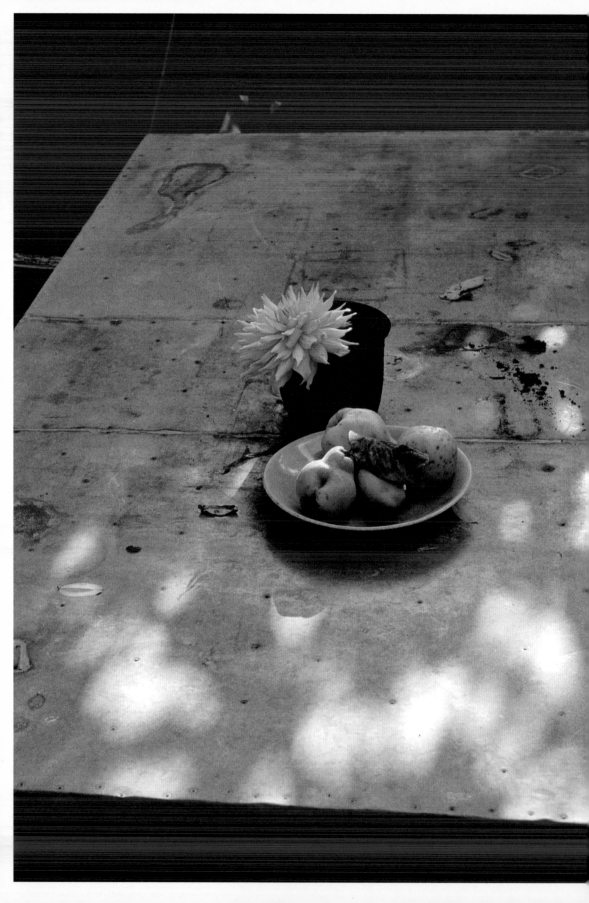

Quince paste

Quince paste is best known for its affinity with sheep's milk cheeses, but I have also used it as a glaze for the Christmas ham instead of marmalade and stirred it into the pan juices of a roast loin of pork. In most cases I would buy it ready-made but, having twice been presented with a box of quinces, I have sometimes ended up making my own. It is a labor of love, stirring the fruit purée and sugar until thick, and can sometimes feel a little extravagant (it needs to be left in a very low oven for several hours or even overnight) and yet there is great satisfaction in making your own. Its production also neatly deals with a glut of quinces in one swoop.

large quinces, unripe if possible – 8
the juice of a lemon
superfine sugar

Peel, core, and quarter the quinces. Put them in a pan with the lemon juice and just enough water to barely cover them. Bring to a boil, then turn down the heat and leave to simmer, partially covered with a lid, for about twenty minutes, until the fruit is soft.

Blitz the fruit in a food processor, then push through a sieve (lots of washing up, but a finer result). Weigh the purée (more mess) and put it into a heavy-bottomed pan with half its weight in sugar. Cook the mixture over low heat, stirring almost constantly, until it is dry and thick. The mixture is likely to splutter up like polenta. Take care. Cook until the paste is almost firm and is heavy to stir around the pan.

Scrape out onto a shallow tray with a rubber spatula. Set the oven at its lowest temperature, and leave the paste in for at least three hours, until set. Pack into jars and cover with lids.

A fragrant winter breakfast

A bowl of pale ivory-pink stewed fruit for those winter mornings when the sky is white and a sugar-frost has caught on the spiderwebs in the garden.

> *enough for 6*
> quinces – 2
> apples – 1¾ pounds (800g)
> lemon juice – 2 tablespoons
> sugar – ¾ cup (150g)

Peel the quinces, remove their cores, and coarsely chop the flesh. Put the peel and cores into a small pan, pour over just enough water to cover, then simmer for fifteen minutes. Set aside.

Meanwhile, cook the quinces in a very little water over low heat for about twenty minutes, until soft and pink. Peel and core the apples, coarsely chop them, and add them to the tender quince with the lemon juice, sugar, and the liquid from the simmered cores and peel. Continue to cook until the apple is tender. Mash to a purée with a fork or potato masher, then beat with a wooden spoon and serve.

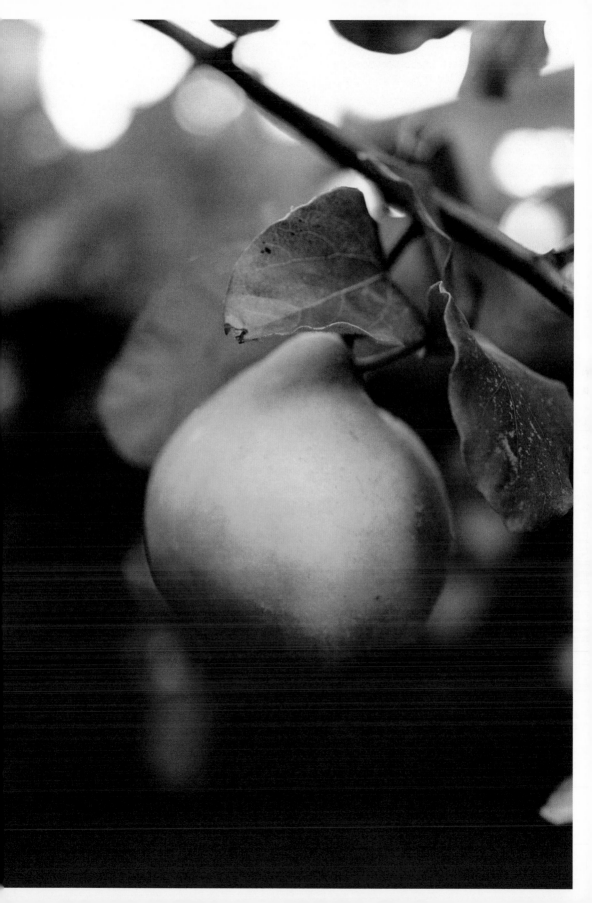

A quince pickle

A razor-sharp, lip-smarting pickle is a permanent fixture of any meal I throw together involving the remains of Sunday's roast. Quinces, shining amber and gold in their pickling liquid, are unusual, offering a pleasing change from the icy crunch of the more usual pickled onion.

> *enough for 2 medium-sized storage jars*
> cider vinegar – 3 cups (750ml)
> golden baker's sugar – 2 cups (400g)
> juniper berries – 12
> black peppercorns – 8
> a bay leaf
> quinces – 3 medium or 4 smaller ones

Pour the vinegar into a stainless steel pan. Add the sugar, juniper, black peppercorns, and bay leaf and bring to a boil. Turn the heat down to a merry simmer.

Peel, halve, and core the quinces, cutting them into six lengthwise. Lower the fruit into the simmering vinegar and leave to cook for fifteen to twenty-five minutes, until the fruit is soft enough to pierce effortlessly with a skewer. Lift the quince out with a slotted spoon and lower into clean storage jars. Pour over the liquid, then seal and leave to cool. They will keep for several weeks.

Raspberries

I can clearly remember the moment I fell totally, hopelessly in love with the scarlet berries. It is seven or maybe eight o'clock one morning in October, the garden is somber with mist, and the heavy air is damp and fungal. The raspberry canes have fallen across the path through want of a stick. I lift them to pass. Hanging down from the canes are crisp brown leaves and bunches of berries, some rotting, others about to collapse, their beads heavy with arterial-red juice. I pick them and they are so soft they break in my fingers, sending beads of red juice down my hand. I eat what I can and lick the rest from my skin. The single leaf by which I am holding the branch tears and the cane crashes back, its sharp thorns scratching my arm, leaving a long gash with little blood dots here and there along its length. I run my tongue along the scratch, then I go back indoors.

The raspberry family suffers from fragility and purple-red juice that stains everything in its path. They are not one berry but a collection of smaller berries—drupelets—fused together. This is why they freeze more successfully than the strawberry. Overripe to the point of leaching their juices, they are the most stimulating of fruit to the senses, more so than a ripe cantaloupe, though less than a dripping honey mango. Their smell has a winelike quality, their flavor can be warm and almost alcoholic, and to look at they are the most alluring of fruits, especially when they come in a little balsa wood basket lined with their own dark green leaves. We eat them in our breakfast muesli, as a layer in a moist sponge cake, but most of all with deep yellow cream and maybe a crisp meringue whose broken crust glistens with sugar.

It is hard to justify doing anything more complicated to a raspberry than serving it as it is, warm from the sun and unadorned or adulterated. Most times that is how I want my berries. If guests are here I will sometimes pile the berries onto a plate lined with raspberry leaves and pass it around the table. They can agonize over the pitcher of cream for themselves. That said, I do love them in a fool, a trifle, or an ice cream, particularly when their juices bleed a little.

Raspberries in the garden

I planted my first raspberry patch almost a decade ago. The fruit likes the cool and the damp, which is why it does so well in Scotland and in particular the Vale of Gowrie. I planted it on the shaded side of the garden at the suggestion of Monty Don, the side whose soil rarely dries out, even in high summer. The canes had arrived as a bundle of short sticks, their roots still damp but looking distinctly dead. I planted them in rich soil on a freezing cold January day, the soil claggy as chocolate cake, convinced they would never survive.

Tradition has it that they are happiest in a slightly acidic soil, but they are generally not as fussy as many other fruits. The trick is not to plant them too deep—2½ inches (6cm) down is enough—and to spread the roots out flat rather than pointing down. I covered mine with topsoil and then a spade or two of manure. The shallowness of the root system, which hates to sit in sodden ground, means you must weed by hand rather than by hoe. The ideal spot is somewhere sheltered but sunny, with moist soil that doesn't become waterlogged in winter. Incredibly, I have such a spot at the rear of the vegetable patch.

The canes need a little care as the year progresses. It is generally accepted that you should cut down new growth to 6 inches (15cm) in height in early spring, once the leaves start to unfurl. As they grow, tie them to wires in early summer, as soon as they are long enough. After summer fruiting, cut out any brown canes, tying in any new green shoots as you go. Autumn fruiting varieties should be cut right down to the ground in midwinter.

For six years, my canes provided almost as many berries as I could eat, and I loved them for that, and the fact that the almost vinous scent of the overripe fruits added a certain sensuality to the garden in autumn, but they had to go. I wanted the bed for other things—beans, tomatoes, parsley, lettuce—so I ripped them out. Except one, that kept coming through the soil each spring. I left it to wind its way up the frame with the beans, its occasional fruits a stinging reminder not to always want more.

Two years ago I realized my mistake in having a fruit patch without the heady pleasure of a row of raspberry canes. This time I planted two varieties, the beloved Autumn Bliss, whose presence in the garden I missed so much, and Fall Gold, the autumn-fruiting yellow variety whose berries are sweet but fragile, with a slight tendency to crumble as you pick them. Never again will my garden be without them.

Varieties

The golden raspberry

Among the most rare and exquisite of fruits, the yellow raspberry has possibly the richest, brightest flavor of all. Autumn-fruiting **Fall Gold**,* sometimes known as All Gold, is one to grow—a chance seedling found among a planting of Autumn Bliss.

Red raspberries

There are two distinct types, known by the season in which they ripen. The first "summer-fruiting" raspberries appear in mid- to late May, the later "autumn-fruiting" varieties can be picked right up to the first frosts.

Summer fruiting

Malling Jewel Ripens in midsummer and is loved for its old-fashioned raspberry flavor.

Glen Prosen Probably at its best if you leave it until it is almost overripe.

Glen Ample Not the easiest to grow, but a very fine fruit if you are successful.

Tullameen* A summer variety that does well in lighter soils. If you leave it on the cane longer than the commercial growers are inclined to, you will be rewarded with a more aromatic flavor.

Autumn fruiting

Autumn Bliss* I was very happy with its late-August cropping that lasted until the first frosts, and with its deep flavor.

Lloyd George A classic from a chance seedling found in a wood in Kent.

Autumn Treasure Delights in deep flavor, strong canes, and a good resistance to root rot. Generally, the deeper-colored berries tend to have the richest flavor.

Galante Exceptionally large fruits and prolific cropping. I have yet to taste this one, but reports are good.

Caroline* Appreciated for its exceptional flavor and its resistance to root rot.

*Available from US sources.

Raspberries in the kitchen

There is little to be gained by cooking a raspberry. Gentle warmth will bring its flavors to the fore, teasing out the berry's sweetness, but a thorough cooking will lose all the fruit's subtlety and destroy its texture. Jam aside, and perhaps the odd handful tucked inside a roasting game bird, I prefer to keep this one well away from the stove.

A few of the berries tumbled into a glass of sweet wine is dessert enough for me. Include them in a salad of melon or blueberries, or crush them with sugar syrup to form a glowing sorbet. All will produce something of great beauty that is worth the trouble we have taken. But the raspberry is often at its happiest when in the presence of cream.

Cream, sweet, yellow, and thick, has an extraordinary effect on these fruits, heightening rather than subduing their flavor. The lexicon of classic raspberry recipes, from fools to ice creams to syllabubs, gives a pretty clear idea of the esteem in which we have historically held this culinary marriage.

The sharper the fruit, the better it is in the presence of dairy products. This is why gooseberries, damsons, and rhubarb make a better fool than strawberry or peach. The raspberry has a nip of acidity that, in my book, sends it soaring over even the best strawberry. And it is that acidity that makes it the perfect contender for a pavlova or a trifle, working in contrast to the layers of blissfully sweet cream and meringue or sponge cake.

Eau-de-vie de framboise, the clear liqueur made from the fruit, is a potent reminder of the fruit at its most ripe and heady. Only the smallest amount is needed to bring a raspberry intensity to a syllabub. In Britain we make a raspberry liqueur that is softer and more quaffable. Framboise is a very sexy addition to dark chocolate truffle mixtures.

The raspberry's leaves can be made into a refreshing tea.

Raspberries and...

Cream Ideally yellow and unpasteurized, either to pour over the fruit or to crush them with to make a fool.

Rose water Either shaken delicately over the fruit or stirred into stewed berries as a more romantic alternative to a fruit liqueur.

Goat cheese Especially the sharp, chalky kind.

Ground almonds As used in a sponge cake to slice and serve with the fruit.

Pistachios Toasted and scattered on the fruit or in a raspberry ice cream.

Sugar To make a jam or simply to sweeten the fruit before serving with cream.

Mascarpone As a filling for a raspberry tart.

Champagne Drop a couple of drippingly ripe ones into each glass, or put one or two berries on your tongue between each mouthful of wine, as if you were popping pills.

Peaches The berries' best friend. I use them in both a fruit salad and a trifle. The two mashed with a fork and stirred into shattered meringues and cream is a ridiculously indulgent dessert.

Chocolate One of the few fruits to be truly happy in the presence of dark chocolate. Serve them whole or as a purée to freshen up a slice of chocolate truffle cake or mousse.

Game birds A few berries can be mashed into the gravy for grouse or partridge to surprisingly successful effect.

* Raspberries should be picked dry rather than after a rain shower. They keep better dry than when they are wet.
* Store them in the fridge, but bring them to room temperature before eating. A warm berry has a deeper flavor.
* Raspberries freeze better than most other fruits because of their structure, being made up of lots of tiny drupelets.
* There is no need to thaw a frozen berry before adding it to a smoothie.
* Prue Leith has a neat recipe for making "instant" raspberry sorbet by simply blitzing frozen berries in a food processor.
* To cook grouse or partridge with raspberries, mash a handful of berries with a little butter and stuff it inside the bird. Roast the bird in a very hot oven, covered with bacon and with a sprig of thyme up its bottom. What emerges is a glistening roast bird with mildly fruit-flavored pan juices. The smell is as good as the taste.
* The soft white hull inside a raspberry is known as a *torus*.

A dish of warm, heady berries

Warmth is a good friend to the raspberry. Put a little fire under this fruit and its juices become intense, rich, and almost heady. The color is arterial, glowing like damson gin. This is meant as a simple dessert, but I must admit to having eaten it for breakfast before now, even with its dash of eau-de-vie.

enough for 6
raspberries, loganberries, or tayberries – 14 ounces (400g)
superfine sugar – up to 4 tablespoons
English raspberry liqueur or eau-de-vie de framboise – 2 tablespoons

Put the berries in a heavy-bottomed saucepan. Scatter over the sugar, then pour in the framboise or raspberry liqueur and 4 tablespoons of water. Bring slowly to a boil, turn down the heat, and leave until the berries appear on the verge of bursting and their juices color the liquid in the pan.

Serve warm, in glasses or small bowls, or spoon it over ice cream, watching the warm juices trickle down the cold vanilla ice.

A raspberry syllabub

The citrus zest and sweet wine go some way toward balancing the rich effect of the whipped cream, as does the streak of crushed berries at the dessert's heart. Nevertheless I serve this elegant summer cream in very small portions. A dish of berries, perfect, headily ripe, and warm from the sun, would be a perfect side offering, as would more of the raspberry purée, crushed and chilled.

enough for 4 to 6
a lemon
superfine sugar – 3 tablespoons
sweet wine (such as a Sauternes or an orange Muscat) – ¼ cup (60ml)
heavy cream – 1¼ cups (300ml)
raspberries – 5 ounces (150g), about 1¼ cups

Grate the lemon zest into a bowl, squeeze in its juice, then add the sugar and sweet wine. Leave to steep in the fridge (it is important the bowl is kept cold) for a couple of hours or, better still, overnight.

Using a large balloon whisk or electric mixer, slowly beat in the cream, getting right to the bottom of the mixture. Watch the texture carefully; I refuse to take my eyes from it until the mixture will sit in thick, soft, billowing folds. It should still leave a slow, falling trail from the whisk. If you take it too far, it will become grainy and separate.

Crush the raspberries with a fork and fold tenderly into the syllabub. Spoon into chilled glasses and leave for at least half an hour in the fridge before serving.

A lemon posset for raspberries, mulberries, and the like

Whenever I am making this classic dessert, I always wonder if there will be enough—it looks such a small amount in the saucepan. Yet once it is poured into glasses and left to set, you realize that it is so rich and lemony that a small amount is all that is required.

Pleasing as it is served in unadorned simplicity, I do think it is the perfect accompaniment for raspberries, mulberries, or loganberries. A crisp cookie such as a brandy snap could be useful here too.

makes 4 small glasses
heavy cream – 2 cups (500ml)
superfine sugar – ¾ cup (150g)
lemon juice – 5 tablespoons (75ml)

Put the cream and sugar in a saucepan and bring to a boil, stirring occasionally to dissolve the sugar. Reduce the heat so that the mixture doesn't boil over and let it bubble enthusiastically for about three minutes, stirring regularly.

Remove from the heat, stir in the lemon juice, and leave to settle. Pour into four small wineglasses or cups and leave to cool. Refrigerate for a couple of hours before serving.

Watermelon and raspberry salad

I am not a great one for using alcohol in cooking, but the faintest hint of raspberry or black currant eau-de-vie is one I can happily live with. This is a dessert for following an exceptionally spicy main course.

enough for 4
a large chunk of watermelon – about 1¾ pounds (800g)
raspberries – 12 ounces (350g), about 3 cups
superfine sugar – a scant tablespoon
framboise liqueur or crème de cassis – a tablespoon

Cut the melon flesh into fat chunks, removing the skin and seeds. Anything too small will just turn to slush. Put them in a bowl with the raspberries. Sprinkle the fruit lightly with sugar and pour over the alcohol. Leave to macerate for an hour or so. Serve chilled.

A frozen ice of raspberries and cream

A simple ice cream made without the need for a machine.

enough for 6
large eggs – 3
superfine sugar – ⅓ cup (80g)
a few drops of vanilla extract or a knifepoint of vanilla seeds
heavy cream – 1¼ cups (300ml)
raspberries – 8 ounces (250g), about 2 cups

You will need a loaf pan approximately 9 by 5 inches (22 by 12cm), lined on the bottom and sides with plastic wrap or wax paper.

Separate the eggs. Add the sugar to the yolks and beat until thick and pale, the color of vanilla ice cream. I find this easiest with a handheld electric mixer. Stir in the vanilla.

Whisk the cream until it is thick but still soft enough to slide a little when the bowl is moved from side to side. You don't want it to be stiff. Fold the cream into the egg yolk and sugar mixture.

Crush the berries with a fork. I like to keep some of their seedy texture here, so I just mash them with a light pressure—enough to bruise rather than mash.

In a clean bowl, beat the egg whites until stiff. Fold them tenderly into the cream mixture, followed by the crushed raspberries. Pour into the lined pan. Tap firmly to level the mixture, then cover loosely with plastic wrap and place in the freezer for a good four to six hours, until frozen. I sometimes think it is best frozen overnight.

To serve, leave out of the freezer, at room temperature, for about fifteen to twenty minutes, then slice into thick pieces with a heavy knife.

A meringue with red berries and cream

Crisp meringue, sugar-frosted like the yew hedges on a winter's day, billowing cream and scarlet fruit.

enough for 8
large egg whites – 6
superfine sugar – 1⅓ cups (280g), plus more for dusting
cornstarch – a heaping tablespoon
mild white wine vinegar – a teaspoon
a handful of sliced almonds

for the filling
heavy cream – 1¼ cups (300ml)
raspberries, loganberries, or tayberries – 14 ounces (400g), about 3½ cups

Preheat the oven to 425°F (220°C). Line a shallow rectangular cake pan or jelly-roll pan, about 13 by 9½ inches (33 by 24cm), with parchment paper. The paper needs to come right up the sides of the pan. Brush lightly with flavorless cooking oil.

Put the egg whites into the bowl of a stand mixer and whisk at high speed until light, fluffy, and stiff. Introduce the sugar gradually, continuing to whisk all the time. Fold in the cornstarch and vinegar. Spread the mixture lightly into the lined pan, smoothing it level as you go, then scatter the top with sliced almonds. Bake for ten minutes, then lower the heat to 325°F (160°C) and cook for a further fifteen minutes or so, until the meringue is golden on top. Place a sheet of wax paper on a work surface, dust it with superfine sugar, then remove the meringue from the oven and tip it upside down onto the paper. The meringue should fall out together with the lining paper. Gently peel the paper from the meringue, cover lightly with plastic wrap, and leave to cool.

Pour the cream into a bowl (it always whips better in a cool bowl) and whip lightly, so that it will almost stand in peaks. Peel off the plastic wrap and spread the cream over the meringue, smoothing it out almost to the edges with a thin spatula.

Scatter the berries over the cream. Take the long edge nearest you and roll the meringue up tightly, like a roulade. Transfer to a long dish and leave to settle for half an hour before serving.

Raspberry yogurt ice cream

The British have a history of making fine dairy products but our love of yogurt is more recent. We produce some splendid farmstead yogurt, not just from cow's and goat's milk but from sheep's milk too, and all of it can be made into very good ice cream. The goat's and sheep's milk versions have a particularly refreshing quality when used with soft fruit, and are my first choice where berries are concerned. Natural foods stores and farm stands are particularly good hunting grounds for locally made natural yogurt.

enough for 4
natural yogurt – 1⅔ cups (400g)
confectioners' sugar – 4 tablespoons
raspberries – 10 ounces (300g), about 2½ cups

Put the yogurt into a bowl and beat in the sugar with a small whisk or fork. Crush the raspberries with a fork and stir them into the sweetened yogurt.

Pour into an ice cream maker and churn until almost frozen. Transfer to a freezer-safe plastic tray and freeze until needed.

Note: You can make this without a machine but it will lose its creamy texture. Simply pour the mixture into a freezer-safe box and freeze for two hours. Stir well with a fork or small beater, bringing the frozen outer edges into the unfrozen middle, then repeat once every hour until frozen.

Purple figs with crushed raspberry cream

Crush a handful of raspberries with a fork. Fold into twice the volume of softly whipped cream, stopping when the fruit has bled into the cream. Cut a cross down each fig from the stalk to the base, then push the sides to open the fruit up. Drop spoonfuls of the crushed raspberry cream into the hollows and serve.

A quick peach and raspberry mess

It is worth making certain your peaches are very ripe before using them for this recipe.

enough for 4
heavy cream – 1 cup (250ml)
meringue shells – 4
raspberries – 14 ounces (400g), about 3½ cups
very ripe peaches – 3

Put a large mixing bowl in the fridge for half an hour to chill. When the bowl is cold, pour in the cream and whisk until it lies in thick, soft folds, before it is stiff enough to stand in peaks.

Crumble the meringues into the cream, making sure to get a mixture of very fine crumbs and large pieces so that the texture is interesting.

Put two-thirds of the berries into a bowl and crush them with a fork—not to make a sauce, but so that they start to give up some of their juices. Cut each peach in half, twist out the pit, then slice the flesh of each half into four or five pieces (you could chop them, if you prefer). Mix the peaches and raspberries together.

Add the raspberry and peach mixture to the cream and meringue, stirring slowly and gently so that the fruit doesn't really color the cream but leaves a trail of juice and fruit throughout the mixture (rather like an old-fashioned raspberry ripple). Fold in the reserved whole raspberries. Pile into glasses or elegant bowls and serve.

Banana, peach, and raspberry brûlée

I struggled with this inclusion. The recipe is something I made virtually every day at a London café for six years. I have always felt the layers of soft fruits smothered in whipped cream and given a thin crust of hot caramel produce something altogether too creamy, too sweet, and too rich. Yet for all that, it is an unsurpassed crowd-pleaser, and I have been asked for the recipe on countless occasions. Take the caramel to deepest coffee color before pouring it, carefully, over the hills and valleys of whipped cream.

enough for 4 to 6
superfine sugar – a generous ¾ cup (175g)
bananas, peaches, and raspberries, mixed – 1½ pounds
(700g) total weight
chilled heavy cream – 1½ cups (350ml)

Put the sugar in a heavy pan and pour in enough water to cover. Set over medium to high heat to boil while you prepare the fruit. Slice the bananas, pit and slice the peaches, and remove any stems from the raspberries. Put all the fruit in a heatproof serving bowl.

Whip the cream until it forms gentle peaks. Take care not to overwhip it. Spoon in high waves over the fruit. The sugar in the pan will start to turn a pale, golden caramel after ten minutes or less—watch it carefully, as it is prone to burning. The caramel is ready when it turns a rich golden brown. Immediately, taking care not to splash or burn yourself, pour the caramel over the cream and fruit. It will at once set to a crisp and shiny coat. Eat within thirty minutes.

Raspberry cranachan

The magical combination of oats and raspberry is experienced nowhere better than in the classic Scottish dessert cranachan. There are as many versions as there are tartans. This is mine.

enough for 4
rolled oats – about 2 cups (175g)
light muscovado sugar – ⅓ cup, packed (80g)
heavy cream – 1¼ cups (300ml)
raspberries – 5 ounces (150g), a generous cup

Put the rolled oats on a baking sheet and toast under a hot broiler until golden. They burn easily, so watch them carefully; it shouldn't take more than a couple of minutes. While the oats are still hot, add the sugar and stir well.

In a cool bowl, whip the cream until it starts to thicken on the whisk. It should loosely hold its shape but not be thick enough to stand in peaks.

Crush the raspberries lightly with a fork. Gently fold the cream, oats, and sugar into the raspberries. Don't overmix. Pile into a serving bowl, or four individual glasses or dishes if you prefer, and chill for a good hour before serving.

A quick raspberry tart

As much as simple fruit salads, fools, and compotes appeal to me, there are moments when only ripe, scarlet fruit, crisp pastry, and whipped cream will do.

The most straightforward interpretation involves laying a sheet of ready-rolled puff pastry on a baking sheet, scoring a rim on all four sides, about ¾ inch (2cm) from the edge, pricking it all over with a fork, and baking in a very hot oven until crisp. I then pile on whipped cream and perfectly ripe raspberries, loganberries, or tayberries. No pâtissier's shining glaze, no dusted sugar crust, in fact no adornment of any kind. Just fruit, pastry, and cream. For a pastry sheet of approximately 7 ounces (200g) in weight, you will need 1 cup (250ml) of heavy cream and 8 ounces (250g), about 2 cups, raspberries.

Peach and summer fruit sundae

Oh joy of joys, such greedy bliss!

enough for 4
superfine sugar – a scant ½ cup (90g)
water – 2 cups (500ml)
a vanilla pod
large peaches – 4
vanilla ice cream – 8 balls, about 3¾ cups (500g)
whipped cream, to serve (optional)

for the summer fruit sauce
raspberries – 5 ounces (150g), about a cup
red currants – 3½ ounces (100g), about a cup, removed from the stalks
confectioners' sugar – 2 heaping tablespoons, or to taste

Make a syrup by putting the sugar, water, and vanilla pod in a saucepan and bringing to a boil. Turn the heat down to a light simmer—the water should be just bubbling—then add the halved and pitted peaches (if the pits refuse to budge, leave them in until the peaches are ready; they will come out more easily then). Let the peaches simmer until tender to the point of a knife. Switch off the heat and let them cool.

Put the raspberries and red currants in a food processor and blitz until smooth, then stir in the confectioners' sugar. If there are any lumps, whiz once more. (Alternatively, push the berries and currants through a sieve, then stir in the sugar.)

Divide the balls of ice cream among four dishes. Add the peaches and a spoonful of their cooking liquid, then spoon over the fruit sauce. Add whipped cream if you wish.

Raspberry tiramisu

Okay, this is about as much a tiramisu as I am, but the principle of booze-soaked sponge cake and mascarpone cream is the same as in the classic Italian dessert. It may make your heart sink to find that it needs to be made the day before, but that is the only way to get the ladyfingers and the cream cheese layer to marry successfully. Rush it and you will be disappointed.

enough for 8
white wine, not too dry – 7 tablespoons (100ml)
crème de cassis – 5 tablespoons (80ml)
a package of ladyfingers
raspberries – 14 ounces (400g), about 3½ cups
mascarpone – 1 pound (500g)
eggs – 3, separated
superfine sugar – 3 tablespoons
heavy cream – a generous ¾ cup (200ml)
a handful of rose petals, if you wish, to serve

You will need an oval or rectangular dish approximately 14 inches (35cm) long. Mix the wine and cassis. Dip the ladyfingers in this and lay them snugly in the dish. Pour over half the remaining liquid (you can dump or drink what's left, it has done its job). Scatter half the raspberries over the ladyfingers.

Beat the mascarpone, egg yolks, and sugar together with a handheld electric mixer. Rinse the beaters, dry them thoroughly, then beat the egg whites until they are stiff and hold firm peaks. Carefully fold the egg whites into the mascarpone mixture. Spread this over the infused ladyfingers and set aside.

Whip the cream, but only until it will sit in soft folds. If it will stand in peaks, you have gone too far. Spread it over the mascarpone mixture. Scatter over the remaining raspberries and cover tightly with plastic wrap. Refrigerate overnight. The next day, scatter with rose petals, should you wish, and serve.

Raspberry fool

I think of fruit fools, be they gooseberry, strawberry, or raspberry, as the very essence of summer. These soft, lazy-day puddings are nothing more than ripe fruit at the height of its season that has been crushed and stirred through with whipped cream, custard, and perhaps a little sugar. I am not certain the sugar is entirely necessary with strawberry or raspberry fools; taste and sweeten as you go. Some crisp almond cookies or shortbread would be good here.

enough for 6
raspberries – 10 ounces (300g), about 2½ cups
heavy cream – ⅔ cup (150ml)
custard (see page 493) – ⅔ cup (150ml)
a little confectioners' sugar, if needed
pistachio nuts – 12

Rinse the berries and crush them roughly with a fork. I think you should stop long before you reach a purée, so that the finished fool will have a more interesting texture. Pour the cream into a chilled bowl and whip it until it stands in soft folds. It shouldn't be stiff. Gently fold in the custard and a good two-thirds of the crushed raspberries.

Should you wish to sweeten the fool, do it now. I suggest a tablespoon of confectioners' sugar, but taste it for sweetness as you go. Stir in the reserved third of raspberries, leaving a trail of red through the pink of the fool. Halve or chop the pistachios and scatter them over the top.

Raspberry ripple yogurt fool

You can spend a lifetime chasing flavors from your childhood and never quite finding them. It has been this way with ice cream, a quiet, plodding hunt for the milky ices I enjoyed as a boy. One of the flavors I hanker after is that of the raspberry ripple frozen pops I bought from the Midland Counties Dairies with my pocket money. Even if I captured the essence of them, I doubt they would hit the same spot, but it is worth trying. This fool was part of that attempt. The result is a finer, more pure thing than I remember, though with much the same flavor. All I need now is to capture it in frozen form.

enough for 4
heavy cream – 1 cup (250ml)
goat's milk yogurt – ½ cup (125g)
raspberries – 8 ounces (250g), about 2 cups
shortbread, to serve

Put the cream into a cold bowl and whisk until it starts to thicken. You want it to be thick enough to sit in heaps rather than stand in peaks. Now gently fold the yogurt into the cream with a large spoon. Don't beat it, which might overthicken the cream, just firmly, smoothly fold the two together.

Crush the raspberries lightly with a fork. I think you should resist the temptation to mash them too much; you want some texture in among all this billowing cream.

Gently fold the cream and yogurt into the raspberries. I find this easiest with a large metal spoon. Again, I don't think you should mix too thoroughly. You want each spoonful to have some of the sharpened cream and a ripple of crushed, scarlet fruit.

Spoon into bowls or glasses and serve with shortbread.

Victoria sponge with raspberries and custard sauce

enough for 6

for the sponge cake
butter, at room temperature – ½ cup (110g)
golden baker's sugar – a generous ½ cup (110g), plus a little for dredging
eggs – 2
self-rising flour – ¾ cup plus 2 tablespoons (110g)

for the custard sauce
heavy cream – ⅔ cup (150ml)
custard (see page 493) – a generous ¾ cup (200ml)
a vanilla pod

for the raspberry sauce
raspberries – 10 ounces (300g), about 2½ cups
kirsch or raspberry liqueur – a tablespoon (optional)
confectioners' sugar – a tablespoon

a few raspberries and fresh rose petals, to finish

Preheat the oven to 350°F (180°C). Butter and line a round 8-inch (20cm) cake pan.

Cream the butter with the sugar in a large bowl until light and fluffy. This is easiest done with an electric mixer or in a stand mixer. Beat in the eggs one at a time. Sift the flour into the mixture and mix very gently until the flour is no longer visible. Spoon the mixture into the prepared cake pan, smooth the top, and bake for twenty to twenty-five minutes, until a skewer inserted in the middle comes out clean. Cool the cake on a wire rack.

To make the custard sauce, put the cream into a chilled mixing bowl and beat until thick. You should aim for a texture that sits in soft folds rather than whipping long enough for it to stand in stiff peaks. Gently fold the custard in. Split the vanilla pod in half, scrape out the seeds with the point of a sharp knife, then stir them into the custard. Set aside in the fridge for an hour or so for the vanilla to work its magic.

Make the raspberry sauce by blitzing the fruit, alcohol, and confectioners' sugar in a blender or food processor. If you wish, you can sieve this to remove any seeds, but I rather like the crunch among the soft sponge cake and custardy sauce. Set aside.

Dredge the surface of the cake with baker's sugar. Cut into twelve narrow wedges. Place two in each of six shallow bowls. Pour the custard sauce around the slices of cake, then drizzle the raspberry sauce into the custard. Decorate with a few raspberries and even a few rose petals, if you wish.

Raspberry panna cotta

Pure raspberries and cream but made in the style of an Edwardian custard-cup pudding. Something for eating with a teaspoon.

makes 6 small puddings
milk – 7 tablespoons (100ml)
heavy cream – 1⅔ cups (400ml)
leaf gelatin – 2 leaves
confectioners' sugar – 4 tablespoons
raspberries – 7 ounces (200g), about 1¼ cups, plus more to serve
rose water – 2 teaspoons
rose petals, to serve

Pour the milk and roughly two-thirds of the cream into a small saucepan. Simmer gently for five or six minutes without letting it boil. The mixture will reduce a little.

Meanwhile, soak the gelatin in a bowl of cold water. After five minutes or so, it will have softened to slithery sheets. Pour the remaining cream into a bowl, add the confectioners' sugar, and beat gently until it starts to feel heavy on the whisk, but stop before it stiffens.

Remove the cream and milk from the heat and stir in the sheets of softened gelatin. Stir in the sweetened cream. Pour the mixture through a sieve balanced over a large measuring cup (don't be tempted to skip this, or the panna cotta will lose something of its purity).

Blitz the raspberries in a food processor for a few seconds (you can sieve out the seeds if you wish, but I prefer not to) and add the rose water. Pour the raspberry purée into the cream mixture and stir gently, then pour into six small cups or white ramekins. Cover each with plastic wrap and chill for three or four hours, until lightly set. Turn them out if you wish by briefly dipping the dishes into hot water, then turning upside down onto a plate and scattering with raspberries and rose petals, or simply eat them from the dish.

Ricotta cake with raspberries

This is about as complicated a dessert as I ever make. There is a sponge cake to bake, flecked with dried apricots and ground almonds, a ricotta and mascarpone filling, and a purée of raspberries to serve alongside. But the finished dessert is worth the trouble for a special occasion. A simpler version might involve a store-bought sponge cake or even simply serving the filling alongside some slices of the sponge cake with a little raspberry purée over the top.

enough for 8 to 10

for the apricot sponge cake
butter – 1 cup plus 2 tablespoons (250g)
golden baker's sugar – 1¼ cups (250g)
large eggs – 4
the grated zest and juice of a lemon
ground almonds – ½ cup (50g)
all-purpose flour – ¾ cup plus 2 tablespoons (100g)
soft dried apricots – 3½ ounces (100g), finely chopped

for the ricotta filling
ricotta – 5 ounces (150g), about ⅔ cup
mascarpone – 8 ounces (250g)
confectioners' sugar – 2 slightly heaping tablespoons
the grated zest of an orange
a few drops of finest vanilla extract
heavy cream – 1 cup plus 2 tablespoons (280ml)

for the raspberry purée
raspberries – 12 ounces (350g), about 3 cups
superfine sugar – ½ cup (50g)
framboise liqueur or kirsch – a few drops

confectioners' sugar and fresh berries, to serve

Preheat the oven to 350°F (180°C). Line the bottom of an 8- to 9-inch (20 to 22cm) shallow square cake pan with a sheet of parchment paper. Cream the butter and sugar in a stand mixer until truly light and fluffy. It should be very pale and creamy.

Beat the eggs lightly and add them in three or four batches to the butter and sugar. They might curdle slightly but don't worry, just keep beating. Add the lemon zest, reserving the juice, then mix the ground almonds and flour together. Slowly fold in the flour and almonds, then add the lemon juice and dried apricots. At this point you should treat the mixture gently. Smooth the mixture into the lined cake pan and bake for thirty to thirty-five minutes. Remove and turn upside down onto a cake rack to cool.

Put the ricotta, mascarpone, and confectioners' sugar in a stand mixer and beat thoroughly to a thick and relatively smooth cream. Beat in the orange zest and vanilla extract. In a separate bowl, softly whip the cream. Stop while it is still in soft folds, before it gets thick enough to stand in peaks. Fold it gently into the ricotta mixture.

To assemble the cake, line the bottom of a long, thin cake pan, about 11 by 3½ inches (28 by 8cm) (though you can improvise with other dimensions easily enough; just use what you have). Cut the sponge cake into three long strips, then cut each half in two horizontally. Line the bottom of the pan with a slice of the sponge cake, using some from a second one where you need to. Spoon one-half of the mascarpone mixture on top of this, smoothing it gently. Cover this with another layer of sponge cake and a second layer of mascarpone cream. Finish with more sponge cake, patching any gaps where necessary. Tightly cover in plastic wrap and refrigerate for a good two hours. Overnight will not hurt. You will inevitably have some sponge cake left over after this, but it will no doubt soon disappear.

Make the raspberry purée by blitzing all the ingredients in a blender or food processor, then pushing everything through a fine sieve. Set aside in a covered bowl until needed.

Run a thin spatula around the edges and turn the cake out onto a long, flat plate. Dust with confectioners' sugar and serve with the purée and berries.

Red currants

In high summer I often start my day with a handful of red currants, snatched from the bush as I walk around the garden before breakfast. If I don't wolf them then and there, I drop the glistening red baubles, pulled from their brittle stalks, into a little bowl and eat them with sheep's milk yogurt. No sugar.

The red currant is not a fruit that responds well to embellishment or to heat—which is why it gets a separate chapter from the black currant, with which it shares fewer characteristics than is often observed. A little pressure can have worthwhile results: burst the raw or lightly cooked berries and their tart juices will flow. The quintessential summer pudding, where raspberries and red currants are pressed between layers of bread to form a juicy but solid mixture, is a case in point. Red currant jelly is another.

The acidity of the rich, claret juice is the whole point of the red currant. It is pleasingly sour among a bowl of sweeter berries, strawberries perhaps, and its sharp pinch is welcome in a fruit salad. Its presence is both charming and useful in a plate of peaches and raspberries. The currant's piercing notes add spice to the sweet peaches and make the berries sing.

Red and white currants, sitting like jewels in their paper baskets, are pleasant enough eaten in small handfuls, like raw peas, but become astringent in quantity. A light dairy product such as fromage frais will temper their bite.

This fruit is celebrated in these pages because of, rather than in spite of, its woefully short season and its limited use at the table. Blink in late July and you will miss them. Most of all I love their exhilarating sharpness and old-fashioned charm. No sweet or bonbon has ever been made with this; no jelly for a children's birthday party. This is the fruit that, if commerce had its way, would be culled—ripped up for more woolly strawberries. That the red currant has survived in these days of monotonous sweet blandness is nothing short of a miracle.

A red currant bush in the garden

One of the first bushes to break into leaf, tiny fresh green leaves that appear when all else is still sleeping, and that signal spring is almost here. The fruit comes as something of a wake-up call too. One day the flowers will be hanging down in lacy, green festoons, the next time you look the berries are almost ripe. By July you can be picking the fine stems with their rows of fruit hanging like costume jewelery. But the birds are attracted to the red variety, so you need to move quickly or cover the bushes with nets.

Every garden needs a red currant bush, if only for the pleasure of snaffling a currant or two when you are down at that end of the garden. Undemanding, and happy to grow on poor soil, they will live quietly in an untended bit of the plot or near the compost heap. They like sunshine and shelter. They fruit on old and new wood, but need regular pruning to keep the bush in shape. Mine thrive on it. Wielding the pruning knife is a job I enjoy each summer, directly after fruiting, when I shorten new growth back to about five leaves from the beginning of the stem. Then in winter, I shorten the branches by at least a quarter of their length, cutting just in front of a bud. I prune as much wood as possible out of the center of the bush to keep it ventilated, reducing the chances of mildew.

My bushes arrived in mid-January, thin, twiggy sticks in a brown sack. As I dug them into the cold soil with a shovel of manure, I doubted their survival. But currants like the cold, it reminds them of their home farther north, and they settled in happily. By late April there were bright leaves, then the first signs of fruit. Not enough for a summer dessert, but just enough to encourage a new gardener.

Varieties

There is not much to choose between varieties other than their fruiting times. I grow Laxton's No. 1 for its reliable, sharply flavored fruit. If I had the space, I would plant three or four varieties to get as long a season as possible.

Junifer Earliest ripening, a lovely start to summer fruit.
Jonkheer Van Tets* Vigorous, upright grower.
Laxton's No. 1 Prolific fruit with a good flavor, ripening early, in mid-July.
Rondom Bountiful fruit on a compact Dutch bush, very late (September) ripening.
Stanza A high-yielding fruit from the Netherlands.
Red Lake* American variety with long, upright branches.
Red Start Late fruiting, despite its name.

Rovada* A Dutch-developed cultivar, the Rovada yields big, beautiful, translucent orbs in long, abundant clusters. Ripens mid- to late July.

*Available from US sources.

Red currants in the kitchen

The extreme acidity of these fruits will help in setting the softer, low-pectin jams such as raspberry or strawberry. Add a good handful or more to the fruits as they simmer.

Red currants catch the light and sparkle like frost on a rose hip if you brush them with very lightly beaten egg white—a quick bash with a fork until the white froths—and then dip them into confectioners' sugar. Their acidity makes them a welcome candidate for decorating a vast and undulating pavlova, though they look better when they're kept in sprigs. Slightly annoying to eat when still on the stalk, but better than a meringue dotted with loose currants. The effect looks spotty no matter how many you pile on.

Beware the juice; it stains, though less so than pomegranate or black currant. Check store-bought specimens for any sign of mildew before you put them in the fridge. Just one bad one will quickly turn the rest. That said, they keep for several days in good condition, though they lose their shine as they age.

Any hue of currant makes an interesting addition to a crème brûlée but dark colors are probably most satisfactory to the eye. There will be an element of curdling around the fruit but no matter. It's the contrast with the smooth, vanilla-scented custard and ice-crisp sugar crust that is the magic here. Their presence will please those who find a plain (and some would say perfect) crème brûlée a little cloying.

I have, once or twice, stirred the little berries into the pan juices of a roast shoulder of lamb, adding a sharp snap to the gravy while at the same time playing on the lamb and red currant jelly theme. The idea was more interesting than the result. Likewise, adding a handful to the roasting juices of a little game bird from the freezer. In principal the addition works, but in practice it looks a bit too clever for its own good. A spoonful of glistening red currant jelly looks far more comfortable.

Red currants and...

Raspberries Classically in a summer pudding, but also in fruit salads and jams. You can make a gorgeous purée for sponge cake and ice cream by mixing the two in equal quantities and pushing them through a sieve.

Bread This bright, tart, strident juice soaks into soft bread to great effect, especially in summer pudding, but I also like to pile the berries on a slice of oven-fresh bread, crisp crusted and warm crumbed, spread generously with cream cheese.

Game Stir the fruit into the pan juices of a roast bird, or serve red currant jelly on the side.

Lamb The punch of good red currant jelly brings out the sweetness in roast lamb or a grilled chop. The jelly made by small, artisan companies seems to be more interesting than the oversweet, overset stuff sold by the more commercial companies.

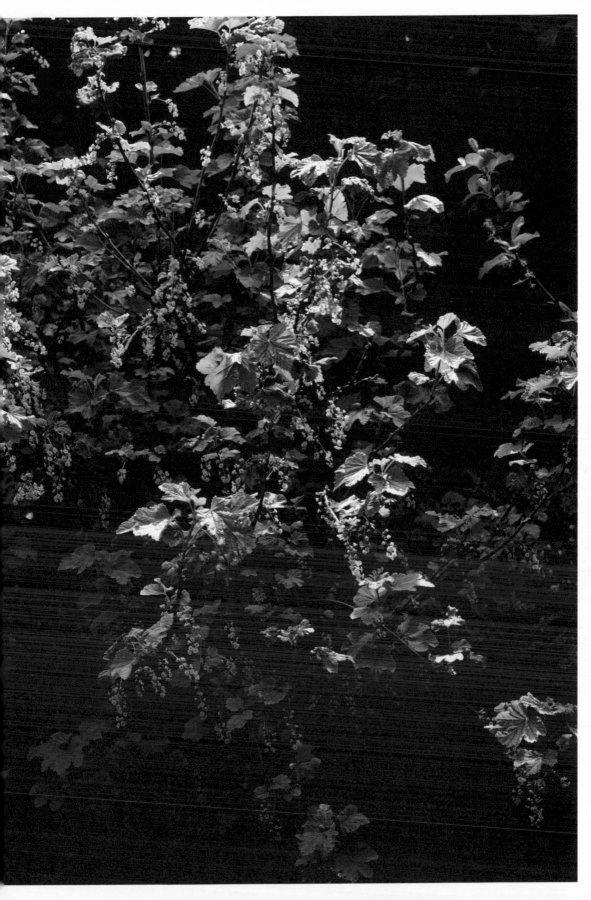

A dish of warm peaches with summer berries

I sometimes use members of the currant family to lift the flavors of sweeter fruits. A little black currant purée will bring life to a dish of strawberries; raw white currants do the same to a salad of oversweet tropical fruits. Peaches, when served warm—under a crumbling pastry crust, say, or afloat in a simple syrup—have an effect that is both sexy and curiously cloying. Spooning a sharp, vividly flavored sauce over them can put a spring in their step. I use a rough-textured sauce of currants and berries that works in perfect contrast to the smooth, slippery notes of the warm peaches. A deep-summer dish of ravishing beauty.

enough for 4
large, ripe peaches – 4
water – 4 cups (a liter)
sugar – to taste

for the sauce
red currants – 8 ounces (225g), 2 cups
black currants – 3½ ounces (100g), about a cup
superfine sugar – 4 tablespoons
water – 2 tablespoons
raspberries – 12 ounces (350g), about 3 cups

Wipe the peaches and put them in a stainless steel pan. Pour in the water and add at least 2 tablespoons of sugar. Bring to a boil, then turn down the heat and leave to simmer gently until the peaches are completely tender. This is unlikely to take more than twenty minutes or so, but will depend on the ripeness of your fruit. Turn off the heat.

Remove the stalks from the currants and put the fruit into a stainless steel saucepan with the sugar and water. Bring slowly to a boil. When the currants start to burst and flood the pan with color, tip in the raspberries. Simmer for two minutes, no longer.

Serve the peaches, drained of their poaching liquid and skinned if you wish (I remove the skins to reveal the glowing color of the poached peaches), with the warm fruit sauce.

A little dish of custard, fruit, and sugar

I like my crème brûlée unadulterated. But I also like the sublime partnership of tart currants and rich dairy products, so a brûlée with a layer of currant compote was an accident waiting to happen. It does curdle slightly where the two meet but I am not especially bothered by this. The flavor and the contrast between fruit, custard, and crisp sugar is too good.

It has taken me a while to get crème brûlée right. I was being impatient, and failed because I hadn't yet discovered how much easier success is if you chill the finished custard before you sugar it, and that you also need to be a little brave. The kitchen blowtorch has changed everything too. Crème brûlée is not complicated, but it needs both courage and a tender touch.

I work on the principle of ½ cup (125ml) heavy cream to each large egg yolk.

enough for 4

for the fruit base
black currants – 5 ounces (150g), about 1⅓ cups
red currants – 8 ounces (250g), about 2 cups
sugar – 4 tablespoons
water – 2 tablespoons

for the custard
heavy cream – 2½ cups (625ml)
a vanilla pod, split along its length
egg yolks – 5
superfine sugar – a heaping tablespoon

for the crust
superfine sugar – 8 tablespoons

Start with the fruit base (it will make too much, so you will have some for breakfast). Pull the currants from their stalks. Put the fruit into a saucepan with the sugar and water and bring to a boil. As soon as the berries start to burst and the juice turns a dramatic purple, remove from the heat and set aside. Leave to cool slightly. Spoon a couple of tablespoons into each of four small ramekins or cups and leave to chill in the fridge. It is best not to include very much juice. Save the rest for later.

Make the custard: put the cream and vanilla pod into a small saucepan and bring to a boil. Before the cream actually boils, turn the heat off and leave to infuse for a good ten minutes. This is to allow the vanilla seeds to scent the cream.

continued

Beat the egg yolks and superfine sugar together lightly, just until they turn pale. Pour the warm cream onto the eggs, removing the vanilla pod as you go, stirring to mix. Wipe the pan, then pour the custard back in, place over low to medium heat, and allow to get hot, but on no account to boil. This is the bit where it is worth concentrating. Stir the custard regularly with a wooden spoon, getting right down into the corners of the pan. After a while you will see movement where the custard is getting hot. At this point, stir enthusiastically—the custard is at its most crucial curdling point—and do not let it boil. The custard is ready when it is starting to thicken a little; it should look almost wobbly.

A word about curdling. If there is any hint of graininess or curdling at this point (and there might well be), then pour the custard quickly into a bowl, dunk it in a shallow sink of cold water, and beat furiously with a whisk. I have rescued many a dodgy custard at this point.

Pour the custard over the chilled fruit and allow to cool. Refrigerate for a good three hours, preferably overnight.

To make the sugar crust, sprinkle the sugar over the cold custard. It should be about ⅛ inch (3mm) thick. For the best results, blowtorch the sugar until it caramelizes. If you don't have such a thing as a kitchen blowtorch, then get the broiler really (really) hot and place the dishes underneath for a few minutes, until the sugar is golden and crisp.

Red currant jelly with sloe gin

Take your own, or a high-quality, softly set artisan-made jam, and melt it in a small saucepan. Add a few tablespoons of British or homemade sloe gin (see page 578), tasting as you go, until you have a bright, sharp, piercingly flavored sauce. Use with game, pork, lamb, or even the Christmas turkey.

Little currant cakes

Ten years old, I would help my aunt make little cakes in her kitchen. The usual fairy cake mixture, some would be transformed into butterfly cakes, others with trickles of colored icing and pastel sprinkles. I'm not sure whether I was proud or embarrassed. Nowadays they would be decorated with a generous swirl of buttercream and called cupcakes. Occasionally, she would insist we put dried currants into the mixture, which I would later fastidiously pick out one by one.

Cookbooks are now awash with recipes for every possible type of cupcake and it is easy to see their charm. What with the instant sugar rush, the warm wave of nostalgia, and the ease with which they are produced, it is no wonder they are so popular. I see no need to add to the tidal wave of recipes, but a sudden notion to toss a handful of currants—red and black—into the raw cake batter resulted in cakes that had the warm butteriness of the genre but here and there a shot of dazzling, sour fruit. For those for whom buttercream holds no attraction.

> *makes 12*
> butter – ½ cup (125g)
> golden baker's sugar – 1¼ cups (125g)
> large eggs – 2
> self-rising flour – 1 cup (125g)
> milk – 2 or 3 tablespoons
> red and black currants (or just black) – 5 ounces (150g), about 1⅓ cups,
>   removed from their stalks

Preheat the oven to 400°F (200°C). Line 12 muffin cups with paper liners. Put the butter, sugar, eggs, and flour into a food processor and blitz until all is well creamed. Introduce enough milk into the mixture (probably a couple of tablespoons) to produce a consistency that will fall lightly from the spoon. Stir in the currants.

Divide the mixture among the muffin cups and bake for about twenty to twenty-five minutes, until risen. They should be light but firm to the touch. They will fall slightly on cooling.

Rhubarb

How could anyone not love something known as the pie plant—or indeed, anything whose stems offer such vibrant color at a time of the year when so much of our fruit is sleeping? Yet rhubarb has never found the broad audience enjoyed by the raspberry or the apple. Instead, it has a loyal, almost cultish following, happy to indulge in its piercing crimson sharpness. Firmly among that number, I hold a crown of rhubarb an essential part of any garden I turn my spade to.

Rhubarb has been used medicinally since 2700 BC, often given to relieve serious constipation. It was the darling of the Victorian kitchen, finding its way into pies, fools, crumbles, and tarts quite by chance. Tired of the escalating price being asked by Chinese exporters, British apothecaries decided they could grow their own, and imported plants from Central Asia. Unfortunately (or perhaps fortunately) they got hold of *Rheum rhaponticum* rather than the required *Rheum palmatum*. The imported plants proved less than successful for medicinal use but, as our luck had it, turned out to be more than edible.

It was down to Victorian market gardener Joseph Myatt to bring this relatively recent addition to our kitchens to the cook's attention. Myatt's persistence, persuading skeptical shoppers at London's Borough Market to try the stalks in a pie, had the same impact on our kitchens as when Mr. Bramley discovered his famous seedling. Rhubarb crumble is now as well known, if not quite as well loved, as apple pie.

The first "forced" rhubarb, those gently tart stalks that appear in the market around Christmas time, came to prominence in the 1800s, thanks to an "accident" at Chelsea Physic Garden. The story goes that it was here in the winter of 1815, when the garden's rhubarb patch was accidentally covered with builder's rubble, that this particularly fine-tasting form was first discovered. The pale pink stalks that were unearthed by the gardeners in early spring were found to be extraordinarily mild and sweet, and a new kitchen ingredient was born.

There are two distinct seasons for rhubarb. First to appear in the store are the long, pale sticks of forced rhubarb, from Christmas to early spring, followed by the stouter, often more astringent, outdoor-grown rhubarb for the rest of the year. The appearance of the forced stalks—pale pink, like sticks of rock, the leaves primrose yellow and tightly furled—is due to the darkness in which they are grown, many in the long, black sheds of Yorkshire's famous rhubarb triangle (actually more of an irregular square), where the precious shoots are kept away from the light. These fine, rather delicate stalks have been grown like this since the 1880s, in an industry set around the Wakefield area.

The tall, lidded terra-cotta rhubarb forcers, or cloches, that are such a common sight in grand kitchen gardens are useful for creating a warm, dark environment (a minished) in which to bring on—force—the plant to produce tender early shoots. I have one in my little rhubarb patch for Stockbridge Arrow, one of three varieties I grow. It was recommended by Janet Oldroyd Hulme, fifth-generation rhubarb grower and known as the "high priestess of rhubarb," as "an excellent all-round performer, a must for every garden." Mrs. Oldroyd Hulme is right, and the glowing sticks with their arrow-shaped leaves provide a good start to the rhubarb year, coming several weeks before my Brandy Carr Scarlet and the late Alan Bloom's Grandad's Favorite.

Late rhubarb, coming shortly after the forced variety has finished, is an easy garden plant to live with. The slugs love their umbrella-like leaves but, asking for little more than a shovel of manure in the winter, the crowns will provide endless spring and summer desserts.

Rhubarb in the garden

Rhubarb revels in rich soil. By rich, I mean moist ground that is well seasoned with rotted manure—preferably somewhere that isn't sodden in winter or bone-dry in summer. I dug a trench under my plants and filled it with horse manure. They seemed to appreciate it.

The crowns, as the roots are called, are usually sent out in the autumn, though pot-grown ones can be put in at any time. They like to have their growing tips just peeping above the surface of the soil. I put a copper collar around mine to ward off the slugs, which love a rhubarb supper almost as much as one from my dahlia patch. I put a forcer over one of the plants in January to bring the stalks on. An old bucket would do.

They like a bit of nitrogen, and a top dressing of pelleted poultry manure or well-rotted farmyard manure applied around, not directly onto, the crown. Other than that, there is little to it. Plants can last for years but they tend to get tired after three or four years, when it is best to split them. I do it Carol Klein's way, splitting each root into two or three pieces with the spade, making certain there are two undamaged buds on each.

To harvest, you pull rhubarb rather than cutting it. Tug each stick downward, then turn to remove. Sometimes it needs quite a tug. Taking no more than half the sticks at a time will allow the crown food with which to rejuvenate itself next year. I stop picking on midsummer's eve.

To force rhubarb, you need to give it extra warmth and protection. Simply put a large flowerpot, terra-cotta forcer, or upturned bucket over the crown in December or January. A little manure pushed around the outside of the pot will warm things up and encourage the tender young shoots to come up early.

Varieties

The hundred or more varieties of rhubarb include many that now only survive in old allotments and kitchen gardens, such as the rare Appleton's Forcing that I am keen to get my hands on. Names from the past include Riverside Giant, Browns Crimson, Muriel (who could turn away a plant called Muriel?), Early Cherry, Early Devon, Stockbridge Emerald, Cutbush's Seedling, and The Streeter. Many of the modern varieties were developed at Stockbridge House near Cawood in Yorkshire. These include all the ones that have Stockbridge or Cawood in their name. Specialty growers such as Brandy Carr Nurseries send crowns out in the spring and autumn and can supply you with rare varieties too if you are patient.

Glaskin's Perpetual* Well known since the 1920s, a green and freckled-pink variety famous for its sweetness. It is unusual in that it can be picked in its first year. According to Christopher Stocks, John Jessie Glaskin was a Brighton baker who won prizes for his hot cross buns. I feel the need to honor him with a dessert incorporating both rhubarb and his spice-speckled bakery goods.

Early varieties
Appleton's Forcing Rare variety much revered for its flavor. The early shoots are red, turning green with maturity. One to bring on under an upturned bucket or terra-cotta forcer.
Timperley Early Red mostly at the base of the stems, this thin-stemmed, heavy-cropping variety is often the first up and can even be forced in time for Christmas. You can pick it until early summer, by which time its sticks will have turned almost completely green. The flavor is deliciously sharp, making it ideal for crumbles. Raised by Mr. Baldwin of Timperley in Cheshire in the 1920s.
Hawke's Champagne A good red color, sweet flavor (some say the sweetest of all), beautiful, heart-shaped leaves, and, once established, acute reliability make this early-season variety a popular choice.

Early Champagne A strong, reliable cultivar that produces exceptionally sweet and early stalks of a deep red.

Stockbridge Arrow A modern variety with blood-red stems, arrow-shaped leaves, and pink rather than the more usual green flesh. Keeps its color well in the garden and will do well outside from late winter onward.

Goliath Lives up to its name, with huge leaves and often thick stalks. The flavor gets a good rating from most.

Grandad's Favorite Named by horticulturist Alan Bloom, a variety with cherry-red stems flashed with green near the leaves. Strong and reliable, it is a prolific cropper.

Prince Albert An exceptionally early variety that has no fear of the cold. A single crown will provide a good crop of long, scarlet stalks.

Midseason (April to early summer)
Cawood Delight Not known for its prolific cropping, this maroon-stemmed variety is exceptional at keeping its shape and color once cooked. Not suitable for forcing.

Strawberry* A fine-tasting rhubarb with good, dark-red skin and pink flesh.

The Sutton Red and green flecks with green, well-flavored flesh. The thick stems often produce enormous leaves and can take up considerable space in the garden. So not one for me.

Late season (June onward)
Valentine* The brilliant red stems end in a heart-shaped leaf. It is exceptionally sweet and prolific.

Victoria* Lovely old variety with rather thick maroon stems and red and green flesh. Often found in traditional kitchen gardens. Apparently easily raised from seed, though I have never tried it.

*Available from US sources.

Rhubarb in the kitchen

Rhubarb is sometimes thought of as purely a pie fruit, or even just something to hide under the tender lid of a crumble. I like to think there is a little more to it than that. The sour quality of the stalks can be as useful in the kitchen as that of cooking varieties of apples, gooseberries, and verjuice. As a razor-sharp accompaniment to rich, fatty meats or fish, rhubarb is somewhat underused. It works in the same way as applesauce with pork, and is appropriate for baked, fried, or grilled mackerel.

While it excels in fatty company, nicely balancing a dish that may be a bit too rich, the stalks can also be added to lamb stews or served as an accompaniment to the darker game birds. I also use it with ham in place of a Cumberland or cranberry sauce. Others have found it a safe home in soups with chickpeas, spinach, or parsnip. (Adventurous cooks might like to get hold of a copy of Mary Prior's wonderful *Rhubarbaria*, published by Prospect Books.)

Rhubarb is arguably at its most comfortable in pies and cakes. The sharp qualities of the sticks work in contrast to the rounded, buttery notes used for cake batters and pastry crusts. A simple, crisp butter cookie can be an effective addition to a dish of slithery poached rhubarb. A single-crust pie, pale, sugar frosted, and served without the intrusion of cream or custard, can be charming, especially if the fruit is of the palest pink.

The excess juice that comes from the stalks as they cook is both a joy and a heartbreak. The flavor, when diluted with sugar, is uplifting, especially at breakfast. But there is often too much for a supporting pastry crust to stay crisp in its company and it can render a cake crumb a soggy mess. The trick is to make a single-crust pie such as the one in the Plum chapter (see page 428), or to bake the fruit first, drain it, then use the cooked stalks to fill a tart. Even then you might need a layer of ground almonds or cookie crumbs (Chez Panisse uses crushed amaretti) under the fruit. I have yet to make a double-crust rhubarb pie whose bottom crust wasn't the wrong side of moist.

That juice can be put to wonderful use. Nigella Lawson uses it for a shimmering jelly, while I have poured it into a glass and filled it up with jagged ice cubes (I like to smash them with an ice pick, *Basic Instinct* style, rather than use ice-cube trays), topping up with sparkling mineral water. There are few more bracing drinks.

Rhubarb and...

Honey Possibly the most appropriate sweetener, introducing a mellowing note to the poached or roasted stalks.

Vanilla A pod and its dislodged seeds can be tucked into a dish of baked rhubarb. A vanilla-scented panna cotta is a pleasing way of introducing a dairy note.

Mackerel and salmon Oily fish like the bite of poached rhubarb to balance their oily qualities.

Cinnamon A sweet, musky note for rhubarb cakes. A stick of the spice can be used in a rhubarb compote.

Ginger Use the dried spice in cakes, the fresh root in compotes.

Pork Contrast the meat's fatty sweetness with a few stalks of roast rhubarb or maybe a purée.

Almonds Use the ground nuts in cakes with the fruit layered in the center.

Yogurt Poached rhubarb, drained, then stirred into yogurt, makes a sharp, kick-ass fool.

Mackerel with rhubarb and sherry vinegar

A purée of rhubarb brings out the inherent sweetness of mackerel well enough, but I prefer the stalks to have some texture and tend to serve them with the fish whole rather than as a sauce. The color, alongside the shimmering silver of the mackerel, makes for a beautiful and extraordinary supper.

enough for 2
rhubarb – 7 ounces (200g)
superfine sugar – 2 tablespoons

for the mackerel
a little all-purpose flour
mackerel – 2, filleted
olive oil
rosemary – a small sprig
sherry vinegar
capers – a tablespoon (optional)

Preheat the oven to 350°F (180°C). Trim the rhubarb and discard the leaves. Cut it into short lengths and put in a roasting pan or baking dish with the sugar. Bake until just soft enough to take the point of a knife, about twenty minutes. Allow to cool, then drain, reserving the cooking juices.

For the mackerel, season the flour with salt and a little black pepper. Lightly coat the skin side of each mackerel fillet with the seasoned flour. Heat a little oil in a large, nonstick frying pan. Gently place the mackerel fillets in the hot pan, skin side down. Chop the rosemary needles and scatter them over the fish. Press the fish down with a thin spatula to keep it from curling. As the underside of the fish starts to crisp lightly, carefully turn over and cook the other side. It shouldn't take longer than two or three minutes on each side. Lift the mackerel fillets out onto warm plates.

Pour a couple of tablespoons of sherry vinegar (or less, to taste) into the hot pan. Add the cooked rhubarb, together with the rhubarb juices. Add the capers if you are using them. Let the rhubarb briefly warm through, then spoon it over the mackerel and serve.

Roast leg of pork with spiced rhubarb

Rhubarb makes a change from the more traditional applesauce in the depths of winter, and shares its ability to balance the richness of the meat. Rather than leave the pieces as a coarse purée, as I would with apple, I whiz the rhubarb into a smooth sauce—a nice contrast to the roughness of the crackling.

enough for 2, with seconds
a piece of pork leg – about 2 pounds (1kg), boned, scored, and rolled
a tablespoon each of sea salt and black pepper
the leaves from 3 bushy thyme sprigs
white wine – 2 glasses

for the sauce
rhubarb – 14 ounces (400g)
sugar – 2 tablespoons
the zest and juice of a small orange
ground cinnamon

Preheat the oven to 425°F (220°C). Put the meat in a roasting pan. Mix together the sea salt, black pepper, and thyme leaves to make a rub for the pork. Massage it into the skin, making sure to get it right down in between the score marks.

Roast the meat for twenty minutes, then lower the heat to 350°F (180°C) and cook for a further twenty-five minutes per pound (500g).

Make the rhubarb sauce. Trim the stalks, removing the leaves (which are poisonous in quantity), and cut into short pieces. Put them into a stainless steel or enameled pan with the sugar and the orange zest and juice. Bring to a boil, then turn the heat down to a slow simmer. Leave until the fruit has virtually collapsed. Whiz in a food processor or blender until smooth. Season to taste with salt and a very little cinnamon.

Remove the pork from the oven and let it rest for fifteen minutes, lightly covered with a dome of foil (too tight and it will soften the crackling). Put the roasting pan on the heat and pour in the white wine, stirring and scraping at the sticky bits in the pan as you go. Bring to a boil, then season carefully and pour into a warm pitcher.

Carve the roast, serving each plate with some of the gravy and passing around the rhubarb sauce.

Rhubarb custard fool with rhubarb syrup

A new take on a nursery stalwart.

enough for 4 to 6
rhubarb – 14 ounces (400g)
water – 3 tablespoons
sugar – 2 tablespoons
heavy cream – a scant cup (220ml)
custard (see page 493) – 1 cup (250ml)

Trim the rhubarb, taking care to discard the leaves. Cut the stalks into pieces about the length of a wine cork. Put the rhubarb into a stainless steel or enameled saucepan (aluminum reacts badly with the acidity of the rhubarb), add the water and sugar, then bring to a boil. Immediately turn down the heat so that the rhubarb simmers gently. You want it to soften but not totally collapse into strings. When the rhubarb is soft, remove it from the syrup with a slotted spoon. Pour the syrup into a small dish and let it cool, then refrigerate it.

Whip the cream lightly. It needs to be thick, but not whipped so far that it forms stiff peaks. It should lie in soft folds. Stir the custard in gently.

Put the drained fruit into the cream and custard and fold gently, so that the fruit forms pale pink streaks through the custard and cream. Set aside in the fridge for half an hour or so. Spoon into glasses and serve, pouring a little of the chilled rhubarb syrup over the top of the fool.

Cinnamon panna cotta with spiced roasted rhubarb

Panna cotta makes a rich and subtle accompaniment to poached or roasted rhubarb. If you want a stronger cinnamon flavor, add half a teaspoon of ground cinnamon to the milk, too.

enough for 4
whole milk – a generous ¾ cup (200ml)
heavy cream – a generous ¾ cup (200ml)
a cinnamon stick
a vanilla pod
crème fraîche – a generous ¾ cup (200ml)
leaf gelatin – ⅕ ounce (6g), 3 small leaves
confectioners' sugar – 3 tablespoons

for the spiced roasted rhubarb
young rhubarb – 14 ounces (400g)
honey – 3 heaping tablespoons
a small orange
a cinnamon stick
star anise – 2

Pour the milk and heavy cream into a small saucepan and add the cinnamon stick. Cut the vanilla pod lengthwise in half, scrape the seeds into the cream with the point of a knife, and drop the pod in too. Bring almost to a boil, turning off the heat just as the liquid is approaching a boil. Stir in the crème fraîche. Cover with a lid and leave for fifteen minutes. This will give the vanilla and cinnamon time to flavor the cream subtly.

Put the gelatin leaves in a bowl of cold water and leave to soften for 5 minutes. Remove from the water and add them, together with the confectioners' sugar, to the cream mixture. Stir until they have dissolved. Pour through a sieve to remove the spices, then divide among four ¾-cup (200ml) molds or ramekins and place in the fridge for four or five hours, until set.

Preheat the oven to 325°F (160°C). Trim the rhubarb, discarding any leaves, and cut it into short lengths. Put the pieces into a baking dish, then trickle over the honey. Grate the orange zest, cut the orange in half, squeeze it over the rhubarb, and add the orange shells and zest to the dish. Add the cinnamon stick and the star anise. Cover with a piece of foil or a lid and bake for thirty minutes, until the rhubarb is soft but has kept its shape.

To release each panna cotta from its mold, carefully lower it into a bowl of tap-hot water for a few seconds, then overturn onto a small dish or saucer. Serve with the rhubarb.

Baked rhubarb with blueberries

Lovely clear flavors here, a dessert for a day when the sky is gray and you need something sharp and fresh.

enough for 2 to 3
rhubarb – 8 ounces (240g)
blueberries – 7 ounces (200g), about 1⅓ cups
superfine sugar – 2 tablespoons
water – 2 tablespoons

Preheat the oven to 325°F (160°C). Trim the rhubarb, taking care to discard the leaves. Cut the stalks into short lengths. Put them into an ovenproof china or glass dish, tip in the blueberries, then add the sugar and water. Bake, uncovered, for forty minutes to an hour, until the fruit is soft and the sugar and water have turned to deep pink juice. Serve warm or thoroughly chilled, without cream or any other embellishment.

Rhubarb with orange

This looks particularly elegant in martini glasses.

enough for 4 to 6
rhubarb – 1½ pounds (750g)
blood oranges – 4
golden baker's sugar
a vanilla pod

Preheat the oven to 400°F (200°C). Rinse the rhubarb, then cut off and discard any leaves. Chop the stalks into short lengths and tip into an ovenproof dish.

Remove the peel from two of the oranges, carefully cutting away any white pith, then slice the fruit thickly and tuck it in with the rhubarb. Squeeze the juice from the remaining oranges and pour it over the rhubarb. Sweeten with a small amount of sugar—a heaping tablespoon will be enough unless your rhubarb is very sharp. Tuck in the vanilla pod. Cover the dish with foil and bake until the rhubarb is tender enough to crush with a fork.

Let the rhubarb cool. You should have soft fruit and clear ruby-pink juices. Spoon everything into glasses, cover each with plastic wrap, and chill for a good hour.

Sloe rhubarb

A surprisingly fine marriage of ingredients here, which leads to a dish of glowing garnet juices. You really don't need cream, and don't even think of making custard. Real sloe gin isn't easy to track down, but Plymouth makes one that is available in North America. Make your own if you have sloes or damsons—see page 578.

enough for 4
rhubarb – 1½ pounds (750g)
sugar – ½ cup (100g)
sloe gin – ½ cup (120ml)
water – 2 tablespoons

Preheat the oven to 325°F (160°C). Cut the rhubarb into short lengths, pulling off any strings as you go. Put it into a glass, stainless steel, or china dish (not aluminum, as it will taint the rhubarb).

Stir together the sugar, sloe gin, and water, then pour it over the fruit. Put the dish into the oven and bake for forty minutes to an hour, depending on the youthfulness of your rhubarb. The toughest will take a good hour. Baste the rhubarb from time to time with the juices.

When the fruit is tender, remove from the oven and leave to cool a little. I think this is best eaten warm rather than hot, though it is very good chilled.

Rhubarb cinnamon polenta cake

You need the coarse polenta meal for this, the one that actually feels a bit gritty. The finer version, with the texture of holiday beach sand, will not do at all. The contrast of the gritty, sugary crust and the slithery fruit is what makes me go back for more. The cake is fragile when warm, so neat cooks will want to serve it cool, together with the reserved juices from the cooked rhubarb.

enough for 8

for the filling
rhubarb – about 1 pound (500g)
golden baker's sugar – ¼ cup (50g)
water – 4 tablespoons

for the crust
coarse polenta – ¾ cup (125g)
all-purpose flour – 1½ cups plus 1 tablespoon (200g)
baking powder – a teaspoon
ground cinnamon – a pinch
golden baker's sugar – ¾ cup (150g)
grated zest of a small orange
butter – 10 tablespoons (150g)
a large egg
milk – 2 to 4 tablespoons
demerara sugar – a tablespoon

Lightly oil or butter an 8-inch (20cm) springform cake pan. Preheat the oven to 350°F (180°C) and put a baking sheet in it to get hot. Trim the rhubarb, cut each stem into short pieces, and put them in a baking dish. Scatter over the sugar and water and bake for thirty to forty minutes, until the rhubarb is soft but still retains its shape. Remove the pieces of fruit from the dish and put them in a colander or large sieve to drain. Reserve the rhubarb juice to serve with the cake.

Put the polenta, flour, baking powder, cinnamon, and baker's sugar in a food processor. Add the grated orange zest and the butter, cut into smallish pieces, then blitz for a few seconds until you have something that resembles breadcrumbs. I sometimes prefer to do this by hand, rubbing the butter into the polenta with my fingertips as if I were making pastry. An extraordinarily peaceful thing to do if one has the time. Break the egg into a small bowl and mix with 2 tablespoons of milk, then blend into the crumble mix, either in the food processor or by hand. Take care not to overmix; stop as soon as the dry ingredients and liquid have come together to form a soft, slightly sticky dough. If it isn't a little sticky, then add a touch more milk.

Press about two-thirds of the mixture into the cake pan, pushing it ¾ inch (2cm) up the sides with a floured spoon. Make sure there are no holes or large cracks. Place the drained rhubarb on top, leaving a small rim around the edge. Crumble lumps of the remaining polenta mixture over the fruit with your fingertips, and don't worry if the rhubarb isn't all covered. Scatter over the demerara sugar.

Place on the hot baking sheet and bake for forty-five to fifty minutes, then cool a little before attempting to remove from the pan. Serve in slices, with the reserved rhubarb juice.

Strawberries

 Our family's move to the Worcestershire countryside brought new responsibilities: chopping wood for the fireplace, chasing copper-colored pheasants off the cabbage patch, taking the dogs for endless walks through the bracken, and collecting eggs from the farm. The last of these involved a slow walk along a narrow, shady path cut along the hillside. In summer, heavily overgrown with ferns, it was dark and damp, even on the brightest of afternoons. At one particularly shaded point, dog-toothed violets, ragged robin, and moss lined the stone walls of the lane, and here and there snow-white strawberry flowers twinkled in the dark. The tiny scarlet berries were few and their crunch as intense as their flavor. As a displaced town dweller, I regarded the idea of strawberries from the wild as both a curiosity and a treat beyond measure.

As we settled into the rhythm of country life, with its annual village fête on the banks of the River Theme, the country shows with their Morris dancers and cake stalls, summer seemed like an endless round of pick-your-own farms. Wherever we drove, the car would always pull up at poppy fields and "pick your owns." At one point its interior seemed to smell permanently of slightly squashed strawberries. It is estimated that there are still a good thousand farms that open their fields to private gatherers. It's a pleasant enough way to spend an hour or two, the good point being that you can choose each berry yourself.

The modern strawberry is a tale of disappointment and delight. I have learned to treat each basket of really good berries I encounter as a box of fleeting, precious jewels, a treat to be enjoyed with unalloyed pleasure; no cream, sugar, or splash of Beaujolais, just the warm berry in all its scarlet glory. That perfect fruit is a rare find, but once you chance upon it life seems, for an instant, to stand still. Eyes closed, you are briefly lost in buttercup meadows, with bees buzzing on the heavy afternoon air. You need to make much of a truly excellent strawberry when you find it, otherwise most of us would probably have given up on this hit-and-miss fruit long ago.

Even at its ripest, the strawberry is not a connoisseur's fruit, in the way of a melting pear or a fig warm from the sun, but more of a cheeky chappie out to please the masses. Strawberry is still the nation's favorite flavor.

Fragility is both the strawberry's charm and its downfall. So tender is its ripe flesh that big business demands something more resilient, a berry that will travel and hold well on the shelf. This has resulted in richly flavored yet delicate varieties being lost and replaced by tougher specimens that will stand a few knocks on the journey from field to plate. Compounded by a propensity for viral infection that can weaken and even wipe out a variety in just a few years, *Fragaria* is a difficult fruit to find at its best. But when you do, and that berry is melting on your tongue, it is as if all your summers have come at once.

The robust varieties of berry can be superb if they are left to ripen fully. An Elsanta that is allowed to ripen gradually and develop its true sweetness will be a revelation to those who have written the variety off as the "supermarket strawberry." Slow ripening produces a deeper flavor because the sugars are given time to develop. This is why the outdoor-ripened fruit in June and July often tastes more interesting than the early hothouse-ripened varieties in late April and May. They are brought to ripeness too quickly. While an unripe apple will be sour, a pear impregnable, and a green orange bitter, an unripe strawberry will simply taste of nothing. Warmth, preferably from the naked sun, is crucial.

By all accounts the berries we enjoy in the twenty-first century are also less red than the dark, bloodied Victorian varieties. The green and white tinges so common now are rarely seen in early portraits of the fruit. At the height of the season, "strawberry girls" were a well-known sight in Regency times, the young women walking around the town balancing a large basket of berries on a cushion on their heads. Buyers would walk away with their fragrant purchase in a pottle—rather like a cone made of wicker. Wine-red berries in a little cane cornucopia—a far more romantic prospect than the blue cellophane carton of today.

It can glow all it wishes, and fill the room with its scent of pineapple, balsam, and honey, but the strawberry will never be my favorite fruit. It lacks the lusciousness of the mulberry, the sensuality of the fig, the mystery of the pomegranate. But once a year I find myself falling for a cardboard basket of misshapen, organic fruits the loud scarlet-red of a Ferrari. It is then, breathing in their honey-sweet scent, the prickle of their yellow seeds on my lips, that I wish they could always be like this.

Strawberries in the garden

The exquisite berries that grow in the dark and shady part of my garden now are a larger form from the wild, the "hautbois," a variety often found wild in Scandinavia and the Low Countries that made its way here in the sixteenth century. Though small, its fruits are less seedy and have an intense flavor. The flowers are acid green. Before I got tough with their rambling manner, I once gathered enough for a plate of tiny sugar-pastry tartlets filled with fromage frais and dusted with a snowfall of confectioners' sugar.

I grow the rest of my plants in rich garden soil in large terra-cotta pots, a layer of heavily rotted manure in the bottom, the fruit hanging enticingly over the edges. Homegrown fruit for anyone with a few feet of outside space. They do well as long as the soil is moist. In the garden, the ripening fruits were consistently half-inched by the squirrels or nibbled at by slugs that found their way over the straw I laid under each plant to keep the crop from becoming muddy. The Florence variety has done particularly well in pots. The bushes remain little more than a spread hand across and survive frost and the occasional drought, yet still produce prolific quantities of richly flavored berries.

In their own bed, the plants like to be about 20 inches (50cm) apart in rich, easily draining soil, but I have found them to be tolerant of both wet and cold. They need a sunny site if they are to ripen aromatically. Green netting will keep off the birds. An underblanket of thick straw will keep them from getting muddy and lift the berries nearer the sunshine. In winter it is a good idea to pull away dead leaves to reduce the chance of infection, but don't expect the plants to live forever; they are naturally short-lived.

Varieties

Strawberry varieties seem to come and go, but with good reason. Their susceptibility to viral infection means that few old varieties survive. Many of the reputed cultivars developed in the first half of the 1820s are now lost forever, including the deep burgundy Black Prince, Keen's Seedling, the reliable British Queen, and the corpulent red Waterloo that Edward Bunyard described as "too carnal in appearance for vegetarians." Bad luck.

Early varieties such as Elvira, Honeoye,* Mae, and Gariguette will be ripe from early to mid-June if we have enough sun. Midseason varieties include Darselect, Hapil, which is good for drier soils, and the heavy-cropping Cambridge Favorite. Late-fruiting varieties, often smaller but with a deep color, include Alice, Florence, the firmer French Daisy, and the exceptionally red Chelsea Pensioner that specialist Ken Muir has high claims for and I too have done rather well with.

Royal Sovereign A gorgeous berry that elicits as much praise now as it did when nurseryman Thomas Laxton introduced it in 1892.

Gariguette The French equivalent of the Royal Sovereign. A long, sugar-sweet berry as bright as a tart's lipstick that is the star of the market stalls of Provence. The fruit is too soft and tender for commercial use here, and so is something for the gardener and allotment holder.

Cambridge Favorite A heavy cropper, this old variety fruits during July. Reliable and tolerant of both disease and neglect, the berry is less red than it might be and has particularly dense leaf growth.

Cambridge Late Pine Bred since 1947, the Cambridge Late Pine is considered by some to be the best-flavored strawberry variety ever. It has a good dark color and is exceptionally fragrant.

Florence The most flavorsome berries I have ever eaten turned out to be Florence, so I ordered several plants and have grown them ever since. Although they have never reached the intensity of those first berries, this is a very finely flavored variety that excels in pots and rarely gets too big.

Chandler* Popular with home gardeners, this early producer yields large, flavorful, juicy berries.

Seascape* Delivers an abundant harvest of large, sweet, good-looking berries.

Earliglow* Prized for its medium-sized, flavorful, aromatic berries. Produces early in the season.

*Available from US sources.

Occasionally you will come across someone selling the seed of cultivated varieties of wood or Alpine berries. These small but well-flavored berries, with a rich flavor and fragrance, include the exceptionally rare and aromatic heirloom Baron von Solemacher.

Strawberries in the kitchen

The grumbling of food writers and consumers, the constant media bashing of the ubiquitous Elsanta variety, and the heart-rending disappointment on children's faces must have finally pricked the growers' collective conscience. Of late, the strawberry of commerce seems to have picked up its little feet, and the promise of sweet, summer-scented berries is often fulfilled. Supermarkets, whose demands for extended shelf life and sturdy flesh had led to the debasing of our proud fruit, seem to have got the message. Varieties grown for flavor rather than shelf life are being offered, necessarily at a premium, and smaller berries too, more intensely flavored and more fragrant. There are still moments of dissatisfaction, but rarer and more forgivable. Disappointment may not be a thing of the past, but I like to think it is getting less usual.

If ever there was a case of leaving well enough alone, then this is it. Churn your berries into an ice cream, dip them in dark chocolate, freeze them as a water ice, or simmer them into a simple homemade jam. Once you start getting clever in the form of mousses, pies, charlottes, crumbles, cakes, and the like, the strawberry's magic will all too often be lost. A fool, where the fork-crushed berries are folded into lightly beaten fridge-cold cream, or a smart tart, is about as sophisticated as things should get.

You have chosen your berries, for their good looks, for their heavy scent, yet once home their flavor somehow fails to deliver. What do you do? Warmth will help. There is no love in a fridge-cold strawberry. If a few hours on a sunny windowsill doesn't work, then slice your cargo into a bowl and dust them with superfine sugar. In an hour, maybe even half that, you will have sweeter berries, slightly softer but of richer color, and there will be juice too. Cutting them into quarters rather than slices will keep the texture firm. A dribble of balsamic vinegar or a glug from the Beaujolais bottle will introduce a mellowness that may surprise. Grated orange zest works too. Lime juice will tease out the shyest flavor, as will lemon.

Strawberries and...

Cream Much debate about the merits of sweet dairy with this fruit, but on a good day, when the fruit is ripe and the cream is particularly yellow and preferably unpasteurized, a dish of strawberries and cream takes some beating. Sharp creams such as mascarpone, crème fraîche, and clotted cream are good here too.

Black pepper I have never really agreed with this, but some find a grinding of pepper, black and very, very fine, brings out the flavor of a shy berry.

Beaujolais The fruity quality of young Beaujolais is good for soaking the fruit in, with a little sugar, before serving. Make sure it is nicely chilled.

Balsamic vinegar The tiniest amount, added to a strawberry ice cream or sorbet as it churns, will make the fruit taste richer and sweeter.

Chocolate Generally I can live without this marriage, but dark and almost bitter chocolate can be an effective partner if used crisp and sparingly. (A thin drizzle allowed to set like a fragile spiderweb on a fruit tart can be excellent.) Soft chocolate mixtures, such as mousse or ganache, will give the fruit a sickly edge.

Orange Make up a dry marinade of superfine sugar and finely grated orange zest for lackluster berries. Set aside for an hour. It will save their lives.

* Bring the box of berries close to your face. If you don't get a hit of ripe strawberry, then put them back. A good batch has a good aroma.
* It is better to wash strawberries before you twist out the green hulls, so the water does not penetrate the fruit and make it soggy.

A strawberry ice for a summer's day

The simplest and best. No other flavoring is needed for this straightforward ice cream, and it is one of the few that is worth making without an ice cream machine. The ripeness of the berries is essential. I always marinate them in sugar for an hour or so before I make the ice, even though I have never heard of anyone else doing it. I believe it makes the flavor all the more intense.

enough for 4
strawberries – 1 pound (450g)
superfine sugar – ½ cup (100g)
heavy cream – 1¼ cups (300ml)

Rinse the berries quickly under cold running water and remove their leaves. Cut each berry into three or four slices, then put them in a bowl, sprinkle with the sugar, and set aside for an hour.

Lightly whip the cream. You want it to be thick enough to lie in folds rather than stiff enough to stand in peaks. Put the strawberries, sugar, and any juice from the bottom of the dish into a food processor and whiz until smooth, then stir gently into the cream. How thoroughly you blend the two together is up to you. I like to leave a few swirls of unmixed cream in the mixture.

Transfer to a freezer-safe box, level the top, cover with a lid or a piece of plastic wrap or wax paper, and freeze for three or four hours. It is worth checking, and occasionally stirring the ice as it freezes, bringing the outside edges into the middle.

Remove the ice from the freezer about fifteen to twenty minutes before serving to bring it up to temperature.

A fromage frais cream with strawberries and passion fruit

A light cream for strawberries. There are several options with this recipe. You can use just heavy cream, fromage frais (full fat), crème fraîche, or a mixture of any two of them. The choice will depend on what sort of piquancy you want. My favorite is a mixture of fromage frais and crème fraîche, a rich but fresh accompaniment to strawberries, and perfect with tiny wild ones.

enough for 4
strawberries – 14 ounces (400g)
the juice of a large orange
passion fruit – 6

for the cream
fromage frais – 10 ounces (300g)
crème fraîche – ⅔ cup (150ml)
egg whites – 2

Line a stainless steel sieve or colander with clean, new cheesecloth, leaving enough overhanging to fold over the top. In a cold bowl, mix the fromage frais and crème fraîche. Do this thoroughly but gently.

Beat the egg whites in a separate bowl until light and stiff. Fold the whites into the cream mixture, taking care not to knock the air out. A large metal spoon is good for this.

Spoon the mixture into the lined sieve. Fold the cheesecloth over the top, place the sieve over a basin, and leave in the fridge overnight (if you have a small fridge, as I do, you may have to take a shelf out to accommodate it).

The next day, unmold the cream, which will have shrunk and become more solid.

Rinse the berries and remove their leaves and stalks. Slice each in half and put them in a glass or china bowl. Squeeze over the orange juice. Cut the passion fruit in half and squeeze over the seeds and juice. Chill for two hours, but no longer, as the berries are inclined to go "fluffy" if they soak too long.

Serve the bowl of strawberries with the mound of cream, letting everyone spoon the fruit over the cream as they wish.

A high-summer jam to serve warm

There are two kinds of jam: the sort you use to preserve a glut of berries to last you through the gray days of winter and the sort for more immediate consumption. The advantage of the latter is that it is not required to have any shelf life and so can be less sweet. The most luscious jams, by which I mean plum, gooseberry, greengage, black currant, and apricot, all have the advantage of a bite of acidity to the raw fruit, resulting in a jam that is rarely oversweet. The strawberry lacks that essential piquancy, which is why most strawberry jams are so tongue-numbingly sweet, and no doubt why they are so popular.

Mid- to late summer, when the roses are almost over, the bees are getting lazy, the lawn worse for wear, and the raspberries almost red enough to pick, is when strawberry prices relax and we can turn our mind to jam. Pots and pots of it, for breakfast toast and afternoon tea, ladled from jars using spoons with sticky handles, spread onto floury scones, and sandwiched between slices of homemade sponge cake, their surfaces sparkling with superfine sugar.

The jam I make is high on fruit, low on the sweet stuff. I bring it to the table still warm from the stove, a pretty dish of it with a faint pink froth on its brow. It won't keep. It is not meant to.

> strawberries – 1½ pounds (750g)
> granulated sugar – ½ cup (100g)
> a squeeze of lemon juice

Rinse and hull the strawberries, but don't dry them. Pile them into a stainless steel or enameled pan with the sugar and lemon juice. Crush the fruit with your hands or a potato masher, then place the pan over low to medium heat. Cook, stirring occasionally, for fifteen to twenty minutes, spooning off the pink froth as you go. The jam should be thick enough to fall slowly from the spoon, like syrup, but nowhere near thick enough to set.

Pour into a bowl and serve with scones (where it will drip down your fingers) or slices cut from a sponge cake, or spoon over goat's milk yogurt, or stir into a mess of whipped cream and crumbled meringue.

Strawberries, passion fruit, and mint

You will need a couple of passion fruits for each portion of strawberries. Check that the passion fruits are ripe, by which I mean heavily wrinkled. Hull the strawberries and cut them in half or even quarters, depending on their size. Halve the passion fruit and squeeze their juice and seeds into a bowl. Very finely chop a couple of mint leaves per person and stir them into the passion fruit, then add the strawberries, and gently toss them about a bit. Cover with a plate and leave for at least twenty minutes, an hour if you can. Serve lightly chilled.

Strawberries, orange, and orange-flower water

The merest breath of orange blossom here. It is a good use for berries that prove less interesting than they appeared in the shop.

> *enough for 4*
> strawberries – 4 handfuls
> oranges – 3
> orange-flower water

Rinse the berries and remove their leaves and stalks. Slice each in half and put them in a glass or china bowl. Peel and slice the oranges, saving any escaping juice and adding it to the berries with the orange slices. Shake over the orange-flower water—you need just the merest drop (believe me, just a drop is heavenly, too much and it will taste like soap).

Chill for two hours, but no longer, as the berries are inclined to go "fluffy" if they soak for too long.

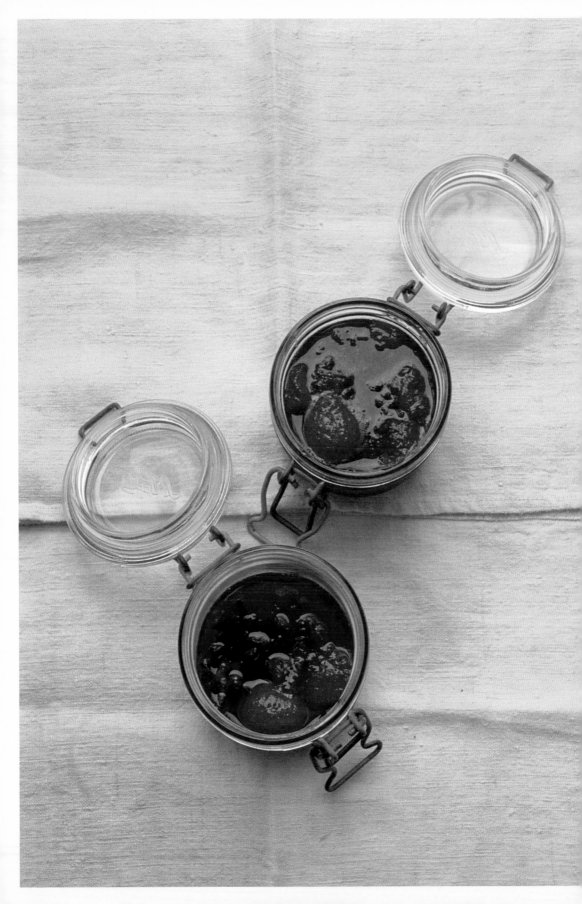

A traditional strawberry jam

Again a fairly light set. I keep this in the fridge, which thickens the jam slightly.

> strawberries – 2¼ pounds (1kg)
> granulated sugar – about 1¾ pounds (800g), about 4 cups
> the juice of a large lemon

Wash and hull the berries. Keep the small ones whole and halve or even quarter the large ones. Put them into a stainless steel pan with the sugar and lemon juice and bring to a boil. Boil rapidly for fifteen minutes or until the fruit is looking soft and translucent.

Skim off the pink froth that appears on the top, then spoon into sterilized jars, seal (see below), and leave to cool.

A few notes: It is essential to prepare the jars correctly if the jam is to keep. You can either warm the thoroughly washed jars in a cooling oven, thereby sterilizing them, or you can immerse them in boiling water for ten minutes. Either way they must be both scrupulously clean and warm when you pour the jam in. Seal the jam with a disk of wax paper. The transparent jam covers that can be bought in kitchenware stores and supermarkets should be applied while the jam is warm so that they shrink tightly over the top of the jar.

Strawberries and cream

Summer is shot through with elegant culinary marriages: white-tipped radishes and ice-cold butter, stewed pale gooseberries and lacework elderflowers, ripe melon and prosciutto, mozzarella and sun-warmed tomatoes, salmon and crisp, dewy cucumber. There is also strawberries and cream.

Of course, you can slice the fruit and pour cream over it. But listen, I have a better idea. You pick the smallest, ripest berries you can lay your fingers on, crimson right through to their little hearts. You hull them, put them in a bowl, then crush them with a fork. The flesh should retain some sort of texture rather than be reduced to a purée or a puddle. Mellow the flavor with a drip or two of balsamic vinegar. Stir in the merest dribble of golden cream. Fiddle no further. I think you owe this one a teaspoon.

Strawberry tarts

Strawberries, pastry, and cream. A threesome made in heaven.

makes 6

for the crust
butter – 7 tablespoons (100g)
superfine sugar – 2 tablespoons
shelled pistachios – 3½ ounces (100g), about ⅔ cup, finely ground
an egg yolk
all-purpose flour – 1½ cups plus 1 tablespoon (200g)

for the filling
heavy cream – 1 cup (250ml)
vanilla extract
strawberries – about 8 small berries per tartlet
a little confectioners' sugar or melted dark chocolate

You will need six tartlet pans with removable bottoms, about 3 inches (8cm) in diameter.

Cream the butter and sugar until pale and smooth. Add the ground pistachios, mix in the egg yolk and then the flour. Add a little water if necessary to make a firm but rollable dough.

On a floured board, roll the dough into a short, fat sausage the circumference of the tartlet pans. Wrap in wax paper or plastic wrap and refrigerate for a good twenty minutes. Preheat the oven to 400°F (200°C).

Cut the pastry into thin disks and place them in the tartlet shells, pushing them gently into the corners. Use wax paper to line each pastry shell, fill with pie weights, then bake for fifteen minutes or so, until the tartlet shells are a pale biscuit color. Remove the paper and pie weights and return to the oven for five minutes to dry them out. Let them cool a little before removing from the tartlet shells.

Gently whip the cream until it will just about hold its shape, adding the tiniest drop of vanilla extract as you go. It should be billowy and voluptuous rather than stiff. Divide between the tartlet shells. Add the strawberries, together with a dusting of confectioners' sugar or a drizzle of melted dark chocolate.

Walnuts

Christmas descends on this old house like a veil of spun sugar. A tree of snow-white lights and resinous scent, church candles in the smoke-stained fireplaces, and bejeweled tartlets of candied peel and crushed walnuts in the oven. I drag bundles of holly and mistletoe home from the farmers' market and trails of ivy from the garden walls. There are bowls of crimson pomegranates and walnuts in their shells. Where the chestnut is the nut of damp, smoky autumn afternoons, the walnut is the Christmas nut, decorating fruit bowls and cheese boards until well into the New Year.

My earliest acquaintance with the walnut was both sinister and sweet. First as the black, pickled nuts like lumps of decaying fungi passed around the table by my father to sharpen up slices of cold roast beef, and then as the buried treasure at the bottom of a Walnut Whip. The pickled walnut still has its faithful fans but gone are the days when the milk chocolate confection had half a walnut in its base as well as a proud one on top.

The meat of the freshly shelled walnut revels in sour or bitter company: preserved in vinegar; scattered in a salad with watercress, endive, or arugula; offered alongside chunks of pomegranate after a meal; or cloaked in darkest chocolate. Eaten too late after harvesting or stored in sunlight, the sweet nut can take on a bitterness all of its own—a quality that has done little to win it any friends.

Fresh, locally grown walnuts are few and far between. The trees are generally too large for domestic gardens and most are found on farms or in parks. Most of those in our shops come from France or Iran. The ones with pale skins are the sweetest, their young flesh briefly mild and, like young hazelnuts, almost milky in taste. As the nuts age, their skin darkens and bitterness becomes a distinct possibility.

The Middle East and Turkey have walnut sauces for fish and game, while Greece excels in pastries made from the nut. Even though we can grow them here, we have no famous traditional dishes based on the walnut, except the pickled walnut, a dark and interesting ketchup, and the long-lamented Fuller's walnut cake, a commercial gateau of walnut cream and crunchy, nut-flecked sponge cake with faintly lemon-scented icing. A cake that still has a following, thirty years after its demise, and that is long overdue for a revival.

I tend to take my walnuts early in the season while they are still pale and young. I toast them, then toss them among winter salads, tuck them into crisp ribbons of coleslaw, and grind them coarsely to add a nubbly texture to a cake. Most are eaten as a naked nut, along with the other Christmas fruits—figs, dates, and mandarins.

The occasional tree appears in the wild here despite it being native to a plain from the Balkans to southwest China. The world's most prolific producer is California, and an ancient 700-acre orchard in the small village of Shahmirzad in Iran. We are lucky that this nut, unlike the Brazil, the pecan, and the almond, will ripen in our climate. The word itself is derived from *wealhhnutu*, meaning "foreign nut" (it came to us via France and Italy). Round and crinkly shelled, this is the nut of feasting and it appears throughout the art world in sumptuous displays of grapes, quinces, pomegranates, and pears, mostly from the brushes of the Dutch masters. For me, it is something to share a plate with a pear or a piece of Appleby's Cheshire or true Caerphilly, or to be dipped into dark chocolate and eaten with vanilla ice cream.

The nut we see here most often is the Persian species, celebrated for its generous size and thin shell (some of the black variety are all but impossible to crack). You can shatter the Persian shells by squeezing two together in the palm of your hand. They can be harvested here as early as September, when the shells are still green, resembling spineless conkers. In this state the nuts within are creamy white in color, crisp, but softer than the dried nut; a treat with the first of the season's apples.

The British are partial to these young, green walnuts. I have rarely seen these—or "wet walnuts," as they are most often known—on sale anywhere else. It is at this point in their life, when the "meat" of the nut is the color of sour milk, that the walnuts are used for pickling and in gritty sauces for game and, in particular, pheasant.

The Armenians preserve the juiciest of them in a thick sugar syrup, eating them by the teaspoonful. In Italy, those that don't end up in a sauce for pasta may be used to flavor the liqueurs Nocino and Nocello.

Those who wait for Santa's stocking before getting the nutcrackers out are missing a trick. By Christmas the nuts are starting to dry out and, though still good, have lost a bit of the spring in their step. Obsessive I may be (and I am) but surely I'm not the only one who attempts to winkle the nut out of its shell in one piece. Even a corner broken is regarded as a failure. Worse, I like to extract those dry, sharp wings that wedge themselves between the two halves of the nut while keeping the kernel intact. One of life's little rituals, like trying to maintain an unbroken length of peel when paring an apple for a pie, or sucking a Murray mint all the way until it disappears without crunching.

The shells, when ground, are used as an environmentally sound abrasive to scale, clean, and polish everything from soft metals and stone to aircraft engines. They form a useful part in the manufacture of dynamite, paint, exfoliators, and much else besides. The husks that so easily stain the hands when you pick the fresh nuts are used as a natural dye. Left whole, an empty walnut shell makes a charming, fairy-tale receptacle for holding a special, tiny gift. (Think ring.)

The wood, much prized by carpenters, gunsmiths, and furniture makers, is dark, dense, and tightly grained. My kitchen drawers are lined with kiln-dried walnut heartwood, each tobacco-colored compartment holding a knife, a ladle, or a measuring cup. The outer wood of the tree is the color of pale honey.

A walnut tree in the garden

You will need as much patience as space. Many take a decade or more to fruit, and some trees can grow to immense specimens 100 feet (30m) tall, far too big for the average domestic garden. They also exude a protective compound—juglone—that is poisonous to many garden vegetables, including tomatoes and apples. Horses, too. Not much will grow under a walnut tree. There are several species of this hardy tree, but it is *Juglans regia* that is most often grown for its nuts. Many species have shells too hard to crack.

Unless you are picking them "wet" in July and August for pickling or simply to munch raw, the nuts are ready to harvest from October onward, when their hulls split or they start to fall off the tree. They are ready when the papery tissue between the kernel and the shell has turned pale brown. The outer cases should be easy to remove, but wearing gloves will keep your fingers from turning brown.

Drying the nuts is essential if you are to store them. You can do this in a single layer in a warm, dry place for a couple of weeks, or do it more quickly over a radiator.

Varieties

A few specialty nurseries can provide young trees, carefully chosen from the hundreds of varieties available to suit our climate and to fruit within four years or so. Just in case you have the space and time, and the kindness, to plant a tree that is more for the next generation than our own, I list a few of the nut-bearing varieties available.

Franquette* A traditional French variety, slow growing but very high quality nuts.
Red Danube A rare red variety from Germany.
Lara French, reliable, and of "moderate vigor."
Buccaneer Vigorous and early. Apparently good for pickling.
Fernor A new French variety that has especially light-colored kernels.
Carpathian* Hardy, lovely black walnut tree with a spreading, open crown and rich, robustly flavored nuts with easy-to-crack shells.
Chandler* Produces an abundant harvest of light-colored, crunchy nuts on a moderately sized tree.

*Available from US sources.

Walnuts in the kitchen

Those cooks who possess neither a walnut tree in their garden nor a post-Christmas glut of whole nuts are likely to buy their nuts ready shelled. It is worth looking out for those that are light in color. They will probably be younger and less inclined to the bitterness that can occasionally develop as the nuts darken and dry. An effective way to remove any hint of bitterness is to soak them in boiling water for ten minutes. For a recipe where the nuts are the point—a sauce with lemon juice and garlic or a walnut cake, for instance—this might not be a bad habit to get into.

Nuts like salt. It brings out their sweetness. I grind over a little sea salt and toast my walnuts until they just start to color—no more than a single shade on a decorator's color card—then eat them while they are still hot. I tuck them into salads at this point too, the most successful being anything involving bitter leaves such as watercress or Belgian endive.

The most famous walnut salad is the Waldorf, named for the New York hotel on whose menu it first appeared in the early 1890s. Legend has it that the restaurant's maître d'hôtel, Oscar Tschirky, first made the salad, a crunchy mixture of celery, apple, and mayonnaise, without the now-synonymous walnuts. They were added by the time the recipe first appeared in print. Another worth making is one with "rabbit ears" of crisp white Belgian endive, Roquefort cheese, and walnuts. This is an absolute gem. Crackling salad leaves, salty cheese, toasted walnuts, and a mustard dressing—it is hard to think of a salad I would rather start my dinner with. I make an alternative with grated pecorino and a very mustardy dressing. It looks cool and elegant but packs a punch. I know of no better use for a walnut.

Most of the kernels not used in a sauce or salad tend to end up in a cake. My own favorite coffee and walnut aside, the nut is most common in a tea bread, perhaps with golden raisins, dark cherries, and a smidgen of allspice. Something to slice and butter. I also make a coarse, less sweet cake with breadcrumbs in lieu of flour. The gravelly texture is softened with a silky frosting scented with orange blossom.

Shallow tarts of walnuts and honey are good for midmorning, as are similar affairs with a little bitter chocolate to take the edge off the sweetness. Walnut cookies, thin and crisp, are an excellent choice for mild cheeses. A few chopped nuts in a crumble topping can be pleasing if you can keep them from burning. A walnut that sits upright is likely to brown a little too quickly. Most successful of all, perhaps, is to include the coarsely chopped nuts in a loaf for cheese. A few tobacco-colored raisins might be welcome too. Thickly sliced, it is the bread for a young and chalky goat cheese or a melting Camembert. A few sprigs of rosemary needles, finely chopped, will add an aromatic edge.

The walnut has another string to its bow in the shape of its golden oil. This has a curious affinity with tomatoes, peaches, and apricots. Trickle a little oil over a grilled peach and you have a piece of poetry on a plate. I like a mayonnaise finished with it (use peanut oil for the bulk, then add a little walnut near the end). A walnut oil mayonnaise comes into its own with a plate of cold, salt-encrusted roast pork and its chewy crackling.

This is not an oil for the frying pan or roasting pan, where its flavor will disappear further with each degree of heat. It burns easily too, as do the nuts themselves. I keep it for salad dressings—it is extraordinary as a balm for a plain salad of soft green lettuce leaves and exciting when spiked with lemon juice and black pepper for an endive and walnut salad. The oil's warm, earthy quality has an affinity with pomegranate seeds, grapes, and fennel.

Walnuts and...

Chocolate Like most nuts, the walnut is exceptionally happy in the company of chocolate, particularly the darker types around 70 percent cocoa solids. I have occasionally included them in the filling for a chocolate tart, the cream in a roulade, and as a secret treat at the bottom of a pot of chocolate mousse.

Maple syrup The flavors flatter each other—a drizzle of the syrup over a walnut cake being a good example.

Honey The halved kernels can be stored in honey as a sweetmeat, to be eaten with long spoons and perhaps a little sharp yogurt. Thick honey and walnuts make an exceptional filling for an autumn tart, and both make good partners for goat cheeses.

Pears Include walnuts in the poaching syrup for pears; add the crushed nuts to cream cheese and use it to stuff the halved pears; introduce a few nuts to the filling of a pear tart.

Cheeses The walnut is a pleasing partner for almost any cheese you can think of. The obvious choices are the milder blues, but goat's and sheep's milk cheeses, and the firm British varieties such as the Cheddars and Cheshires, can produce happy marriages.

Caramel Coat the lightly toasted kernels in crisp caramel for a more fragile version of nut brittle. I sometimes pass them round with coffee after dinner.

Celery Match the two in salads, especially with Russet apples, or add the toasted and salted nuts to a celery soup.

Peaches A walnut stuffing, made with the coarsely ground nuts, soft cream cheese such as mascarpone, and a little honey, can be used with halved peaches and baked until the filling has melted and the fruit is soft.

Figs Include a handful of nuts in a dish of baked figs with honey; work them into a fig and pomegranate salad; offer them together as a simple dessert.

* Most walnuts don't need nutcrackers. The point of a knife, inserted into the fat end of the shell, should be enough to open them with a flip of the wrist. For a tough nut, I resort to the oyster knife.

* The high level of unsaturated fat in walnut oil assures that it will not keep well. I store this oil in the fridge.

* Oil from tropical regions has been found to be higher in saturated fats than that produced from nuts grown in a temperate climate.

* English walnuts will keep in the shell for several months in a cool, dry place.

* Shelled walnuts store best in an airtight container.

A simple salad of leaves and new walnuts

Sometimes, you just cannot beat a simple green salad with masses of spankingly fresh leaves and a mild, nutty dressing.

enough for 4 as a side salad
salad leaves, such as butter lettuce, romaine, oakleaf, or frisée – 8 handfuls
shelled new walnut halves – a couple of handfuls

for the dressing
tarragon vinegar – 2 teaspoons
French mustard – a level teaspoon
sunflower oil – 2 tablespoons
walnut oil – 3 tablespoons

Put the tarragon vinegar in a jar to which you have a tight-fitting lid. Add the mustard, a grinding of salt and black pepper, then the oils. Screw on the lid and shake hard to mix.

Wash and dry the salad leaves. Gently toss with some of the dressing. Don't overdress; each leaf should just be moist, no more. Toss with the new walnuts, untoasted and unskinned.

A "new" Waldorf salad

The classic salad is simply chopped celery, apples, and walnuts bound with mayonnaise. Some like its mildness and slightly sticky texture. I prefer the classic ingredients brought together in a somewhat lighter dressing, with more bite to it than the usual recipe. A good one for accompanying a punchy cheese, slices of smoked mackerel, or cold meats such as speck.

enough for 2 as a side salad
large, sweetish apples, preferably Russet – 3
large celery sticks – 2
walnut halves – 12

for the dressing
crème fraîche – 2 tablespoons
chopped parsley – 2 tablespoons
chopped mint – 2 tablespoons
mayonnaise – ⅔ cup (150ml)

To make the dressing, mix all the ingredients in a bowl. Coarsely chop the apples, celery, and walnuts and toss them with the dressing.

A salad of Belgian endive, pecorino, and new walnuts

enough for 2
medium-sized Belgian endive heads – 4
new walnuts in their shells – 8
chopped flat-leaf parsley – 2 tablespoons
grated pecorino or Parmesan – 4 heaping tablespoons

for the dressing
Dijon mustard – 1 tablespoon
white wine vinegar – 2 teaspoons
walnut oil – 1 tablespoon
peanut oil – 2 tablespoons

Trim the endive, removing any leaf that isn't utterly white and perfect.
Separate the leaves, rinse and pat dry carefully, then put them in a
salad bowl.

Crack the walnuts, remove the nuts from their shells, and season
lightly with salt. Toast them briefly under a hot broiler or in a small pan
over medium heat. Keep your eye on them all the time; they burn within
seconds. They should be barely colored.

Put the mustard, vinegar, and walnut and peanut oils in a blender with
a little salt and pepper and whiz for a few seconds. Pour the dressing into
the salad bowl, then add the nuts, chopped parsley, and grated cheese.
Toss the salad gently and serve immediately.

A salad of marinated goat cheese, figs, and pomegranate

A classy little starter, this, full of crisp leaves and fresh tastes.

enough for 4
small goat cheeses – 4
bushy sprigs of thyme – 4
black peppercorns – 12, lightly crushed
bay leaves – 4
olive oil – ⅔ cup (150ml)
walnut oil – 7 tablespoons (100ml)
salad leaves – 4 large handfuls
a large pomegranate
figs – 4
red wine vinegar – 2 to 3 tablespoons
walnut halves – 24

Cut each cheese in half horizontally. Put the disks of cheese in a flat dish, sitting snugly, then tuck in the sprigs of thyme, the lightly crushed peppercorns, and the bay leaves. Pour over the oils, cover with plastic wrap, and leave in a cool place overnight.

Rinse and dry the salad leaves. Halve the pomegranate and pick or knock out the seeds. Avoid the bitter pith; you want just the jewel-like seeds. Cut a cross in the top of each fig and press its shoulders with your fingers and thumbs so that it opens out like a flower (actually I think they more resemble baby birds singing in their nest).

Pour the oil from the cheeses into a bowl, holding them in place with a spatula. Add a little salt and the vinegar to the oil, whisking lightly to give a sharp dressing. Taste as you go, adding more or less vinegar depending on its acidity. Toast the walnuts in a hot, dry nonstick pan.

Divide the salad leaves among four plates. Lay two slices of cheese on each plate, one fig, a scattering of pomegranate seeds, and the hot walnuts. Spoon over a little of the dressing.

Penne, walnuts, Gorgonzola, and sage

Supper in ten minutes; what more could anyone ask on a cold midweek night in midwinter? The flavor here is deliberately mild and soothing (the exact opposite of a puttanesca). The pasta coheres gently with the sauce rather than swimming in it. I usually make an endive salad to follow, something crisp and slightly bitter. Even then, all I want to do is drop off to sleep afterward. That's what creamy pasta recipes are for.

enough for 2
penne or other small, tubular pasta – 10 ounces (300g)
creamy Gorgonzola – about 10 ounces (300g)
heavy cream – 7 tablespoons (100ml)
walnuts – a dozen or more, young and freshly shelled
sage leaves – about 6 will do

Put the pasta on to cook in a deep pan of generously salted boiling water. Test it throughout the cooking, but it should be ready after about nine minutes. I like my pasta to have a bit of bite. Drain the pasta in a colander, reserving a couple of tablespoonfuls of the cooking water.

Put the empty pan immediately back on the stove and turn the heat down low, then add the cheese, cream, and reserved cooking water. Stir for a minute or less, until the cheese starts to melt and you have an impromptu sauce. Tip the pasta back into the pan with the walnuts and sage leaves, then tip onto warm plates.

Vanilla walnut sundae

It was Stephen Fry who I feel discovered the best possible use for this particular nut. On visiting a world-famous Vermont ice cream manufacturer, he was encouraged to come up with his own "flavor." It was a stroke of typical Fry genius that led him to woo the assembled crew with a simple mixture of vanilla ice cream, bitter chocolate, and toasted walnuts. Never has a recipe made me leave my seat so quickly and head for the kitchen. Simple, perfect.

Fig and walnut cake

A big family cake made in much the same way as carrot cake.

serves 8 (at least)
soft dried figs – 8 ounces (250g)
shelled walnuts – 3½ ounces (100g), a scant cup
eggs – 3
golden baker's sugar – 5 tablespoons (65g)
light muscovado sugar – 5 tablespoons (65g)
peanut oil – a generous ¾ cup (200ml)
flour – 2 cups (250g)
baking powder – a gently heaping teaspoon
ground cinnamon – a teaspoon
a pinch of ground nutmeg
yogurt – 7 tablespoons (100ml)
a drop or two of vanilla extract

for the icing
cream cheese – 8 ounces (250g)
mascarpone – 7 ounces (200g)
softened butter – 3½ tablespoons (50g)
a drop or two of vanilla extract
confectioners' sugar – 1¼ cups (150g)

Preheat the oven to 350°F (180°C). Line the bottoms of two 8-inch (20cm) cake pans with lightly buttered or oiled parchment paper. Coarsely chop the figs and walnuts. The nuts should be chopped slightly finer than the fruit.

Mix the eggs, sugars, and oil using an electric mixer and beat until pale and fluffy. Sift the flour with the baking powder, cinnamon, nutmeg, and a pinch of salt. Add the yogurt to the cake mixture, alternating with the flour and spices. Stir in the vanilla, the figs, and the walnuts.

Divide the mixture between the two lined pans and bake for thirty-five to forty minutes, until firm like a fruitcake. Remove from the oven, leave to settle for a few minutes, then run a thin spatula around the edges and carefully turn onto a cooling rack. Remove the paper from each cake.

Make the icing. Beat the cream cheese, mascarpone, butter, and vanilla until smooth, then beat in the confectioners' sugar. Spread a layer on the top of one of the cake layers, place the other cake on top, then move to a cake stand or plate. Spread the remaining buttercream over the top and sides of the cake.

Walnut, chocolate, and honey tart

Dense, sweet, and crumbly. A tart for serving with coffee. Also good cold in a lunch box.

enough for 6 to 8

for the crust
butter – 10 tablespoons (150g)
all-purpose flour – a generous 1½ cups (200g)
a large egg, beaten

for the filling
butter – 10 tablespoons (150g)
crystallized honey – 6 ounces (180g), about ½ cup
light muscovado sugar – a generous ⅔ cup, packed (180g)
heavy cream – ⅓ cup (80ml)
a drop or two of vanilla extract
dark chocolate – 5 ounces (140g), coarsely chopped
walnuts – 7½ ounces (220g), a scant 2 cups, coarsely chopped

crème fraîche, to serve

To make the pastry, cut the butter into pieces and rub into the flour with your fingertips, then mix in the egg to give a firm dough. Roll out and use to line a 9- to 9½-inch (22 to 24cm) shallow tart pan. Leave to rest in the fridge for a good twenty minutes. Preheat the oven to 400°F (200°C).

Cover the pastry shell with parchment paper and fill with dried beans or ceramic pie weights. Cook in the preheated oven for about ten minutes, until the pastry is lightly biscuit colored. Carefully remove the paper and beans and return the pastry shell to the oven for five minutes, until dry to the touch.

For the filling, melt the butter in a small pan, add the honey and sugar, and then pour in the cream and a couple of drops of vanilla extract. Boil hard for two minutes, then remove from the heat and lightly fold in the chopped chocolate and walnuts. Pour the filling into the tart shell.

Turn the oven down to 375°F (190°C) and bake for twenty minutes, until golden. Remove and leave to cool for a good half hour before serving with crème fraîche.

Classic coffee and walnut cake

I thought long and hard before including this cake here. The recipe is in my 2005 book, *The Kitchen Diaries*, and initially I didn't want to repeat it. What is more, it wasn't a recipe I wanted to tinker with or alter in any way. But I also feel that a chapter dedicated to the walnut is incomplete without such a classic recipe. So here it is again. It is more than my "dessert" island dish, it is the cake I want on my lips as I leave this world. Fat chance.

enough for 8 to 10
butter – ¾ cup (175g)
golden baker's sugar – ¾ cup plus 2 tablespoons (175g)
large eggs – 3
self-rising flour – 1⅓ cups (175g)
baking powder – 1 teaspoon
instant coffee granules – 2 teaspoons
walnut pieces – 2 ounces (65g), about ½ cup

for the buttercream
butter – a scant cup (200g)
confectioners' sugar – 3⅓ cups (400g)
instant coffee granules – 2 teaspoons
walnut pieces – 2 ounces (60g), about ½ cup

You will need two 8-inch (20cm) springform cake pans. Line the bottoms of the pans with parchment paper. Preheat the oven to 350°F (180°C).

Beat the butter and baker's sugar until light, pale, and fluffy. You could do this by hand but it is far easier and, frankly, better with an electric mixer. Crack the eggs into a bowl, break them up with a fork, then add them a little at a time to the butter and sugar, beating well after each addition.

Mix the flour and baking powder together and gently mix into the butter and sugar, either with the mixer on low speed or by hand, with a large metal spoon. Dissolve the coffee granules in a tablespoon of boiling water, then stir them into the mixture. Chop the walnuts and fold them in gently.

Divide the cake mixture between the two pans, smooth the tops lightly, and bake for twenty to twenty-five minutes. I have noticed mine are pretty much consistently done after twenty-three minutes. Remove from the oven and leave to cool.

To make the buttercream, beat the butter with an electric mixer until soft and pale, then add the confectioners' sugar and beat until smooth and creamy. Stir a tablespoon of boiling water into the coffee granules, then mix it into the buttercream. Fold in the walnut pieces.

As soon as the cake is cool, turn one layer upside down on a plate or board, spread it with a good third of the buttercream, then place the second cake layer on top. Spread the remaining buttercream on top and round the sides.

A raisin and walnut loaf for pears and cheese

Two thick slices cut from a warm whole wheat loaf studded with walnuts, a golden, washed-rind cheese, and two crisp, grainy pears all set out on a thin beech board. It's a perfect Saturday lunch, and one worth making a loaf for. Apples too, appreciate the nutty, chewy quality of a fruit loaf.

makes 2 small loaves
whole wheat bread flour – 2 cups minus 2 tablespoons (250g)
white bread flour – 2 cups minus 2 tablespoons (250g)
fresh yeast – 1½ ounces (40g)
black treacle or dark molasses – a tablespoon
salt – a gently heaping teaspoon
warm water – 1½ cups (350ml)
juicy raisins – 8 ounces (250g), about 1⅔ cups
shelled walnut halves – scant 2 ounces (50g), about ⅓ cup

Put the flours into a large bowl (or the bowl of a stand mixer) and crumble in the fresh yeast. Add the treacle and the salt, then mix in the water with a wooden spoon (or the paddle attachment of the stand mixer). Keep mixing until all is smooth and there are no lumps of yeast. Turn the dough out onto a generously floured surface and knead for three or four minutes. I am never too fussy about my kneading method, and find simply working the dough with my hands until it feels springy and alive, moist but not sticky, does the trick.

Flour the bowl and return the kneaded dough to it. Cover with a clean cloth and leave in a warm place for an hour. It should have risen to almost twice its size.

Turn the dough out onto the floured surface again and push the raisins and walnuts into it, kneading lightly as you go. Cut the dough in half and form into two balls. Place on a floured baking sheet and leave to proof once again for an hour until nicely risen. Preheat the oven to 425°F (220°C).

Bake the loaves for twenty-five minutes, then allow to cool on a wire rack.

Walnut cardamom cake with orange-flower frosting

With a texture I can only describe as "scrunchy," this simple, shallow cake has masses of walnut flavor. It is mercifully less sweet than the majority of cakes, good for tea or perhaps something to eat with coffee. A cake for nut fans.

enough for about 8
eggs – 6
superfine sugar – ¾ cup (150g)
shelled walnuts – 8 ounces (250g), about 2 cups
fresh white breadcrumbs – 2½ ounces (75g), about 1¾ cups
green cardamom pods – 5
the grated zest and juice of a large orange

for the frosting
the juice of a tangerine or clementine
the juice of half a lemon
confectioners' sugar – 1½ to 2 cups (175 to 250g)
orange-flower water (optional) – a couple of drops

Line a square 9-inch (22cm) cake pan with very lightly oiled parchment paper. Preheat the oven to 350°F (180°C).

Separate the eggs. Put the yolks and sugar into a stand mixer fitted with a whisk attachment and beat until thick, pale, and light. This is likely to take a good five or ten minutes.

Chop the walnuts. They should be neither coarsely chopped nor finely ground but somewhere in between, rather like fine gravel, so that the texture of the finished cake is both spongelike and chewy. Mix them with the breadcrumbs. Crack open the cardamom pods and discard the papery cases, then crush the black seeds finely using a mortar and pestle. Add them to the nuts together with the grated orange zest and juice.

Beat the egg whites until stiff. Gently fold the nut mixture into the egg yolks and sugar, then incorporate the beaten egg whites. I do this with a large metal spoon, gently but firmly folding the egg whites in, scooping right down to the bottom of the mixture. It is essential to mix thoroughly but not to overmix, so that the mixture stays light.

Tip the mixture tenderly into the cake pan, using a rubber spatula so as not to waste a drop, then bake for thirty minutes, until firm in the middle. A skewer, pierced in the middle of the cake, should come out without any uncooked batter on it. Leave to settle in the pan for fifteen minutes before turning the cake out onto a cooling rack and carefully peeling off the paper.

continued

Make the frosting: put the fruit juice into a small bowl and stir in enough confectioners' sugar, with a drop or two of orange-flower water, to give a smooth mixture just thick enough to pour. Smooth it over the top of the cake, allowing it to run down the sides here and there. Leave to set before serving.

Walnut–maple sugar cookies

Crumbly cookies, sweet with the warm, honeyed flavor of maple sugar and tart with dried cranberries. Maple sugar is extraordinarily difficult to find in Britain. I include the recipe for American and Canadian readers and those lucky enough to get hold of this warm and buttery sugar. You could use light brown sugar if the maple variety eludes you.

If you feel the family cannot cope with thirty cookies at once (they don't keep well), freeze any remaining mixture for another day.

makes about 30
maple sugar – a generous ⅓ cup (80g), plus a little extra for dusting
salted butter – 10 tablespoons (150g), cut into cubes
a large egg
self-rising flour – ½ cup plus 1 tablespoon (75g)
ground almonds – about 1 cup (100g)
shelled walnuts – 2½ ounces (75g), about ⅔ cup
dried cranberries – 2½ ounces (75g), about ½ cup

Preheat the oven to 375°F (190°C). Put the sugar, butter, and egg into a mixing bowl and cream together until quite smooth. You really don't need to be terribly thorough about this, but even so you will find a handheld electric mixer much less trouble than doing it with a wooden spoon. Stir in the flour and ground almonds, coarsely chop the walnuts, and add those along with the dried cranberries, folding them in with a spoon until everything is well mixed.

Take walnut-sized lumps of the mixture in your fingers and roll them gently in a little more maple sugar, then place them on a nonstick baking sheet, pushing them down gently with the back of a spoon. They will be all the more interesting for being left knobbly and rough-hewn. One-third inch (1cm) on each side of them will allow them to spread without touching the next. Bake for ten to twelve minutes, then remove and leave to cool a little before transferring carefully to a cooling rack.

Warm Christmas tartlets of candied peel and walnuts

A fragile alternative to the mince pie, rich with peel and spice. I like to serve these warm, with a pitcher of cream.

makes 18

for the pastry
cold butter – 10 tablespoons (150g)
all-purpose flour – 2⅓ cups (300g)

for the filling
honey or golden syrup – ⅔ cup (200g)
walnuts – 3½ ounces (100g), a scant cup
candied orange and lemon peel – a scant 2 ounces (50g)
dried cranberries – a scant 2 ounces (50g), about ⅓ cup
mixed spice or pumpkin pie spice – a pinch
soft amaretti – 4, or 3½ ounces (90g) of cake crumbs
an egg, lightly beaten

You will need eighteen tartlet pans, 3 inches (7.5cm) in diameter and ⅓ inch (1cm) deep.

For the pastry, cut the butter into small pieces and rub it into the flour with your fingertips until it resembles fine breadcrumbs. You can add a tiny pinch of salt if you want to. Drizzle in a very small amount of water—I would start with just a teaspoon or two—bringing the mixture together to form a soft, but not sticky, rollable ball. Pat the pastry into a fat sausage the same diameter as your tart pans, cover with plastic wrap, and chill for twenty minutes. This will give the pastry time to rest, making it less likely to shrink when it's in the oven.

Preheat the oven to 350°F (180°C). Warm the syrup in a small pan set over low heat. Add the walnuts, coarsely chopped, the finely diced peel, the cranberries, and the spice, then crumble in the amaretti or cake crumbs. Remove the pan from the heat, leave to cool for five minutes, then quickly and lightly stir in the beaten egg.

Cut the roll of pastry into 18 thin slices and use them to line the tart pans. Trim the edges with a small knife. Divide the mixture among the tartlet shells—you don't want to overfill them—then bake until golden and bubbling, about fifteen to twenty minutes.

The finished tarts are very fragile, so allow them to cool a little before attempting to remove them from their pans. Serve with cream.

White currants

A white currant bush is beautiful enough to have around even if you choose to leave its fruit for the birds. From the first acid-green buds that open in March to the frilled swags of diminutive white flowers that fall from the branches in lacy trusses in July, this is a sensational shrub. The fact that it has rows of berries with which to make a fairytale fruit tart or to toss with golden raspberries or wild blackberries is almost irrelevant.

My initial love for this berry comes from sitting, as an eleven-year-old, among its electric-green leaves and glassy white berries in early summer. A group of bushes hung with cascading fruit is a magical place for a child to hide. As the sun streams through the lime-green leaves and transparent fruit, it creates an enchanted place from which to view the world.

The fruit makes a good open tart. The sparkling tartness is a credible contrast to the sweet, buttery crust. The filling must not overpower, like a true custard or pastry cream might. Better is probably a mixture of mascarpone and softly whipped cream or a layer of *fromage blanc*. Perhaps best of all are the little paper-wrapped cream cheeses called Petit Suisse. Good luck in finding those.

Some would suggest that there are better uses of your outdoor space. It would be difficult to disagree. Yet what other bush can offer such delicate charms, such pretty fruit, such brief, teasing pleasure? It is as if you have found and opened up a secret Victorian jewel box, and every working vegetable garden needs a little romance among the potatoes.

White currants in the garden

A white currant bush needs little attention, save a quick pruning after fruiting to remove any weak branches and keep the tree in shape. Take all the branches back a few inches each autumn with secateurs. The birds are less interested in this than the red, so netting is relatively unnecessary. The bushes will thrive in rich soil but can take a little shade. Mine does. Expect flowers in early May and clusters of ripe fruit from late June.

Varieties

There are nineteen varieties in the National Fruit Collection, including the poetically named old Bar-le-Duc à Fruits Blancs, Verriere Blanche, Weisse Aus Juterbog, and the White Antagonist and White Transparent from the 1940s. Versailles Blanche—the one I grow—and the relatively new White Pearl are the most popular in nurseries now and probably the only ones you will be offered. White Imperial, which yields an abundance of large, translucent fruits with a pale rose blush and a particularly sweet flesh, is common in US nurseries.

I must mention that there is also a rare and special pink currant that I would dearly love to grow, a fruit of such exquisite beauty that it charms all who see it. The flesh is pink, the skin translucent. The names alone seduce: Couleur de Chair, Gloire de Sablons, and Rosa Hollandische, all of which first appeared in 1958. An earlier variety, the October Currant, is a survivor from the early 1920s. I long to get hold of a bush or two.

White currants in the kitchen

A salad of gray lentils and transparent currants is as understated and graceful as a dish of food could be. Even more so if you offer it in the somber colors of a gray or jade-green bowl. The contrast of nutty lentils and sharp berries that burst in the mouth is extraordinary.

The season is fleeting, and the only possibility of preserving these rare fruits is in a fruit jelly, the white substituted for the more usual red. They will freeze, but emerge curiously foggy, without their characteristic glasslike clarity. Red and white currants are interchangeable. Anything you can do with a red you can do with a white. The latter tends to be more intriguing; a lot of people have never seen them, and they have, arguably, a subtler flavor. I have a fancy to make a white summer pudding of currants and golden raspberries. One day, I shall. And I will eat it in the garden, by moonlight.

White currants and...

Golden raspberries A dessert of such purity and simplicity, like a dish of precious jewels.

Lentils Dark green or brown lentils have an earthy note that makes a successful and unusual marriage with the astringent edge of the little currants.

Cream cheese The more lactic dairy products, such as cream cheese, fromage frais, and molded cream and/or cheese desserts like *les crémets*, have a mild acidity that only enhances the currants' flavor. Petit Suisse, the soft fresh cheese sold in tiny paper wrappings, in particular.

Blackberries A rather beautiful combination for lovers of tart, refreshing fruit salads.

A tart of fromage frais and white currants

A year after planting, I picked my first decent crop of Versailles Blanche currants. I wanted to celebrate their delicate beauty and translucency. I could, I suppose, have set them in a golden jelly (elderflower, perhaps, or Sauternes), turned them into a conserve, or mixed them with another suitable fruit. Instead they became a fruit tart, their sharpness taken further with a light filling of strained yogurt and fromage frais. I picked a sweet crust to support them, to balance the bracing freshness of the rest of the ingredients.

enough for 8

for the filling
fromage frais – about 1 pound (500g)
plain yogurt – 2 cups (450g)
confecioners' sugar – 3 slightly heaping tablespoons, plus more
    for dusting
the grated zest of a small orange
white currants – 1 pound (450g)

for the crust
butter – 5 tablespoons (75g)
lemon, orange, or ginger cookies – 10 ounces (300g)

Mix the fromage frais and yogurt. Line a colander or sieve with cheesecloth. Pour the mixture into the sieve, place the whole thing on a shallow dish to catch the drips, and put it in the fridge (you may well have to take a shelf out to fit it in). Leave overnight.

To make the crust, melt the butter. Crush the cookies to a coarse, open crumb, then mix them with the melted butter. Tip them into a loose-bottomed tart pan, about 9 inches (22cm) in diameter, then smooth them in, pushing them into the corners with your fingers. Chill for twenty minutes.

For the filling, tip the strained cheese mixture out of the cheesecloth into a bowl. Stir in the confectioners' sugar and grated orange zest. Smooth the filling into the chilled tart crust. Pull the currants from their stalks and pile them on top of the tart filling. Dust generously with confectioners' sugar. Leave for a few minutes before slicing.

An elegant compote

You can use this for red currants, too. I wouldn't want to destroy its simplicity by serving it with cream, but a nice, crisp cookie would be welcome.

enough for 2 or 3
superfine sugar – ½ cup (100g)
water – 1¼ cups (300ml)
white currants – 8 ounces (250g), about 2 cups

Make a light syrup with the sugar and water by bringing them slowly to a boil in a small pan, then leaving to bubble for three or four minutes. Remove the currants from their stems and tip them into the warm syrup. Turn off the heat immediately and leave the currants be while they cool down. You could serve them warm or thoroughly chilled; they are delicious either way. A dessert of tender elegance.

A midsummer dessert of quiet perfection

A small plate or saucer. A tenderly unwrapped Petit Suisse cheese or chalk-white fromage frais. A palmful of white currants scattered over the surface. A drizzle of heavy cream. An ivory and white dessert of utter charm and purity.

A salad of lentils and white currants

The first mention of lentils with fresh currants was in *Real Fast Food*.
I used red then, but at the time suggested using white if you could get hold
of them. I am honestly not sure where the idea came from, I only know it
was something I made a lot at one time, and I still find the mixture of the
sharp fruit with the nutty, bland lentils an invigorating one. This is a side
dish, and one that I would use to accompany a cold roast—particularly
lamb, pork, salmon, or guinea fowl. You could make a deeper-flavored
dressing if you like, but the flavor of the white currants would be lost.

enough for 2 as a side dish
small green lentils – 6 ounces (175g), a scant cup
olive oil – 3 tablespoons
white wine vinegar – a tablespoon
white or red currants – 4 ounces (125g), about 1 cup
a few mint sprigs
parsley – a small bunch

Wash the lentils in a sieve under running water. Lentils are invariably dusty.
Cook them in boiling, lightly salted water for twelve to fifteen minutes,
until they are tender but retain a nutty bite. They shouldn't be soft. Drain
and place in a bowl. Dress while they are still warm with the olive oil,
vinegar, and some salt and pepper.

Top and tail the currants and add them to the lentils. Remove the leaves
from the mint and parsley, then add them, chopped or whole. Stir the salad
gently, so as not to crush the little white jewels.

A few other good things: medlars and sloes

The garden's yew and box hedges went in as soon as the ground was dug. Even before the fruit trees. The idea was to break up the long, thin space into small "rooms" and to enclose and protect the vegetable and fruit beds. Having spent much of my childhood in farming country, I learned to appreciate this ancient form of partitioning and marking the land. The tearing out of traditional hedges in the name of farming efficiency is undoubtedly one of the most destructive acts of vandalism this country has seen. So many of the hedges of my childhood, alive with hawthorn and hazel, with blackbirds and voles, hedgehogs, wild roses, and cherries and the inevitable rowans with their scarlet-orange berries, are gone.

Now well established, the hedges here in this garden are principally of box and yew. I wish I had thought to include more variety—a sloe bush or two, a wild rose, the creamy white froth of hawthorn that so entranced me as a child on the long, long walk to school. But what mattered at the time was a rich, dark green background against which the white blossom of the damsons, plums, apples, and pears would be at their most beautiful. The appearance of a wild plum in the midst of one of the yew hedges has brought much joy. Blackbirds nest in the hedges each spring and I fancy they are the same pair. They are here again now, as I write, darting in and out with tidbits for their young.

Each autumn, just as the frosts start threatening, I go to friends who know where there are sloes to pick. We come back with bags full, with which to make bottles of crimson gin, and a few rose hips for jelly.

There is a medlar here too, standing among the rhubarb and gooseberries. These are the trees that live in old gardens, farmyards, and, occasionally, country lanes. Mine gives me enough for one, maybe two, jars of aromatic jelly a year. But that is all I ask of it.

The medlar

The quaint, hopelessly crooked medlar tree was planted for the same reason I insisted on having a quince, a mulberry, and a hazelnut in the garden—I was taken by the romance and mystery of it. There is something enchanting about the idea of growing a fruit that you rarely see in the market, that appears only in very old recipe books, and that came shot through with visions of medieval walled gardens and monastery kitchens. How could anyone resist?

Five years on, the quince and mulberry are doing well, but the medlar has been spectacular since day one, giving white, gardenia-like blossom in spring, followed by a hundred or more fruits hidden amid the rust and golden leaves each autumn. Some years, such as 2009, the blossom is rose-colored, others, like 2010, perfectly white. I can't recommend it enough for someone looking for an interesting, decorative, edible fruit tree for a small garden.

But what on earth do I do with the fruit that smells of rancid wine and resembles nothing so much as a cat's bottom? (Cat's ass was, somewhat appropriately, the medieval name for this fruit.) The only recipes I could find were for jelly, and until recently I was not a preserving kind of guy (the term *jelly bag*, like *piping bag*, usually sends me running for the hills). The idea of baking them appealed less, even with the promise of scooping their flesh out and mixing it with sugar and cream. Medlar cheese sounded like a bridge altogether too far. But then I thought of the glistening amber jelly quivering on the same fork as hot roast pork and a nib of crackling or a slice of cold, rose-pink pheasant and thought I'd give it a try. Anyway, in reality a jelly bag is an inexpensive item that sleeps quietly in the linen closet next to the hot water bottle for the rest for the year.

Picked unripe and hard, the fruits need to be bletted—in other words left to soften—before you use them. History dictates that you should do this by burying them in sawdust, but piling them on a plate in the kitchen works well enough for me. This is a fruit you look at, wondrously, at the farm stand, buy in a fit of enthusiasm and intrigue, then promptly leave in the bottom of the fridge until you find them, rotted to a pulp, a month later.

Making medlar jelly sounds like someone has too much time on his or her hands, but I wanted to taste the fruits of the most beautiful tree in my garden, the one that always does so well by me. I wanted to find a use for them beyond piling them on the table for the appropriate autumnal oohs and aahhs.

Once they have softened, you bring them to a boil with water and sugar, squash them a little (too much will make the jelly cloudy), then strain the result through a jelly bag, boil it with sugar, and pour it into jars. I would imagine a pair of pantyhose might work too, but I can't pretend I have tried it. Sir Harry Luke's book *The Tenth Muse* (Putnams, 1954) mentions that, curiously, Worcestershire sauce is worth adding to the preserve, but I tend to make it without any intrusion, to get the true flavor.

My medlar is the Nottingham variety, though for no other reason than I liked the shape of the tree—which looked bent and ancient from the start. The Dutch variety offers larger fruit, but can take up rather more room than most small gardens can spare. Royal, which yields pretty nut brown fruits, and Breda Giant, a Dutch cultivar that produces particularly big fruits, are available from US sources.

Medlar jelly

A bronze-colored preserve for eating with cold roast meat. If you have no firm medlars, only "bletted" (softened) ones, then you can still make a perfectly good jelly.

makes 1 jar
bletted medlars (see below) – 1¾ pounds (800g)
firm medlars – 7 ounces (200g)
water – 5 cups (1.2 liters)
lemons – 2
sugar

Make sure the medlars are well bletted and remove any leaves. Cut each fruit in half and drop into a heavy-bottomed saucepan. Pour over the water. Cut the lemons into six pieces and add them to the fruit. Bring to a boil, then turn the temperature down so that the liquid simmers gently, partially cover with a lid, and leave to cook for an hour. Take care that the liquid doesn't evaporate, and give the fruit an occasional squash with a wooden spoon. Avoid the temptation to stir or mash the fruit, which will turn the finished jelly cloudy.

Pour the fruit and its liquid into a jelly bag suspended over a large jug or bowl (I hang mine from the faucet over the sink). Let the juice drip into the jug, giving it the occasional squeeze, until it has all dribbled through.

Put the juice back into a clean saucepan and boil for four minutes, then add an equal amount of sugar (this is likely to be about a pound [500g] or 2 cups). When the sugar has dissolved, pour the mixture into clean, warm jars and seal. I use Mason jars with rubber seals. Leave to cool.

To blet medlars

Medlars are usually bought rock hard and have to be softened. Pull them off their leaves and place the whole fruits on a shallow plate. Don't pile them up. Leave them at cool room temperature for a week or two until they turn deep brown and are soft, almost squashy, to the touch. They are then ready to cook.

Roast partridge, juniper, thyme, and medlar gravy

enough for 4
young, plump partridges – 4
thyme – 6 bushy little sprigs
juniper berries – 12
butter – 3½ tablespoons (50g)
unsmoked bacon – 8 thin slices
pears – 2
a squeeze of lemon juice
a glass of vermouth or white wine
medlar jelly (see page 572) – 3 tablespoons

I always check the birds all over for any stray feathers or bits of shattered bone before I start. Preheat the oven to 425°F (220°C).

Pull the leaves from the thyme branches and mash them with the juniper berries, butter, and a hefty pinch of sea salt and black pepper, using a mortar and pestle. Reserve a tablespoon for cooking the pears, then spread the butter all over the birds, but particularly on their breasts.

Lay each slice of bacon flat on a cutting board, then stretch with the flat of a knife blade to give a longer, thinner slice. Wrap the bacon slices around the birds and place in a roasting pan.

Cut the pears into thick slices, core them, toss them in a little lemon juice, and cook briefly in the reserved herb butter in a shallow nonstick pan. When both sides are pale gold, transfer them to the roasting pan. Roast for twenty minutes, then peel off the bacon, setting it aside if it is crisp enough or leaving it in the roasting pan if not. Return the birds to the oven for a further ten minutes' roasting.

Remove the birds and pears from the pan and leave to rest in a warm place, covered with foil. Put the roasting pan over low to medium heat, pour in the vermouth or white wine, and leave to bubble for a few minutes, then add the jelly, stirring until it has dissolved. Correct the seasoning, then serve the birds, pouring over the medlar gravy from the pan.

The blackthorn and its fruit

I am a winter person, never happier than on a clear, frosty morning. The ash-gray branches of bare trees against a crisp sky; cinnamon leaves and blood-red hips still holding onto charcoal twigs; a kitchen that smells of juniper. This is my time, just as others long for the dog days of summer.

Spotting a blackthorn hedge dotted with tiny sloes, or finding baskets of the fruit for sale on a frozen November morning at the farmers' market, is even more exciting for me than a field full of asparagus in May. Sloes make me want to get out the gin bottle. Hard to think that such a velvet-throated drink as sloe gin could come from so sour and impenetrable a fruit. Even the stones within are tough. Crows and hawfinches are the only birds with beaks strong enough to crack them.

The blackthorn, or sloe, is native to Europe, and widespread throughout the country. Although the names are interchangeable, blackthorn is most often used to describe the bush, while the term *sloe* is generally kept for the fruit. If allowed to grow into a tree, the blackthorn can reach over twelve feet (four meters) in height, though most are found as part of a mixed hedgerow.

The creamy-white blossom appears in early spring and brings a soft froth to hedges up and down the country. You can make a syrup from the blossom, though I have yet to try it. The result is said to taste of almonds. The fruit itself is beautiful, smaller and darker than a damson, and bullet hard. Its bitterness will leave your mouth numb.

While for many, the wood of the blackthorn is still a preferred choice for making a shillelagh, the principal use of the fruit is the gorgeous drink, sloe gin. The glowing-red drink is without question my favorite cold-weather tipple. Many a bitterly cold winter's night I have sat with a fire burning in the hearth and a bottle of this glorious red liqueur at my side. It is made easily enough by pricking or bashing the fruit and leaving it to steep for a few weeks in a bottle with gin or vodka.

Pricking the sloes so that the alcohol can absorb their juice is a job I enjoy, and choose to do with a needle stuck into a cork. A mention of this in print once brought hundreds of emails from readers telling me of their "quick" way that involved putting the fruits in the freezer, then hitting them with a bottle or a hammer instead. Yes, I could have done that, but they had missed my point entirely that for me the task is not about speed, it is something I like to take pleasure in, slowly working my way through a colander of inky-blue fruits one by one. I found it odd and somehow sad that even the calmest and most ancient of kitchen pleasures had to be reduced to something to be "done and dusted" as quickly as making instant ramen.

Sloe gin

Pricking the diminutive fruits with a needle is less fussy than it sounds—a job to do on a damp Saturday afternoon. The jars, filled with sugar, gin, and fruit, need turning regularly until the sugar has dissolved, then tucking away in a dark corner for a couple of months while the magic gets to work. Christmas seems an appropriate time to break open a jar. I can rarely wait that long.

> sloes (or damsons) – 2 pounds (900g)
> superfine sugar – 3½ cups (700g)
> gin – around 6 cups (1.5 liters)

Wipe the sloes, discarding any that are squashy or bruised. Prick the fruit all over with a needle and put them into glass preserving jars, layering them with the sugar. Fill each jar just over half full. Pour enough gin over the fruit to fill the jars, keeping the gin bottles for later. Seal them, then leave in a cool, preferably dark place for about three months. Turn the jars over from time to time—I do it every few days—or give them a respectful shake. Filter the gin through a cheesecloth-lined funnel into the reserved gin bottles. Seal and store in the cool place, where it will keep for several months.

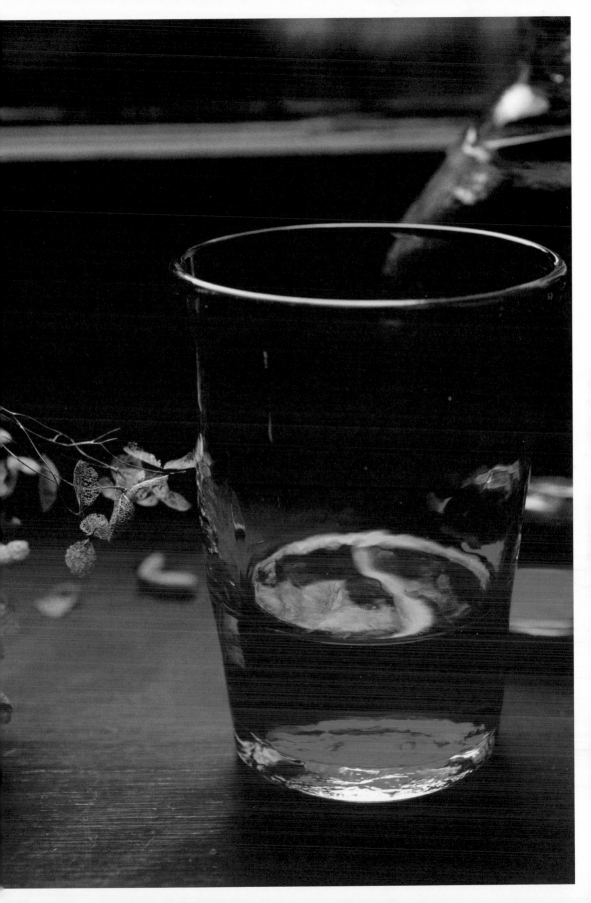

Roast duck with apples and sloe gin

A wild duck such as a mallard is enough for two—just. You will also need some roasted or mashed potatoes or pumpkin and some vegetables too. Use British sloe gin only, never American, which bears little relation to the genuine article. Or make your own (see page 578).

enough for 4
wild ducks – 2
an onion
butter – about 3½ tablespoons (50g)
juniper berries – 10
small, sharpish dessert apples – 4
sloe gin – a wineglass
stock – a wineglass

Preheat the oven to 425°F (220°C). Put the birds in a roasting pan, not too close together. Peel the onion, cut into quarters, and stuff each of the birds with two of the pieces. Rub a thin layer of butter over the birds, then tuck a small knob of butter inside each. Using a mortar and pestle, crush the juniper berries with a little coarse sea salt and half a dozen black peppercorns. Rub the mixture over the ducks.

Score the skin of the apples around the middle and tuck them into the pan. Roast for fifteen minutes, then turn the heat down to 350°F (180°C) and continue roasting for twenty to thirty minutes, or until the skin of the birds is a fine color and lightly crisp. Lift out the ducks and put them in a warm place to rest. Put the roasting pan over medium heat, pour in the sloe gin and stock, and stir with a wooden spoon to dissolve any pan-stickings into the liquid. Season with salt and pepper and leave to bubble for a good couple of minutes. When the sauce has started to thicken slightly, pour into a small hot pitcher.

Cut the birds in half and place a half on each of four warmed plates, together with an apple. Stir the gravy and pour it over.

Baked fruits with sloe gin

The marriage of fruits and sloe gin produces a heady dessert with glowing, garnet juices. You really don't need cream, and don't even think of making custard. If you can't make your own sloe gin (see page 578)—sloes are not exactly something you can pick up at the supermarket—look for a British brand, such as Plymouth or, if you are very fortunate, Bramley and Gage.

enough for 4
plums, rhubarb, apricots, damsons, or peaches – 1½ pounds (700g)
sugar – ½ cup (100g)
sloe gin – half a cup
water – 2 tablespoons

Preheat the oven to 350°F (180°C). Put the fruit in an ovenproof dish, cutting it in half or into thick pieces no bigger than will comfortably sit in a spoon. Scatter the sugar over evenly, then pour in the sloe gin and water. Place the dish in the oven, covered with a lid or foil if you wish, and bake for forty minutes or so (much will depend on the type of fruit you are using), until the fruit is starting to burst.

Remove from the oven and leave to cool a little. I think this is best eaten warm rather than hot, though it is also very good chilled.

About the author

Nigel Slater is the author of a collection of bestselling books, including the classics *Real Fast Food, Appetite,* and the critically acclaimed *The Kitchen Diaries.* He has written a much-loved column for *The Observer* for eighteen years and is the presenter of the award-winning BBC series *Simple Suppers.* His memoir, *Toast —The Story of a Boy's Hunger,* has won six major awards, including British Biography of the Year, and has been adapted into a BBC film. *Ripe* is the companion volume to *Tender: A cook and his vegetable patch.* Visit www.nigelslater.com.

Also by Nigel Slater

Tender
Eating for England
The Kitchen Diaries
Toast—The Story of a Boy's Hunger
Thirst
Appetite
Nigel Slater's Real Food
Real Cooking
The 30-Minute Cook
Real Fast Puddings
Real Fast Food

A note on the type

Claude Garamond (c. 1480–1561) cut type for the Parisian scholar-printer Robert Estienne in the first part of the sixteenth century, basing it on the type cut by Francesco Griffo for Venetian printer Aldus Manutius in 1495. Garamond refined his typeface in later versions, adding his own concepts as he developed his skills as a punchcutter.

Adobe Garamond, the type used in *Ripe,* was designed by Robert Slimbach in 1989. The roman weights were based on the true Garamond, and the italics on those of punchcutter Robert Granjon. This font has been expanded to include small caps, titling caps, expert fonts, and swash caps, which were typical in the fifteenth and sixteenth centuries.

Britain's foremost food writer Nigel Slater returns to the garden in this sequel to *Tender*, his acclaimed and beloved volume on vegetables. With a focus on fruit, *Ripe* is equal parts cookbook, primer on produce and gardening, and affectionate ode to the inspiration behind the book—Slater's forty-foot backyard garden in London.

Intimate, delicate prose is interwoven with recipes in this lavishly photographed cookbook. Slater offers more than 300 delectable dishes—both sweet and savory—such as **Apricot and Pistachio Crumble**, **Baked Rhubarb with Blueberries**, and **Crisp Pork Belly with Sweet Peach Salsa**. With a personal, almost confessional approach to his appetites and gustatory experiences, Slater has crafted a masterful book that will gently guide you from the garden to the kitchen, and back again.